The Cambridge Companion to Krautrock

This Companion is the first academic introduction to the 1960s/70s 'Krautrock' movement of German experimental music that has long attracted the attention of the music press and fans in Britain and abroad. It offers a structured approach to this exceptionally heterogeneous and decentralised movement, combining overviews with detailed analysis and close readings. The volume first analyses the cultural, historical, and economic contexts of Krautrock's emergence. It then features expert chapters discussing all the key bands of the era including Can, Kraftwerk, Tangerine Dream, Neu!, Faust, Ash Ra Tempel, Cluster, and Amon Düül II. The volume concludes with essays that trace the varied, wide-ranging legacy of Krautrock from a variety of perspectives, exploring in particular the impact of German experimental music in the Anglosphere, including British post-punk and Detroit Techno. A final chapter examining the current bands that continue the Krautrock sound closes this comprehensive overview of the Krautrock phenomenon.

UWE SCHÜTTE worked as a Reader in German in British higher education until Brexit. Now based in Berlin, he is Privatdozent at the University of Göttingen. Schütte has edited some ten volumes and written more than fifteen monographs on contemporary German-language literature and German pop music, with a focus on W. G. Sebald and Kraftwerk.

Cambridge Companions to Music

Topics

The Cambridge Companion to Ballet
Edited by Marion Kant

The Cambridge Companion to Blues and Gospel Music
Edited by Allan Moore

The Cambridge Companion to Caribbean Music
Edited by Nanette De Jong

The Cambridge Companion to Choral Music
Edited by André de Quadros

The Cambridge Companion to the Concerto
Edited by Simon P. Keefe

The Cambridge Companion to Conducting
Edited by José Antonio Bowen

The Cambridge Companion to the Drum Kit
Edited by Matt Brennan, Joseph Michael Pignato and Daniel Akira Stadnicki

The Cambridge Companion to Eighteenth-Century Opera
Edited by Anthony R. DelDonna and Pierpaolo Polzonetti

The Cambridge Companion to Electronic Music
Edited by Nick Collins and Julio D'Escriván

The Cambridge Companion to the 'Eroica' Symphony
Edited by Nancy November

The Cambridge Companion to Film Music
Edited by Mervyn Cooke and Fiona Ford

The Cambridge Companion to French Music
Edited by Simon Trezise

The Cambridge Companion to Grand Opera
Edited by David Charlton

The Cambridge Companion to Hip-Hop
Edited by Justin A. Williams

The Cambridge Companion to Jazz
Edited by Mervyn Cooke and David Horn

The Cambridge Companion to Jewish Music
Edited by Joshua S. Walden

The Cambridge Companion to Krautrock
Edited by Uwe Schütte

The Cambridge Companion to the Lied
Edited by James Parsons

The Cambridge Companion to Medieval Music
Edited by Mark Everist

The Cambridge Companion to Music and Romanticism
Edited by Benedict Taylor

Composers

Instruments

The Cambridge Companion
to Krautrock

Edited by
UWE SCHÜTTE
University of Göttingen

CAMBRIDGE
UNIVERSITY PRESS

University Printing House, Cambridge CB2 8BS, United Kingdom

One Liberty Plaza, 20th Floor, New York, NY 10006, USA

477 Williamstown Road, Port Melbourne, VIC 3207, Australia

314–321, 3rd Floor, Plot 3, Splendor Forum, Jasola District Centre,
New Delhi – 110025, India

103 Penang Road, #05–06/07, Visioncrest Commercial, Singapore 238467

Cambridge University Press is part of the University of Cambridge.

It furthers the University's mission by disseminating knowledge in the pursuit of
education, learning, and research at the highest international levels of excellence.

www.cambridge.org
Information on this title: www.cambridge.org/9781316511077
DOI: 10.1017/9781009036535

First published 2023

A catalogue record for this publication is available from the British Library.

Library of Congress Cataloging-in-Publication Data
Names: Schütte, Uwe, 1967– editor.
Title: The Cambridge companion to Krautrock / edited by Uwe Schütte
Description: [1.] | Cambridge, United Kingdom ; New York, NY : Cambridge University
Press, 2022. | Series: Cambridge companions to music | Includes index.
Identifiers: LCCN 2022022780 (print) | LCCN 2022022781 (ebook) | ISBN 9781316511077
(hardback) | ISBN 9781009005272 (paperback) | ISBN 9781009036535 (ebook)
Subjects: LCSH: Krautrock (Music) – History and criticism. | Popular music – Germany –
History and criticism. | BISAC: MUSIC / General
Classification: LCC ML3534.6.G3 C36 2022 (print) | LCC ML3534.6.G3 (ebook) | DDC
781.660943/09047–dc23/eng/20220520
LC record available at https://lccn.loc.gov/2022022780
LC ebook record available at https://lccn.loc.gov/2022022781

ISBN 978-1-316-51107-7 Hardback
ISBN 978-1-009-00527-2 Paperback

This volume is dedicated to my colleagues at the German section at Aston University, which was closed shortly after Brexit: Claudia Gremler, Elisabeth Wielander and Stefan Manz. You always had my back, tolerated my incompetence in administrative matters for two decades and filled in for me when I was in Berlin rather than Birmingham.
Thank you.

Contents

Illustrations

Contributors

ULRICH ADELT is Professor of American Studies and Director of African American and Diaspora Studies at the University of Wyoming, Laramie. He is the author of *Blues Music in the Sixties: A Story in Black and White* (New Brunswick: Rutgers University Press, 2010) and *Krautrock: German Music in the Seventies* (Ann Arbor: University of Michigan Press, 2016).

JENS BALZER lives in Berlin and writes for German weekly paper *Die Zeit*. His book publications include: *Pop: Ein Panorama der Gegenwart* (Berlin: Rowohlt, 2016), *Pop und Populismus: Über Verantwortung in der Musik* (Hamburg: Ed Körber, 2019), *Das entfesselte Jahrzehnt: Sound und Geist der 70er* (Berlin: Rowohlt, 2019), *High Energy: Die Achtziger – das pulsierende Jahrzehnt* (Berlin: Rowohlt, 2021), *Schmalz und Rebellion. Der deutsche Pop und seine Sprache* (Berlin: Dudenverlag, 2022), and *Ethik der Appropriation* (Berlin: Matthes & Seitz, 2022).

MARCUS BARNES is a seasoned music journalist, copywriter, and author from London. He is the direct offspring of Jamaican soundsystem culture (his father was part of a Rastafarian soundsystem and his mother a fan). As the former techno editor at renowned music magazine *Mixmag*, he cultivated close ties to the global techno community, writing about, and investigating, the roots and wider cultural impact of electronic music extensively. Marcus has contributed to the *Guardian*, the *Independent*, *Time Out*, and the BBC, and also worked with Sony, Virgin Records, Atlantic, and many more major labels. His published works include *Around the World in 80 Records Stores* (London: Dog N Bone, 2018).

ALEXANDER CARPENTER is Professor of Music and Director of the Wirth Institute for Austrian and Central European Studies at the University of Alberta. A musicologist, music critic, and cultural historian, his research interests include popular music, Arnold Schoenberg and the Second Viennese School, film music, the intersections between music and psychoanalysis, and zombies in popular culture. At present, he is writing a monograph on the early history of gothic rock for Lexington Press.

PATRICK GLEN is Teaching Fellow in the School of Performance and Cultural Industries at the University of Leeds. He has held a fellowship in the Centre for Contemporary History at the University of Wolverhampton and previously worked at University College London and the University of Salford. He is the author of *Youth and Permissive Social Change in British Music Papers, 1967–1983* (London: Palgrave Macmillan, 2019) and is now writing a book on the social meanings and politics controversies surrounding British music festivals during the 1970s.

PERTTI GRÖNHOLM is Adjunct Professor and University Lecturer in the Department of European and World History at the University of Turku. His research themes range from the politics of history and collective remembering, the history of utopia and dystopia, to the history of technology and pop music. As regards the last theme, Pertti has lectured and written journal articles and book chapters on Kraftwerk, Mika Vainio, Pan Sonic, and other makers of electronic pop and experimental music.

ALEXANDER C. HARDEN is an independent researcher based in the United Kingdom. After studying electroacoustic composition at the University of Birmingham and developing a creative portfolio inspired by *kosmische Musik* techniques, he completed a PhD in narratology and popular music analysis at the University of Surrey. Alexander now focusses on areas of record production and early electronic popular musical practice and holds an International Association for the Study of Popular Music (UK & Ireland Branch) Andrew Goodwin Memorial Prize for his essay 'A World of My Own'.

JEFF HAYTON is Associate Professor of History at Wichita State University in Kansas. He has published numerous articles on popular culture, rock 'n' roll and German history. He is the author of *Culture from the Slums: Punk Rock in East and West Germany* (Oxford: Oxford University Press, 2022). He is now working on a study of mountain climbing in East Germany called 'Summits and Socialism: Mountaineering in the German Democratic Republic, 1945–1990'.

ALEXANDER HENKLE studied English and philosophy at the University of Wyoming. His undergraduate thesis, 'Revolutionary Desire: Nonsense in Language and Literature', theorises nonsensicality and pitifully investigates Lewis Carroll, Tristan Tzara, and Gertrude Stein. He is pursuing an MA in English at the University of New Mexico, focussing on modernist and avant-garde literatures.

JAN-PETER HERBST is Reader in Music Production at the University of Huddersfield where he is Director of the Research Centre for Music, Culture and Identity (CMCI). His primary research area is popular music culture, in particular rock music and the electric guitar, on which he has published widely. Currently, Jan is undertaking a funded three-year project that explores how heaviness is created and controlled in metal music production. His editorial roles include *IASPM Journal* and *Metal Music Studies*, and he currently edits the *Cambridge Companion to Metal Music* and the *Cambridge Companion to the Electric Guitar* (with Steve Waksman).

RYAN ISEPPI, PhD, is a writer and educator living in Detroit, Michigan. He is an alumnus of the University of Michigan, where he wrote about the relationship between Krautrock and the West German counterculture. He completed a Fulbright fellowship in Hamburg in 2013. He also previously hosted the Krautsider Music radio show on WCBN-FM Ann Arbor.

MICHAEL KRIKORIAN is Assistant Professor of Piano and Music Technology at California State University, Fresno. He holds a DMA in piano performance with additional minor fields in music theory, music composition, and scoring for visual media from the University of Southern California, an MM in Piano Performance from the Manhattan School of Music, and a BA in Piano Performance from CSU, Fresno. His collaborative research presentations have focussed on the demystification of contemporary pedagogical keyboard works and the use of popular music in applied music lessons for elementary to advanced level pianists. Michael composes for the concert stage and for visual media.

HEATHER MOORE is a doctoral student at the University of Southern California, where she is pursuing a PhD in historical musicology. She holds a dual-emphasis MA in music history and literature, and piano pedagogy from California State University, Fullerton, as well as a BM in piano performance from Chapman University. Heather's research revolves around the intersection of music and politics within twentieth-century Germany, with particular emphases on the German Democratic Republic and popular music of the Cold War era.

SEAN NYE is Associate Professor of Practice in Musicology at the University of Southern California. His recent publications include *Modeselektor's 'Happy Birthday!'* (London: Bloomsbury Academic, 2022) for the 33 1/3 Europe series. His teaching and research encompass topics such as electronic music, hip-hop, German studies, and science fiction. Prior to joining the University of Southern California, Sean was a fellow in the Berlin Program for Advanced German and European Studies at the Free University of Berlin and a DAAD graduate fellow at the Humboldt University of Berlin.

DAVID PATTIE is Associate Professor in Drama and Theatre Arts at the University of Birmingham. He has published widely on the work of Samuel Beckett, contemporary theatre, Scottish theatre and popular music. He is the co-editor (with Sean Albiez) of *Kraftwerk: Music Non-Stop* (London: Continuum, 2012), *Brian Eno: Oblique Music* (London: Continuum 2016), and *The Velvet Underground: What Goes On* (London: Bloomsbury Academic, 2022).

SASCHA SEILER is currently Visiting Professor at the Department of World Literature, University of Mainz. He has published widely in the field of popular culture as well as Latin American and North American literature. His books include monographs on the influence of popular culture on German literature since the 1960s and the aesthetics of disappearance. Sascha has edited several volumes on different subjects like culture and terrorism or transatlantic literary relations, the most recent being on the German author Wolfgang Welt. He is currently writing a monograph on folk and occult horror in film, literature, and music.

UWE SCHÜTTE was Reader in German at Aston University, Birmingham (until Brexit) and is now Privatdozent at Göttingen University. He lives in Berlin and has edited some ten volumes and written more than fifteen monographs on contemporary German-language literature and German pop music, with a focus on W.G. Sebald and Kraftwerk. Recent publications include *Annäherungen: Sieben Essays über W.G. Sebald* (Cologne: Böhlau, 2019), *Kraftwerk: Future Music from Germany* (London: Penguin, 2020), *W. G. Sebald: Leben und literarisches Werk* (Berlin: De Gruyter, 2021), and *GODSTAR: Die fünf Tode des Genesis P-Orridge* (Meine: Reiffer, 2022).

DETLEF SIEGFRIED is Professor of History at Copenhagen University. His research focusses mainly on the twentieth century and the histories of West Germany and Europe, popular cultures and consumption, left-wing radicalism, intellectuals, and the history of historiography and social sciences. His publications include *Time Is on My Side: Konsum und Politik in der westdeutschen Jugendkultur der 60er Jahre* (Göttingen: Wallstein, 2006) and *Modern Lusts: Ernest Borneman: Jazz Critic, Filmmaker, Sexologist* (New York: Berghahn, 2020).

ALEXANDER SIMMETH, PhD, is a writer and educator based in Detroit, Michigan. He primarily works on popular cultures in Europe and the United States, focussing on music, film, and travel. His publications include the chapter 'The Future Past: Reflections on the Role of History', in Peter W. Lee's volume *Exploring Picard's Galaxy: Essays on Star Trek: The Next Generation* (Jefferson: McFarland, 2018) and *Krautrock Transnational: Die Neuerfindung der Popmusik in der BRD, 1968–1978* (Bielefeld: Transcript, 2016).

DAVID STUBBS is a journalist and author. He started working life at the UK music magazine *Melody Maker*, before going on to work for numerous publications including *New Musical Express*, *Vox*, the *Guardian*, *The Wire* and *The Quietus*, among many others. He has written a number of music books, including studies of Jimi Hendrix, Eminem, and *Fear of Music: Why People Get Rothko But Don't Get Stockhausen* (London: Zero, 2009). He is also the author of *Future Days: Krautrock and the Building Of Modern Germany* (London: Faber, 2014) and *Mars by 1980: The Story of Electronic Music* (London: Faber, 2019). He lives in London.

Acknowledgements

I am grateful to Anne Haffmans at Mute, Mareike Hettler at Grönland, Sean Newsham at Bureau B, and Sandra Podmore at Spoon for support in obtaining band images and rights clearance. As several image rights holders refused to grant permission, some band chapters sadly contain no illustrations. Particular thanks, though, go to Heinrich Klaffs and Wolfgang Wigger for making available great live images they took during the heyday of Krautrock. Jacques Schumacher contributed a cool photo of Inga Rumpf while Ilona Ziok helped with fine pictures of Ash Ra Tempel and Manuel Göttsching.

Göttsching also helped to clarify several facts pertaining to his career in an uncomplicated way – thanks! Lucy Renner-Jones checked my translation of Jens Balzer's contribution. As goes without saying, this volume would not have been possible without the invaluable and reliable support of Kate Brett at Cambridge University Press.

Finally, acknowledgments are due to the Deutscher Akademischer Austauschdienst (DAAD) London office. A three-year grant under the Promoting German Studies scheme, running from 2018 to 2021, was supposed to kickstart ongoing collaborative research in German pop music, bringing together the British and German academic communities. In addition to the Covid-19 pandemic, Brexit put a spanner in the works. The strategic decision to discontinue modern languages at my former institution finally made sure that all future research projects were rendered impossible.

I am delighted, though, that at least this volume could be completed. Leaving academia and England for good after thirty years, I like to think of this *Companion to Krautrock* as my farewell gift. Best of British to you all!

Note on Translation

All quotations from German sources were translated by the respective contributors.

Introduction

UWE SCHÜTTE

Arguably, Krautrock is a primarily British phenomenon. Contrary to common assumptions, the term is by no means a British creation but has been circulating within the German music scene since 1969 at the latest.[1] However, the expression lost its original (self-)ironic quality when it eventually surfaced in the English music press in the early 1970s. British hacks adapted 'Krautrock' as their label of choice for the experimental rock music that emanated from Germany from the late 1960s to the mid-1970s. Music journalists and audiences largely preferred to perceive the outlandish, peculiar-sounding music – which often vehemently rejected the conventions of anglophone pop and rock music – through the ubiquitous Nazi stereotypes and Teutonic clichés peddled in British popular culture.

Leading music critic Nick Kent, to give a telling example, mirrored prevailing British Germanophobia when characterising German bands like Kraftwerk and Neu! in 1974 as 'stout-hearted Krauts who have set out – facial muscles characteristically tensed-up as they lurch manically over their various keyboard instruments'; in his perception, Germans are overly-cerebral 'experimental quacks' who make 'mind-numbingly boring' music comprised of 'nihilistic electronic landscapes they were droning their way through interminably'.[2] But as in the case of 'Made in Germany' – originally a designation of origin that was intended to deter British consumers from buying German products – the derogatory expression turned into a hallmark of quality as the reception of German experimental music soon reversed from defamation to adoration.[3]

Germany and Krautrock: An Uneasy Relationship

Krautrock is likewise a very British phenomenon in that the reverence, if not worship, of bands like Can, Kraftwerk, Faust, Neu!, and many more featured in this volume never took place in Germany. 'The Germans never

---

[1] A Simmeth, *Krautrock Transnational: Die Neuerfindung der Popmusik in der BRD, 1968–1978* (Bielefeld: Transcript, 2016), p. 54.

[2] N Kent, Can: Ve Give Ze Orders Here, *New Musical Express* (16 February 1974).

[3] See my case study on Kraftwerk: U Schütte, From Defamation to Adoration. The Reception of Kraftwerk in the British Music Press, 1974–1981, *Angermion* 13 (2020), pp. 1–23.

do appreciate what's on their own doorstep', Mark E. Smith, late lead singer of Mancunian post-punk outfit The Fall, remarked in conversation with Irmin Schmidt of Can. As many of the Krautrock players featuring in Christoph Dallach's 2021 interview collection *Future Sounds: Wie ein paar Krautrocker die Popwelt revolutionierten* (*How a Few Krautrockers Revolutionized the Pop World*) attest, the German musicians were often taken aback at the rapturous welcome they received upon first playing in Britain.

The reverse of such appreciation is the lack of interest (and indeed: lack of pride) Germans continue to take in homegrown bands that revolutionised the idiom of global pop music. Indeed, it is only international fame that saved many lesser-known Krautrock bands from disappearing out of the public eye in Germany. At the root of this perplexing situation is the inferiority complex that haunts German culture: the experience of utter disgrace felt by young Germans growing up in the aftermath of Nazism and the Holocaust. German culture was perceived as indelibly tainted while the tradition of the vibrant popular culture of the Weimar period was cut short by fascism. What would be referred to as the '68er generation' hence largely turned to Elvis, Bob Dylan, The Beatles, and The Rolling Stones in protest against the staunchly conservative values of their parents' generation. The very notion of pop music being a liberating force, as well as a cultural expression offering opportunities for subcultural identity formation, became synonymous with Anglo-American models.

In the road movie *Im Lauf der Zeit* (*Kings of the Road*, 1976) by director Wim Wenders, one of the characters remarks upon hearing a certain pop song: 'Die Amis haben unser Unterbewußtsein kolonisiert' (The Yanks have colonised our subconscious). Only a minority of young post-war Germans opposed the ready acceptance of this cultural invasion. Among them was Ralf Hütter from Kraftwerk, who explained: 'We woke up in the late '60s and realized that Germany had become an American colony .... There was no German culture, no German music, nothing. It was like living in a vacuum.'[4]

What was later designated as Krautrock originated in a defensive reaction against the dominance of Anglo-American artists. German experimental music was an attempt to newly define what pop music should be and how it could sound. For this reason, it would be rewarding to critically examine Krautrock from the perspective of post-colonial studies. Often

---

[4] Quoted in T Barr, *Kraftwerk: From Düsseldorf to the Future (with Love)* (London: Ebury, 1998), p. 74.

without any musical training, young people tried to create an emancipatory, anti-nationalist art form that opposed the anglophone cultural
imperialism – Krautrock offered an opportunity to create a new, uncon-
taminated national identity from a minority position, but also would be
a transnational music, readily open to foreign cultural influences beyond
the anglosphere. It was to be an innovative form of music that aimed at no
less than 'denazification': rebuilding German culture and morally and
politically cleansing the musicians themselves, as leftist pop music critic
Frank A. Schneider remarked.[5]

This political-aesthetic programme was largely successful, although it
became increasingly superfluous as German society and politics were
liberalised under the chancellorship of social democrat Willy Brandt
during the 1970s. Krautrock eventually disappeared and was succeeded
towards the early 1980s by the Neue Deutsche Welle (German New
Wave) movement, which was largely inspired by the British post-punk
movement. New wave and post-punk were hence paying back their
artistic dues; Krautrock returned, in adapted and hybridised form, to
Germany. The chain of transnational exchanges and mutual feedback
mechanisms – which could also be observed in the trans-Atlantic transformation of electronic Krautrock music (by Kraftwerk and other
bands) into styles such as electro, house, and techno – had been set in
motion.

A Krautrock Renaissance

In Germany, Krautrock bands were all but forgotten during the late 1980s
and 1990s. It was only the renewed interest in Britain that initiated
a sustained revival. A key role in this resurgence was played by the musician
Julian Cope, formerly singer of the Liverpool band The Teardrop Explodes.
His idiosyncratic *Guide to the Great Kosmische Music*, as his 1995 primer
Krautrocksampler was subtitled, caused an astonishing Krautrock renaissance, reportedly leading to many British record shops selling out of the
albums enthusiastically praised by Cope. His book also inspired the emer-
gence of the Kosmische Club in July 1996, founded and run by Leon
Muraglia, which quickly developed into one of the best-known clubs in
London.

---

[5] F Schneider, *Deutschpop halt's Maul! Für eine Ästhetik der Verkrampfung* (Mainz: Ventil, 2015),
pp. 18–21.

The advent of the Internet unquestionably proved key in the rediscovery of Krautrock: the archive was flung wide open, as it were, making music widely available that previously often only existed as a rumour or as highly expensive, sought-after collectors' items. First mostly through illegal file-sharing blogs, later via commercial streaming services, even the deeper reaches of the Krautrock corpus became accessible. But the Internet boost was not just about the music: fan websites mushroomed while many musicians established an Internet presence, enabling direct contact and distribution opportunities. This in turn increased demand for reissues, to which new German labels such as the Bureau B and Grönland Records responded from the early 2000s, making almost all the important releases on the classic Krautrock labels available again.

From the 2010s onwards, public interest in Krautrock became palpable in Britain: in 2009 BBC Four screened the TV documentary *Krautrock: The Rebirth of Germany*, and in 2012 BBC Radio 6 Music followed suit with the programme *The Man Machine: Kraftwerk, Krautrock and the German Electronic Revolution*. The first Krautrock book in English appeared in 2009: *Krautrock: Cosmic Rock and Its Legacy*, a richly illustrated coffee-table book edited by Nikos Kotsopoulos. It was followed by David Buckley's band biography *Kraftwerk Publikation* in 2012 and, two years later, by *Future Days: Krautrock and the Building of Modern Germany* by the music critic David Stubbs, which provided a truly comprehensive and competent account of the genre. Yet another standard work on a major band was published in 2018, the voluminous *All Gates Open: The Story of CAN*. It contains a comprehensive biography penned by Rob Young and a collage of interviews conducted by Can's keyboarder Irmin Schmidt with some twenty-five musicians and artists on the reception and legacy of the band.

The beginnings of academic interest in Krautrock hark back to a special issue of the journal *Popular Music and Society* in 2009, which has five articles by American researchers.[6] As John Littlejohn reminds us in his introduction, Krautrock is 'the single most important strand of modern popular music to originate outside the United States or England. . . . For such an important music, there exists surprisingly little research.'[7] The journal issue, which included articles on bands such as Faust, Neu!, and Kraftwerk, could of course only scratch the surface but it was an important first step. Two years later, *Kraftwerk: Music Nonstop*, edited by Sean Albiez

---

[6] *Popular Music and Society* 32:5 (2009).
[7] J Littlejohn, Introduction, *Popular Music and Society* 32:5 (2009), pp. 577–8 (577).

and David Pattie, laid a solid foundation for research into this, the most influential band to emerge from the Krautrock context.[8] Its eleven chapters cover a variety themes and topics and demonstrate the richness of the research questions raised by Kraftwerk's oeuvre.

Finally, two important monographs, both appearing in 2016, demarcate the beginning of serious and sustained research into Krautrock: Alexander Simmeth's German doctoral thesis *Krautrock transnational* and Ulrich Adelt's study *Krautrock: German Music in the Seventies*. Simmeth investigated the immense influence exerted by the most important German bands. From the viewpoint of an historian, he analysed the transnational feedback processes in which Krautrock music became hybridised across national and cultural borders.[9] Adelt surveyed the heterogenous field of Krautrock and provided a reliable theoretical framework for future research. His careful analysis showed Krautrock to be a discursive formation that invokes notions of essential Germanness and universal New Age spirituality, blurs rigid distinctions between a specific socio-political context of protest and a much broader interrogation of identity and stretches across different forms of media.[10]

The electronic branch of Krautrock, and in particular Kraftwerk, remains at the forefront of public interest and academic investigation. The international two-day conference I organised in Birmingham in January 2015 drew a capacity audience and created considerable interest among the research community, fans and the media. The edited volume *Mensch-Maschinen-Musik* from 2018 comprised papers given at the conference as well as at a follow-on event in October 2015 in Düsseldorf during the first Electri_City Conference,[11] which accompanied *Electri_City*, the oral history of electronic music from Düsseldorf, edited by Rudi Esch. My Kraftwerk primer, entitled *Kraftwerk: Future Music from Germany*, appeared with Penguin in 2020 and an adapted German version will follow in 2024 to celebrate fifty years since the release of *Autobahn*.

Kraftwerk are also the cornerstone of a travelling exhibition on the development of electronic music, which was first shown in 2019 at the Philharmonie de Paris with further stops at the Design Museum in London 2020 and Düsseldorf in 2021/22. The first dedicated Kraftwerk exhibition took place in 2015 at the Röhsska museum in Gothenburg, while the

---

[8] S Albiez & D Pattie, *Kraftwerk: Music Non-Stop* (London: Continuum, 2011).

[9] Simmeth, *Krautrock Transnational*.

[10] U Adelt, *Krautrock: German Music in the Seventies* (Ann Arbor: University of Michigan Press, 2016).

[11] U Schütte, *Mensch-Maschinen-Musik: Das Gesamtkunstwerk Kraftwerk* (Düsseldorf: Leske, 2018).

Barbican in London was the site of the 2020 exhibition entitled *Tangerine Dream: Zeitraffer* (Time Lapse/Fast Motion), which explored the work of these pioneers of *kosmische Musik* through photographs and videos, original synthesisers, cassettes, and vinyl.

The relative lack of German interest in Krautrock must be measured and understood against this roughly sketched background. Only the serious international recognition of Kraftwerk, Can, Neu!, et al. as influential musical innovators brought home the significance of Krautrock as a home-grown cultural achievement. Yet there are hardly any German equivalents to the BBC documentaries or indeed the knowledgeable books by British music journalists.

The first German survey of German music from the 1968 era and beyond, *Krautrock: Underground, LSD und kosmische Kuriere*, by Henning Dedekind, appeared in 2008 with a small Austrian publisher; evidently no German publisher was interested. It is a similar story for Christoph Wagner's excellent *Der Klang der Revolte: Die magischen Jahre des westdeutschen Musik-Untergrunds* (*The Sound of the Revolt: The Magical Years of the West German Music Underground*) from 2013. This richly illustrated volume appeared with Schott, a publisher specialising in musical notation rather than books on pop music.

More recently, to conclude this overview, the US-based German journalist Jan Reetze published *Times & Sounds: Germany's Journey from Jazz and Pop to Krautrock and Beyond* in 2020, followed by a German version in 2022. This idiosyncratic book provides an extensive survey of the history of German popular music from the immediate post-war period to the present. In it, Krautrock takes centre stage, but all sorts of side lines are discussed and, once again, only a small publisher was interested.

Female Voices Uncovered

It took until summer 2021 before Christoph Dallach's aforementioned interview compilation *Future Sounds* became the first German Krautrock book proper to appear with a trade publisher, Berlin's Suhrkamp Verlag. Dallach interviewed both leading and unknown musicians from Germany and Britain, along with prominent journalists, key producers, and important record company managers, providing a rich and polyphonic oral history of the development of Krautrock and its cultural, historical, and socio-economic context. *Future Sounds* was positively received in the media and finally drove home the importance of Krautrock to a German reading audience, but this is not its only merit: the book also gives overdue credit to the female musicians and other women whose important contributions were previously largely ignored in histories of Krautrock.

In addition to allowing Renate Knaup-Krötenschwanz, lead singer of Amon Düül, to discuss her marginalisation in an all-male band, Dallach's book rediscovers the avant-garde music of female bands like Zweistein (consisting of the sisters Suzanne and Diana Doucet) or the unusual musician and instrument maker Limpe Fuchs. Furthermore, *Future Sounds* features female voices such as the graphic designer Gil Funccius, who conceived impressive album artwork for Embryo, Wallenstein, and Amon Düül, among others. Similarly, Dallach's book recognises Hildegard Schmidt, wife of Can keyboarder Irmin Schmidt, for the crucial role she played as manager of the music group.

Another important book published in 2021 is devoted to the rediscovery of a pioneering female music journalist: *Die Zukunft war gestern* (*The Future Was Yesterday*) collects many of the best features and reviews by Ingeborg Schober. She was not only one of the first music journalists in the Federal Republic but also one of the best to boot. Her pioneering, partly autobiographical book *Tanz der Lemminge* (*Dance of the Lemmings*, 1979) gave a vivid and detailed portrayal, not just of Amon Düül, but also the communal scene that proved so crucial to the development of Krautrock. As a woman working in the predominantly male world of music journalism, Schober long fought against prejudices and later became a role model for aspiring female journalists.

Always eager to discover exciting new music, Schober writes on many Anglo-American bands that proved ground-breaking, such as Talking Heads, The Human League, and Ultravox. It was her pronounced interest in experimental sounds, though, that meant that she not only discovered but also strongly advocated Krautrock acts like Can, Neu!, and Kraftwerk, despite widespread German prejudice against home-grown bands. It is therefore no exaggeration to state that Schober considerably helped shape the German Krautrock scene.[12]

The 'Sound of Revolt'

While the present volume aims to provide readers with an academically solid and focused overview of the major Krautrock bands, along with the key contexts and an examination of the legacy of the movement, there is an

---

[12]　I Schober, *Die Zukunft war gestern: Essays, Gespräche und Reportagen* (Meine: Reiffer, 2021).

important proviso. As must be readily admitted, any such endeavour is bound to fail given the complexity of the Krautrock phenomenon. Krautrock simply cannot be defined effectively as the product of specific German political, economic, historic, and cultural specifics, since international outliers have existed since the term originated.

For example, in 1970, the multinational quartet Dom released their only major album, *Edge Of Time*, which shares several stylistic similarities with Krautrock but included members from Germany, Poland, and Hungary. In the following year, the Belgian band Brainticket released their debut *Cottonwoodhill*, inspired by Tangerine Dream, Amon Düül II, and Can, which again shared many of the musical characteristics of these bands' early work.[13] Likewise, the music by the all-French band Magma, which sang in the constructed language of Kobaïan, is partly reminiscent of the composer Carl Orff and fits seamlessly into the sonic palette of German Krautrock bands.

A better way to consider and define the heterogenous artistic body of Krautrock is hence to posit that the common aesthetic quality uniting these bands and artists was the emphasis placed on experimentation with sound and song structures. Through these musical means, Krautrockers of all denominations constructed what can be described, with Josh Kun's notion of the 'audiotopia', as an alternative, utopian space. This aesthetic space constructed from experimental sounds did not necessarily mark an attempt to create a German-sounding pop music.

After all, much of Krautrock music was inclusive of non-German elements and influences and thus sought to create a hybridised version of Germanness that challenged essentialist and fixed notions of what it meant to be German. As such, it resonated strongly with musicians outside Germany, who also felt political dissatisfaction with their own culture and its pop music. Or as Kun puts it: 'Music can be of a nation, but it is never exclusively national; it always overflows, spills out, sneaks through, reaches an ear on the other side of the border line, on the other side of the sea.'[14] And that is just what Krautrock did.

As a German phenomenon, however, it needs to be understood as the main but surely not only expression of what Christoph Wagner labelled the 'sound of revolt'.[15] Though Krautrock proved to be the most important and influential musical expression that originated in the fertile period between 1967 and 1973 in Germany, it was by no means the only musical revolution

[13] Thanks to Alex Harden for bringing these examples to my attention.

[14] J Kun, *Audiotopia: Music, Race, and America* (Berkeley: University of California Press, 2005), p. 20.

[15] C Wagner, *Der Klang der Revolte: Die magischen Jahre des westdeutschen Musik-Untergrunds* (Mainz: Schott, 2013), pp. 15–37.

at the time. In a spirit of optimism, young Germans radically broke with the affirmative *Schlager* music produced by the culture industry in the revolutionary atmosphere of a general politicisation of society.

This radical change equally affected the area of jazz: free improvisation emerged with musicians such as Peter Brötzmann and Alexander von Schlippenbach, and jazz musicians such as Wolfgang Dauner branched out into electronic music; the unadventurous singer-songwriter scene, too, saw a paradigm shift with the advent of political *Liedermacher* (literally: song makers) like Franz Josef Degenhardt, while the folk scene turned psychedelic with Witthüser & Westrupp and others.[16] Ton Steine Scherben, to provide one last example, stuck to Anglo-American models with their music but used highly political lyrics that openly agitated for revolutionary action.[17]

That is to say, in more sober academic language, the transition period from the late 1960s to the early 1970s was – to use the terminology of historian Reinhart Koselleck – a *Sattelzeit* (saddle time, or threshold time). Still, as Magma and other experimental French bands demonstrate, Krautrock was part of a continental radical transformation that was fundamentally but not exclusively German.

Air from Another Planet

When visiting Germany, British observers like the music critic Ian MacDonald were not just fascinated by Krautrock, they also noticed that audiences behaved noticeably differently. When joining concert-goers to listen to 'cosmic groups' in the winter of 1972, MacDonald stated that 'the audience common denominator on the rock circuit is that fabulous monster: The Revolutionary Head'.[18] To MacDonald, German music fans appeared far more sincere, politicised, and unruly than their British counterparts. Similarly, he noticed the unfamiliar features of the German music scene, such as a pronounced tendency for self-help, idealism, and initiative,

---

[16] E Holler, The Folk and Liedermacher Scene in the Federal Republic in the 1970s and 1980s, in D Robb (ed.), *Protest Song in East and West Germany since the 1960s* (Woodbridge: Boydell & Brewer, 2013), pp. 133–68.

[17] M Putnam, Music as a Weapon: Reactions and Responses to RAF Terrorism in the Music of Ton Steine Scherben and Their Successors in Post-9/11 Music, *Popular Music and Society* 32:5 (2009), pp. 595–606.

[18] I MacDonald, Germany Calling, *New Musical Express* (9 December 1971).

resulting in economy-priced concerts, independent distribution, or self-prompted shows.

The 'threshold time' between the 1960s and 1970s was clearly shaped by the strong belief in utopia; the faith that, after the immense catastrophe of the Holocaust and out of the rubble of the bombed cities, a better, brighter future was (or at least seemed) attainable. The futuristic impetus of Krautrock originates from this very spirit of departure. But the sense of being at the cusp of a new age – and this is a crucial point – could be grasped when listening to the utterly new sounds created by synthesisers. In very much the same way, going to a concert now often meant to witness machines making music. No wonder, then, that futuristic metaphors and/ or sales tags like *kosmische Musik* abounded, along with science-fiction-type album titles like *Cyborg* (Klaus Schulze) or *Alpha Centauri* (Tangerine Dream), and that was long before Kraftwerk released their defining album *Mensch-Maschine* (*Man-Machine*) in 1978 and began to replace musicians with robot mannequins.

Fast forward forty years to July 2018: when Ralf Hütter invited the German astronaut Alexander Gerst – who was orbiting earth on the International Space Station – to join Kraftwerk live from space for a performance of 'Spacelab' at their Stuttgart appearance, he used the words, 'Lasst uns zusammen Zukunftsmusik machen!' (Let's play future music together).[19] 'Future music', as a concept, is key here. For starters, well into the twenty-first century, the very innovation of Kraftwerk and other Krautrockers to shed all norms and conventions of rock music proved more than prophetic. Not only does electronic pop music constitute the (cultural industrial) norm today but, more importantly, the experimentation that characterised 1970s German music carries on in current bands like Radiohead, The Flaming Lips, or Camera.

At the same time, the notion of 'future music' refers us back to Richard Wagner. In 1861, Wagner expressed his view that it is not enough for music to be contemporary: it had to be ahead of itself and its time. The composer's duty, according to Wagner, is to call up from the future those aesthetic forms that may already be present in the germ but have not yet been made audible.[20] This line of thinking, of course, betrays a very modernist aesthetic. Furthermore, Wagner understood his considerations of the future of

[19] U Schütte, Update 2021: 'Lasst uns zusammen Zukunftsmusik machen', in U Schütte (ed.), *Mensch-Maschinen-Musik: Das Gesamtkunstwerk Kraftwerk* (Düsseldorf: Leske, 2021), pp. 358–65 (363–4).

[20] R Wagner, *Zukunftsmusik: Brief an einen französischen Freund als Vorwort zu einer Prosa-Uebersetzung seiner Operndichtungen* (Leipzig: Weber, 1861).

music as socio-philosophical: only a new, liberated society can bring forth the desired, unheard type of music. As hardly needs to be stressed, this same belief also underwrites the emergence of Krautrock during the late 1960s.

In 1907/8, Arnold Schönberg composed his string quartet no. 2, op. 10, incorporating a line from the poem 'Entrückung' (Rapture) by Stefan George: 'Ich fühle luft von anderem planeten' (I feel air from another planet).[21] Schönberg's piece occupies a threshold position in his oeuvre; the composition enters new sonic territory with its non-hierarchically structured harmony and the suspended tensions between consonance and dissonance. Something new, something unheard of, can be sensed though it has not yet arrived – air from planets other than earth.[22] The astral metaphor provides an evident link to the *kosmische Musik* that Krautrock produced. Both Schönberg and the young German musicians experimenting with previously unheard, otherworldly sounds very much believed that their music allowed one to breathe such novel air – not in a fantastic neverland or an unattainable, distant future, but here and now, as a harbinger of things to come.

This idea, in turn, connects with the philosophy of utopian thinker Ernst Bloch. In his writings on music in *Der Geist der Utopie* (*The Spirit of Utopia*), published in revised form in 1923, he considers music to be a toolkit for utopian thinking. Accordingly, Bloch argues music must not be 'related all too historically to the past, instead of being illuminated from the direction of the future: as Spirit in utopian degree'.[23] To illustrate the ability of music to instil a genuine sense of emergence in the listener, Bloch affirmingly quotes from *Selina*, a fragmentary novel by the writer Jean Paul (1736–1823). The heroine, Selina, poses this question:

Why, when music redoubles our sad or happy emotions, even creates them, do we forget how more supremely and forcibly than any other art it tosses us abruptly back and forth between happiness and sadness, in the blink of an eye – I ask, why do we forget her outstanding characteristic: her power to make us homesick? Not for the old, abandoned land, but for the virgin land; not for a past but for a future?[24]

---

[21] M Pfisterer, 'Ich fühle luft von anderem planeten': Ein George-Vers kommentiert den Beginn der Neuen Musik. Analyse eines Themas von Arnold Schönberg, in H Kühn & P Nitsche (eds.), *Bericht über den Internationalen Musikwissenschaftlichen Kongress Berlin 1974* (Kassel: Bärenreiter, 1980), pp. 416–24.

[22] H Mayer, Musik als Luft von anderen Planeten, in H Mayer (ed.), *Versuche über die Oper* (Frankfurt: Suhrkamp, 1981), pp. 153–62.

[23] E Bloch, *The Spirit of Utopia* (Stanford: Stanford University Press, 2000), p. 54.

[24] Ibid., p. 157.

This nineteenth-century description of utopian longing for better times, the notion of homesickness for the future captures perfectly the very same sentiments, hopes and expectations that Krautrock expressed and instilled in contemporary listeners in 1960s and 1970s Germany. More so, as the longevity of that experimental music attests, its seemingly timeless sound is still able to achieve this effect in listeners today.

To sum up, the future music that is Krautrock needs to be situated in its overarching cultural historical context to be fully understood and appreciated for its manifold social, political, cultural, and musical achievements. Only against this background does it emerge as part of a longstanding countercultural tradition, that is to say: as an artistic protest against the gravity of the unsatisfactory circumstances that we find ourselves trapped in. A never-ceasing musical release of fresh air from another planet.

PART I

Context

1 | Krautrock

Definitions, Concepts, Contexts

ULRICH ADELT

Even five decades after its emergence, the term 'Krautrock' remains contested among artists affiliated with the music. In Christoph Dallach's 2021 oral history of Krautrock, Klaus Schulze called the term 'dreadful', while Wallenstein drummer Harald Grosskopf found it 'wonderful'; Mani Neumeier of Guru Guru thought of the term as 'not even unsympathetic', whereas Jaki Liebezeit rejected the 'rock' part even more than the derogatory 'kraut', and preferred to think of his band Can as a 'pop group'.[1] This diversity of opinions extends to heated discussions on social media by self-described Krautrock fans as to which bands should be included and excluded and how to rank the included ones as to their importance and significance.[2]

Generally, Krautrock is used as a catch-all term for the music of various West German rock groups of the 1970s that blended influences of African American and Anglo-American music with the experimental and electronic music of European composers. Many Krautrock bands arose out of the West German student counterculture and connected leftist political activism with experimental rock music and, later, electronic sounds. There are no precise dates for Krautrock, and while the heyday of the movement was roughly from 1968 to 1974, one could also argue that it lasted well into the 1980s. Krautrock was primarily a West German art form and differed significantly from East German *Ostrock*, with the latter's emphasis on more traditional song structures. Krautrock and its offshoots have had a tremendous impact on musical production and reception in Britain and the United States since the 1970s. Genres such as indie, post-rock, EDM, and hip-hop have drawn heavily on Krautrock and have connected a music that initially disavowed its European American and African American origins with the lived experience of whites and blacks in the United

---

[1] C Dallach, *Future Sounds: Wie ein paar 'Krautrocker' die Popwelt revolutionierten* (Berlin: Suhrkamp, 2021), pp. 15, 12, 11.

[2] A good indication is a list of fifty seminal albums in my 2016 monograph on Krautrock that generated a fiery exchange of opinions among subscribers to a Facebook group (265 comments in total, including a few by Amon Düül II singer Renate Knaup). The post on the Facebook Krautrock group is from 16 October 2016.

States and Europe. At the same time, while reaching for an imagined cosmic community, Krautrock, not only by its name, stirs up essentialist notions of national identity and citizenship.

Viewed as a genre, Krautrock seemingly points to a specific national identity, but it continuously transgresses spatial borders and defies rigid classifications. Therefore, even its one seemingly definitive component (its 'Germanness') is dubious. Historically, the term itself was only one among many describing West German popular music from the 1970s. Until about 1973, the music magazines *Musikexpress* and *Sounds* used *Deutsch-Rock* ('German Rock') to label the new groups from West Germany. Alexander Simmeth dismisses the theory that the British music press invented the term Krautrock and cites producer Konrad 'Conny' Plank's music publishing house Kraut, which was established in 1969, as well as an Amon Düül song from the same year, 'Mama Düül und ihre Sauerkrautband spielt auf' (Mama Düül is Playing with Her Sauerkraut Band), as early namesakes.[3]

Yet, it should be noted that the word 'kraut' is short for 'sauerkraut' only in its English definition – in German *Kraut* refers to, among other things, herbs, weeds, and even drugs (for Mani Neumeier, Krautrock referred to the *Kraut* 'that you smoke' rather than the *Kraut* 'that you eat'[4]). Arguably, the actual term Krautrock was introduced by British DJ John Peel and taken up by the British music press, which interchangeably also used other terms like 'Teutonic rock' or 'Götterdämmer rock'. In an ironic move in response to the popularisation of the term, the band Faust called the first song on their 1973 album *Faust IV* 'Krautrock'.

For a long time, the West German music press used 'Krautrock' as a term to dismiss specific artists. Even as late as 1982, a special edition on the 'Neue Deutsche Welle' (New German Wave) by the music monthly *Musikexpress* repeatedly invoked negative connotations of Krautrock as sounds that were considered passé: Hanover punk bands were countering 'pompous Kraut-Rock a la Eloy or Jane'; Düsseldorf bands like Kraftwerk and Neu! were developing innovative electronic music concepts, 'while musicians in the rest of Germany were still ploughing through Krautrock by the sweat of their brow'.[5] The dismissal of Krautrock was part of a more

---

[3] A Simmeth, *Krautrock transnational: Die Neuerfindung der Popmusik in der BRD, 1968–1978* (Bielefeld: Transcript, 2016), p. 54.

[4] Dallach, *Future Sounds*, p. 12.

[5] *Musikexpress Special: Neue Deutsche Welle* (Hamburg: Drei Sterne, 1982), pp. 5, 16.

general trend in the German music press to view domestic productions as less important than British or American ones.

Incidentally, it was Krautrock's success in Britain that made the term more acceptable in West Germany. In 1974, the Hamburg label Brain issued a triple-album compilation of West German music under the title *Kraut-Rock*. In his liner notes, Winfried Trenkler wrote: 'Rock from the Federal Republic [of Germany] doesn't have to hide behind Anglo-American rock, in particular when German musicians don't even try to sound like their famous colleagues from the USA and England.'[6] Apart from the musicians cited earlier, most of the German public, if aware of the term, does not seem to find it offensive and many music aficionados even embrace it as a seal of approval.

While German and American publications did not apply positive connotations of the term for a long time, the British music press gave it a more positive spin. The publications *Melody Maker* and *New Musical Express* soon raved about West German bands, some of which, like Faust and Amon Düül II, became more successful in Britain than in their home country; Tangerine Dream's album *Phaedra*, for example, even reached the UK Top 20 in 1974. It should be noted that the positive use of 'Krautrock' in Britain only became more common after an initial barrage of World War II stereotypes, as Uwe Schütte has shown for the example of Kraftwerk.[7]

Another term commonly used for some German music from the 1970s is *kosmische Musik* (cosmic music). It was introduced by Rolf-Ulrich Kaiser to market Krautrock artists like Ash Ra Tempel, Tangerine Dream, and Klaus Schulze. Although also rejected by many artists associated with it, *kosmische Musik* remains a useful term to describe the synthesiser-heavy, meditative anti-rock of some West German musicians of the 1970s since a cosmic, 'New Age' identity was one way in which Krautrock musicians conceptually and sonically re-imagined 'Germanness'.

Taken together, the ongoing debates about Krautrock among fans and scholars, the context of its musical diversity, and, in particular, its spatial ambiguity and conflicted expression of German national identity show the relevance of what I prefer to call a 'discursive formation' (rather than the more restrictive notion of 'genre') in re-imagining regimens of sound, space, and place in non-hierarchical ways.

---

[6] W Trenkler, liner notes for *Kraut-Rock: German Rock Scene* (Brain, 1974).
[7] U Schütte, From Defamation to Adoration: The Reception of Kraftwerk in the British Music Press, 1974–1981, *Angermion* 13:1 (2020), pp. 1–24.

The Reception of Krautrock

The reception of Krautrock inside and outside of Germany shows the instability of a musical formation that was generally only recognised as anything cohesively 'German' by non-Germans. Initially, Krautrock did not leave much of a legacy in its country of origin. Artists who had been commercially successful – like Kraftwerk, La Düsseldorf, and Michael Rother – gradually retreated from the scene, while other artists like Faust are still fairly unknown in their home country. Some groups – like Tangerine Dream – remained successful throughout the 1980s but were rarely associated with their 1970s output or any concept of 'Krautrock'. The term itself, which had never been accepted by most of the musicians associated with it, was increasingly used by publications like the German *Sounds* in the 1980s to classify music that was seen as overblown and outdated – the bloated progressive rock of bands like Eloy, Grobschnitt, and Triumvirat. German punk and Neue Deutsche Welle, in contrast, briefly appeared as a fresh alternative that responded to the trends coming from Britain and even to Germany's *Schlager* (literally 'hit') legacy.

Since the 1990s, Krautrock has been successfully re-branded as a genre in countries that include Germany and Britain, but also the United States and Japan. For instance, in April 1997, British *Mojo* magazine ran a thirty-page special under the title 'Kraftwerk, Can and the Return of the Krautrockers'. An instrumental figure in the 1990s revival of Krautrock was the British musician Julian Cope, who published the now out-of-print *Krautrocksampler* in 1995. In his thoroughly entertaining but highly subjective account, Cope argues that Krautrock 'was borne on the high East wind that soared above the rage of the 1960s British and American scenes' and comprises 'some of the most astonishing, evocative, heroic glimpses of Man at his Peak of Artistic Magic'.[8] As the first readily available discussion of something that could be recognised as 'Krautrock' and as an introduction to bands that proved to be influential afterwards, the book became quite popular among British and American music insiders and musicians. As Cope has pointed out, his main reason for writing the book was 'to introduce the word "Krautrock" in a more positive, pouting glamrock way'.[9] Partly as a result of Cope's book, entire genres of British and

---

[8] J Cope, *Krautrocksampler: One Head's Guide to the Great Kosmische Music – 1968 Onwards* (Yatesbury: Head Heritage, 1996), pp. 2, 3.

[9] J Cope, Q&A 2000ce: Krautrock, July 2000, www.headheritage.co.uk/julian_cope/qa2000ce/krautrock.

American popular music openly borrowed from Krautrock groups like Can, Kraftwerk, Neu!, and Tangerine Dream, including, but not limited to, punk, post-punk, post-rock, industrial, disco, various forms of EDM like techno, ambient, and house, hip-hop, and indie rock. Even bestselling groups like Radiohead and Wilco clearly indicated that they were indebted to West German music from the 1970s.

The renewed interest in Krautrock as subcultural capital specifically in American indie rock discourses is exemplified by the reception of the music in the online publication *Pitchfork Media*, founded in 1995. In 2004, *Pitchfork* published their 'Top 100 Albums of the 1970s'. With a disproportionate amount of German music, the list included three LPs by Can (*Ege Bamyasi*, *Tago Mago*, and *Future Days*), two by Kraftwerk (*Trans Europa Express* and *Die Mensch-Maschine*), and one each by Cluster (*Zuckerzeit*), Neu! (*Neu!*), Faust (*Faust IV*), and Giorgio Moroder (*From Here to Eternity*). Also included were the two Krautrock-inspired LPs by Iggy Pop (*The Idiot* and *Lust for Life*), as well as David Bowie's *Low*, which topped the list. In interviews conducted in 2013 with a number of the *Pitchfork* editors responsible for reviving Krautrock as an important influence on popular music, they described the appeal of the music as an alternative to standard Anglo-American and African American models and how for them it represented a certain coolness through being 'weird' and 'otherworldly'.[10]

In addition to 'popular' interest in Krautrock (in the sense of trickling out into popular consciousness after its subcultural value had been introduced by gatekeepers like Julian Cope), the past decade has seen a significant increase in scholarship on the music. Earlier English-language accounts by well-known musicians and journalists like Cope and Lester Bangs often suffered from a fascination with what they perceive as the Germanness of an exotic Other – for instance, although many Krautrock musicians explicitly distanced themselves from the past, the Germany chapter in Jim DeRogatis' seminal book about psychedelic rock from 2003 was entitled 'The Krautrock Blitzkrieg'.[11] Another early approach was to simply list all West German groups, no matter how obscure, as Stephen and Alan Freeman did in their 1996 compendium *Crack in the Cosmic Egg*.[12] Two non-scholarly German

---

[10] U Adelt, *Krautrock: German Music in the Seventies* (Ann Arbor: University of Michigan Press, 2016), pp. 170–4.

[11] Cope, *Krautrocksampler*; L Bangs, Kraftwerkfeature, *Creem* (September 1975), pp. 30–1; J DeRogatis, *Turn On Your Mind: Four Decades of Great Psychedelic Rock* (Milwaukee: Hal Leonard, 2003).

[12] S and A Freeman, *Crack in the Cosmic Egg: Encyclopedia of Krautrock, Kosmische Musik, & Other Progressive, Experimental & Electronic Musics from Germany* (Leicester: Audion, 1996).

books by Henning Dedekind and Christoph Wagner provided meandering and detailed histories of Krautrock with the inclusion of some groups deliberately excluded from Julian Cope's Krautrock canon, such as Missus Beastly, Kraan, Anima, and Checkpoint Charlie.[13]

Musical Context

Because of the music's stylistic diversity, a musicological definition of the term Krautrock is equally as difficult as a semantic or historical definition. The influence of music traditionally perceived as German, such as the compositions of Bach, Beethoven, and Brahms, on what would evolve around 1968 as Krautrock is negligible (the history of any distinctively 'German' music mostly dates back to the nineteenth century and is more a product of writers and politicians than of classical composers).[14] Krautrock also stood in stark opposition to popular forms like *Schlager*, German-language pop songs with simple melodies and sentimental lyrics, and *Volksmusik* ('oom-pah music'), traditional regional styles mostly from Bavaria. Finally, Krautrock rejected heavily Anglo-Americanised or African American–derived forms of post-war popular music like the toned-down German-language rock 'n' roll of Peter Kraus and the early 1960s German beat bands like The Rattles and The Lords, who merely imitated their Anglo-American models.

Despite its rejection of Anglo-American influences, Krautrock did pay tribute to some of the psychedelic rock bands and other countercultural artists from Britain and the United States, namely Pink Floyd, Frank Zappa, and Jimi Hendrix. Yet, instead of merely developing another replication of the major Anglo-American and African American styles that dominated the airwaves, Krautrock artists also drew from two distinctive musical developments that were outside of mainstream rock's framework, both geographically and structurally: experimental composition and free jazz.

The Darmstadt Summer Courses, 'instituted in 1946 to bring young Germans ... up to date with music unheard under the Nazis',[15] became increasingly international over the years and involved composers like

---

[13] H Dedekind, *Krautrock: Underground, LSD und kosmische Kuriere* (Höfen: Hannibal, 2008); C Wagner, *Der Klang der Revolte: Die magischen Jahre des westdeutschen Musik-Underground* (Mainz: Schott, 2013).

[14] Compare C Applegate and P Potter (eds.), *Music and German National Identity* (Chicago: University of Chicago Press, 2002), pp. 2–3.

[15] P Griffiths, *Modern Music and After* (New York: Oxford University Press), p. 35.

Edgar Varèse, Karlheinz Stockhausen, and Pierre Boulez. The Darmstadt school's embrace of total serialism and resistance to neoclassicism foreshadowed many of Krautrock's developments (as did musique concrète and minimalism). Stockhausen, who taught two of the musicians who later founded the Krautrock group Can, collaborated with the Studio for Electronic Music in Cologne as early as 1953 and began 'sampling' and electronically manipulating non-Western music and national anthems in his compositions *Telemusik* (1966) and *Hymnen* (1966–7). Another vital influence on Krautrock clearly outside of Anglo-American traditions were German free jazz musicians like Peter Brötzmann, Manfred Schoof, and Alexander von Schlippenbach, part of a central European (Scandinavian/German/Dutch) scene that was departing from the harmonic and rhythmic conventions still retained in American free jazz.

Sonically, Krautrock came to encompass a range of styles, from the electronic music of Klaus Schulze and the jazz rock of Kraan to the political songs of Floh de Cologne, the folk rock of Witthüser & Westrupp, and music that is even harder to classify but had a long-lasting impact, like that of Faust, Cluster, or Popol Vuh. Krautrock was influenced by African American music but also involved the conscious departure from blues scales, as those were the building blocks of Anglo-American rock music. Unlike psychedelic rock groups in the United States, many Krautrock performers had a background in European classical music and ties to the electronic music of 'serious' composers. Krautrock's embrace of the dilettante, abstract, and experimental contrasted with British progressive rock's focus on composition and Romantic themes. The early use of synthesisers, non-traditional song structures, and the employment of a steady, metronomic beat (generally referred to as *motorik*) instead of rock 'n' roll's backbeat also set Krautrock apart from Anglo-American music of the 1970s. Through their connections to the avant-garde art world, through their more intellectual approach, and through abandoning traditional song structures, Krautrock bands were in some aspects more daring and radical than comparative groups in Britain and the United States like Pink Floyd, the Beatles, or the Beach Boys.

As the music scene in West Germany was flourishing in the 1970s, it became increasingly harder to generalise about Krautrock. While many groups included classically trained musicians, diverted from the blues scales of American psychedelic rock groups like the Grateful Dead, released albums on small labels like Ohr, Pilz, and Brain, moved to the country to live in communes, and employed electronic instruments, none of these characteristics applied to all Krautrockers. Among the many different and unconnected local scenes were Düsseldorf, with the slick electronics of Kraftwerk, Neu!, and Wolfgang Riechmann; Hamburg, with the experimental rock of Faust; Cologne, with the groove-heavy minimalism of Can; Munich, with the psychedelic progressive rock of Amon Düül II; and West Berlin, with the synthesiser drones of Klaus Schulze, Ash Ra Tempel, and Tangerine Dream. To some extent, the stratification of Krautrock is a West German phenomenon, where one of the examples of the denazification-motivated decentralisation after World War II led to making the provincial town of Bonn the capital. The stylistically pluralist and heterogenous nature of Krautrock can hence be related to the federalist nature of West Germany.

Also, Krautrock was an exclusively West German phenomenon. To explain the absence of the music in East Germany, it is useful to consider the differences of the counterculture between East and West. Students in East Germany had more fundamental needs, which were expressed by singer-songwriters, many of whom were harassed or banned by the Communist government. The sole political party, SED, or *Sozialistische Einheitspartei Deutschlands* (Socialist Unity Party of Germany), strenuously tried to prohibit Western rock music, which made it a sought-after commodity and difficult to consistently access. East German rock groups like the Puhdys walked a fine line between supporting the government and subtly critiquing it, and musically mostly imitated British and American bands while adding German lyrics.[16]

Since Marxism was part of the establishment in the East, many young people viewed the United States as a potential liberator, and there was not the same urge to reject Anglo-American influences as 'imperialist' as in Krautrock.[17] Jazz and rock were sought after as a 'window to the West'.[18] With the difficulty of obtaining and accessing music from Western countries, Krautrock was also simply not big enough to make it over to East Germany. Despite the absence of Krautrock in East Germany, understanding the divided nation is crucial for the politics of the music, in particular West Berlin groups like Tangerine Dream and Ton Steine Scherben, who were tied to West Germany ideologically but not geographically.

---

[16] Compare M Rauhut, *Rock in der DDR: 1964–1989* (Bonn: Bundeszentrale für politische Bildung, 2002).

[17] Compare R Ritter, '1968' und der Wandel der Protestkultur in der Musik im Ostblock: Ausgewählte Beispiele (CSSR, DDR, Polen, Ungarn), in Beate Kutschke (ed.), *Musikkulturen in der Revolte: Studien zu Rock, Avantgarde und Klassik im Umfeld von '1968'* (Stuttgart: Steiner, 2008), pp. 207–24 (p. 209).

[18] Ibid., p. 212.

Krautrock and Spatiality

There are a number of theoretical approaches one could apply to Krautrock. For instance, the historical context of West Germany's student revolution of 1968 has been thoroughly analysed by Alexander Simmeth, and gender would be an important lens to consider (with Krautrock groups defying the hypermasculinity of 'cock rock' yet overwhelmingly featuring male artists).[19] Here, I want to highlight spatiality as a concept that helps to understand the significance of the music and can even work to broaden the scope of what could be included (for instance, while many fans might disagree, I consider Donna Summer as part of Krautrock, challenging racialised and gendered notions of the music.)[20] Considering the spatiality of Krautrock can help re-thinking concepts of sound, belonging, and genre.

I hesitate to call Krautrock a 'genre' or 'movement' and would rather describe it as a 'discursive formation'. According to Foucault, 'the unity of a discourse is based not so much on the permanence and uniqueness of an object as on the space in which various objects emerge and are continuously transformed'.[21] Foucault applies this instability of seemingly fixed systems of classification to medical science, economics, and grammar, but it also informs the fragmented relationships between different musical expressions discussed under the contested term Krautrock. Connected merely by their destabilising of the seemingly coherent notion of national identity, Krautrock musicians rarely worked with each other (or even knew of each other) and did not form local scenes that expressed larger issues in regional ways. Indicative of a discursive formation, 'influences' on and by Krautrock artists did not operate in linear ways, a central figure did not emerge, and even the term Krautrock was only retroactively applied from outside of Germany. For Foucault, discursive formations are an attempt to apply some regularity to 'systems of dispersion' (like Krautrock), to describe 'series full of gaps, intertwined with one another, interplays of differences, distances, substitutions, transformations'.[22]

Rather than through a purely musicological or historical lens, I view Krautrock as being constructed through performance, articulated through various forms of expressive culture (among them, communal living,

---

[19] Simmeth, *Krautrock transnational*. For 'cock rock', compare S Waksman, *Instruments of Desire: The Electric Guitar and the Shaping of Musical Experience* (Cambridge: Harvard University Press, 1999).

[20] Adelt, *Krautrock*.

[21] M Foucault, *The Archaeology of Knowledge* (New York: Pantheon, 1972), p. 32.

[22] Ibid., p. 37.

spirituality, visual elements but, most importantly, sound) by people not even directly interacting with each other but still structurally related. This explains how Krautrock succeeded through time and space and does not merely reflect historical events.

Barry Shank has addressed the complex and dynamic relationship between music and identity in which real politics can emerge: 'The act of musical listening enables us to confront complex and mobile structures of impermanent relationships – the sonic interweaving of tones and beats, upper harmonics, and contrasting timbres – that model the experience of belonging to a community not of unity but of difference.'[23] Shank goes on to state that, rather than reifying identity, musical forms help 'capturing an emergent sense of the world'.[24] While Shank's examples are mostly Anglo-American, Krautrock serves to illustrate the transnational dimension of the politics he so aptly describes.

By employing a derogatory term for Germans in its name, Krautrock is clearly linked with national identity, but, particularly in times of increased globalisation, the nation-state appears as the mediator between the local and the global.[25] The study of Krautrock allows for an anthropologically motivated study not just of what Deleuze and Guattari have called 'de-territorialisation', but also of 're-territorialisation', a re-localising of culture in new or changed contexts. Néstor García Canclini describes the process of de-territorialisation and re-territorialisation as 'the loss of the "natural" relation of culture to geographical and social territories and, at the same time, certain relative, partial territorial re-localisations of old and new symbolic productions'.[26] Canclini's context is 1990s Latin America, but with the disruption of World War II, Krautrock artists also expressed a fragmented, porous transnational identity that, in Canclini's words, lacked 'consistent paradigms' and experienced the loss of 'the script and the author'.[27] Krautrock's de-territorialisation, its negation of the nation-state as a stable identifying force, plays with national identity through expressing an international or cosmic non-German Germanness and through ironically invoking older, seemingly stable forms of Germanness. The latter re-territorialisation also involves non-German subjects

---

[23] B Shank, *The Political Force of Musical Beauty* (Durham: Duke University Press, 2014), p. 1.

[24] Ibid.

[25] Compare I Biddle and V Knights, National Popular Musics: Betwixt and Beyond the Local and the Global, in I Biddle and V Knights (eds.), *Music, National Identity and the Politics of Location: Between the Global and the Local* (Burlington: Ashgate, 2007), pp. 1–15.

[26] N Canclini, *Hybrid Cultures: Strategies for Entering and Leaving Modernity* (Minneapolis: University of Minnesota Press, 2005), p. 229.

[27] Ibid., p. 243.

identifying with a transformed and transmogrified Germanness as evidence of Krautrock's 'globalisation'.

In addition to de-territorialisation, hybridisation helps to understand the transnational dimension of Krautrock. Despite critiques of biologism and the obviation of issues like class and gender, cultural hybridity can be useful for describing the exchanges that take place between the centre and the periphery or between different peripheries.[28] Hybridity can function as a form of resistance but does not necessarily entail oppositional politics. Canclini warns of reducing the study of hybridised popular culture to either deductivist or inductivist notions (i.e. assuming either that cultural production is exclusively determined by hegemonic sectors or that subaltern forces are solely responsible for shaping popular culture). Krautrock's hybridity appears in a variety of ways, from Kraftwerk's blurring of 'man' and 'machine' to the linguistic slippages of Neu!'s appropriation of advertising slogans and the syncretic spirituality of Popol Vuh, who blended Eastern religions with a reformed Christianity.

It should not come as a surprise that the spatiality of popular music is one of the major factors that create its hybridity. As George Lipsitz has noted in describing a poetics of place:

Recorded music travels from place to place, transcending physical and temporal barriers. It alters our understanding of the local and the immediate, making it possible for us to experience close contact with cultures from far away. Yet precisely because music travels, it also augments our appreciation of place. Commercial popular music demonstrates and dramatizes contrasts between places by calling attention to how people from different places create culture in different ways.[29]

Lipsitz's description of popular music as both transcending and reaffirming a sense of place applies to Krautrock's double discourse of the national and the transnational. In a different approach, Josh Kun has developed the notion of 'audiotopias', in which music itself appears as a spatial practice: 'Music is experienced not only as sound that goes into our ears and vibrates through our bones but as a space that we can enter into, encounter, move around in, inhabit, be safe in, learn from.'[30] One might add that as an alternative space, music is not always safe but disruptively appears in what

[28] See N Papastergiadis, Tracing Hybridity in Theory, in P Werbner and T Modood (eds.), *Debating Cultural Hybridity: Multi-Cultural Identities and the Politics of Anti-Racism* (London: Zed Books, 1997), pp. 257–81.

[29] G Lipsitz, *Dangerous Crossroads: Popular Music, Postmodernism and the Poetics of Place* (New York: Verso, 1994), pp. 3–4.

[30] J Kun, *Audiotopia: Music, Race, and America* (Berkeley: University of California Press, 2005), p. 2.

Lipsitz calls 'dangerous crossroads'. Josh Kun goes on to argue that political citizenship does not necessarily equate cultural conformity, and that 'music can be of a nation, but it is never exclusively national; it always overflows, spills out, sneaks through, reaches an ear on the other side of the border line, on the other side of the sea'.[31]

It follows from the ability of music to transgress and trespass invoked by Kun and Lipsitz that the relationship between national identity and music is always interpenetrative.[32] In their seminal book on popular music, identity, and place, geographers John Connell and Chris Gibson talk about the contested enterprise of linking music and nation-states when 'boundaries are porous, constantly being broken, necessitating new national anthems and new attempts to sustain imagined communities in the face of trans-national flows'.[33] I disagree with Connell and Gibson's assessment that national sounds are by definition 'retrospective and nostalgic',[34] and posit that unlike national anthems, Krautrock allows for a more flexible expression of nationality that necessitates moving across borders, as well as questioning essentialist and fixed notions of what it means to be German.

Conclusion

I have exercised different modes of theorising Krautrock here: analysing the semantics of the term, tracing the reception of its sounds, and taking a stab at its musicological characteristics; one could add the underlying historical contextualisation of World War II and the student revolution of 1968. I have mentioned gender as yet another promising aspect to study in further research on the topic. In the last section, I have illustrated how national/transnational identity and spatiality can serve as concepts that connect Krautrock's history, identity formation, and overall politics.

Drawing on the history and music of Krautrock, I perceive its de-territorialisation and hybridisation in different ways. Groups like Can, Kraftwerk, and Neu! created a post-war German identity that engaged with and set itself apart from the Nazi past and the influx of Anglo-American music

---

[31] Ibid., p. 20.

[32] Compare J O'Flynn, National Identity and Music in Transition: Issues of Authenticity in a Global Setting, in I Biddle and V Knights (eds.), *Music, National Identity and the Politics of Location*, pp. 19–38 (p. 26).

[33] J Connell and C Gibson, *Sound Tracks: Popular Music, Identity and Place* (Abingdon: Routledge, 2003), p. 143.

[34] Ibid.

by blending man-made and machine-made music, negotiating internationalism, stereotypical 'Germanness', and anti-capitalism. Other Krautrock bands
like Amon Düül I and II, Faust, and Ton Steine Scherben explored living in
communes as alternative spaces and expressed notions of community and
conflict in vastly different ways, while responding to similar modes of oppres-
sion. Performers of *kosmische Musik* like Ash Ra Tempel, Tangerine Dream,
Klaus Schulze, and Popol Vuh developed post-national notions of New Age
cosmic identity and spirituality, which involved the consumption of psychedelic drugs and the invention of new sounds, in particular through the
employment of the synthesiser. Popol Vuh also exemplifies the parallels
between Krautrock and the New German Cinema of the 1970s, as there are
connections between the landscapes of Werner Herzog's films and the soundscapes provided by the band (the soundtracks by bands like Tangerine Dream
and Can are also promising topics for future research). Finally, I would like to
argue that it is necessary to stretch the definitions of Krautrock as transnational by including Italian-German producer Giorgio Moroder's collaborations with African American disco singer Donna Summer as well as the three
years British pop star David Bowie spent in West Berlin in the 1970s.

As has become abundantly clear, when viewed as a discursive formation,
Krautrock eludes any strict definition, easy theorising, or quick summa-
tion. Its boundaries remain contested and its understanding unfinished.
This, however, is the intellectual work that Krautrock continues to challenge us to do, and I for one am happy that I am not done thinking about its
ramifications.

Recommended Reading

U Adelt, *Krautrock: German Music in the Seventies* (Ann Arbor: University of
    Michigan Press, 2016).
N Kotsopoulos, *Krautrock: Cosmic Rock and Its Legacy* (London: Black Dog, 2010).
A Simmeth, *Krautrock transnational: Die Neuerfindung der Popmusik in der BRD,
    1968–1978* (Bielefeld: Transcript, 2016).
D Stubbs, *Future Days: Krautrock and the Building of Modern Germany* (London:
    Faber & Faber, 2014).
C Wagner, *Der Klang der Revolte: Die magischen Jahre des westdeutschen Musik-
    Underground* (Mainz: Schott, 2013).

2 | Krautrock and the Radical Politics of 1968

DETLEF SIEGFRIED

Krautrock emerged in the late 1960s and early 1970s and cannot be understood without the upheaval of '1968'. In some respects, 1968 actually had a more political contour in West Germany than in other Western European countries – with the exception of France, perhaps. There were three main reasons for this: the immediate pre-history of the 'Third Reich', the fact that the country was at the crossroads of the Cold War, and a philosophical tradition of thought that was always on the trace of fundamental truths.

Attitudes towards National Socialism had shaped the youth revolt in West Germany, and it was already fully formed before 1968. The vast majority of the older generations had been entangled with National Socialism through active complicity or all-too-passive acceptance, and therefore could not claim a guiding role in the present. Imprints of National Socialism continued to exist in a hidden anti-Semitism, anti-communism, and authoritarianism. A considerable section of society and politics opened the door to the elimination of democracy through the introduction of the *Notstandsgesetze* (Emergency Laws) in 1968, which allowed the government to curb civil rights in the case of uprisings, leading to suspicions of the door being potentially opened to a new dictatorship. The social force that was able to loosen these ties to the past was the young generation, especially young intellectuals. Detachment from Nazi ties as a prerequisite for social reform was an almost unquestioned basic argument in debates about sexuality, forms of housing, and political measures.

West Germany's position on the eastern front of the West and the division of Germany with the GDR as the antithesis of the Federal Republic had already created an anti-communist climate in the 1950s that shaped political and cultural discourses in general. Abstract art was a manifestation of Western freedom, which in turn was threatened by rock 'n' roll; communist agitation was also repeatedly suspected behind strikes and demonstrations. Unlike all other countries of Western Europe – except for the fascist dictatorships in Spain and Portugal – the Communist Party had been banned since 1956. A left-wing opposition thus had no parliamentary mouthpiece and was relegated to the streets.

Rudi Dutschke, the informal leader of the student movement, was born in East Germany and thus was particularly strongly politicised. The fact that a young Nazi sympathiser attempted to assassinate him in Easter 1968, the late effects of which were to kill him in 1979, contributed to the enormous radicalisation of the West German student movement. A particularly militant expression of radical thinking could be observed in the irreconcilable criticism that many actors directed at 1960s consumer society. This kind of society was represented not least by the United States, who were also delegitimised by the Vietnam War at the time. Symptomatic of this militancy was the arson attack on two Frankfurt department stores on 2 April 1968, carried out by Andreas Baader, Gudrun Ensslin, Thorwald Proll, and Horst Söhnlein, a week before Dutschke's assassination – an act that is not unjustly regarded as a precursor to the terrorism of the Rote Armee Fraktion, or RAF (Red Army Faction). Political radicalism, in the shape of militant action and communist groups, continued to represent a relevant part of the political outcome of 1968 during the 1970s.

However, one must look at the whole of 1968 and understand it as a melding of new cultural currents and radical politics. While research in countries like Britain or Denmark has always emphasised the cultural revolution, in West Germany the focus was for a long time on politics and thus the student movement. Only in recent years has the perspective broadened to include the cultural aspects of 1968 and its significance as a youth revolt. Here, music plays a central role as an emotional bonding element and semantic carrier of meaning. Folk and pop music, especially from the United States and Britain, represented a youth culture, trans-ported the ideal of a lifestyle separated from the older generation, and propagated political ideas that oscillated between participation and revolu-tion. In West Germany, these musical imports were at the same time opposed by the political reservation that they were being used by the culture industry to make profits and manipulate consumers.

Scepticism towards the culture industry was more widespread in West Germany than elsewhere and led to the development of a genre of its own – Krautrock – which was quite heterogeneous both musically and politically but was characterised by the endeavour of German musicians to develop a style of their own that set themselves apart from the American and British models. In this way, the German scene reacted to a feeling of over-saturation that had already set in by the autumn of 1967: flower power, the expansion of consciousness, and psychedelic and pop art dominated magazines and record shelves without having any provocative effect. The emergence of Krautrock can thus only be understood in the specific

German political context of 1968, from which, at the same time, it partially distanced itself.[1] The intermingling of pop culture and politics in the 1968 period fell apart shortly after – into a radical political scene on the one hand and a lifestyle-oriented music and drug scene on the other. However, contrary to received wisdom, in the practices of the Krautrockers, musical preferences were combined with radical political ideas and activities for a long time, partly even into the punk scene that emerged years later.

Catalysts: Rolf-Ulrich Kaiser and the Waldeck Festival

The mixing and unmixing of culture and politics can be traced particularly vividly in the story of Krautrock's most important protagonist, Rolf-Ulrich Kaiser. This story is closely connected with the precursors of Krautrock, the festivals at Waldeck Castle, and the Essen Songtage of 1968. Kaiser, born in 1943, was one of the most enigmatic figures of the counterculture. He came from the folk-and-protest-song scene, had political interests, and recognised the signs of the times early on, rising with the beat and underground culture and falling because of its professionalisation, which he himself had helped to spur. As organiser of the Essen Songtage, an author and publisher of several books, and a record producer, he played a central role in the breakthrough of the underground in West Germany between 1966 and 1972. He persistently worked through the question of how the rebellious core of the new culture could be further disseminated and at the same time preserved from culture-industrial dilution.

Kaiser advocated a mixed concept of left-wing positions in terms of content and experimental aesthetics. This mixed concept became particularly visible in the years around 1968; during the early 1970s, the aesthetic side gained a preponderance. Kaiser sensed new tendencies earlier than others and immediately put them into practice – through interventions at Burg Waldeck festivals, talent cultivation, his own festival, magazine distribution, and book and record production. No other player in the West German counterculture combined reflection on new trends so early and effectively with the production of pop cultural material. This made him an avant-gardist on the one hand, but on the other hand he appeared as an

---

[1] Cf. A Simmeth, *Krautrock transnational: Die Neuerfindung der Popmusik in der BRD 1968–1978* (Bielefeld: Transcript, 2016), pp. 190 ff.; U Adelt, *Krautrock: German Music in the Seventies* (Ann Arbor: University of Michigan Press, 2016), pp. 45 ff.

opportunist who knew how to turn a new mass movement into cash. Kaiser himself saw his initiatives as part of an economy of counterculture that did not strive for commercialisation but for popularity. A culturally critical public – especially on the left – did not accept the drive to commercialisation as exemplified by the concert agency Lippmann + Rau or rock bands that earned money in and with the counterculture.

An important focal nucleus of West German underground culture was the festivals held at Burg Waldeck in south-west Germany between 1964 and 1969. Songwriters such as Franz Josef Degenhardt, Dieter Süverkrüp, and Walter Mossmann came to prominence through their performances, while at the same time international folk stars such as Phil Ochs or Odetta provided a connection to developments in other countries.[2] In the context of the student movement, the festival became radicalised and, in 1968 and 1969, also offered a space for young German bands (like Xhol Caravan or Checkpoint Charlie). Moreover, it became a forum for discussion about German counterculture. The initiators of the Waldeck, somewhat older intellectuals, were considerably more sceptical about the potential of beat music than Kaiser. At this point already, in the debate about a possible renewal of the Waldeck Festival of 1967, he was accused of wanting to 'commercialise' the festival.[3] The fact was that Kaiser had pleaded, firstly, not only to accept the rise of folk music to mass culture, but to welcome it joyfully, and secondly, to spike it with that rebellious sting through politicisation that would ensure the spread of its emancipatory content and stop it flattening out commercially.

The Monterey Festival had shown what an electrified mass culture could achieve, and Waldeck 1967 had shown that the German folk song offered heightened political potential. It was important to combine the two into a new event concept. When the political protest movement spread after 2 June 1967 – when Berlin policeman killed a student during a demonstration – Kaiser noticed the new thrust that his concept received from this movement and spiced it up with fashionable vocabulary. The 'new song', he declared in 1968, gave a 'foretaste of what the revolution is capable of achieving'.

So directly related to content ... the talk of danger through corrupting success reveals itself as a liberal-bourgeois farce. The Fugs sell 100,000 copies of a single LP,

---

[2] H Schneider, *Die Waldeck: Lieder, Fahrten, Abenteuer: Die Geschichte der Burg Waldeck von 1911 bis heute* (Potsdam: Berlin-Brandenburg, 2005), pp. 313 ff.; M Kleff, *Die Burg Waldeck Festivals 1964–1969: Chansons Folklore International* (Hambergen: Bear Family Records, 2008).

[3] D Kerbs, Das Waldeck-Festival: Zu dem Bericht im Juliheft *Deutsche Jugend* 15 (1967), pp. 381–2 (381); R-U Kaiser, Chanson Folklore International, *Deutsche Jugend* 14 (1966), pp. 304–7 (304).

Franz-Josef Degenhardt fills 1,000-man halls even in medium-sized towns; and yet both their song lyrics have become nastier and more aggressive. It only becomes dangerous for the new song forms when they lose contact with the content of the revolution-to-be-achieved and fall in love with mere formal experimentation. Then, however, they are immediately manipulable, consumable. The new German songs are far from being in such danger. For they still have enough unconsumable fare to bring to consumers.[4]

The Revolution Begins: Internationale Essener Songtage

Kaiser became famous through the International Essen Song Days in 1968. He had pleaded in vain for the annual meeting, which had become traditional, to no longer be held in the youth-movement context of Waldeck Castle, but to be moved to an urban space.[5] Through urbanisation, the festival was to be brought closer to society, absorbing its current tempo and new musical forms. Essen was born out of the impulse of the American underground, mixed with London and Amsterdam influences, and the heterogeneous elements of the counterculture that were meanwhile also blossoming more strongly in the Federal Republic – from the protest singers to the early communes and experimental pop bands to the Provo subcultures. Under the sign of the non-commercial fusion of pop and politics, the Songtage were the most important event of the West German counterculture in the late 1960s.

They were embedded in a theoretical framework that Kaiser had created: political pop music could become mass culture, but in order not to be at the mercy of the exploitative interests of companies and public media, the 'new people' needed independent means of production and performance spaces.[6] From 25 to 29 September 1968, not only well-known American underground greats like The Fugs and Mothers of Invention, along with British artists like Alexis Korner, Brian Auger, and Julie Felix, performed in Essen, but also singer-songwriters like Dieter Süverkrüp and Franz Josef Degenhardt and hitherto mostly unknown German music groups like Amon Düül, Guru Guru Groove, Xhol Caravan, and Tangerine Dream.[7]

---

[4] R-U Kaiser, Das neue Lied und die Revolution, *Deutsche Jugend* 16 (1968), pp. 127–32 (132).

[5] R-U Kaiser, *Das Songbuch* (Ahrensburg/Paris: Damokles, 1967), p. 40; O & H Kröher, *Rotgraue Raben: Vom Volkslied zum Folksong* (Heidenheim: Südmarkverlag, 1969), p. 99.

[6] Cf. R-U Kaiser (ed.), *Protestfibel. Formen einer neuen Kultur* (Bern: Scherz, 1968), pp. 195 ff.

[7] D Siegfried, *Time Is on My Side: Konsum und Politik in der westdeutschen Jugendkultur der 60er Jahre* (Göttingen: Wallstein, 2006), pp. 601 ff.; D Mahnert & H Stürmer, *Zappa, Zoff und Zwischentöne: Die Internationalen Essener Songtage 1968* (Essen: Klartext, 2008).

With 40,000 participants, the biggest pop festival in Europe at that time, it represented a European Monterey from which impulses emanated beyond just the commercial. Pop music was in the foreground, but the political element was more heavily weighted here than in the American or British scenes. Music and happenings were complemented by political texts, radical cabaret, and discussion rounds.

Essen showed, firstly, that alongside the politically grounded protest culture, a broad pop-cultural field had established itself, which in part contained political components. However, one may doubt that it represented, as the organisers claimed, 'the beginning of the end of conventional and only commercially oriented music exploitation'.[8] First, while the festival did provide a forum for bands like Amon Düül and Tangerine Dream, who combined electronic, improvisational sound patterns with political demands, attracting media attention for the first time and winning record contracts, this did not mean the end of the commercial exploitation system, but rather its opening and differentiation. Second, it became clear from the reactions of the audience and the public that the electrified version of the underground attracted larger crowds of young people than the traditional, more chanson-based scene of protest singers. Their audiences were and remained limited. Third, it became apparent that there were narrow limits to the political radicalisation of the masses. While many visitors probably shared the connection between pop and politics, but felt little inclination to engage in activities of their own in this context, only a small group was prepared to push the concept of individual political action further at the expense of music.

Thus, in the early autumn of 1968, it became clear that a more radicalised political wing was separating itself from the bulk of the counterculture. On the other hand, the connection between pop and politics had proven itself precisely through the festival, and many of its protagonists – not least the *spiritus rector* himself – held on to it until the early 1970s. To some observers, it seemed as if pop music in the variant visible here had a politicising effect. The writer Erasmus Schöfer, at any rate, was convinced after Essen that 'the phenomena of beat and pop were latently critical of society in their broad impact on the young generation and would gradually come to an awareness of this character of theirs'.[9]

---

[8] Broder/Degenhardt/Kaiser/Witthüser, Spiegel-Redakteur missbraucht Spiegel, 20.10.1968, *Deutsches Kabarett-Archiv*, Mainz, LN/N/1.

[9] *Rhein-Neckar-Zeitung* (2 October 1968); *Badische Zeitung* (2 October 1968).

Politicisation of the Music Scene Since 1970

Between 1968 and 1970, the two elements of the counterculture of 1968 –
radical politics and 'youth culture' – drifted apart again. Yet there was no
lack of attempts to hold them together. The politicisation of pop came from
various sources: the protagonists of pop journalism, bands, some recipients, and the state. Just how important pop culture had become could be
seen in summer 1970, when about 500,000 young people attended the
various pop festivals in the Federal Republic, including a large part of the
left-wing scene.[10] The climax and end point was the Love and Peace
Festival, which took place on the island of Fehmarn in early September.
Instead of a European Woodstock, however, Fehmarn turned into
a provincial Altamont – the culmination of those negative phenomena
that determined the image of the festival summer of 1970.

The conclusions that radical left-wing masterminds drew from this
experience were broad. Pop music was attractive to large masses and thus
profitable. Instead of protesting the miserable conditions under which the
festivals were held – inflated prices, failing bands, and aggressive security –
and changing them through political action, the visitors remained in an
apathetic consumerist attitude. In their eyes, this showed that 'capitalists in
hippie look'[11] had also incorporated this originally rebellious segment into
the capitalist manipulation context. One could only refuse this appropriation, even if one liked the music offered there. In spring 1971, right at the
beginning of the new festival season, several subculture activists – among
them Henryk M. Broder, Jens Hagen, and Helmut Salzinger – called for
a boycott of pop concerts and festivals. One of the underground magazines
argued:

You voluntarily go to a prison and still let the jailers earn from it! . . . How long is
this going to go on: Love and peace inside, beating policemen outside, gangs of
stewards just waiting to strike, dogs, barbed wire, barriers and organisers bundling
notes. All this with your consent! Don't take part in this anymore!!![12]

But the festivals were also politicised from above when the Bavarian
Ministry of the Interior issued a general ban on festivals in July 1972.
According to the ministry, open-air pop festivals represented a 'serious
disturbance of public order' caused by loud music, endangerment of

---

[10] S Paul, Pop-Festivals und ihre Folgen, *Sozialistische Zeitschrift für Kunst und Gesellschaft* 4
      (1970), pp. 79–82 (80).
[11] *Elan* 10 (1970), p. 7.   [12] *'Ran* 5 (1971), p. 41.

minors, hygienic deficiencies, devastation of the landscape, but above all the mass consumption of narcotics.[13] As a result, more than fifty rock bands sent an open letter to the Bavarian minister of the interior demanding the withdrawal of this measure.[14] For many commentators, it was clear that the drug problem was only a pretext to put an end to a new, unwelcome youth culture. Politicians were only interested in eradicating the mass experience 'that it is possible to live together without social constraints in a very nice way and much more freely than it is possible in this state so far'.[15]

The journalist Ingeborg Schober pointed out that in West Germany social problems were responded to with bans, while in neighbouring countries like Denmark or the Netherlands, youth centres and free rock concerts were financed by the state, without the occurrence of many of the negative side effects of commercial festivals.[16] In general, this debate forced the scene itself to differentiate more precisely and propelled the tendencies towards self-organisation. This could best be realised at self-made festivals with a regional reach. But it was precisely these festivals that were being deprived of the opportunity to develop alternatives to the greed of the promoters, not focusing primarily on profit.[17]

In general, a national component could not be overlooked in the anti-commercial self-image of the German scene. The underground magazine *Germania* saw it this way: while the British and American bands were already completely paralysed by the consumer industry, the potential for the German scene, which was 'still three years behind', was to ward off the threat of commercialisation through self-organisation.[18] In essence, the rise of German rock bands in the early 1970s, under the sign of authenticity and self-organisation, was underpinned by national tones directed against commercial dominance from abroad.

Tim Belbe and Thomas Wollscheid from Xhol Caravan contrasted the 'consumer music' produced by the music industry of the 'Anglo-Saxon countries' with the 'music of indigenous groups', which was characterised by 'free' production and 'honest' statements and was thus 'folk music of our time'.[19] The 1973 appeal of the 'IG Rock' (rock music union) stated that 'foreign groups are flooding the Federal Republic of Germany so massively' that German bands hardly had any performance opportunities left, and that when international greats toured, the opening programme was also

[13] *Riebe's Fachblatt* 9:4 (1972), p. 7.   [14] *Riebe's Fachblatt* 11:6 (1976).
[15] K Martens in *Riebe's Fachblatt* 10:5 (1972), p. 7.   [16] *Sounds* 10 (1972), p. 12.
[17] *Flash* 13 (28 September 1972), p. 5.
[18] *Germania* 9:1 (1971).   [19] *Song* 1 (1970), p. 28.

'dictated by foreign countries', against which joint action by 'all German musicians' was necessary.[20] The feeling of dominance from outside was coupled with considerable self-confidence. Surveys in 1972/73 showed that about one-third of concert-goers and over half of German rock musicians seriously expected German pop groups to be able to 'outflank' their British and American competitors in a few years.[21]

Between 1971 and 1973, several associations were set up to promote cooperation between bands – in Hamburg there was a 'Rock Lib Front', in southern Germany a 'Band-Coop', in Mainz a 'Rock-Büro' and in West Berlin a 'Rock Front'. By cutting out producers, middlemen, and promoters, the groups were expected to be able to maintain their freedom and market their products more cheaply. Finally, these approaches to self-organisation were to form nodes of a countercultural network, as the theoretician of West German counterculture, Rolf Schwendter, had in mind as a model of a counter-economy within the capitalist system.[22]

The ideal groups were rock bands who produced and distributed their music independently and played for a small fee, or often for 'free', such as Ton Steine Scherben, Franz K., Hotzenplotz, or Can. Although three-quarters of West German rock musicians thought the principle of self-organisation was advantageous, most attempts at cooperation promptly failed.[23] Professional bands who were not primarily politically oriented quickly realised that overcoming competition in the pop scene was an arduous business and speculated that, in view of the desolate situation, 'a big, commercially raised agency for German groups' would be more likely to help.[24] The slogan of mutual aid, in any case, as the group Kraan saw it, had instead promoted exploitation under countercultural auspices: if the bands did not play cheaply, or preferably for 'free', they were ostracised as a 'commercial group'.

The economy of anti-commercial consumption included other practices that enabled low-cost participation in popular culture. They not only had the advantage of costing nothing or little, but also gained an ideological superstructure through the morality of anti-consumerism, which had a long tradition in Germany. These practices not only included the forcing of free concerts, but also the production and distribution of bootlegs, theft from book or record shops and the individual hijacking or collective

---

[20] *Riebe's Fachblatt*, 3/4 (1973), pp. 6, 10.
[21] R Dollase, M Rüsenberg & H-J Stollwerk, *Rock People. Die befragte Szene* (Frankfurt: Fischer, 1974), p. 115 ff.
[22] R Schwendter, *Theorie der Subkultur* (Hamburg: EVA, 1993).
[23] Dollase, Rüsenberg & Stollwerk, *Rock People*, p. 209.   [24] *LOG-Zeitung* 6:1 (1973).

storming of concert halls. Especially between 1969 and 1971, groups of young people – often numbering 100 to 200 – stormed the halls at concerts of popular bands like Steppenwolf, Canned Heat, and Pink Floyd to gain free admission.

Unlike the rock 'n' roll and beat riots of the 1950s and mid-1960s, these actions contained a weighty political component that was in the spirit of the times. 'They are very young', said concert organiser Peter Hauke of the participants. 'All under 20. Mostly students who hide behind political arguments. And say this is just a political demonstration against capitalism.'[25] Their slogan, 'The concert halls are ours!', once again made clear their claim of ownership over pop music. Actions were primarily directed against the concert organisers, but also against bands who did not fulfil audience expectations. The radical-left scene cheered on such activities as social revolutionary self-activity. In 1971, The West Berlin underground gazette *883* justified this concept in detail:

Within the underground, it was possible for us to communicate freely with each other for the first time. We could express ourselves freely among ourselves, could smoke pot, fuck, etc., without being bothered too much by bourgeois values. The underground was the way of life of the new, struggling left . . . . But capitalism, which is fighting for its life, is dependent on either commercialising or smashing up emerging socialist islands. A gigantic pop industry has emerged; . . . By trying to [enjoy music] without having to spend our hard-earned money, through street fights at pop concerts, we reduce the profit rate of the promoter pig.[26]

Most concert-goers, on the other hand, appeared to be all too compliant consumers. They were therefore considered 'direct allies of the pigs' and had to reckon with physical attacks on another occasion when *883* called for a boycott of all pop concerts: 'If you pay, you get punched in the face.'[27] Less radical activists tried to de-escalate. Tom Schroeder, for example, also considered pop music to be the property of the public but warned against 'putschist individual actions' and called for the use of 'organisation, discipline and imagination'.[28] He called for the opening of larger halls for this new mass culture – barracks, exhibition halls, or football stadiums – to reduce ticket prices to a minimum.

Because entrepreneurs who did not act with the required seriousness thrived, the ideological construction that had already been omnipresent in

---

[25] *Underground* 4:4 (1970), p. 30.   [26] *883*, vol. 83 (3 July 1971), p. 7.
[27] NN, Macht Schluss mit dem Terror der Veranstalter!, *883*, vol. 71 (15 November 1970).
[28] *Underground* 4:4 (1970), p. 30.

the 1960s was once again booming on this battlefield of consumer culture: mindless 'managers' tried to exploit the young people who had been manipulated by artificially arousing their needs. However, the scene itself was already taking a closer look. While promoters like Hauke or the agency Mama Concerts, founded in 1970, were considered primarily profit-oriented, Lippmann + Rau was able to defend a profile as an ethically motivated and fair promoter. Papers like *Underground* and *Sounds* gave Fritz Rau – the organiser of the disastrous Jethro Tull concert in Frankfurt on 21 February 1970 – plenty of space to explain his position.[29] In fact, Rau provided a far from superficial analysis of the novel practice of storming concerts to enforce a right to free music consumption: The industry had 'operated a bit too much with buzzwords like "underground" and "pop revolution"', so that now a 'friction' had arisen:

Young people suddenly find themselves in a vacuum: on the one hand the habitus of the revolutionary and on the other hand all this embedded in the practices of our consumer society. Of course, young people feel this dichotomy, and in my opinion, this is also the reason why these riots have happened.[30]

From Rau's point of view, too, this political activism represented a German specificity that was not to be observed in the large north-western European live cultures in England and Scandinavia.[31]

In fact, it cannot be overlooked how strongly the German rock scene stood out from other national scenes due to its political underpinnings. In Britain or Denmark, for example, youthful musical taste was regarded as a leisure time enjoyment whereas in West Germany it was essentialised as the expression of a generation-specific spirit of opposition. In his feature 'Germany Calling' for the *New Musical Express*, Ian MacDonald saw a special feature in the fact that the German scene was much more political and militant than the British one.[32] In an interview with *Pop* magazine in 1973, Led Zeppelin singer Robert Plant complained at length about the politicisation of their music in Germany, which had already led to riots on their first tour in spring 1970, and summed up his view in a nutshell: 'The German audience is O.K. in and of itself, just far too political.'[33] After boycott actions against his concerts, Edgar Broughton also considered German fans to be partly 'more arrogant than elsewhere'; they were 'less hippie-like and much more political'.[34] The band Ten Years After even

[29] Ibid.; *Pauke* 4:2 (1971).   [30] *Sounds* 4 (1970).   [31] *Underground* 4:4 (1970), p. 28.
[32] *New Musical Express* (9 December 1972), p. 18.
[33] *Pop* 11 (1973), quoted in *Sounds* 2 (1974), p. 20.
[34] *Sounds* 27 (1971); Wagner, *Klang der Revolte*, p. 27.

claimed they saw 'madness sparkling in the eyes of the German audience' at their gigs.[35]

In its anti-commercial self-image, it already becomes clear to what extent the German rock scene linked its musical preference to radical political claims. A quantitative insight into the connection between music and radical politics is provided by the research conducted by Rainer Dollase and colleagues in the early 1970s. As many as 17 per cent of concert-goers said they were led to a 'socially critical attitude' by the music.[36] Musicians attributed an even stronger political component to it, with 53 per cent of them generally intending to contribute to social change and 42 per cent setting themselves the goal of promoting socio-critical attitudes among their audience – not only through political song lyrics or statements, but also through the composition and arrangement of the tunes.

Even if such ideas remained more than vague, the political aspirations of rock music among producers and recipients alike were remarkably high and in this formed a specific feature of the time and of national culture. The German audience could also appear as particularly political because music was not to be consumed passively but was meant to lead to political practice. Thus, at the end of their concerts, Floh de Cologne always called for the audience to become active in left-wing youth associations, and Ton Steine Scherben were known for their mobilising power, especially during demonstrations.

From Ohr to Cosmic Couriers: Revolution as Ecstasy

In 1970, Kaiser realised that the real existing counterculture was actually changing society. By changing their lives, following more informal values and building their own networks of production, distribution, and communication, the followers of the counterculture changed 'not only their own situation, but also the balance of society as a whole'.[37] Kaiser was still interested in further expanding this countercultural network – especially its media sector. Among the many initiatives with which he fertilised the counterculture was the discussion about the further development of a 'hedonistic left'.[38] The debate about how 'rationalist' (i.e. political) and

---

[35] Quoted in ibid., p. 33.   [36] Dollase, Rüsenberg & Stollwerk, *Rock People*, pp. 210 ff.
[37] *Sozialistische Zeitschrift für Kunst und Gesellschaft* 10:4 (1970), p. 75.
[38] *Roter Mohn* 4 (1 May 1971).

'emotional' (i.e. music- and drug-centred) sub-cultures could be held together began in spring 1970 and ended with a split into two currents, with Kaiser belonging to the faction focusing on pop, drugs, and religious beliefs, while Rolf Schwendter was the protagonist of a more politically contoured direction.

What particularly upset many critics of Kaiser was the fact that in 1970, in addition to his powerful position in the press, he also set up an independent record label for the countercultural sector of pop music, together with an old veteran of the record industry. Peter Meisel (Hansa Musik Produktion), who also produced German *Schlager* stars, joined Kaiser to found the label Ohr (ear) in spring 1970.[39] Meisel, who was considered a 'pike in the carp pond' of the record industry in the mid-1960s, had taken Amon Düül under his wing and produced two successful LPs with them.[40] Connected to Metronome's distribution network, Meisel and Kaiser looked after five German rock bands in June 1970, covering a broad musical spectrum and with a partly political, in any case anti-commercial claim, including Embryo, Tangerine Dream, and Floh de Cologne. Later, bands like Amon Düül I, Birth Control, and Guru Guru joined them.[41]

At first, the German pop scene had high hopes for Ohr, because having their own label was the first step towards holding their own in a market dominated by British and American bands. For the bands, the cooperation with Kaiser and Meisel had advantages, because they now had sufficient technical possibilities to produce records for the first time and were being promoted systematically. On the other hand, members of the counterculture had already been irritated in 1968 by the PR avalanche unleashed by Kaiser and Broder, which had promised a lot but could by no means deliver everything. Now, as the founder of Ohr, Kaiser once again preyed with financially heavy promotion on a clientele that was not only unprepared for it, but also resolutely rejected the usual commercial hype.

In addition, he hung ideological labels on his bands, for example claiming that they were committed to a particularly altruistic ethic (which led to irritations in marketing) and ended up selling them as mediums of cosmic supernaturalism. The application of grandiloquent advertising to the underground scene contributed significantly to Kaiser's already damaged reputation, eroding dramatically from 1970 onwards.[42] From the more

---

[39] *Der Musikmarkt* 13 (1972), p. 42; *Musik-Informationen* 7 (1970), p. 10; *Spiegel* 29 (13 July 1970), p. 126.

[40] Cf. *Vorwärts* (19 January 1966).   [41] *Musik-Informationen* 7 (1970), p. 10.

[42] Cf., e.g. *Sounds* 2 (1971); *Riebe's Fachblatt* 8/9 (1973), pp. 1, 8 f.

pragmatic point of view of the bands, the fact that no political or aesthetic constraints were imposed was to Ohr's credit. In fact, the connection between an established representative of the record business and an up-and-comer from the folk and underground scene was innovative in that Ohr systematically placed German rock music on the market for the first time, thus preparing the national and international Krautrock boom. In 1972, leading industry magazine *Musikmarkt* identified a 'considerable asset' in this market segment and praised Kaiser for having 'significantly promoted' this development. Of course, approval by a mouthpiece of commerce irrevocably damaged Kaiser's reputation in the counterculture: 'He was one of the first to grasp the market opportunities for a new German pop music and beat the advertising drum accordingly.'[43]

In autumn 1971, Kaiser and Meisel founded a second label called Pilz (mushroom), which presented a programme oscillating between folk rock and contemplative electronic music with groups such as Bröselmaschine, Hölderlin, and Popol Vuh. The commercial success of these two ventures was considerable; in the 1972 polls of the German magazines *Musikexpress*, *Sounds* and *Schallplatte*, they occupied thirty-seven places, with the Ohr band Birth Control ranking first in each case.[44] With his last creation, the Kosmische Kuriere record label of 1973, Kaiser concentrated almost exclusively on spherical sounds and also took off for unattainable heights. From around 1971 onwards, he became increasingly vehement in his advocacy of a mystical view of the world, which was mainly fed by the ideas of Timothy Leary. Kaiser saw himself as a 'dealer' who helped spread those substances with which a new 'sensitivity' could be created: hashish, LSD, and rock music. As such, he did not primarily want to earn money, but to spread an alternative consciousness and strengthen the sense of community in the counterculture.

In his view, drug use helped to overcome individual and social failings: drug users 'hear more finely, react more sensitively, dress more fantastically, live more peacefully and take care of each other. Their hearing is sharpened, their eyes look deeply, their feeling responds sensitively.'[45] Robert Feustel described the overriding context thus: 'the hope of finding a way out of the valley of failed modernity hangs on the chemical substance'.[46]

---

[43]   *Der Musikmarkt* 13 (1 July 1972), p. 42.   [44]   *Sounds* 5 (1972).

[45]   R-U Kaiser, *Rock-Zeit: Stars, Geschäft und Geschichte der neuen Pop-Musik* (Düsseldorf/Vienna: Econ, 1972), pp. 253 ff. (263).

[46]   R Feustel, *Ein Anzug aus Strom. LSD, Kybernetik und die psychedelische Revolution* (Wiesbaden: Springer, 2015), p. 3.

Conclusion

It is true that in the two typically separated subcultures elements of each other's preferences were still present – pop music consumption in radical political subcultures and leftist positions in the subcultures of music and drug consumers. Nevertheless, with their explosive growth, the scenes also became increasingly separated from each other. More political bands on the one hand – Floh de Cologne, Ton Steine Scherben, or Franz K – split with bands more interested in new musical paths like Amon Düül, Can, or Tangerine Dream. That they were nevertheless united by their countercultural origins is illustrated by the fact that they all were subsumed retrospectively under the rubric of Krautrock. The stronger attraction of the sensually disordered is demonstrated by the example of the Munich pop journalist Ingeborg Schober. In 1967, at the age of twenty, she went to London, fell completely into the pop frenzy there, and returned in summer 1969 to Munich, which had become more radical – politically as well as culturally. In an interview with her, director Wim Wenders described his first encounter with the band Amon Düül at a festival at the Academy of Arts in spring 1968. According to Wenders, the band modelled their approach on bands like Velvet Underground or Hapshash and the Coloured Coat:

It was terribly chaotic. And I remember that in those first sessions they also suddenly stopped in the middle because nobody knew how to continue. And at the same time, I really, really appreciated that. And that's why Amon Düül were a real myth for me at the time, because they were a band that was looking for something. That was the meaning, the content of this music – a search. And they had a few pieces that they played over and over again, which were then different each time and each time a piece further. The pieces were based on very rhythmic scraps and then became longer and longer in the rhythmic arcs, and more and more balanced and also more and more beautiful.[47]

In such statements, political claims still shine through – a reference to society and the emancipatory potential of self-activity – but had moved far from the directly political claims of left-wing radicalism that emerged in a much purer form in the music of bands like Ton Steine Scherben.

---

[47] Quoted in I Schober, *Tanz der Lemminge. Amon Düül – eine Musikkommune in der Protestbewegung der 60er Jahre* (Reinbek: Rowohlt, 1979), p. 31.

Recommended Reading

U Adelt, *Krautrock: German Music in the Seventies* (Ann Arbor: University of Michigan Press, 2016).

D Siegfried, *Time Is on My Side: Konsum und Politik in der westdeutschen Jugendkultur der 60er Jahre* (Göttingen: Wallstein, 2006).

A Simmeth, *Krautrock transnational: Die Neuerfindung der Popmusik in der BRD 1968–1978* (Bielefeld: Transcript, 2016).

C Wagner, *Der Klang der Revolte: Die magischen Jahre des westdeutschen Musik-Underground* (Mainz: Schott, 2013).

3 | Krautrock in the British and American Music Press

ALEXANDER SIMMETH

Printed in the September 1975 issue of *Creem* magazine and accompanied by the drawing of an imperial eagle and a swastika, the Detroit-based music journalist Lester Bangs wrote:

Everybody has been hearing about kraut-rock, and the stupnagling success of Kraftwerk's Autobahn is more than just the latest evidence in support of the case for Teutonic raillery, more than just a record, it is an indictment. An indictment of all those who would resist the bloodless iron will and order of the ineluctable dawn of the Machine Age.[1]

This quote condenses several core points concerning Anglo-American media perceptions vis-à-vis German popular music in the mid-1970s: embedded in German stereotypes, Krautrock was perceived as an 'electronic' phenomenon, as cold and emotionless 'machine music', as a new kind of pop music defying basic Anglo-American elements and roots, and, above all, as a style that would profoundly change the course of pop in the years to come.

In many ways, 1975 can be seen as a peak in the classic phase of Krautrock, most certainly in terms of its transnational recognition and its presence in the Anglo-American music press.[2] Boldly entering the American market and widely discerned as a game changer for pop music and pop culture as a whole, it had solidified its lasting influence and the almost mystical adoration it enjoys today. Only very few people in the pop-cultural diaspora of late 1960s West Germany, however, would ever have imagined such a development; early Krautrock experiments were often met with scepticism and German media outlets mirrored that sentiment. After a short glimpse at the initial media coverage in Germany, this chapter explores the appearance and the discursive formation of Krautrock in the Anglo-American music press and highlights differences in their respective perceptions, such as the varying popularity of individual groups and musicians, as well as shifting paradigms in the ascriptions of stereotypes and clichés.

---

[1] L Bangs, Kraftwerkfeature, *Creem* 9 (1975).

[2] A Simmeth, *Krautrock Transnational: Die Neuerfindung der Popmusik in der BRD, 1968–1978* (Bielefeld: Transcript, 2016), pp. 227–45, 292–311.

Amateurs and Dilettantes? Initial Press Coverage in Germany

Already in the early 1970s, Krautrock's beginnings outside the Anglo-American norms of pop-cultural production were often seen as a pillar of its success;[3] the freedom to develop unique soundscapes and performative spaces were rooted in necessity at first and would not have been possible in predetermined forms of an established industry. In late 1960s West Germany, however, those unusual experiments still drew contempt, most certainly in large parts of the early West German media coverage. In particular, the feature pages of German newspapers and news magazines up to the early 1970s were full of articles and reports subjecting Krautrock with harsh criticism over new albums, concert performances, or any attempt of the young scene to establish a market outside the 'almost 100 per cent Anglo/American closed shop'.[4]

Often painting a picture of amateurish dilettantism, critics dismissed Amon Düül II, for example, as 'pot-smoking children of affluence'[5] trying to copy their Anglo-American heroes and producing nothing but unintelligible noise. Right after successfully organising the Internationale Essener Songtage in 1968 – a ground-breaking pop festival not only on a German but also on a European scale – the leading West German news magazine *Spiegel* symptomatically accused organiser Rolf-Ulrich Kaiser of facilitating nothing but 'utter incompetence'.[6]

There were exceptions from the rule, however. New magazines dedicated to progressive pop music that grew out of subcultural beginnings in late 1960s Germany were the first to be interested in the young experimental scene at home. The magazine *Sounds* (not to be confused with the British publication of the same name) was at the forefront: the first xeroxed issues were published irregularly, until it turned into an increasingly professional monthly in 1970.[7] By then, it had developed into the leading West German pop magazine for progressive music, heavily influencing the discourse about the newest musical trends and developments among

---

[3] I MacDonald, Germany Calling, *New Musical Express* (9 December 1972).

[4] *Sounds* (UK) (24 October 1970).

[5] R Rudorf, Also so genau kann man das alles nicht sagen, *Frankfurter Rundschau* (27 September 1969).

[6] Größtes Ding, *Spiegel* 41 (1968). For the West German media coverage of Krautrock, cf. Simmeth, *Krautrock*, pp. 117–33.

[7] D Siegfried, *Time Is on My Side: Konsum und Politik in der westdeutschen Jugendkultur der 60er Jahre* (Göttingen: Wallstein, 2006), pp. 553–6.

a pop-cultural avant-garde, including Krautrock. The rise of new music magazines coincided with the appearance of a distinct West German pop journalism based on the Anglo-American paradigm:[8] largely in conjunction with Krautrock, writers such as Ingeborg Schober and Winfried Trenkler emerged who, like Rolf-Ulrich Kaiser, were among the first to understand the importance and transformative character of the phenomenon.

On a broad scale, however, West German journalists, decision makers, executives, and other leading figures in the music industry still skimmed Anglo-American print media for the newest trends abroad, eager to import what had already been successful somewhere else.[9] Still during the 1970s, thousands of British music magazines made it to West Germany every week, as did print publications from the United States (although in much smaller numbers).[10] It is no surprise that things in West Germany started to change only with growing British interest in Krautrock. Ironically, in the first broad multi-page article scrutinising the West German scene in 1972, English music critic Ian MacDonald explicitly pointed out the fact that Germans obviously accepted their 'own' artists only after they had been recognised abroad.[11]

Indeed, once the music weeklies in Britain started to pick up the phenomenon that same year, West German periodicals followed, painting a decisively more positive picture of the domestic bands. Next to newspapers and magazines as well as more conventional music publications, even highly circulating teenage magazines such as *Bravo* or *Pop* (with runs of more than a million copies) began to show interest, with little text but lots of pictures and posters, celebrating musicians for their unlikely success in Britain.

Britain – 'Germanness' as a Common Denominator

It was in 1972 that Krautrock made it into the British music press, and the interest in the new West German phenomenon immediately gained traction. It was Krautrock's 'rockier' manifestations such as Amon Düül II,

---

[8] K Nathaus, Nationale Produktionssysteme im transatlantischen Kulturtransfer: Zur 'Amerikanisierung' populärer Musik in Westdeutschland und Großbritannien im Vergleich, 1950–1980, in W Abelshauser, D Gilgen, A Leutzsch (eds.), *Kulturen der Weltwirtschaft* (Göttingen: Vandenhoeck & Ruprecht 2012), pp. 202–27.

[9] Siegfried, *Time*, p. 542; D Baacke, Being Involved: Internationale Popzeitschriften in der Bundesrepublik, *Deutsche Jugend. Zeitschrift für die Jugendarbeit* 16 (1968), pp. 552–60.

[10] Simmeth, *Krautrock*, pp. 124–5.   [11] MacDonald, Germany Calling.

Can, and Faust that enjoyed early widespread popularity. However, in terms of market share and media attention, they would remain all but fringe phenomena in the United States, where interest would only pick up years later and almost entirely focus on the electronic variations such as Tangerine Dream and Kraftwerk, also popular in Britain.

Despite different stylistic ranges, however, the music press in both countries perceived Krautrock, in all its varieties, as specifically 'German'. Krautrock always has been categorised on national origin, and even though national or regional categorisations in pop music (e.g. Southern Rock, Brit Pop, K-Pop, etc.) usually share at least some kind of common stylistic ground, Krautrock does not. Trying to find any kind of similarities, say between Kraftwerk and Amon Düül II, would be a challenging endeavour. The perceived 'Germanness' of all stylistic varieties of Krautrock, no matter how different, is the leitmotif of its Anglo-American reception in the 1970s – and of this essay.

In Britain of 1972, Krautrock faced an entirely different media environment than back in Germany.[12] Five music weeklies in large newspaper format served the market, among them *Melody Maker* and the *New Musical Express*; in addition, a varying number of independent or subcultural music magazines followed and pushed the newest developments. Furthermore, print publications amplified interest in Krautrock on other media channels, in contrast to West Germany, most notably John Peel's legendary radio shows on the BBC. In the early 1970s, Peel heavily promoted Krautrock as 'the most interesting and genuinely progressive music anywhere in the world',[13] an appreciation Peel's listeners[14] as well as the music weeklies shared, leading to substantial British interest in the following years.

For example, Barry Miles, a writer and activist in the British counterculture since the 1960s, saw 'the true sound of the decade coming from Germany'.[15] For Michael Watts, *Melody Maker*'s US editor in the early 1970s, it was 'a new European music, like it's never been heard in this country before'[16] and 'genuinely different to anything that Britain or America has thrown up'.[17] *Disc*, another British music weekly, similarly described Krautrock's soundscapes as 'so apart from everything we've ever

[12] S Frith, *The Sociology of Rock* (London: Constable, 1978).
[13] J Peel, in *The Listener*, 12 April 1973.
[14] J Peel, *The Olivetti Chronicles. Three Decades of Live and Music* (London: Transworld, 2008).
[15] B Miles, The Tangs – Live from the Studio Computer, *New Musical Express* (29 November 1975).
[16] M Watts, Amon Duul, *Melody Maker* (24 June 1972).
[17] M Watts, Can You Dig It, *Melody Maker* (5 February 1972).

heard ... devoid of the usual R'n'B and soul roots'.[18] Early on, the phenomenon was perceived not only as the most recent innovation, but as decisively different and entirely new, seemingly detached from pop music's Anglo-American heritage.

When MacDonald's aforementioned multi-page report about Krautrock was published in late 1972, the first on this scale in Britain, he dubbed it the 'strangest rock scene in the world'.[19] He found not only the music and appearance of the bands strange, however, but also and much more generally the modes of production and distribution. For a British observer, he noted, the lack of professionalism was striking, as was the radical anticapitalist stance of many musicians who often actively resisted professional management. In turn, MacDonald praised Krautrock's freedom to experiment, its freedom from cultural-industrial constraints, and, as a result, its challenge to 'virtually every accepted English and American standpoint'.[20] He was one of the first to draw the connection between a lack of professionalism and the freedom to experiment, which added to the perception of otherness already prevalent in British media.

When Krautrock acts began to tour Britain in 1972, their stage performances further solidified this perception. One aspect linked to the increased politicisation of Krautrock musicians, and repeatedly pointed out on stage, for instance, was the missing hierarchy: seemingly without band leaders, 'no glittery stardust hype, no crotch-brandishing macho rockers, no mikeswinging crowd pleasers',[21] all that made Krautrock acts again appear entirely different from Anglo-American performers. However, as with the large stylistic variety of Krautrock's soundscapes, its stage performances hardly had any common pattern: Amon Düül II made a commune-like, spontaneous appearance; on stage, Can were described as a highly sophisticated collective; Faust employed visual art installations; Tangerine Dream sat with their backs to the audience in front of their instruments; and Kraftwerk eventually vanished from stage entirely, replaced by mannikins in suits. Despite their varied performances, the music press would come to identify a common thread that could be used to classify them as a more unified, homogeneous movement. The perceived otherness based on Krautrock's soundscapes, performances, and modes of production demanded, it seems, a categorisation, and that categorisation was 'Germanness'.

---

[18] P Erskine, Never a Duul Moment, *Disc* (1 July 1972).   [19] MacDonald, Germany Calling.
[20] MacDonald, Germany Calling.
[21] K Dallas, Tangerine Dream, *Melody Maker* (22 June 1974).

One of the first recurring themes of British Krautrock reception in that respect was its supposed relation to the music and ideas of Richard Wagner. 'Wagnerism' had shaped the British imagination of Germany and 'Germanness' for almost a century, and it permeated into the 1970s pop discourse to a surprising extent.[22] At first, it was directed towards Amon Düül II during their initial stage appearances in Britain, when observers saw them 'influenced by the great classical music tradition that's so much part of German life – in particular Wagner'.[23] For Duncan Fallowell, a British Krautrock connoisseur who travelled in the West German scene extensively in the 1970s, Amon Düül's performances evoked 'spacey gothic landscapes, lots of growling electronics, drums like a Panzer division, the whole Wagner in black leather bit'.[24] Others simply called them, again using Wagnerian imagery, 'aggressively Teutonic'.[25]

Even though references to Wagner became less explicit over time, they never quite vanished. Kraftwerk's music, design, and performances of the late 1970s, to point at a particularly prominent example, would be related to the Wagnerian idea of a *Gesamtkunstwerk* (total work of art). Writer Andy Gill saw Kraftwerk as 'the only completely successful visual/aural fusion rock has produced so far'.[26] Mentioning Emil Schult's visual artwork – a decisive and often undervalued contribution to the band's concept – Gill added that 'the music couldn't be other than it is. The form determines the content . . . The form can probably only be fully understood in relation to the German cultural and psychological make up.'[27]

The notion of modernity, also inseparably linked to Wagnerism and another leitmotif of British Krautrock coverage of the 1970s, further contributed to the imagination of a specific 'Germanness'. This narrative was based on the fact, as most observers continued to point out, that Krautrock had severed its ties to Anglo-American musical roots – a core objective of the West German musical movement – but also on the extensive or even exclusive use of electronic instruments, still new in popular music at the time. In the Anglo-American pop market of the early 1970s, it was mainly those two aspects that branded Krautrock as 'modern', as the newest development, or even as pop music's future: Amon Düül II, for example, were regarded as 'terrifying modern';[28] Can as 'quite a distance ahead';[29]

[22] A Ross, *Wagnerism: Art and Politics in the Shadow of Music* (New York: Farrar, Straus and Giroux, 2020).

[23] Erskine, Duul Moment.   [24] D Fallowell, Can, *Melody Maker* (30 October 1971).

[25] Watts, Amon Duul.   [26] A Gill, Mind Machine Music, *New Musical Express* (29 April 1978).

[27] Ibid.   [28] J Sivyer, Amon Duul, *Melody Maker* (2 December 1972).

[29] J Johnson, Can, *Melody Maker* (6 May 1972).

and Faust even as the 'perfect definition of the term avant-garde'.[30] While sometimes Anglo-American acts had to serve as reference – Pink Floyd, for instance, were told that Tangerine Dream had 'advanced far beyond them electronically'[31] – Kraftwerk's *Mensch-Maschine* (*Man-Machine*) album was called 'modern electronic music'[32] by the end of the decade.

Imagining the future of pop music, provoked by Krautrock's soundscapes, even entered another dimension in the British (and later American) reception of the 1970s. With the Space Age still in its earlier stages and science fiction experiencing a boom in literature and film, linking Krautrock to outer space seemed like a logical next step. Even Amon Düül II were lauded for their 'space effect'[33] and, referring to Stanley Kubrick's still new epic, proposed as 'a possible soundtrack from a possible *2001* Part 2'.[34] However, it was most of all Krautrock's electronic variations that sparked futuristic connotations, most prominently Tangerine Dream and, a little later, Kraftwerk. Tangerine Dream's stage outfit during concerts in the mid-1970s were met with astonishment by British audiences in the face of their enormous amounts of electronic equipment, with blinking, wandering diodes on synthesisers towering over the three musicians.

For many, it appeared more like the helm of a spaceship than the stage of a concert performance and it visually amplified the futuristic electronic soundscapes, creating a multisensory experience that left the audience 'mesmerised'.[35] In 1978, Kraftwerk took the imagery a step further by creating their futuristic 'man machine aesthetic' based on classic modernism, but also evoking cyborgs or androids. At the time of its release, the album was described as 'hard-edged, mechanised to the ultimate, de-humanised, even inhuman'.[36] By then this 'Prussian ice-age of Kraftwerk'[37] had replaced 'something as gentle as'[38] Tangerine Dream, but nonetheless, the futuristic remained prominent.

Ghosts From the Past: Nazi Clichés

Another very different notion of Germany and Germanness – not connected to modernity or even the future, but much rather to the past – was a continuously prominent companion of Krautrock's reception in the

---

[30] R Seal, Faust, *New Musical Express* (27 July 1974).   [31] Miles, The Tangs.
[32] I Birch, The Kraft of Dusseldorf, *Melody Maker* (15 July 1978).
[33] J Sivyer, Amon Duul II, *Melody Maker* (24 June 1972).   [34] Sivyer, Amon Duul.
[35] Dallas, Tangerine Dream.   [36] Kraftwerk: Man Machine, *Melody Maker* (6 May 1978).
[37] Birch, Kraft of Dusseldorf.   [38] Dallas, Tangerine Dream.

1970s: German stereotyping based on World War II and Germany's Nazi past. British popular culture in the 1970s was soaked with depictions of Germans as militarist, warmongering Nazis goosestepping through the screen or magazine pages. The fascination ran deep and disseminated throughout British pop culture itself: expressing admiration for Nazi aesthetics or using them as a (very effective) form of provocation was not foreign even to British pop stars such as Mick Jagger or David Bowie. Likewise, the first generation of London punks frequently sported swastikas in another extreme manifestation of this phenomenon. It was this environment that also set the tone for the British music press's analysis of 'Kraut'-rock.

Looking at the term Krautrock, the common narrative goes as follows: the term was invented by the British music press as an expression of disdain or at least mockery for pop music produced by *krauts*, a derogative term for Germans, but eventually turned into a quality seal for some of the most inventive and progressive sounds of the decade.[39] However, at least in its simplicity, this narrative is unlikely true. The term had already appeared in the West German music scene in 1969, long before British writers and journalists took any notice;[40] even in 1973, when Faust as well as Conrad Schnitzler both released tracks titled 'Krautrock', the term was far from ubiquitous in the British music press. 'German Sound', often used interchangeably, remained far more common.

In any case, Germany's Nazi past was an ever-present asset in British Krautrock reception and again it spanned the entire stylistic range of the phenomenon. To stick with the two examples already mentioned, it affected Amon Düül II at the beginning of the decade just as much as Kraftwerk at its end, when their album was described as 'the soundtrack for an afternoon teabreak at Krupp's . . . almost off to invade Poland'.[41] Nazi connotations were partly intertwined with Wagnerian notions (compare the 'drums like a Panzer division'[42]), but was often more blatant and explicit. In most cases, the irony was easy to decipher, although not always.

Clearly ironic, full of cultural references, and one of the most extreme examples of promoting Nazi connotations and symbolism was Lester Bang's 1975 article on and interview with Kraftwerk, quoted at the beginning of this essay. Written in Bang's unique and radical style, it not only appeared in the Detroit-based *Creem* magazine, but also, in a slightly edited

---

[39] *Krautrock: The Rebirth of Germany*, dir. B Whalley (BBC, 2009).
[40] Simmeth, *Krautrock*, p. 54.
[41] A Jones, Many Hands Make Kraftwerk, *Melody Maker* (22 April 1978).   [42] Fallowell, Can.

version and under a more explicit caption, in the British *New Musical Express*.[43] Published across the entire Anglo-American market on the pinnacle of Krautrock's transnational fame, the article is in many ways a prime example of Krautrock's depiction in the British and American music press of the 1970s.

With the title, 'Kraftwerk – The Final Solution to the Music Problem?',[44] referring to the Nazi genocide of European Jews in World War II, and a two-page depiction of the Kraftwerk musicians collaged into photos of swastika flags and Nazi rallies, the framing of Bangs' article in the *New Musical Express* could hardly have been more graphic. Indeed, it marked a stark intensification of the Nazi symbolism used more sparingly in the *Creem* version of the same review. This is symptomatic in the sense that Nazi connotations played a much larger role in British media than they did in the United States, although such connotations were present in both. Even more important, it is also symptomatic in the sense that nothing in Bangs' interview with Kraftwerk, the basis for the article, hinted in any way at Kraftwerk having sympathies for Nazism or Nazi aesthetics.

Quite the contrary: Bangs, not surprisingly considering his radical and provocative approach, seems to have implied Nazi connotations more than once, although without Kraftwerk entertaining them. In fact, Kraftwerk, clearly well-prepared for the interview and with a clear-cut vision and strategy, laid out their narrative of a 'zero hour' in German popular culture at the end of World War II, Anglo-American cultural dominance in West Germany's post-war decades, and their push to create a new, explicitly central European cultural identity, drawing on 1920s German classic modernism 'unspoilt' by the Nazis.[45]

Before arriving in the United States, as their US manager Ira Blacker put it retrospectively, Kraftwerk already had 'very distinct ideas as to their identity'.[46] There is evidence that Kraftwerk's famous concept of the man-machine developed out of a dialectic between actively constructing this identity and its very reception in the Anglo-American music press, that the media stereotyping based on Kraftwerk's attempts to construe a new identity in turn influenced the very process of identity building itself. However,

---

[43] Bangs, Kraftwerkfeature; L Bangs, Kraftwerk. The Final Solution to the Musical Problem? *New Musical Express* (6 September 1975).

[44] Bangs, Final Solution.

[45] U Schütte, *Kraftwerk: Future Music from Germany* (London: Penguin, 2020); U Schütte, From Defamation to Adoration: The Reception of Kraftwerk in the British Music Press, 1974–1981, *Angermion* 13:1 (2020), pp. 1–24.

[46] Simmeth, *Krautrock*, p. 306.

resorting to various cultural fragments from the pre-Nazi era and cutting ties to dominant Anglo-American popular culture were common themes among Krautrock artists in general. What set Kraftwerk apart was their highly stylised, conceptual approach that went far beyond music and included visual arts as well as performative aspects, not least in interviews. In the context of Lester Bangs' interview in 1975, Kraftwerk described the 'German mentality' as 'more advanced',[47] an example of (self-)ironic play with anglophone clichés about German national identity.

However, it turned out to be a very controversial quote in West Germany because most observers there had initially read the interview under the drastic Nazi imagery employed by the *New Musical Express*. Kraftwerk repeatedly rejected any such accusations, which were, in fact, rooted in the Anglo-American media reception; the band itself always promoted a cosmopolitan identity, and some of their core themes such as individualism versus collectivism, human and technology, or digitisation clearly hit the zeitgeist of the 1970s and beyond. And it is those latter aspects to which the discourse turned by the end of the decade, away from national clichés and stereotypes, towards a more universal imagination.

Future Music from Outer Space: Krautrock in America

The American market for pop journalism in the 1970s was decisively different from its British counterpart, despite the permanent exchange of ideas and countless mutual contributions.[48] On the one hand, trade journals played a significant role, most of all the highly influential *Billboard* magazine, which also circulated widely among West German leaders in the music industry.[49] In the late 1960s and 1970s, ground-breaking new magazines such as *Rolling Stone* or *Creem* appeared and, after humble beginnings, successfully established themselves on the market.[50] It was *Rolling Stone* that published the first multi-page features on Krautrock for the American market in 1972 and 1973. With Krautrock acts (especially most of the groups mentioned in both articles) being marginal in the United

---

[47] Bangs, Kraftwerkfeature.

[48] R S Denisoff, *Tarnished Gold: The Record Industry Revisited* (New Brunswick, NJ: Transaction, 1986). N Johnstone, *Melody Maker: History of 20th Century Popular Music* (London: Bloomsbury, 1999).

[49] P Wicke, *Vom Umgang mit Popmusik* (Berlin: Volk und Wissen, 1993), p. 57.

[50] D Ginsburg, Rock Is a Way of Life. The World of Rock 'n' Roll Fanzines and Fandom, *Serials Review* 5 (1979), pp. 29–46; S Jones, *Pop Music and the Press* (Philadelphia: Temple University Press, 2002); Frith, Sociology.

States at the time – despite an already strong interest among music professionals[51] – the motivation for those two features is not entirely clear.

One likely reason might have been that *Rolling Stone* picked up on the interest in the British media. However, the driving force seems to have been Rolf-Ulrich Kaiser's tireless efforts to promote his labels and groups in the United States. The first article in 1972 de facto showcased his portfolio and was based on promotional material Kaiser had sent over the Atlantic. Not hiding a certain degree of confusion and bewilderment, *Rolling Stone* then noted that 'rare indeed it is that we have the opportunity to observe another culture in the throes of its own transition. . . . There is something going on here, but we don't know what it is at the moment.'[52]

The second article in 1973 described English author Charles Nicholl's visit to one of Kaiser's last release parties for his label Kosmische Kuriere in West Germany. Nicholl, cognoscente of the Anglo-American counterculture of the 1970s and writing for the London office of *Rolling Stone*, at first found it 'hard to avoid a patronising nostalgia for the mid-Sixties, as if the reverberations from the West Coast had only just been translated into a rather stodgy German terminology. The exotic costumes. The hazy cosmic jive. And acid. The ghost of Timothy Leary.'[53] However, the music presented that day obviously appealed to Nicholls, who described an impromptu live performance by Tangerine Dream as 'something special'.[54]

Unfortunately for Kaiser, however, large-scale interest for Krautrock in the United States only picked up one year later in 1974. By then, he had already disappeared from the scene, unable to harvest what he had so relentlessly been trying to seed for years. Richard Branson signed Tangerine Dream to his Virgin label, and Kraftwerk made it to the American market through Ira Blacker and his company Mr. I. Mouse Ltd; both bands would dominate the early Krautrock discourse in the United States.

The interest in those new appearances was immense: the trade journal *Cash Box* saw them as a sign of 'Germany's increasing influence on the international music scene',[55] while *Variety* saw rock music beginning a 'Teutonic phase of its evolution' with 'virtually every U.S. label . . . in the market for the so-called "German Sound"'.[56] With Tangerine Dream

---

[51] I Schober, *Tanz der Lemminge. Amon Düül, eine Musikkommune in der Protestbewegung der 60er Jahre* (Reinbek: Rowohlt, 1979), p. 194.

[52] Die Deutschen Rockmusiker, *Rolling Stone* (26 October 1972).

[53] C Nicholls, Germany's New Sound, *Rolling Stone* (30 August 1973).   [54] Ibid.

[55] Blacker to Rep German Firms, *Cash Box* (28 December 1974).

[56] Rock Enters Teutonic Phase, *Variety* (2 April 1975).

and Kraftwerk dominating its reception in the United States in the second half of the 1970s, Krautrock was, as mentioned, primarily understood as an electronic phenomenon: the 'German electronic trend'[57] was 'pushing new frontiers'.[58]

To no big surprise, then, technology and the 'hypnotically structured'[59] electronic sounds were two of the primary elements at the core of this reception. In that context, new terms and descriptions appeared in the pop-cultural language that would make a return one and a half decades later, again with considerable German contribution: 'techno' and 'trance'. *Creem*, for instance, described Krautrock as a 'techno flash',[60] music critic Robert Hilburn called it, slightly more traditionally, 'techno-rock',[61] and according to *Circus* magazine, Krautrock's electronic soundscapes put listeners into a state of 'trance'.[62] Not everyone was necessarily happy with the increasing role of electronic elements infused into pop music by the Germans, however. Critic Larry Rohter lamented that 'the age of synthetic music is upon us'[63] and found that to be 'menacing',[64] while musicologist Robert Palmer, equally sceptical, saw mere 'simulations'[65] at play.

But the days in which the American Federation of Musicians demanded a ban of electronic instruments were over,[66] and the fascination for new musical technology far outpaced the traditionalist's incredulity. For most critics and writers listening to Kraftwerk or, in this case, Tangerine Dream, it was 'fascinating to see what technology can accomplish',[67] a perception many musicians and music professionals obviously shared. A tangible example of Krautrock's influence on the music scene already in the 1970s was the observation that, at a 1977 Tangerine Dream show in California, 'musicians frantically wrote notes and musical notations'.[68] Kraftwerk, of course, were equally considered to be part of the technological avant-garde; science fiction author Jim Aikin, a critic for the pioneering trade magazine

---

[57] Kraftwerk – Autobahn, *Billboard* (11 January 1975).

[58] Autobahn, *Cash Box* (11 January 1975).

[59] J Rockwell, German Kraftwerk, a Rock Band, Holds Beacon Fans Rapt, *New York Times* (7 April 1975).

[60] Techno-Flash, *Creem*, 3 (1975).

[61] R Hilburn, Kraftwerk: Surge in Techno-Rock, *Los Angeles Times* (26 March 1977).

[62] Kraftwerk – Autobahn, *Circus* 6 (1975).

[63] L Rohter, The Synthetic Tangerine, *Washington Post* (5 April 1977).

[64] L Rohter, The Musical Voltage of the Mellotron, *Washington Post* (3 April 1977).

[65] R Palmer, Pop – Dream in Sequence, *New York Times* (7 April 1977).

[66] An AFM Ban on the Moog Synthesizer? *Rolling Stone* (19 April 1969).

[67] Meyr, Tangerine Dream (3) Laserium, *Variety*, (13 April 1977).

[68] M Falcon, Tangerine Dream, *Cash Box* (18 June 1977).

Contemporary Keyboard, laconically declared Kraftwerk's 1978 album *Mensch-Maschine*, a 'technical triumph'.[69]

It is not a coincidence that in the 1970s, a writer of science fiction would endorse new musical technologies. As already seen in Britain, Krautrock's soundscapes were broadly understood as 'future sounds', and what was true for Amon Düül II back in England was most certainly true for the electronic acts favoured in the United States. For many observers, 'German Sound'[70] was alternatively, a 'sound like science fiction',[71] a 'genuine listening experience ... from outer space',[72] 'space tripping ... future music',[73] or, as Kaiser had already insisted half a decade earlier, 'cosmic music for cosmically inclined audiences'.[74] Being the avant-garde of electronic pop music and a forerunner of newest musical technology, however, did not only evoke cosmic visions. Again, the art was tied back to the national origin of its creators – Germany – with all the known clichés.

The usual set of German stereotypes entered many reviews and feature pages. Far beyond Nazi pictures and symbolism, one of them was the supposedly cold and emotionless German linked to technological mastery. Lester Bangs, even before publishing his Kraftwerk feature, called electronic Krautrock 'music made by machines on ice';[75] Rohter referred to it as 'mechanical music for a machine age',[76] while *Circus* claimed it was 'totally in control, unemotional and detached'.[77] 'Machinelike',[78] icy, detached: for many readers, typical German traits; for many writers, convenient stereotypes to employ.

Conclusion

The leitmotif of both American and British Krautrock reception in the 1970s was the continuing popularity of German stereotypes and clichés, with the music press coverage in both countries differing only in nuances. From Amon Düül II to Kraftwerk, Krautrock in all its vastly different stylistic variations was perceived as 'unmistakably Germanic',[79] and it

---

[69] J Aikin, Kraftwerk, *Contemporary Keyboard*, 8 (1978).

[70] J V, Tangerine Dream: Rubycon, in: *Stereo Review*, 11 (1975).   [71] Techno-Flash.

[72] N. N., Tangerine Dream, Rubycon, *Cash Box* (3 May 1975).

[73] M Hooker, Space Tripping with the Boys from Berlin, *Los Angeles Times* (24 April 1977).

[74] D Nusser, Tangerine Dream, *Billboard* (30 April 1977).

[75] L Bangs, Kraftwerk: Autobahn, *Creem* 6 (1975).   [76] Rohter, Mellotron.

[77] Kraftwerk – Autobahn, *Circus* 6 (1975).

[78] R Townley, Germany's Kraftwerk: Metal of the Road, *Rolling Stone* (3 July 1975).

[79] Fallowell, Can.

was not before the end of the decade that those ascriptions and stereotypes slowly started to fade away. By then, it was the broad consensus among critics and pop journalists that Krautrock had, as music critic John Rockwell put it, 'evolved a musical style so removed from the blues-based fervour of 1950s rock that it is hard to think of this music as rock-and-roll at all, except that it's sold through the same market'.[80]

From the start, but even more by the end of the decade, the 'future sounds' of Krautrock were widely regarded as a transformative contribution to pop music and culture; far beyond the early commercial success of the well-known acts mentioned in this chapter, its more obscure and experimental manifestations, as well as solo projects and new formations from Düsseldorf to West Berlin and beyond entered British and American music journalism. Starting in the 1990s, then, renewed interest in the phenomenon finally re-discovered it in its full breadth, far beyond the stars of the initial decade, and far beyond the stereotypes and clichés that dominated the initial reception.

Independent of changing patterns of attention and appreciation, the shift in the Anglo-American music press's understanding of Krautrock in the 1970s suggests that Krautrock's mission to create a new and transnational cultural identity, for themselves and for West Germany, can ultimately be considered successful. British as well as American observers clearly placed Krautrock outside the Anglo-American realm of pop music, viewing it as a distinct West German phenomenon detached from pop music's Anglo-American roots. In addition, and as a result, Krautrock's soundscapes and performative elements were not only considered modern, but also futuristic pop music, not just a passing trend, but a transformative contribution, and the first fundamental contribution to pop music from outside the Anglo-American sphere.

Possessing a distinct kind of otherness compared to the world of pop in the 1970s, reactions to Krautrock sometimes fell back on preconceived notions of 'Germanness' and inconsistent German stereotypes – some writers actually misunderstood, others simply played with clichés, some referred to the past, others to the future. Tying Krautrock back to its national origin, however, seems to have changed those very preconceived notions of Germanness in the Anglo-American music press at the same time. By the end of the decade, clichés and stereotypes faded from the pages of music magazines, and with them Wagner, swastikas, and the looming spectre of the icy German.

---

[80] J Rockwell, The Pop Life, *New York Times* (30 June 1978).

Recommended Reading

P Glen, NEU! Europe: Krautrock and British Representations of West German
    Countercultures during the 1970s. *Contemporary British History*, 35:3 (2021),
    pp. 439–65.
U Schütte, From Defamation to Adoration: The Reception of Kraftwerk in the
    British Music Press, 1974–1981, *Angermion* 13:1 (2020), pp. 1–24.
D Siegfried, *Time Is On My Side: Konsum und Politik in der westdeutschen
    Jugendkultur der 60er Jahre* (Göttingen: Wallstein, 2006), pp. 601–44.
A Simmeth, *Krautrock Transnational: Die Neuerfindung der Popmusik in der BRD,
    1968–1978* (Bielefeld: Transcript, 2016), pp. 117–33, 227–45, 292–311.

4 | Infrastructure of the German Music Business

JAN-PETER HERBST

The Krautrock phenomenon formed part of a global revolution in pop music and culture in the 1960s and 1970s, but in sharp contrast to the Anglo-American world, Germany's music business infrastructure for countercultural rock music was initially underdeveloped. That was different in Britain and the United States, where a surge in independent record labels and studios with the latest recording technology followed the rock 'n' roll era. With multitrack recording expanding, artists began to use the studio as an instrument, and more independent producers like George Martin, Brian Wilson, and Phil Spector appeared on the scene. Rock music became more complex and increasingly focused on the record as a work of art. Experimental use of new studio tools, inspired by the production techniques of The Beatles and The Beach Boys and the progressive and psychedelic rock styles of acts like Pink Floyd, Yes, and King Crimson, accompanied a shift from singles to album LPs.[1]

Linked to this development was the widespread opening of recording studios independent of major record companies, such as Associated Independent Recording (London, 1965), Trident Studios (London, 1968), Sound City Studios (Los Angeles, 1969), and Electric Lady Studios (New York, 1970), and the establishment of dedicated rock engineers like Tony Visconti, Glyn Johns, and Alan Parsons. The economic infrastructure was changing simultaneously, with established major labels recognising the widespread desire for rock music and the need for new release opportunities. Decca was the first major that in 1966, staffed by young, enthusiastic rock fans, created the sub-label Deram for rock music, releasing Procul Harum and Ten Years After. EMI and Philips followed suit and opened the sub-labels Harvest and Vertigo, respectively, in 1969, with Pink Floyd, Deep Purple, Black Sabbath, and Uriah Heep on their rosters. Rock music production was progressing, and rapidly becoming more professional, leading to many now-classic albums.

---

[1] V Moorefield, *The Producer as Composer: Shaping the Sounds of Popular Music* (London: MIT Press, 2010), pp. 40–1.

Live music, also in a state of flux, gave club culture more relevance. Well-known examples are the Whisky a Go Go in Los Angeles (1964) as a prime venue for rock music, or the now legendary Cavern Club in Liverpool, which gained prominence through performances by The Beatles (1961–3). A significant event for the development of international popular music culture was the Monterey Pop Festival in 1967, which marked the beginning of the 'Summer of Love'. Woodstock followed it in 1968, and the Altamont Free Festival in 1969. All three festivals made history and inspired pop festivals all over the world. On the business side of things, dedicated rock managers emerged with renowned professionals such as Brian Epstein (The Beatles), Peter Grant (Led Zeppelin), and Allen Klein (The Rolling Stones). Due to the popularity of Anglo-American rock music, a supportive infrastructure was quickly established in Britain and the United States, contributing to the music's global success.

In West Germany, there was a profoundly different situation. The infrastructure was much less developed, but it was precisely this disadvantage that provided the breeding ground for Krautrock.[2] The German music industry was built on *Schlager*, a commercial form of pop music intended to appeal to the sentiments of the public,[3] produced by major labels in their own studios. Independent record labels for rock music did not exist, nor was there an adequate club and concert infrastructure for such music. Moreover, roles like music managers were practically forbidden until the mid-1970s. The *Arbeitsamt* (Federal Employment Agency) held a special department for artists and had a monopoly on managing musicians, but it lacked suitable personnel for rock music.[4] So bands either took over their management duties themselves or recruited an external 'band member', neither of which was usually suited for the job. Moreover, both approaches were violations of the law and carried hefty fines.

These structural deficits disadvantaged German artists, but they were also one of the reasons why such an unusual form of rock could develop in Germany with Krautrock. The lack of structure provided ample space for creativity and exploration outside Anglo-American norms, without which Krautrock would probably not have developed as it did. The structural

---

[2] U Adelt, *Krautrock: German Music in the Seventies* (Ann Arbor: University of Michigan Press, 2016), pp. 1–14; A Simmeth, *Krautrock Transnational. Die Neuerfindung der Popmusik in der BRD, 1968–1978* (Bielefeld: Transcript, 2016), pp. 203–26; D Stubbs, *Future Days: Krautrock and the Building of Modern Germany* (London: Faber, 2014), pp. 21–32.

[3] J Mendívil, *Schlager* and Musical Conservatism in the Post-War Era, in U Schütte (ed.), *German Pop Music: A Companion* (Berlin: De Gruyter, 2017), pp. 25–42.

[4] J Reetze, *Times & Sounds: Germany's Journey from Jazz and Pop to Krautrock and Beyond* (Bremen: Halvmall, 2020), pp. 214–15; Simmeth, *Krautrock*, p. 208.

disadvantage was transformed into an artistic concept. While the late 1960s were still a developmental time for Krautrock, the period between 1970 and 1974 was marked by professionalisation, institutionalisation, expansion, and transnationalisation.[5] Innovative independent record labels, recording studios, and distribution networks emerged for progressive rock music, enabling experimental German rock artists to produce records and release them internationally. Many of the industry professionals involved were just as relevant to the creative output as the artists.

Clubs and Festivals

German progressive rock bands did not benefit from an established infrastructure of performance venues in the 1960s. Early Krautrock bands had to be content with performing at art galleries and exhibitions, bars and universities, such as the canteen of the Technical University of West Berlin, an important meeting place at the time.[6] Dedicated rock clubs were rare, one of which was the Star Club in Hamburg (1962–9). Best-known for providing a stage for The Beatles in 1962, it also impacted Krautrock, given that influential recording industry figures were involved in the live events and house label Star Records. For example, Amon Düül II, Popol Vuh, and Can were signed by Siegfried Loch, an artist and repertoire representative at Philips Records and later head of the German branch of American label Liberty Records.[7] Inspired by Andy Warhol's Factory and the Dom in New York, a club culture began to develop in West Germany by the late 1960s.

Zodiak Free Arts Lab played a crucial role in Berlin. Founded by musicians Conrad Schnitzler and Hans-Joachim Roedelius, the club had, despite its short existence between 1968 and 1969, a profound influence on what later became known as the 'Berlin School' of electronic music.[8] As an avant-garde space for musicians, artists, creatives, and the counterculture, Zodiak hosted daily open-stage sessions with little distinction between audience and artists. It encouraged anyone to pick up an instrument and experiment with free jazz, progressive rock, and avant-garde styles. The boundaries between performing and rehearsing were fluid. Many Krautrock bands originated there one way or another from those jam

[5] Ibid., pp. 135–245.

[6] Ibid., pp. 69–70, 198; U Schütte, *Kraftwerk: Future Music from Germany* (London: Penguin, 2020), pp. 40, 46.

[7] Reetze, *Times & Sounds*, pp. 79–90.   [8] Simmeth, *Krautrock Transnational*, pp. 112–13.

sessions: multimedia artists Agitation Free were the house band, Edgar Froese and Klaus Schulze of Tangerine Dream were regulars, and Kluster formed directly from the sessions. Besides Zodiak, composer Thomas Kessler's Electronic Beat Studio, a publicly funded semi-professional studio in a music school, provided electronic instruments and recording facilities for early Berlin Krautrock bands.[9] Ash Ra Tempel were formed in this studio.

Düsseldorf became as equally important as Berlin with the development of a 'Düsseldorf School'. Kraftwerk, its most famous representative, alongside Neu!, La Düsseldorf, and later acts such as DAF, Der Plan, and Propaganda, made Düsseldorf Germany's capital of electronic pop music.[10] Just as in Berlin, the early scene was concentrated in a few central locations. Near the renowned Düsseldorf Art Academy with contemporary artist Joseph Beuys and a thriving art gallery run by Konrad Fischer, Creamcheese (1967–76) was Germany's first psychedelic club to combine pop music and art.[11] Even more so than Zodiak, Creamcheese emphasised multimedia elements, realised through light and video projections, art installations, and music, to unite the senses. Spectacular events and performances from bands like Pink Floyd, Genesis, and Deep Purple brought the club considerable media attention. Prominent Krautrock bands Kraftwerk, Can, and Tangerine Dream also performed at Creamcheese.[12]

Other cities also had clubs relevant to Krautrock. In Frankfurt, the Sinkkasten jazz club and Heidi Loves You basement bar became hubs for the local psychedelic scene, and Munich had the PN Hit House with house band Amon Düül.[13] Even though no club came close to Zodiak and Creamcheese, they all had something in common in that Krautrock musicians initiated and shaped the operation of these clubs, which helped establish a social and performative infrastructure for progressive rock music.[14] In contrast to earlier venues like Hamburg's Star Club that hosted strictly organised live performances by mainstream bands, the new progressive clubs encouraged experimentation and promoted the interplay of art and music. But these clubs were rare, so it was difficult for bands to tour the country.

While clubs provided the breeding ground for bands and their progressive styles, one event was fundamental to the institutionalisation of Krautrock: International Essen Song Days from 25 to 29 September 1968.

---

[9] Adelt, *Krautrock*, p. 96.   [10] Schütte, *Kraftwerk*, p. 13.
[11] Simmeth, *Krautrock Transnational*, p. 113.   [12] Schütte, *Kraftwerk*, pp. 19–20.
[13] Reetze, *Times & Sounds*, p. 56.   [14] Simmeth, *Krautrock Transnational*, pp. 115–16.

Inspired by the Monterey Pop Festival of 1967, music journalist Rolf-Ulrich Kaiser, who later founded the Krautrock labels Ohr, Pilz, and Kosmische Kuriere, conceived the event as a non-profit festival. The generous support of Essen's Department of Youth made it possible to sell tickets at low prices.[15] Over these five days, more than 200 musicians from Germany and abroad played forty-three performances at eight venues. Among the foreign bands were Frank Zappa and the Mothers of Invention, Alexis Korner, and The Fugs. Notwithstanding a considerable financial loss, the festival profoundly impacted German pop culture. With 40,000 visitors, it was Europe's biggest pop music event at the time and marked the beginning of a festival boom in Germany.

Festivals becoming integral to pop culture triggered the debate between commercial interest and the countercultural authenticity central to Krautrock.[16] Essen Song Days was also a noteworthy event in another respect; Krautrock bands like Tangerine Dream, The Guru Guru Groove, and Xhol Caravan benefitted from both a broader audience and more media attention than was possible with performances at arty clubs and galleries. What followed was the formation of professional networks and Krautrock bands receiving their first record contracts: Amon Düül, Tangerine Dream, Xhol Caravan, and Birth Control were signed to the Hansa label by Peter Meisel, *Schlager* producer and owner of Hansa Studios in Berlin.[17] Due to its myriad influences on German pop culture, Essen Song Days was a momentous milestone, marking Krautrock's inception; some even see it as the beginning of German countercultural pop music.[18]

German Record Labels for Independent Rock Music

By the late 1960s, dedicated record labels for rock music did not yet exist in Germany, but it was not long before a new infrastructure of Krautrock-specific independent labels formed. *Schlager* producer Peter Meisel had no vision for handling the newly signed bands Amon Düül, Tangerine Dream, Xhol Caravan, and Birth Control. Without a clear production concept, he recorded Amon Düül's semi-improvised performances in a chaotic session.[19] Meisel was unsure about the result and waited until the band's offshoot project, Amon Düül II, released *Phallus Dei* (*Penis of God*, 1969).

[15] Adelt, *Krautrock*, pp. 8–9.   [16] Simmeth, *Krautrock Transnational*, pp. 102–4.

[17] Reetze, *Times & Sounds*, p. 145.

[18] See Adelt, *Krautrock*, pp. 8–9; Simmeth, *Krautrock Transnational*, pp. 94–5.

[19] Reetze, *Times & Sounds*, p. 146.

Assured by this release, Meisel finally released Amon Düül's debut album, *Psychedelic Underground*, in 1969 through his major international distributor, Hamburg-based Metronome. The following year meant the beginning of a historical collaboration for Krautrock: together with Rolf-Ulrich Kaiser, organiser of Essen Song Days, Meisel founded the first record label for German progressive rock music, Ohr, in 1970.

Set up in Meisel's premises in Berlin-Wilmersdorf and using his *Schlager* network, Ohr offered the burgeoning new psychedelic rock scene professional music production and distribution services,[20] as well as Kaiser's imaginative marketing campaigns.[21] Within its first three years of existence, Ohr released thirty-two LPs and enabled countless Krautrock bands to reach an international audience, including Tangerine Dream, Ash Ra Tempel, Guru Guru, and Embryo. The early releases, produced in Thomas Kessler's Beatstudio, sounded a bit raw, unlike many later releases that had internationally competitive quality, owing to the collaboration with Germany's two primary Krautrock producers, Conny Plank and Dieter Dierks.

Kaiser signed many bands in the label's first year, which prompted distributor Metronome to limit Ohr's activities. Kaiser and Meisel then started another label, Pilz, distributed by the German chemical giant BASF, which had just set up the music label Mouse and a distribution system that was used for Pilz releases.[22] Pilz was supposed to release more folk-oriented music, whereas Ohr should focus on psychedelic rock, but this distinction did not hold in practice. Within the first two years, both labels had sold 250,000 copies of eighteen albums but hardly made a profit because of high production costs.[23] Kaiser's ambition was to raise the market share of German bands from under 1 per cent to 90 per cent in less than a year.[24] Since he had to compensate for often poor artistic quality, his huge advertising and promotional campaigns took increasingly absurd turns. Towards the end of his short-lived career spanning six years, Kaiser claimed that his bands were bigger than The Beatles and played on Mars.[25] Such delusions of grandeur made Meisel sever his ties with Ohr and Pilz in 1973. Many artists like Tangerine Dream and Klaus Schulze also wanted to pull out of their contractual obligations, which they finally achieved through lawsuits.[26]

---

[20] Simmeth, *Krautrock Transnational*, pp. 216–17.

[21] See Reetze, *Times & Sounds*, pp. 269–73; Stubbs, *Future Days*, p. 392.

[22] Reetze, *Times & Sounds*, p. 269.   [23] Adelt, *Krautrock*, p. 91; Reetze, *Times & Sounds*, p. 271.

[24] Reetze, *Times & Sounds*, p. 271.   [25] Stubbs, *Future Days*, pp. 392–3.

[26] Stubbs, *Future Days*, p. 389.

In 1972, before these incidents, leading Ohr employees Bruno Wendel and Günter Körber had already left the company to set up their own Krautrock label, Brain Records, distributed by Metronome. Becoming the main competitor, Brain attracted many acts from Kaiser's roster. In the four years between 1972 and 1976, Brain released fifty-eight Krautrock albums and sold about one million copies of records by Neu!, Embryo, Tangerine Dream, Edgar Froese, Klaus Schulze, Popol Vuh, Kraan, Cluster, Harmonia, and Guru Guru, making it the biggest German rock label.[27] Körber left Brain in 1975, intending to pursue a different model; he founded the one-person company Sky Records that served a narrowly defined niche market within the blossoming rock music scene.[28] After twenty-five years in business, Sky ultimately closed in 2000, having only released reissues in its final years. Brain is practically inactive but still releases albums, compilations, and reissues of its leading artists, such as Klaus Schulze, Grobschnitt, Harmonia, Birth Control, Cluster, Accept, the Scorpions, Neu!, and Jane.

One of the few German Krautrock labels left today is Bureau B, a sub-label of Tapete Records. Founded as a specialist label for electronic and experimental German music of the 1970s and 1980s,[29] Bureau B regularly releases reissues of Brain and Sky, including records by Conrad Schnitzler, Hans-Joachim Roedelius, or Cluster, often with the original design, but also new releases in the Krautrock tradition. Similarly, the Grönland label, founded by German pop star Herbert Grönemeyer, spearheaded the Krautrock revival in Germany by re-releasing all long-out-of-print albums by Neu! in 2001. Box sets compiling key Krautrock bands like Harmonia or the solo oeuvre by former Can member Holger Czukay followed suit.[30]

Back to Rolf-Ulrich Kaiser: after his business partners Wendel and Körber left, in 1973 Kaiser started a third record label called Kosmische Kuriere (Cosmic Couriers) with his partner Gille Lettmann, distributed by Metronome. The label represented Kaiser's New Age interests and the rather pronounced preoccupation with the mind-altering drug LSD. Its name is inspired by the term populist psychologist Timothy Leary used for LSD dealers.[31] Sonically the label *kosmische Musik* referred to releases by Ash Ra Tempel, Klaus Schulze, Wallenstein, The Cosmic Jokers, and Popol

---

[27] Simmeth, *Krautrock Transnational*, pp. 212–13.

[28] Simmeth, *Krautrock Transnational*, p. 254.

[29] S Ziehn, Bizarres Wiederentdeckt: Gunther Buskies vom Label Bureau B im Corso-Gespräch, Deutschlandfunk, www.deutschlandfunk.de/bizarres-wiederentdeckt.807.de.html?dram:article_id=256353.

[30] Grönland, About us, www.groenland.com/en/about-us.   [31] Adelt, *Krautrock*, p. 91.

Vuh. Of his three labels, it was Kosmische Kuriere that allowed Kaiser to most effectively realise his ideas of promoting alternative spiritualities as well as his vision of 'deterritorialized, post-national cosmological identity, which involved the consumption of psychedelic drugs and the invention of new sounds, in particular through the use of the synthesizer'.[32] During his business years, Kaiser helped boost blossoming careers of groups such as Tangerine Dream, Ash Ra Tempel, Klaus Schulze, and Popol Vuh, but this did not save him from declaring bankruptcy in 1975. His erratic, presumably drug-influenced behaviour towards the end of his career had made him a laughing stock, before he disappeared from the music scene altogether.

His pivotal role as a visionary and promoter of Krautrock, however, cannot be overstated.[33] In addition to founding Essen Song Days, he provided the production and distribution infrastructure for Krautrock with his three labels, which indirectly led to the conception of other influential record companies like Brain and Sky. Kaiser's downfall, though, cannot be reduced to drugs; he was simply too ambitious in his quest to change society through pop music. With his disappearance, Krautrock had passed its zenith.[34] Still, several Krautrock artists took the risk of opening their own labels. By 1977, around 100 existed, occupying 9 per cent of the market, but most eventually ended in financial disaster.[35]

Independent labels like Ohr, Pilz, Kosmische Kuriere, Brain, and Sky were not the only ones interested in German psychedelic rock music. For one thing, all but Pilz were distributed by Hamburg-based Deutsche Metronome, the German offshoot of a Swedish major record company. For another, major labels discovered the market potential of Krautrock. In 1971, Stuttgart-based Intercord opened a sub-label for progressive music called Spiegelei. Even more impactful was Polydor, the pop label of Deutsche Grammophon, whose sub-company BASF later became relevant as the distributor of Pilz Records.

One of the most widely reported signings in the already unconventional Krautrock practices was Faust. The outlet was sold to Polydor in 1970 by journalist Uwe Nettelbeck, who (unofficially) acted as their manager, producer, and marketing expert. Strikingly unconventional and generous, Polydor set up a top-class recording studio, providing living quarters for the entire band.[36] The label had hoped for a German version of The Beatles[37] but was somewhat stunned upon hearing the results of a year's

---

[32] Ibid., p. 83.   [33] See Simmeth, *Krautrock Transnational*, pp. 223–4.   [34] Ibid., pp. 223–5.
[35] Ibid., p. 210.   [36] Adelt, *Krautrock*, pp. 61–2; Simmeth, *Krautrock Transnational*, pp. 137–8.
[37] Adelt, *Krautrock*, p. 60.

work in the studio, heavily influenced by LSD use and experimentation with recording technology. The debut album *Faust* (1971) sold poorly in the British key market; it was still worse in Germany, with less than 1,000 copies sold. Their second album *So Far* (1972) also failed.

Krautrock in the International Market

Just as important as German major labels were German branches of foreign corporations, many of which recognised the economic potential of Krautrock even before independent labels emerged. Given that selling records without losing royalties to German partners was lucrative, foreign companies were keen on opening national branches in Germany. Before Krautrock's emergence, American outfit Liberty/United Artists, founded in 1967 with Siegfried Loch as head of the German branch, was already involved in German rock music. Liberty released early albums by Can, Amon Düül II, and Popol Vuh, which gave artists professional structures and international distribution, and ensured affordable overseas prices, making them successful in Western Europe and Japan.[38]

Another important player was Virgin in Britain, initially a mail-order company specialising in importing international LPs. After Polydor had dropped Faust, Virgin CEO Richard Branson signed the band and released *The Faust Tapes* (1973), a compilation of unreleased recordings from the Polydor era. Neither *The Faust Tapes* nor the following Virgin-produced *Faust IV* (1974) had any major success in Germany, so Faust disbanded[39] before receiving recognition in their home country for their achievements abroad. In retrospect, Faust produced some of the most influential records of the decade, considerably impacting British and American bands.[40]

Virgin was not only relevant for Krautrock because of Faust; they were also pivotal for acts like Tangerine Dream achieving major successes in Britain. Their third album for Ohr, *Atem* (1973), was already becoming the most commercially successful import album in Britain, also winning John Peel's Best Album of the Year award.[41] After Tangerine Dream parted ways with Rolf-Ulrich Kaiser, Virgin signed the band and released their fourth album, *Phaedra* (1974). As with Faust, the album did not sell well in Germany. Nonetheless, Tangerine Dream, enthusiastically received in

---

[38] Simmeth, *Krautrock Transnational*, pp. 73, 211–12.   [39] Adelt, *Krautrock*, p. 67.
[40] Ibid., p. 59.   [41] Simmeth, *Krautrock Transnational*, p. 171.

France and even more so in Britain, became the first German band to perform at London's Royal Albert Hall in 1975.[42]

Many other international partnerships existed; some were successful, some were not. British Vertigo successfully released albums by Can, Amon Düül, and Faust, but the first two Kraftwerk albums did not sell well. Kraftwerk, however, succeeded in the United States, where they were released through Mercury, EMI Electrola, and Capitol. Amon Düül also achieved a high-profile signing with American major label Atlantic to produce the double album *Made in Germany* (1975), which flopped incredibly.[43]

Krautrock was received very differently in its home country and abroad. As representative examples of the larger Krautrock movement, Faust and Tangerine Dream were commercially successful in Britain, France, Spain, Italy, Japan, Australia, and the United States, though they flopped in Germany. Demand for international touring was highest for Tangerine Dream, Ash Ra Tempel, Neu!, Guru Guru, Embryo, Amon Düül II, and Can.[44] Even though record labels were right in their hope that the international success of domestic rock bands would eventually raise their appeal in Germany, this became only partly true. Popularity and sales never came close to that of other countries. In the early 1970s, less than 1 per cent of all rock album sales were by German bands; British and American records dominated the German market. While frontrunners at Ohr and Pilz sold about 15,000 records, average releases ranged between 1,000 and 3,000.[45] Such low revenues did not allow bands to tour overseas.

However, it gave them the important 'authentic' or 'underground' identity, which would have been threatened by commercial success – a difficult position for music producers and labels considering pop music's inherent commercial interest.[46] Nowhere was this better demonstrated than in the downfall of Rolf-Ulrich Kaiser's business due to bankruptcy. Virgin was better positioned with Tangerine Dream, featuring synthesiser-driven anti-rock and a quintessentially 'German' sound.[47] Their revenue alone exceeded that which Brain made in Germany with *all* of their artists.[48] Of the many Krautrock records, peaking in 1972 with 222 releases, none reached the German charts.[49]

But the international comparison should not distract from the fact that in the 1970s, the time of the second global economic crisis, the German

---

[42] Adelt, *Krautrock*, p. 99.   [43] Stubbs, *Future Days*, pp. 105–6.

[44] Simmeth, *Krautrock Transnational*, pp. 136–7.   [45] Reetze, *Times & Sounds*, pp. 227–9.

[46] Simmeth, *Krautrock Transnational*, pp. 194–5.   [47] Adelt, *Krautrock*, p. 95.

[48] Simmeth, *Krautrock Transnational*, p. 248.   [49] Reetze, *Times & Sounds*.

music market grew to become the second largest in the world after the United States. The share of German rock bands may have been comparatively small, yet the German music industry professionalised in countercultural genres, especially with Krautrock production supported by major and independent record labels.[50] The government abolished its monopoly on managing creatives, and independent professionals like managers, engineers, studio owners, and record producers entered the scene.

Producers and Studios as Facilitators of Krautrock

Record labels and their distribution arms are essential to make music accessible beyond the local scene. Equally important are recording studios, audio engineers, and producers, without whom recorded music would not exist. In the 1960s, it was common for major labels to own studios and employ staff to produce primarily commercial *Schlager* music. With the emergence of Krautrock, independent studio operators, producers, and engineers, roles often held by one person, were on the rise, mirroring developments in the Anglo-American sphere. Label owners and managers like Rolf-Ulrich Kaiser, Peter Meisel, Uwe Nettelbeck, and Günter Körber could be described as producers in the broader sense because they influenced artists' musical visions without necessarily being involved in studio work. The new independent producers, by contrast, operated technology and conducted the recording sessions.

Since they were not record label employees, their job involved many roles besides commission work: finding promising artists, producing music at their own risk, giving record licences to labels, or releasing them through their own publishing outlets. Initially, this new breed of record producers was not popular with major labels, but it did not take them long to recognise these specialists' creative and commercial potential for niche genres, missing in their *Schlager*-centred infrastructure. Two Krautrock producers stood out like no others, Konrad 'Conny' Plank and Dieter Dierks. They shook up the German record industry and were pivotal to the quality and success of most domestic psychedelic rock bands.

Conny Plank underwent formal training as an audio engineer before leaving Saarland Broadcasting in 1966 to start working at Rhenus Tonstudio in Cologne, where he was involved in the very first recordings of Krautrock, including *Klopfzeichen* (1969) by Kluster and *Tone Float*

---

[50] Simmeth, *Krautrock Transnational*, p. 205.

(1969) by Organisation, who later became Kraftwerk. Interested in experimental electronic music, he advised his clients to build on Anglo-American influences but be original with it.[51] Plank worked in various studios around the country, recording Krautrock bands in the cheaper off-peak hours at night, most notably at Windrose-Dumont-Time and Star Studio in Hamburg.[52] In 1973, he finally opened his own studio in a former barn in rural Wolperath near Cologne, a fifty square metre former pigsty he reconstructed in a DIY fashion.

Plank's mentality matched the counterculture zeitgeist of Krautrock. Unlike the Anglo-American understanding of a producer, Plank saw himself more as a co-producer or 'mediator' between musicians, sounds, and tape, not wanting to determine his artists' music.[53] Instead, he was keen to foster a democratic environment where musicians could live out their creativity. For his artistic input, Plank, in his modesty, rarely claimed credit, while other contemporaries sure did, as the example of Eberhard Kranemann shows:

I know ... the early music of Kraftwerk without Conny Plank: and so I know exactly the work that Conny Plank did for the band. The sound of the band in the early stages was 70–80% Conny Plank; and not Florian and Ralf. It was so important what he was doing at the mixer with the sound and what kind of music he selected and how he supported Ralf and Florian. The sound is very important for Kraftwerk; and the sound has been made by Conny Plank, the great master.[54]

According to reports, from the ideas Plank regularly played on the synthesiser, Kraftwerk chose the ones they liked; yet he was only credited as an engineer, not as producer or co-composer. Today Plank is acknowledged as 'West Germany's answer to Brian Eno ... part producer, part collaborator, part ideas man'.[55] With his style, which Plank described himself as 'live dub mixing', he intended to treat the studio as an instrument. Hence he contributed artistically to various compositions by the artists he produced.[56] Although not an official band member, Plank had a significant impact on the music of the first four albums by Kraftwerk, as well as on Neu!, Guru Guru, and Can.[57]

In addition to his creative merit, Plank's role as a networker and business facilitator deserves attention. Indifferent to the commercial aspect of his craft, he recorded several Krautrock bands for free, enabling Cluster to get

[51] D Buckley, *Kraftwerk: A Biography* (London: Omnibus, 2015), p. 68.
[52] Reetze, *Times & Sounds*, pp. 258–9.   [53] Buckley, *Kraftwerk*, pp. 35–6.   [54] Ibid., pp. 66–7.
[55] Buckley, *Kraftwerk*, pp. 35–6.   [56] Simmeth, *Krautrock Transnational*, p. 256.
[57] Adelt, *Krautrock*, p. 33.

a record deal with major label Philips.[58] By producing on his own, Plank frequently put bands in a better position to negotiate record deals with labels.[59] With his Kraut Musikverlag, he founded a publishing company that gave him and his clients essential business connections.[60] When the Krautrock boom was over, Plank produced electro-pop bands like Ultravox and Eurythmics and played in his own band, Moebius & Plank. He died of cancer in 1987.

Dieter Dierks is the second eminent German Krautrock producer, who began his career as a self-taught engineer. He initially used the attic in his parent's house, which did not suffice for long. So Dierks had a studio built in the yard. Soon the house was turned into a family-run hotel to accommodate bands, allowing them to work whenever they felt creative. Much of the music Rolf-Ulrich Kaiser released on his three labels was recorded and produced by Dierks, including Ash Ra Tempel, Can, Popol Vuh, Embryo, Guru Guru, Tangerine Dream, Klaus Schulze, Birth Control, and Wallenstein. From the outset, Dierks was interested in experimental music and took the curious Krautrock bands seriously. Like Conny Plank, Dierks was not driven by commercial success. What he had in mind, however, was a music production empire comprising his studio, the record label Venus Records, and his Breeze Music publishing company. By the mid-1970s, he had a state-of-the-art recording studio of his own, with custom-built equipment like a forty-track mixing console and a thirty-two-track tape recorder, which was among the best in West Germany.[61]

Dierks, still expanding, enlarged the studio with three more recording spaces and a control room in the basement under the hotel section, allowing several bands to work simultaneously. He also acquired a mobile sixteen-track recording unit, used for live recordings and rental to radio and television stations. With this mobile unit, 'Rockpalast' nights at Essen's Grugahalle were recorded between 1977 and 1986.[62] Moreover, the first album recordings of German hard rock pioneers Accept and the Scorpions, released on Brain, took place at Dierks' studio. Today, the studio is still in high demand as one of the best-equipped in the world.

In Krautrock's heyday, most albums were recorded at either Plank's or Dierks' studio. Some bands had facilities, most famously Kraftwerk with their Kling-Klang studio in Düsseldorf, and Can with their Inner Space

---

[58] Stubbs, *Future Days*, pp. 337–8.   [59] Simmeth, *Krautrock Transnational*, pp. 287–90.
[60] Reetze, *Times & Sounds*, p. 259.   [61] Simmeth, *Krautrock Transnational*, pp. 284–6.
[62] Reetze, *Times & Sounds*, p. 258.

Studio, first at Schloss Nörvenich (Castle Nörvenich), then in a former cinema near Cologne. Guru Guru, Cluster, Harmonia, and Klaus Schulze followed suit, preferring rural areas for their studios.[63] The main reason for setting up a studio was to boost creativity.[64] Having one's own private studio was an essential part of Krautrock's aesthetic. Access to one was beneficial because it allowed for exploration and improvisation free from time pressure and external influences like audio engineers and producers.[65]

Conclusion

Germany's popular music industry owes a lot to Krautrock. In the 1960s, there was an infrastructure for *Schlager*, indeed a popular genre, but none for counterculture or youth. With the emergence and sudden proliferation of Krautrock towards the end of the decade, this changed quickly. Major labels discovered the economic potential of countercultural music, and new independent record labels helped jumpstart the international careers of countless Krautrock bands. Professionals independent of major companies and state organisations, but pivotal for Krautrock's aesthetic and worldwide dissemination, entered the scene and made Krautrock an international success story within less than ten years. A rapidly developing, well-functioning and globally operating production infrastructure, inspired by the Anglo-American industry and yet distinct from it, contributed to the Krautrock ecosystem. Germanness is, intentional or not, the most clear-cut characteristic of Krautrock. Critical, though, for the music to be heard beyond Germany's borders were international experiences and the business contacts of key players. Among them were record label representative Siegfried Loch and entrepreneur Peter Meisel, the genre's two primary producers, Conny Plank and Dieter Dierks and, of course, Rolf-Ulrich Kaiser. They all helped to lay the structural foundation for Neue Deutsche Welle (New German Wave), rock, and metal that followed Krautrock in the 1980s and 1990s. Krautrock's successes of the 1960s and 1970s, made possible by independent record labels, studios, and distribution networks, encouraged, if not created, an openness towards countercultural music made in Germany.

---

[63] Simmeth, *Krautrock Transnational*, p. 90.

[64] D Buckley, *Kraftwerk: A Biography* (London: Omnibus, 2015), p. 92.

[65] Adelt, *Krautrock*, p. 26; Reetze, *Times & Sounds*, p. 179; Simmeth, *Krautrock Transnational*, p. 145.

Recommended Reading

U Adelt, *Krautrock: German Music in the Seventies* (Ann Arbor: University of Michigan Press, 2016).

N Kotsopoulos, *Krautrock: Cosmic Rock and Its Legacy* (London: Black Dog, 2010).

A Simmeth, *Krautrock Transnational: Die Neuerfindung der Popmusik in der BRD, 1968–1978* (Bielefeld: Transcript, 2016).

D Stubbs, *Future Days: Krautrock and the Building of Modern Germany* (London: Faber, 2014).

R Young, *All Gates Open: The Story of Can* (London: Faber, 2018).

5 | The Sound of Krautrock

HEATHER MOORE

In terms of musical style, the sizeable catalogue of music that falls under the label of Krautrock is as diverse as it is experimental. The instrumentation of Krautrock groups ranges from soloists surrounded entirely by synthesisers to standard rock formations of vocals, guitar, bass, keyboard, and drums. Krautrock songs could be shorter than the average pop hit, or take up an entire side of a vinyl record. Some critics have drawn comparisons between the genre and psychedelic, acid, punk, progressive, and art rock on the one hand, while others insist that it 'owe[s] more to the avant-garde than to rock & roll'.[1] In short, when it comes to musical characteristics, Krautrock is all over the map.

The sheer diversity of this genre can be seen, for instance, in a comparison of two pieces that, despite being markedly different, are both widely regarded as quintessential examples of Krautrock.[2] On 'Part II' of Tangerine Dream's classic 1975 album *Rubycon*, the track begins with a low, oscillating drone, not unlike the sound of an air raid siren that has been slowed down and set to play in an endless loop. Hollow electronic pitches weave in and out of the sonic fabric, seemingly conversing with a series of metallic hits before being drowned out by a dissonant, undulating synthetic choir. This nightmarish soundscape develops for nearly five minutes, finally giving way to a rhythmic sequencer that signals the next large section of the seventeen-minute piece, which comprises the entirety of the second album side.

By contrast, Can's 'Halleluwah' (*Tago Mago*, 1971) opens with a rhythmic, repeated bassline and a tight, funk-like drum beat on an acoustic kit. The guitar alternates between syncopated chords and long, drawn-out pitches, making ample use of tremolo, while vocalist Damo Suzuki sings nonsensical lyrics over a melody derived from the classic blues scale: 'Did anybody see the snowman standing on winter road / With broken guitar in his hand, onion peeling sleepy eye?'

---

[1] Kraut Rock, All Music, www.allmusic.com/subgenre/kraut-rock-ma0000002687?1626735447443.

[2] The Ultimate Krautrock Playlist, NME, www.nme.com/blogs/nme-blogs/the-ultimate-krautrock-playlist-47357.

The difficulty in pinning down a specific 'sound' for this diverse body of music can be traced to the history of its development. Krautrock came into existence as the result of a larger cultural movement in West Germany. Since the end of World War II, West Germans had grappled with forming a German identity not tied to their Nazi past; on top of that, American popular culture had become a dominating force, often overshadowing the elements of German cultural heritage that were still acceptable in the wake of the Third Reich's cultural appropriation.[3]

Moreover, throughout the late 1950s and 1960s and culminating in 1968, younger generations of Germans began protesting with increasing vigour against the perceived ills of their government, believing that the Federal Republic was 'constantly threatened by the re-emergence of the Third Reich and by the possibility of a new world war and genocide'.[4] Musicians were heavily involved in this period of social upheaval. In addition to direct participation in these protests, artists began to search for a new sound, striving to break away from 'bad German Music and imitations of American music', in Dieter Moebius' words, and create music that reflected the new Germany.[5] In other words, Krautrock was initially better defined by what it was *not*, rather than what it specifically *was*. Krautrock musicians began to abandon the characteristics of both Anglo-American popular musics such as beat and rock 'n' roll, and the prevailing German style of the time, *Schlager* (literally, hits), endeavouring to create something 'new, special and most of all original'.[6]

This originality took many forms. Klaus Schulze, Tangerine Dream, and Ash Ra Tempel often created music that featured primarily electronic instruments, experimental recording techniques, and a minimalistic approach to form and harmonies, a style often more akin to a soundscape than a song in the traditional sense. Their style, sometimes referred to as 'Berlin School' or *kosmische Musik,* influenced ambient and New Age genres. In contrast, groups like Kraftwerk, La Düsseldorf, Neu!, and Cluster embraced a sparse, mechanical sound, characterised especially by what came to be known as *motorik* beats in the drums (or drum

---

[3] U Poiger, *Jazz, Rock, and Rebels: Cold War Politics and American Culture in a Divided Germany* (Berkeley: University of California Press, 2000), p. 1.

[4] B Kutschke, Anti-Authoritarian Revolt by Musical Means on Both Sides of the Wall, in B Kutschke & B Norton (eds.), *Music and Protest in 1968* (Cambridge: Cambridge University Press, 2013), p. 189.

[5] D Stubbs, *Future Days: Krautrock and the Building of Modern Germany* (London: Faber, 2014), p. 336.

[6] D Moebius, Cluster Interview with Dieter Moebius Psychedelic Baby (2 December 2012), www.psychedelicbabymag.com/2012/12/cluster-interview-with-dieter-moebius.html.

machines). The result was a 'hypnotic, piston-pumping' style in which 'drummers pounded out tightly-wound beats, bassists thumped pulsing notes, and zoned-out singers warbled over it all in an absurdist drone'.[7]

All the while, other groups like Guru Guru, Popol Vuh, and Amon Düül incorporated jazz and ethnic musical styles, while Faust and Can used non-musical sounds and spliced tape recordings.[8] In short, while West German musicians of the 1970s largely agreed on a desire 'to put aside everything we had heard in rock'n'roll, the three-chord pattern, the lyrics ... the urge of saying something completely different', as Jean-Hervé Péron from Faust put it, their idea of what that would entail varied drastically.[9] However, these radically different approaches to newness shared certain characteristics. Krautrock musicians embraced innovative approaches to instrumentation, timbre, the voice, texture, and form, generating a new musical vocabulary that they could call their own.

The Sounds of Krautrock

The musicians involved with Krautrock were heavily invested in sound; the goal of sonic originality informed most of their musical decisions. This began at the initial stage of the composition process. Krautrockers selected instruments that could contribute to an original style: existing instruments were played in an unusual way, while new instruments added a degree of unfamiliarity to the sound. Techniques including sampling, tape manipulation, and sequencing contributed further to Krautrock's foreign sonic character, as did innovative recording locations and methods.

When it comes to instrumentation, Krautrock artists were less focused on the means of making their music than the ends. As David Stubbs points out, it was the 'continued, imitative use of traditional instruments played in the received, traditional rock'n'roll manner that was most inauthentic' to these musicians, rather than the instruments themselves.[10] Thus, while electronic sounds play a significant role in Krautrock's style, many bands that carry this label used synthesisers and other fully electronic instruments

---

[7] D Tewksbury, Tonight: The Merciless Circularity of Beak, *Los Angeles Magazine* (13 February 2013).

[8] S Albiez, Sounds of Future Past: from Neu! to Numan, in T Phleps (ed.), *Klangtexturen in der Pop- und Rockmusik: Basics, Stories, Tracks* (Bielefeld: Transcript, 2003), p. 131.

[9] D Stubbs, Invisible Jukebox: Faust, *Wire* 275 (2007), p. 18.

[10] D Stubbs, Why Was the Synthesizer So Crucial to Krautrock?, MHP Books, Melville House, www.mhpbooks.com/why-was-the-synthesizer-so-crucial-to-krautrock/.

in a limited capacity. Indeed, because this technology was both expensive and rare in West Germany in the early days of Krautrock, many groups of the late 1960s and early 1970s used traditional instruments but played and recorded them in unusual ways.[11]

In addition to a typical rock line-up of guitar, bass, drums, and sometimes piano or organ, Krautrockers incorporated woodwind and brass instruments as well as non-Western sounds. For example, Amon Düül's psychedelic *Paradieswärts Düül* (*Towards Paradise*, 1970) contains bass, piano, flute, bongos, harp, African percussion, drum set, and guitar, along with solo vocals and choir. Including these atypical instruments served to untether the music's sound from the mainstream rock and *Schlager*.

For the more customary instruments, like guitar, Krautrock groups used unusual playing styles and modified sounds to differentiate their music from pop traditions. Instruments were fitted with contact microphones, effects pedals, and anything else the musicians could use to alter their sound, creating a processed, manipulated timbre that was sometimes so different from the original that it was nearly indistinguishable from an actual synthesiser.[12] The guitar in Neu!'s 'Negativland' (*Neu!*, 1972), for example, flows between choppy rhythmic patterns, screeching free-noise solos, and distorted drones, building to an aggressive, buzzing wail. Beneath it, the bass and drums play a relentless ostinato pattern that lasts almost the entirety of the ten-minute track, except for a few abrupt stops and restarts, switching between 'off' and 'on' with the cold suddenness of a track being muted.

Though the resulting collage of noise sounds akin to the manipulated electronic works of the classical avant-garde, no synthesisers are listed in the album's liner notes: the personnel merely includes Michael Rother on guitar and bass, and Klaus Dinger on drums, vocals, guitar, and taishōgato (a Japanese stringed instrument). The combination of non-Western instruments and rock instruments played in an innovative fashion allowed Krautrockers to escape the sonic world of the mainstream even without delving into newer electronic technologies.

Despite the difficulty early bands faced in attaining them, electronic instruments would become a hallmark of the Krautrock sound. Krautrock musicians adopted synthesisers and drum machines, relatively obscure as well as expensive (at the time) instruments that provided fertile ground for sonic creativity. Some even created their own electronic instruments, allowing for a fully unique musical voice. Krautrockers now had the

[11] Ibid.   [12] Ibid.

tools to generate an entirely new set of sounds that could serve as building blocks for the musical identity detached from tradition they sought to create.

Machine Music

In effect, Krautrock groups like Kraftwerk and Can brought electronic music out of the academic realm, taking inspiration from the experiments of Karlheinz Stockhausen and other contemporary art music composers. The majority of public exposure to synthesised sounds before the 1960s came in the form of film and television soundtracks: the theremin featured in the soundtrack to the alien invasion film *The Day the Earth Stood Still* (1951), the musique concrète of the introduction to *Doctor Who* (1963–present), and so on.[13] Pioneered in avant-garde art music circles of the first half of the twentieth century, these instruments first became available to the general public in the mid-1960s with the introduction of the Moog synthesiser.[14]

The development of the smaller and more affordable Minimoog in 1970 – the first synthesiser to be sold in music stores – resulted in a sharp increase in the instrument's overall popularity, as it was now small enough to store and bring to recording studios or live performances.[15] However, though some Anglo-American rock groups had experimented with synthesisers, they were often played in ways that gave them a similar function to the guitar or piano, rather than in an idiomatic fashion. It was only 'when synthesizers were freed from endeavouring to simulate analogue instruments [that] they came into their own as tools to exploit a broad and diverse field of new electronic sound timbres and textures'.[16]

This idiomatic use of synthesisers became a hallmark of Krautrock, from the lush electronic soundscapes of the Berlin School to stark, sequenced patterns and sparse techno-pop. Often, synthesisers and modified sounds took precedence over traditional instruments. Tangerine Dream's eerie album *Phaedra* (1974) was dominated by a Moog synthesiser; the Mellotron, flute, and bass guitar parts were added later, almost as an afterthought.[17] Some bands even forewent traditional instruments

---

[13] Albiez, Sounds of Future Past, p. 138.

[14] T Pinch & F Trocco, *Analog Days: The Invention and Impact of the Moog Synthesizer* (Harvard: Harvard University Press, 2004), p. 53.

[15] Ibid., p. 233.   [16] Albiez, Sounds of Future Past, p. 138.

[17] B Osborne, Game Changer: How Tangerine Dream's 'Phaedra' Set the Template for Ambient Electronics, *DJ Magazine* (29 July 2019).

altogether, opting for a fully synthetic line-up. Kraftwerk, after an early period of experimental rock, abandoned their flutes, guitars, and drum kits in favour of a wide array of synthesisers, including a Minimoog, ARP Odyssey, EMS Synthi-A, and Prophet-5, as well as electronic drums, vocoders, and sequencers.[18]

Like synthesisers, drum machines were a new and relatively obscure addition to the palette of options afforded to Krautrock musicians. While experiments with electronic rhythm instruments dated back to the early 1930s, fully programmable drum machines were not introduced to the market until 1972 with EKO's ComputeRhythm. However, drum machines only became a staple of 1980s electronic music with the introduction of the Roland TR-808.[19] Just as synthesisers provided the opportunity to explore new melodic and harmonic timbres, these machines allowed for a sonically different rhythm section. They are particularly present on the polished, mechanical side of the Krautrock spectrum, featuring heavily in Kraftwerk's albums.

The spirit of sonic originality was so imbued in many of these musicians that some even created instruments of their own. Amon Düül's Kalle Hausmann, for example, built ring modulators and other custom synthesisers for his performances on *Tanz der Lemminge* (1971) and *Carnival in Babylon* (1972).[20] Kraftwerk are particularly known for their technological innovations; they used a custom-built vocoder for the albums *Ralf & Florian* (1973) and *Autobahn* (1974), and even invented an electronic drum kit with sensor pads, for which they filed a patent between 1975 and 1977.[21] Edgar Froese spoke of creating 'a new musical identity' through creating and modifying synthesiser patches, arguing that

It may sound superfluous, but we're not talking about a musical philosophy – it is more a technical necessity in order to find an incomparable musical basis . . . as a synth player you need to be original, even if you can't make a sound 'better' but make it more original, more like your personal handwriting.[22]

This 'incomparable musical basis' was the artistic goal behind Krautrock, and the musicians involved with this genre achieved it through both the use

---

[18] L Eilers, Kraftwerk: Their Legendary Synths, Sequencers, and Sounds, gearnews, www .gearnews.com/kraftwerk-their-legendary-synths-sequencers-and-sounds/.

[19] A Crute, The History of Drum Machines, MusicTech, www.musictech.net/guides/essential-guide/drum-machines-history/.

[20] J Gross, John Weinzierl Interview, *Perfect Sound Forever* 8 (2008).

[21] Kling Klang: The Electronic Garden, *Aktivität* 10 (April 1998).

[22] E Froese, L Kay & D Kay, Interview with Edgar Froese of Tangerine Dream by Inquisitor Betrayer, The Rocktologist, www.therocktologist.com/interview-with-edgar-froese-of-tangerine-dream.html.

of new electronic instruments such as synthesisers and drum machines and the transformation of the sound and style of traditional instruments, from standard rock equipment like guitars and drums to orchestral and non-Western instruments.

Vocals in Krautrock

The voice, too, was assigned a different role in Krautrock than it typically served in British and American music, both in terms of its delivery and its use of language. Krautrock singers treated vocal lines more like sound poetry, more akin to progressive and psychedelic rock than beat music or *Schlager*. More attention was given to the way in which the voice was used, rather than the lyrics or conventional talent; the voice served as an avenue for further sonic exploration, rather than a mere medium for lyrical expression.

Can's Damo Suzuki, for example, infused the band's songs with invented words, piercing shrieks, buzzing lips, and guttural groans, often singing with more of a shout than a defined pitch. On top of this experimental use of the voice, vocals were often so thoroughly manipulated that they could be mistaken for a synthesiser; this can be heard in Faust's 'Exercise with Voices' (*Faust Tapes*, 1973), a nightmarish soundscape of processed, word-less vocals rising and falling as various instruments and noises penetrate the texture. Perhaps most famous for innovative vocal timbres among Krautrock groups were Kraftwerk, who made frequent use of vocoders to create a dehumanised, robotic effect. Kraftwerk were among the first bands to feature this technology, which had first been used in the 1971 dystopian film *A Clockwork Orange*; their 'roboticisation' of vocals would have a profound and lasting impact on popular music across the globe.

As with other aspects of Krautrock's sound, vocal style varied widely from one musician to the next. Can's original singer, Malcolm Mooney, sang with a rhythmic, unembellished style, while his replacement, Damo Suzuki, delivered his curious blend of English, Japanese, and invented words with a sense of breathy melodicism. Moreover, many bands did not consistently use a certain style. Faust's vocals, for example, are widely varied. One of their songs, 'Flashback Caruso', comes across as folk rock, with Rudolf Sosna singing Beatles-esque lyrics over a piano-dominated jam session. 'J'ai Mal Aux Dents', in contrast, gives the voice a rhythmic function, with the phrase 'J'ai mal aux dents / J'ai mal aux pieds aussi' repeating continuously in time with the drums and guitar as Jean-Hervé Péron recites, rather than singing, seemingly nonsensical English lyrics.

Both voice lines are compressed and nasal, and are sometimes balanced fairly evenly in the mix, making it difficult for the listener to focus on one over the other. These songs appear on the same album, *The Faust Tapes* (1973), and are as different from the other tracks as they are from each other. In short, vocal styles varied greatly across the spectrum of Krautrock; however, their function was the same: originality. From atypical melodies and nonsensical lyrics to vocoders and studio effects, Krautrock vocals were performed with a unique style and function, creating another degree of separation between themselves and the Anglo-American and German mainstream.

Sonic Explorations

These were not the only methods Krautrockers used to create a unique sonic signature, however. These musicians were deeply interested in sound itself, and used techniques like sampling, tape manipulation, and sequencing, as well as innovative recording locations and methods, to further differentiate their music from what had come before. In the words of Kraftwerk's Ralf Hütter:

Sound sources are all around us, and we work with anything, from pocket calculators to computers, from voices, human voices, from machines, from body sounds to fantasy to synthetic sounds to speech from human voice to speech synthesis from anything, if possible. We don't want to limit ourselves.[23]

Krautrockers' sonic explorations took many forms. It was not uncommon for these musicians to incorporate recordings of themselves crushing glass, hitting sheet metal, and throwing bricks.[24] Can's Holger Czukay became known for 'bridging the gap between pop and the avant-garde' through his incorporations of vocals and other sounds from short-wave radio broadcasts, a practice that would pave the way for sampling practices of the 1980s and beyond.[25] Likewise, bands often manipulated recordings of their own music, experimenting with playback speed, EQ, and other aspects of the

---

[23] R Hütter & M Richardson, Kraftwerk, *Pitchfork* (9 November 2009).

[24] Froese, Kay & Kay, Interview with Edgar Froese; Albiez, Sounds of Future Past.

[25] J Leidecker, Variations #3: The Approach, Radio Web MACBA, https://img.macba.cat/public/rwm/uploads/20120201/03Variations_transcript_eng.pdf.

  J Pareles, Man, Alive to Machine Possibilities, *New York Times* (15 April 2012).

base recording to add 'musical dirt'.[26] According to Edgar Froese from Tangerine Dream, recording and manipulating these sounds was not only 'much more fun', but also helped these artists to create 'new sounds definitely no one else has', again feeding into their desire for sonic originality.[27]

Location played a significant role in the recording process as well. Many Krautrock groups explored alternatives to conventional studios, affording them the freedom to record without interference from studio owners and employees (who were sometimes less enthusiastic about the bands' experiments) and creating the opportunity for a different-sounding environment. The nature of these studios varied significantly. Can elected to record in a castle, Schloss Nörvenich, with nothing but 'two stereo tape decks, four microphones, two small speakers, and a few malfunctioning amplifiers, in addition to the band's instruments'.[28] Kraftwerk, on the other hand, founded their own studio, Kling Klang, which they outfitted with a vast array of electronic equipment. The band saw the studio almost as a laboratory and considered it to be such an essential part of their sound that they eventually modified it to be fully portable and have toured with it since the early 1980s.[29]

Overall, Krautrock musicians' focus on sound quality and timbre informed many of the artistic decisions they made before even composing their works. They selected instruments, performance and recording techniques, and studio locations with the specific intent of creating a unique sonic identity. This philosophy also translated to the methods with which they composed their music.

Texture as Structure

Just as they used instruments and recording equipment to create a new *sonic* identity, Krautrock musicians used innovative compositional methods to develop a new *musical* one. Form was treated with a distinctly different approach than that of standard popular music, often

---

[26] Froese, Kay & Kay, Interview with Edgar Froese.   [27] Ibid.
[28] U Adelt, *Krautrock: German Music in the Seventies* (Ann Arbor: University of Michigan Press, 2016).
[29] M Beecher, Kraftwerk Revealed!, *Electronics & Music Maker* 9 (1981), pp. 62–7.

only loosely planned, if not entirely improvised. The structure of Krautrock tracks is generally based on changes of texture rather than common song forms or narrative lyrics. Said textures play a large role in the development of the loose stylistic categories of 'oceanic' and 'machine', which have come to be among the most recognisable qualities of Krautrock.

Musical form provided another avenue for the differentiation of Krautrock from mainstream popular practices. Krautrock musicians sought to 'get away from the A-B-A format in music', as Guru Guru's Mani Neumeier puts it, as part of the process of 'mak[ing] some sort of music that has not been there before'.[30] Indeed, few Krautrock songs follow any semblance of this verse–chorus format. This may be due in part to the emphasis on vocal timbre over lyricism. The verse–chorus form is largely based on lyrical content: choruses contain catchy, unchanging refrains with memorable musical material – the song's 'hook' – while verses advance the song's narrative with different lyrics and, usually, subdued instrumental parts.[31] The vague experimentalism of Krautrock vocals is not conducive to this type of songwriting. Instead, Krautrock form is largely derived from musical texture, which, in turn, involved certain performance practices specific to this movement.

Sean Albiez, in his study of the 'sonic futurscape' of electronic music during the height of Krautrock and beyond, outlines two larger categories of the electronic avant-garde in popular music: 'machine rock', which embraces a sense of kineticism and motion, and 'oceanic rock', which embodies a sense of stasis and expansive spaces. Both, importantly, involve movement: machine rock represents the time spent moving, while oceanic rock expresses the moments of stillness in between.[32] These textural styles align to an extent with the subsets of Krautrock belonging to the Berlin and Düsseldorf Schools, respectively.

The term Berlin School refers to an oceanic variety of Krautrock commonly used by West Berliners Klaus Schulze, Manuel Göttsching, and Tangerine Dream, among others. These artists tended to create music of an ambient nature, with drones, slow or non-existent tempi, and gradual shifts in harmony, texture, and timbre. Sequenced patterns created motion, while sweeping melodies and non-musical sounds could be layered above the drones to add colour and timbral shifts. Oceanic Krautrock is

---

[30] F Gingeleit, The Drumming Man: An Interview with Mani Neumeier of Guru Guru, *Aural Innovations* 19 (2002).

[31] J Summach, The Structure, Function, and Genesis of the Prechorus, *Music Theory Online* 17:3 (2011), pp. 1–13.

[32] Albiez, Sounds of Future Past, pp. 141–7.

overwhelmingly electronic, and is particularly associated with the use of the Mellotron, an electronic instrument akin to an analogue sampler that produces choir-like sounds; orchestral instruments were sometimes used as well. Rock-associated sounds like guitar, drums, and vocals seldom make an appearance. Albiez describes the overall feeling of oceanic music to be 'contemplative, resting but sonically and texturally still searching for the new';[33] it is expansive, but not always serene, embracing a sense of the sublime.

This style is exemplified in much of Tangerine Dream's oeuvre, particularly their works in the mid to late 1970s. Their album *Phaedra* (1974) is considered to be a hallmark of the Berlin School.[34] The title track epitomises the oceanic. It begins with an eerie, breathy synthetic drone, evoking feelings of the deepest expanses of outer space. A sequencer enters the mix, barely audible at first, sprinkled with high-pitched hollow tones. The piece builds, the sequencers gradually increasing in volume, pitch, and speed; processed noises and synthesised patterns build layer upon layer into a cacophony of sound. Eventually, it collapses into a nightmarish soundscape of indeterminate noises and melancholy electronic melodies, fading away after nearly twenty minutes.

While the *kosmische Musik* of the Berlin School conveys a sense of the unknown expanses of the universe, the 'machine music' of Düsseldorf groups like Kraftwerk and Neu! has a highly controlled, mechanical quality. A significant component of this was the *motorik* drum beat first pioneered by Can's Klaus Dinger. *Motorik*'s beat is straight, unembellished, and in 4/4 time, almost metronomic in its consistency and sparseness. Other groups, like Kraftwerk, utilised drum machines or sequencers to this end, but the result was the same: a consistent, disciplined march towards an unknown destination. On top of this rhythm, a bassline establishes a groove, over which additional synthesisers and vocals are layered.[35] The style also embraces machine-like timbres and sounds: non-electronic instruments and vocals are often heavily processed, and mechanical sounds frequently contribute to the texture. Furthermore, machine music features a significant amount of repetition: rhythm and basslines are often ostinatos, while the lyrics and motifs played over them are constantly reiterated.

[33] Ibid., p. 145.

[34] A Harden, Kosmische Musik and Its Techno-Social Context, *Journal of the International Association for the Study of Popular Music* 6 (2016), pp. 155–73.

[35] I Brockhaus, *Kultsounds: Die prägendsten Klänge der Popmusik 1960–2014* (Berlin: Taschen, 2017).

Kraftwerk are perhaps the best-known example of machine music. Their 'Trans Europa Express' is built upon a dry, sequenced beat, over which a motif of short, rising synthesiser chords repeats. Over the course of the thirteen-minute song, the rhythm and basslines do not change, pushing the music along with the controlled insistence of a moving train. In addition to the rising chord motif, three other sounds appear throughout the song: a short synth-strings melody (which, along with the initial motif, is sometimes transcribed to the minor mode), a higher-pitched electronic drum pattern, and vocals. The lyrics, which mostly comprise repetitions of the song's title, are delivered rhythmically and without melodic contour, coming across as mechanical even when the band's signature vocoder is not used.

Across the spectrum of Krautrock, texture, rather than lyrics or established musical forms, informed the music's structure. Sections were determined by the addition or removal of certain sounds, a modular approach far removed from the verse–chorus model.[36] 'It's components, it's conceptual', stated Froese of this approach. 'There's development, gradual. Whereas in classical music there is drama. That's not our thing.'[37] This modular structure and gradual development was not necessarily planned; indeed, many Krautrock bands relied on aleatoric practices and improvisation, or, as Tangerine Dream's Thorsten Quaeschning prefers to describe it, 'real-time composing', while creating their albums.[38]

This was structured to varying degrees. Can's pieces were largely improvised, but with a semi-planned structure, similar in some ways to jazz improvisation.[39] It differed, however, in its willingness to break away from traditional formal practices, as discussed by Holger Czukay:

Most of the bands I know that improvise, if at all, follow a certain pattern. Then they get to a point where they have the chance to destroy everything and develop completely new ideas. But at this exact point, which is so crucial, almost all groups go back to the theme! It's all over right there. What's different about us compared to almost all other bands is that at that point we keep playing.[40]

After recording a jam session, Can would then overdub and manipulate the initial recording. Tangerine Dream's works were even more improvisatory: according to Peter Baumann, all their works were written spontaneously in

---

[36] Pareles, Man, Alive to Machine Possibilities.   [37] Ibid.

[38] Fifteen Questions Interview with Tangerine Dream, 15 Questions, https://15questions.net/interview/fifteen-questions-interview-tangerine-dream/page-1/.

[39] Adelt, *Krautrock*, p. 11.

[40] K Borchert, Can mit neuer Platte: Zukunftstage haben begonnen, *Musikexpress* 12 (1973).

the studio, without even a predetermined structure. 'It was intuitive', he stated in an interview. 'I can't remember there ever being a big discussion about the music itself. It just fell into place.'[41] This practice was fairly common among Krautrock groups.

Even after a track was created and released, many Krautrockers were open to the idea of modifying and re-releasing it, allowing for multiple versions of a musical concept. Kraftwerk say their compositions are 'endless scripts', open to change and improvisation.[42] Indeed, their songs are subject to near-constant reworking, most recently in the two box sets *Der Katalog* (2009) and *3-D Der Katalog* (2017). Many of Tangerine Dream's live albums contain pieces that are radically different from their original versions (as well as works that have never been included in their studio albums); moreover, they have released several remixes of their existing material, such as the dance-style *Dream Mixes* (1996). Froese staunchly defends this process, stating that '[n]othing on the planet has an immortal value, nothing will survive forever. . . . [T]he artist must have the freedom of choice to destroy his own art or at least rebuild structures and change the whole composition in order to pursue a new train of thought.'[43]

This laissez-faire approach to form at every stage of composition allowed, once again, for great variety among Krautrock pieces. Some tunes, like Kraftwerk's 'Transistor', are just one or two minutes long; indeed, almost half of the tracks on the album from which it came, *Radio-Aktivität* (1975), are shorter than three minutes. Others, like a great deal of Klaus Schulze's works, last fifteen to twenty minutes or longer, to the point that several Krautrock records consist of just one track on the A- or B-side.

Through these innovative approaches to form and texture, Krautrockers developed a musical style that was thoroughly divorced from popular practices of the past. They eschewed traditional approaches to musical form, leaving much of the music's development to chance and spontaneity. The structure that does exist within these pieces, moreover, is modular, distinguishable by changes in texture rather than through a lyrical narrative or verse–chorus format. These textures were likewise unique, making use of their already-innovative choices of instruments and timbres to create the

[41] P Baumann & C May, Tangerine Dream's Peter Baumann on Synth Improvisation and Studio Wizardry, The Vinyl Factory, https://thevinylfactory.com/features/peter-baumann-tangerine-dream-interview/.

[42] Richardson, Kraftwerk.

[43] E Froese, FAQ, Tangerine Dream Official Website, www.tangerinedreammusic.com/en/community/faq_detail.asp?id=68&tit=Fans+sometimes+argue+that+you've+ruined+the+original+version+of+a+sound+or+record+by+adding+new+layers+and%2For+changing+parts+of+the+original+composition%2E.

sublime soundscapes of oceanic rock or the automated kineticism of machine music. However, despite their endeavours to break from tradition, their music was not created in a vacuum. Krautrock was influenced, to certain extents, by other styles of music, even if they utilised aspects of these styles in different ways.

Musical Influences

Musicians of the Krautrock movement were united by a desire to create something that was sonically unique, a stark departure from the musical styles that dominated German culture at the time. However, they were not entirely devoid of musical influences, regardless of whether this was desired. The pioneers of Krautrock came from a wide range of musical backgrounds. Some were cooks and carpenters who picked up their instruments out of casual interest, while others had completed conservatory-level training, studying with the pre-eminent avant-garde composers of the time. Before founding the groups that would become flagships of the Krautrock scene, many played in different styles, from free jazz to beat rock to skiffle (a melding of blues and folk styles); moreover, some had developed an appreciation for musical styles from different parts of the world.[44] Many elements of this wide palette of musical styles come through in Krautrock, but the most prominent are non-Western styles, avant-garde art music, and other experimental popular styles.

Many artists of the Krautrock movement borrowed heavily from non-Western musical traditions. Can frequently incorporated Afro-Cuban rhythms and basslines, while Neu! attributed their emphasis on repetition to Pakistani music.[45] Bands sometimes even sampled musicians and everyday sounds from other countries; Agitation Free's *Malesch* (1972), for instance, contains recordings of an Egyptian market in addition to jams inspired by Middle Eastern cultures. Beyond this, many Krautrockers incorporated non-Western instruments, as discussed earlier.

In the case of classical music, most Krautrock musicians derived inspiration from contemporary composers, rather than the 'lengthy Germanic classical tradition' which was considered to be limited in its capacity to inspire originality.[46] This is not to say that there was no borrowing from

[44] J Wallenfeldt (ed.), *Sounds of Rebellion: Music in the 1960s* (New York: Britannica, 2013).

[45] Interview with Michael Rother: 50 Years of Making Music, Derek's Music Blog, https://dereksmusicblog.com/2016/01/03/interview-with-michael-rother-50-years-making-music-2/.

[46] Pareles, Man, Alive to Machine Possibilities.

this extensive repertoire: some works, such as Manuel Göttsching's *Inventions for Electric Guitar* (1975) or Popol Vuh's *Hosianna Mantra* (1972), utilise traditional classical forms, while others, like Klaus Schulze's 'Wahnfried 1883' (a nod to Richard Wagner) or Kraftwerk's 'Franz Schubert' seem to emulate the styles of the composers they reference.

By and large, though, Krautrock has far more in common with the experimental styles of the mid-twentieth century. Their experiments with tape music and sampling are connected to the works of Karlheinz Stockhausen and György Ligeti, with whom some of them had studied, while the focus on repetition, modular forms, and drones, which feature so heavily in Krautrock, relates closely to minimalist composers like Terry Riley, Steve Reich, and Philip Glass. However, other Krautrockers are ambivalent about this connection, feeling a stronger kinship with other experimental popular genres. The vast array of musicians and bands to whom they have credited influence includes Frank Zappa and The Mothers of Invention, The Beatles, Pink Floyd, Jimi Hendrix, Miles Davis, Ornette Coleman, and The Velvet Underground, all of whom were pioneers of art rock, free jazz, and other similarly experimental genres. Though there are at times stark differences in the styles and practices of these groups and Krautrock – not unlike the variety found within Krautrock itself – they shared a common goal of innovation and originality.

Despite their goal of musical originality, Krautrock musicians were influenced to a certain degree by other styles. Some, like non-Western musics and avant-garde classical techniques, were incorporated into Krautrock, while others, like art rock and free jazz, were inspirational in their similar attitude towards music-making. However, it could be argued that even the genres that Krautrockers rejected – not only traditional classical music, but also *Schlager* and Anglo-American rock – influenced the development of Krautrock's unique sound.

For it was these styles that created the need, in these musicians' eyes, for such innovations in the first place. Krautrock's negative reaction to these mainstream genres created a new space, one that was open and dynamic, and could be filled with any style. This music is not at all uniform in its instrumentation, musical content, or style, but there is one unifying factor: it was something entirely new.

Recommended Reading

U Adelt, *Krautrock: German Music in the Seventies* (Ann Arbor: University of Michigan Press, 2016), pp. 1–110.

S Albiez, Sounds of Future Past: From Neu! to Numan, in T Phelps (ed.), *Klangtexturen in der Pop- und Rockmusik: Basics, Stories, Tracks* (Bielefeld: Transcript, 2003), pp. 129–52.

B Kutschke & B Norton (eds.), *Music and Protest in 1968* (Cambridge: Cambridge University Press, 2013), pp. 188–204.

D Stubbs, *Future Days: Krautrock and the Building of Modern Germany* (London: Faber, 2014), pp. 151–208, 277–311.

PART II

Music

6 | Kraftwerk

UWE SCHÜTTE

Kraftwerk are a special case indeed. Founded in 1970 by Ralf Hütter and Florian Schneider, the Düsseldorf-based group were the most artistically significant German music group of the 1970s. They exerted a formative influence on global pop music with their innovative approach to transpose academic, or 'new' electronic music into the realm of pop music. The defining characteristic of Kraftwerk's work is the prominent incorporation of artistic concepts to which Hütter and Schneider had been exposed at the Düsseldorf Art Academy and within the local art scene. Accordingly, they saw themselves as performance artists rather than musicians.

Both musicians, and in particular Schneider, came from wealthy backgrounds. They had the financial means to purchase expensive synthesisers and other technical equipment for their Kling-Klang studio. Also, ownership of their label released Kraftwerk from the commercial restraints of a record company. Their strategic use of artistic autonomy was inspired by Andy Warhol and, like Warhol's operation, Kraftwerk constituted a 'myth machine'.

According to Dirk Matejovski, from *Autobahn* (1974) onwards, Kraftwerk formulated 'an aesthetic concept that became ever more perfectly developed'. Initially Hütter and Schneider issued enigmatic interview statements of their artistic intentions to steer reception, but then 'ceased all self-commentary in the 1980s'. The resulting 'mystification through communication breakdown' enabled the Kraftwerk myth to emerge.[1] Johannes Ullmaier proposes an alternative to the self-created mythologies and tendencies towards monumentalisation that originate especially from the Anglosphere: he proposes a more sober view of the band that undermines hero-worshipping narratives. In his view, the development of Kraftwerk's oeuvre is perceived 'as a gradual, ... situational niche creation via clever, international, trial-and-error market analysis and adaptation'.[2]

---

[1] D Matejovski, Einleitung, in D Matejovski (ed.), *Kraftwerk: Die Mythenmaschine: Konzeption und Ästhetik eines popmusikalischen Gesamtkunstwerks* (Düsseldorf: DUP, 2016), pp. 7–10 (7, 8, 9).

[2] J Ullmaier, Kraftwerk, Kraftwerk unter anderem: Anmerkungen zu einem deutschen Mythos, in U Schütte (ed.), *Mensch-Maschinen-Musik: Das Gesamtkunstwerk Kraftwerk* (Düsseldorf: Leske, 2018), pp. 333–57 (342).

This chapter opens an overview of key Krautrock bands. Yet the extent to which Kraftwerk can be strictly classified as Krautrock requires critical evaluation. Such a subsumption is certainly unproblematic regarding their first three albums alone, *Kraftwerk* (1970), *Kraftwerk 2* (1972), and *Ralf & Florian* (1973). But it was precisely this trio of albums that Kraftwerk – in a move no other band discussed in this volume ever did – disavowed and exorcised from their œuvre. Instead, they made their next album, *Autobahn* (1974), the official starting point of their discography. Whereas its B-side is still strongly influenced by the Krautrock sound of the first three albums, the title track, which takes up the entire A-side, heralded no less than a paradigm shift in the history of German popular music: the advent of electronic pop music.

Kraftwerk's claim to autonomy in the field of pop music is based on their definition of their artistic production as a pop-cultural *Gesamtkunstwerk* (total work of art) and a 'work in progress'. Not only can their output be divided into phases but also into two opposing modes of production: a conventional mode characterised by their ground-breaking concept albums (from 1974 to 1981) and then, from the 1990s onwards, a mode of curation. In the latter, they subjected their work to a permanent process of technical revision, stylistic adaptation, and intermedial expansion, which turned it into a transmedial, 'open work of art' (in Umberto Eco's sense).

Finally, the most remarkable feature of Kraftwerk may well be that, more than fifty years after first emerging, they continue to give live performances, now under the sole artistic leadership of founding member Ralf Hütter. In addition to regular tours and festival appearances, Kraftwerk play concerts at prestigious venues such as symphony halls, world-class museums, and prestigious theatres. Their *Gesamtkunstwerk* approach, which unites sound and vision, has led to an immersive stage show with continuous 3D video projection and a multi-channel sound system based on wave field synthesis technology that creates sculptural sound effects.[3]

Formative Influences

Hütter and Schneider were inspired to develop the concept of electronic pop music in the 1970s by local Rhineland musicians such as Karlheinz Stockhausen, Mauricio Kagel, Pierre Boulez, Pierre Schaeffer, and György

[3] Turbines to Triangulation: This is Kraftwerk, D&B Audiotechnik, www.dbaudio.com/global/en/applications/touring-and-concerts/turbines-to-triangulation-this-is-kraftwerk/.

Ligeti. These avant-garde composers worked at the famous Studio for Electronic Music, which was founded in 1951 at the WDR public radio station. Equally significant for Kraftwerk were the technical experiments in electronic sound synthesis by the physicist Werner Meyer-Eppler, who was the first person to use the term electronic music in German in 1949.[4] Hütter and Schneider paid their homage with 'Die Stimme der Energie' (The Voice of Energy, 1975), a variant on a speech synthesis experiment conducted by Meyer-Eppler in 1949.

Via the Düsseldorf Art Academy and the local gallery and museum scene, Kraftwerk were influenced by the modernist avant-garde and contemporary Pop Art. Hütter and Schneider also adopted the strategy to subordinate their artistic project to conceptual principles. The latter encompasses far more than the mere fact that their œuvre consists of concept albums only. The band name itself, which translates as 'power station', has a conceptual function, since the electricity electronic music requires is generated in a power station. The conceptual approach is also evident in the artistic tactic of disappearing as private individuals behind the uniform group identity. This allowed Hütter and Schneider to reject the myth of authenticity surrounding rock musicians and style themselves as an artistic collective of 'sound researchers'[5] and 'music workers'.[6]

Warhol's influence, as already explained, looms large over the early work of Kraftwerk. The recurring use of pylons on the minimalist sleeves of the first two, untitled albums was evidently a nod to his serial art. Another important model was local Düsseldorf artist Joseph Beuys, whose conceptual art strategies were adapted by Kraftwerk in various ways. An important link to Beuys's conceptual approach was provided by his student Emil Schult, who assumed the role of an unofficial band member. Schult guided Hütter and Schneider on how to align their artistic output to overarching conceptual ideas. Furthermore, he not only wrote most of the lyrics but also designed many record covers. Similarly, many ideas for Kraftwerk's stage presentation stemmed from Schult. For instance, he devised the neon signs featuring the first names of the musicians that can be seen on the back sleeve of *Ralf & Florian*.

[4] E Ungeheuer, *Wie die elektronische Musik 'erfunden' wurde ... Quellenstudien zu Werner Meyer-Epplers musikalischem Entwurf zwischen 1949 und 1953* (Mainz: Schott, 1992).

[5] Hütter, quoted in A Koch, *Kraftwerk* (St Andrä-Wördern: Hannibal, 2005), p. 33.

[6] Compare, for example T Rapp & F Thadeusz, Maschinen sind einfach lockerer: Interview mit Ralf Hütter, *Spiegel* 50 (2009), pp. 138–40 (138).

Illustration 6.1 Kraftwerk dolls. © Ilse Ruppert.

Industrielle Volksmusik from Germany (1970–1974)

Music journalists have made various attempts to label Kraftwerk's electronic style of pop music. In addition to 'synth pop', Kraftwerk themselves suggested labels such as 'electro pop', 'robo pop', and 'techno pop' – the latter being one of the tracks on the album *Electric Cafe* (1986). Asked about the original artistic idea behind Kraftwerk's music, Hütter told an interviewer: 'To create music that reflects the moods and sentiments of modern Germany. That's why we named our studio Kling-Klang [literally ding-dong], because those are typical German onomatopoetic words. We call our music *industrielle Volksmusik* from Germany.'[7]

This odd concept name, which literally means 'industrial folk music', requires critical analysis since it neither regards industrial music nor folk music in the received sense. The emphatic qualification 'German' is easier to comprehend: it reflects Krautrock's impetus to create an alternative to the dominant, cultural imperialist model of Anglo-American rock/pop music. Kraftwerk, however, did not search for inspiration in cosmic expanses (like 'Berlin School' bands such as Tangerine Dream or Ash Ra Tempel), in the music of foreign cultures (like Can, Agitation Free, Popol

---

[7] P Kracík, Computer Unsterblichkeit, in U Schütte (ed.), *Mensch-Maschinen-Musik: Das Gesamtkunstwerk Kraftwerk* (Düsseldorf: Leske, 2018), pp. 291–300 (295). The interview was conducted in 1992 and translated from Czech.

Vuh etc.), in modernist aesthetics like the cut-up technique (like Faust), or in jazz (like Embryo). Rather, Hütter and Schneider decided to focus on forgotten German cultural traditions (such as the *Gesamtkunstwerk*, Bauhaus, or Expressionism) and often emphasised their Germanness, especially to anglophone interviewers. Thus, according to Melanie Schiller, 'not least because of their German band name, they were an exception'[8] among the important Krautrock bands.

Kraftwerk also gave their songs exclusively German titles. The tracks on the first four albums can be categorised as follows: firstly, terms from electrical engineering, such as 'Strom' (Current), 'Wellenlänge' (Wavelength), or 'Spule 4' (Coil 4); secondly, German onomatopoetic or compound words such as 'Kling-Klang' (ding-dong), 'Ruckzuck' (in a jiffy), or 'Tongebirge' (Mountains of Sound); thirdly, programmatic terms from the field of music: 'Tanzmusik' (Dance Music) or 'Heimatklänge' (Sounds of Home). Therefore, the 'industrial' in *industrielle Volksmusik* does not primarily refer to factories – although the modernist redefinition of noise as music played a role in Kraftwerk's work, along with their self-designation as 'music workers' – but rather to modern technology, in particular electronic machines that allow a new type of music to be made.

Kraftwerk understand this electronic music – against the background of the industrialisation and modernisation of post-war Germany – as constituting 'Heimatmusik' (ethnic/homeland music). As the band once proudly stated in a press release: 'We make *Heimatmusik* from the Rhine-Ruhr area.'[9] Kraftwerk's key work 'Autobahn', a homage to the extensive network of motorways in their home federal state of North Rhine-Westphalia, is a case in point. This piece of music is 'industrial' not only by virtue of its electronic nature but also in view of sound effects such as a car door slamming, engine noises, and vehicle horns. These noises, which Kraftwerk simply took from a library record, evoke the sonic presence of the Volkswagen engine that, as it were, drives the very *motorik*[10] of the track.

The meaning of the polyvalent concept of '*Volksmusik*' becomes more apparent if we consider instrumental pieces like 'Heimatklänge' or

---

[8] M Schiller, Wie klingt die Bundesrepublik? Kraftwerk, Autobahn und die Suche nach der eigenen Identität, in U Schütte (ed.), *Mensch-Maschinen-Musik: Das Gesamtkunstwerk Kraftwerk* (Düsseldorf: Leske, 2018), pp. 34–49 (37).

[9] *EMI Presse Report* 14 (1978), pp. 9–10 (10).

[10] Concerning this term, see the essays by Heather Moore, David Stubbs, and David Pattie in this volume.

'Tanzmusik'. The romantic simplicity of their melodies is striking. They are clearly alluding to the German folk song tradition but, at the same time, they highlight the electronic instrumentation that makes them modern versions of traditional folk songs. *Autobahn,* as an album, unites both properties in the contrast between the monotony of the 'industrial' title track and a 'folk' composition like 'Morgenspaziergang' (Morning Walk), which features electronic birdsong and gentle flute sounds. Kraftwerk's *Volksmusik,* though harking back to folk tradition, must hence be understood as the 'music of the people (Volk)', that is, the *populus*; ultimately, it is a literal translation of the English term 'pop music' into German. The seemingly opaque expression *industrielle Volksmusik* could thus be simply rendered as 'electronic pop music' in English.

Although *Autobahn* was not completely electronically recorded, the album steered pop music into hitherto unexplored realms. This quantum leap, however, went largely unnoticed at first. As of the release, there was only one review in the German music press. It rated the title track as a 'a car ride with whimsical music and a lot of drive' but found that 'the vocals, which are used for the first time, as yet lacked their own style'.[11]

The initial reception in Britain – inevitably riddled with Germanophobic clichés – was similarly disparaging. 'Odd noises, from percussion and synthesiser drift out from the speakers without any comprehensible order while a few words are muttered from time to time in a strange tongue. . . . Miss,'[12] rated one reviewer, while another opined, 'Synthesizer-tweakers Hutter and Schneider try for a concept – a drive down the motorway – and convincingly blow the few avant-garde credentials fans of their earlier work awarded them. . . . Simple minds only.'[13]

In the United States, however, *Autobahn* became a surprise success; the magazine *Cash Box,* for example, had only praise: 'Ethereal, inspired and well-conceived, Kraftwerk relates through electronic wizardry and soaring synthesizer tracks the moody feeling of motoring along the road. . . . Lovely and interesting.'[14] A heavily cut single version of the title track soared to number twenty-five on the Billboard charts, subsequently catapulting the album to number five on the album charts, where it remained for more than four months. Kraftwerk were now a force to be reckoned with.

---

[11] HJ Krüger, Kraftwerk: Autobahn, *Sounds* 12 (1974).
[12] Kraftwerk: Autobahn, *Melody Maker* (3 May 1975).
[13] Kraftwerk: Autobahn, *New Musical Express* (15 February 1975).
[14] Kraftwerk: Autobahn, *Cash Box* (22 March 1975).

Retro-Futurism (1975–1977)

Autobahn indeed marks the inauguration of Kraftwerk's core œuvre in that – at least as far as the title track is concerned – it represents their first attempt to achieve a pop-cultural *Gesamtkunstwerk* aesthetic: musical style, car noises, lyrics, cover image, and stage presentation merge seamlessly to form a coherent concept. *Radio-Aktivität* (*Radio-Activity*, 1975), then became Kraftwerk's first complete concept album. The record was also fully self-produced in the band's own Kling-Klang studio and recorded entirely electronically. With a playing time of thirty-eight minutes, the album resembles an experimental radio play as it emulates a radio broadcast, forming a continuous collage of sound effects, instrumentals, spoken word sections, and pop songs.

The play on words in the title is a fundamental aspect of the album: *Radio-Aktivität* refers both to nuclear energy, a controversial topic in Germany at the time, and the radio as a medium for transmitting political propaganda as well as musical entertainment. This ambivalent neutrality was implied by the album sleeve, which replicated the front and back of a National Socialist *Volksempfänger* radio. What emerged out of this 'radio set', however, was avant-garde electronic pop music. *Radio-Aktivität* thus undertook a merger of opposites that proved to be one Kraftwerk's core artistic strategies. This constitutive ambivalence was reflected in the hyphen of the title and the bright yellow Trefoil radioactivity warning sticker that adorned each cover.

This unprejudiced treatment of the topic of nuclear energy caused disgruntlement in left-wing ecological circles, especially since Kraftwerk had themselves been photographed in white protective suits in a Dutch nuclear power plant. The Chernobyl nuclear disaster in April 1986 led Hütter and Schneider, however, to abandon their ambivalent stance on nuclear energy: the demand 'Stop radioactivity!' was added to the new recording of 'Radioactivity' for the compilation *The Mix* (1991); also, the line 'Wenn's um uns're Zukunft geht' (When our future is at stake) was replaced by the unequivocal 'Weil's um uns're Zukunft geht' (Because our future is at stake). For their June 1992 performance at the Greenpeace-organised anti-Sellafield benefit in Manchester, Kraftwerk also presented a new robot voice intro with a warning about radiation exposure from the Sellafield nuclear facility, which was later supplemented by other places associated with radiation accidents (Chernobyl, Harrisburg, and Hiroshima).

This modification demonstrates paradigmatically Kraftwerk's understanding of their œuvre as an open work of art subject to a constant process of adaptation and updating. Their sensitivity to political considerations, however, resulted in a loss of ambivalence since it was precisely the tension between diverse thematic interpretations and a neutral presentation that had comprised *Radio-Aktivität*'s aesthetic value. The musician John Foxx (Ultravox) had described the original version of the title song to be 'as neutral a Warhol statement as all their songs tend to be'.[15]

This quality of neutrality, in turn, can be linked to Warhol's artistic ideal of acting as a machine,[16] and forms a bridge to the man-machine concept because in 'Kraftwerk there is no individual, experiential emotional language. They reject all emotionality and sensibility. The band members try to present themselves as emotionless musicians.'[17] Marcus Kleiner therefore considers *Radio-Aktivität* to embody Kraftwerk's trademark 'coldness' that stands in direct contrast to the Anglo-American tradition. The latter can be described as a 'narrative of heat and sweat and a history of excitement and sensuality', which Kraftwerk countered with an 'electronic coolness that has influenced the history of pop music history to the present'.[18]

Today, the *Radio-Aktivität* sequence – performed in a mix of German, English, and Japanese and consisting of the tracks 'Nachrichten' (News), 'Geigerzähler' (Geiger Counter), and 'Radioaktivität' (Radioactivity) – is a highlight of every live concert. Visually, the performance is accompanied by video projections of animated warning symbols, excerpts from the original 1975 Expressionist video, and graphics showing nuclear reaction processes, while, musically, there is the shrill beeping of a Geiger counter, earth-shaking bass beats, and a beautifully simple melody – the whole, in total, constituting a magnificent pop-musical work of art.

Trans Europa Express (1977), released at the height of the punk explosion, most strikingly embodies Kraftwerk's important stylistic principle of retro-futurism. Thus, the band's nostalgic black-and-white cover photo marks a striking contrast to the zeitgeist of the time: the conservatively dressed musicians look like a group portrait from the 1930s or 1940s. While resembling a string quartet, on *Trans Europa Express* Kraftwerk defined a futuristic sound that made the album an electronic music blueprint that 'inspire[ed] a new generation of electronic music producers to make sense

---

[15] Quoted in D Buckley, *Kraftwerk: Publikation* (London: Omnibus, 2011), p. 78.

[16] See 'The reason I'm painting this way is that I want to be a machine, and I feel that whatever I do and do machine-like is what I want to do.' GR Swenson, Interview Andy Warhol, in Jacob Baal-Teshuva (ed.), *Andy Warhol 1928–1987* (Munich: Prestel, 1993), pp. 131–2 (131).

[17] M Kleiner, Cool Germany: Elektronische Entsinnlichung in Kraftwerk's Radio-Aktivität, in U Schütte (ed.), *Mensch-Maschinen-Musik: Das Gesamtkunstwerk Kraftwerk* (Düsseldorf: Leske, 2018), pp. 50–63 (62).

[18] Ibid.

of a developing post-industrial techno-world based on acceleration and electronics'.[19]

Contrary to the gloomy urban realism of British punk, Kraftwerk evoked nostalgic images of the 'elegance and decadence' of the European continent on 'Europa endlos' (Europe Endless) and referred to the romantic tradition with the instrumental 'Franz Schubert'.[20] Pertti Grönholm argues that such references to the past in combination with innovative electronic music aim to merge utopian ideas with melancholy images to create an aesthetic tension that confronts the present with unfulfilled promises of a better future:

Kraftwerk constructed a cultural and historical space that worked as an imaginary utopian/nostalgic refuge in the cultural situation of 1970s West Germany. . . . It excludes sentimentality and rejects the idea of a Golden Age but, instead, re-imagines the past as a continuum of progressive development and as a source of inspiration and ideas.[21]

Trans Europa Express also exposes, as already implied in *Autobahn*, the ambivalent connotation of a means of transportation – in this case rail – in the historical context of Nazi Germany. While the project to build a national network of highways – the *Reichsautobahn* – was a propaganda tool of Hitler's regime, the European rail network was used for the deportation of Jews to the extermination camps in the East. After the war, a transnational railway system was introduced to foster the idea of European integration: the Trans Europ Express (TEE) network was in operation from the late 1950s to the early 1990s. In its heyday, it connected 130 cities across Western Europe with regular services every two hours.

Kraftwerk's 'Trans Europa Express', often considered one of their masterpieces, proved crucial to the development of electronic music. David Buckley considers it 'the most influential possibly in their entire career'.[22] It consists of a sequence of three tracks that merge seamlessly into one another: the song 'Trans Europa Express' is followed by the instrumental 'Metall auf Metall' (Metal on Metal), which was originally followed by the short outro 'Abzug' (the sound of a train departing) as a separate track.

[19] H Rietveld, Trans-Europa Express: Tracing the Trance Machine, in S Albiez & D Pattie (eds.), *Kraftwerk: Music Non-Stop* (London: Continuum, 2011), pp. 214–30 (214).

[20] Compare M Haglund, Franz & Robert: The Romantic Machine, in A Hagström (ed.), *Influenser, referenser och plagiat: Om Kraftwerk estetik* (Göteborg: Röhsska Museet, 2015), pp. 153–9 (153–4).

[21] P Grönholm, When Tomorrow Began Yesterday: Kraftwerk's Nostalgia for the Past Futures, *Popular Music and Society* 38:3 (2015), pp. 372–88 (372).

[22] Buckley, *Kraftwerk*, p. 114.

The thirteen-minute suite is based on relentlessly propulsive repetitions that imitate the velocity of a train. In this musical simulation of a train journey, the hammering sound of the railway wheels on the rails is transferred into music instead of translating the movement of the car journey into a *motorik* beat, as on 'Autobahn'. Kraftwerk thus succeeded in converting industrial sounds into machine-generated music. Following in the footsteps of similar efforts by Dadaists and Futurists in the 1920s and 1930s to bring industrial modernism into art, Kraftwerk's machine music allowed electronic pop music to become a perfect, danceable synthesis of avant-garde and pop.

This is especially true of 'Metall auf Metall', the central piece of the 'Trans Europa Express' suite. According to David Stubbs, it is 'one of a handful of the most influential tracks in the entire canon of popular music', while Simon Reynolds described it as 'a funky iron foundry that sounded like a Luigi Russolo Art of Noises megamix for a futurist discotheque'.[23] The repercussions of the furious, dissonant metal machine sound was used throughout British pop music in the 1980s: by Peter Gabriel ('I Have the Touch'), Depeche Mode ('Master and Servant'), Visage ('The Anvil'), as well as by the left-wing industrial collective Test Dept, but also the Düsseldorf industrial pioneers Die Krupps ('Stahlwerksynfonie', i.e. Steelworks Symphony) or Einstürzende Neubauten in Berlin, who took the title of the Kraftwerk piece literally.

However, the futuristic sounds from Germany with which Kraftwerk sought to express their 'cultural identity as Europeans'[24] had a most decisive influence on African American minorities in urban centres such as New York and Detroit. There, they were adapted into new music styles such as electro or techno and re-contextualised as a means of expressing minority identity concepts. In the early 1980s, the New York DJ Afrika Bambaataa used the 'Trans Europa Express' suite for its uplifting hypnotic effect as a musical background to inflammatory speeches by activist Malcolm X.[25] According to Bambaataa, Kraftwerk never knew 'how big they were among the black masses in '77 when they came out with *Trans-Europe Express*. When that came out, I thought that was one of the weirdest records I ever heard in my life.'[26]

---

[23] Both quotes: D Stubbs, *Future Days: Krautrock and the Building of Modern Germany* (London: Faber, 2014), p. 189.

[24] P Alessandrini, Haute tension, *Rock & Folk* 11(1976), pp. 54–7 (54).

[25] B Brewster & F Broughton, *Last Night a DJ Saved My Life: The History of the Disc Jockey* (New York: Grove Press, 2000), p. 243.

[26] Quoted in D Toop, *Rap Attack: African Jive to New York Hip Hop* (London: Pluto Press, 1984), p. 130.

On the epoch-making track 'Planet Rock' (1982), Bambaataa fed the sonic exoticism of *industrielle Volksmusik* into the energy stream of the Afro-futurist tradition. By doing so, he unwittingly set in motion transatlantic electronic music feedback loops that have been operating ever since: 'European art music', according to Robert Fink, 'is cast, consciously or not, in the role of an ancient, alien power source'.[27] Martyn Ware (Human League/Heaven 17) summed up the artistic merit of the album as follows: '*Trans-Europe Express* had everything: it was retro yet futuristic, melancholic yet timeless, technical, modern and forward-looking yet also traditional. You name it, it had it all.'[28]

Post-humanism in the Computer Age (1978–1981)

Mensch-Maschine (*Man-Machine*, 1978) is Kraftwerk's key work, since the concept of the man-machine lies at the core of their *Gesamtkunstwerk* aesthetics. 'Strictly speaking, rather than the LP being a concept, the group themselves were now the concept, and the LP was merely a vehicle to further it',[29] Pascal Bussy concludes. The term 'man-machine' has appeared in Kraftwerk's promo statements since 1975 and remains an integral part of live performances today, with a robot voice explicitly announcing the band as 'the man-machine Kraftwerk' at each concert.

In addition to 'Das Modell' (The Model), Kraftwerk's biggest pop hit, *Mensch-Maschine* contains the conceptually significant song 'Die Roboter' (The Robots). This signature tune is linked to the doppelgänger mannequins of the four musicians that have replaced the real group members on album covers and promotional photos since 1981. Even more conceptually significant, these puppets appear on stage as substitutes for the 'music workers' at every live performance. Their proud statement 'Wir sind die Roboter' (We are the robots) can hence be related to the dummy lookalikes as well as the band members. In this respect, the mechanical doubles embody a concretisation or personification of the abstract concept of the man-machine.

The highly influential cover, devised by the Düsseldorf graphic designer Karl Klefisch, shows the real, heavily made-up musicians appearing as

---

[27] R Fink, The Story of ORCH5, or, the Classical Ghost in the Hip-Hop Machine, *Popular Music* 24:3 (2005), pp. 339–56 (352).

[28] R Esch, *Electri_City: The Düsseldorf School of Electronic Music* (London: Omnibus, 2016), p. 161.

[29] P Bussy, *Kraftwerk: Man, Machine and Music* (London: SAF, 2001), p. 99.

artificial robot beings with pale faces. The distinct colour scheme of red, white, and black refers to the colours of the German imperial war flag as well as the National Socialist swastika flag while the (typo)graphic design of the cover directly refers to Bauhaus and Soviet constructivism. Accordingly, *Mensch-Maschine* can be linked to the attempt made in constructivism to establish a connection between revolutionary art and revolutionary politics; in Kraftwerk's case, the band presents the pop-revolutionary concept of electronic future music. That is to say, the politically encoded hope for a better future is artistically imagined as a futuristic vision of a post-human synthesis of man and machine.

This technological eschatology is clearly celebrated by Kraftwerk. Yet, the Nazi experience does undermine the optimism of an invariably better future. Kraftwerk, as it were, remain mindful of the danger that the next paradigm shift in the evolution of humanity might easily lead to a relapse into totalitarian rule. The title of the instrumental 'Metropolis', which refers to the Fritz Lang's Expressionist film of the same name – featuring the first robot in film history – also invites such a dystopian reading. After all, Lang's prophetic vision was of a society that was deeply divided, both socially and politically; the critic Siegfried Kracauer famously condemned the film as proto-fascist in his influential book *Von Caligari zu Hitler* (*From Caligari to Hitler*, 1947). As ever so often, Kraftwerk's retro-futuristic recourse to the German cultural tradition reveals a profound ambivalence.

The album mirrors the pronounced futurism of *Mensch-Maschine* and, at the same time, refers to a time before modernity. The fact that the cover gives 'L'Homme Machine' as the French translation of the album title creates a link to the 1748 treatise of the same name by the early Enlightenment philosopher Julien Offray de La Mettrie. His polemical book offered a radically materialistic view of the unity of body and soul and had a large influence on philosophers from 'Hobbes and Pascal to Spinoza, Malebranche and Leibniz'. Subsequently, in Enlightenment discourse, 'the 'automaton' became a contemporary cipher for the most diverse aspects in the anthropological and socio-political discussions'[30] of the true nature of man.[31]

---

[30] S Perrig, Nichts als Pappendeckel und Uhrfedern!'. Vorelektronische Roboterfiktionen aus dem Feld der Literatur, in G Friesinger & K Harrasser (eds.), *Public Fictions: Wie man Roboter und Menschen erfindet* (Innsbruck: Studienverlag, 2009), pp. 66–77 (69).

[31] Cf. U Schütte, Halb Wesen und halb Ding. Nostalgische Vergangenheit und posthumane Zukunft in Die Mensch-Maschine, in U Schütte (ed.), *Mensch-Maschinen-Musik: Das Gesamtkunstwerk Kraftwerk* (Düsseldorf: Leske, 2018), pp. 88–115.

Mensch-Maschine thus positions itself in a broad, cultural-historical net of references and allusions. Despite its clearly futuristic orientation, the album simultaneously incorporates retro elements; one need only look critically at the doppelgänger dummies on stage during their performance of 'Die Roboter'. As David Pattie soberly observes: 'The robots do not look like the incarnations of a cyborgian future – if anything, they seem to hark back to a mechanical past.'[32] Once again, we encounter a deep-rooted ambivalence.

And it is such complexity that keeps Kraftwerk's album relevant to today's discussions about post-humanism. Leading experts in the field define objective post-humanist thought as follows: 'The predominant concept of the "human being" is questioned by thinking through the human being's engagement and interaction with technology.'[33] As hardly need be highlighted, this sounds like a summary of Kraftwerk's artistic project.

With *Computerwelt* (*Computer World*, 1981), Kraftwerk released another decidedly futuristic album, which in retrospect proved quite prophetic. A key musical merit of *Computerwelt* is that Kraftwerk recorded the album almost entirely in analogue, which only underlines its visionary character. This time, Kraftwerk 'do not predict a robotised, sci-fi future. However, they do predict, with complete accuracy, that our modern-day lives will be revolutionised'[34] by computer technology: console games, pocket calculators, and online dating, on the one hand, and computer-assisted surveillance, digital finance, and the total digitalisation of society, on the other, are the topics of the album.

Hard to miss on *Computerwelt* is its warning against social alienation and the political misuse of technology. The original German lyrics of the title track contain lines missing from its English-language version: 'Interpol und Deutsche Bank / FBI und Scotland Yard / Finanzamt und das BKA / haben unsre Daten da' (Interpol and Deutsche Bank / FBI and Scotland Yard / tax office and the BKA / have our data at their disposal). In an interview with *Melody Maker*, Ralf Hütter explained the aim of the album as 'making transparent certain structures and bringing them to the forefront . . . so you can change them. I think we make things transparent, and with this transparency reactionary structures must fall.'[35]

---

[32] D Pattie, Kraftwerk: Playing the Machines, in S Albiez & D Pattie (eds.) *Kraftwerk: Music Non-Stop* (London: Continuum, 2011), pp. 119–35 (125).

[33] R Ranisch & S Sorgner, Introducing Post- and Transhumanism, in R Ranisch & S Sorger (eds.), *Post- and Transhumanism: An Introduction* (Frankfurt: Lang, 2014), pp. 7–27 (8).

[34] Buckley, *Kraftwerk*, p. 165.

[35] N Rowland, Kraftwerk's Computer World, *Melody Maker* (4 July 1981).

Illustration 6.2 Kraftwerk live, 1981. © Wolfgang Wigger.

This explicitly political statement must be understood against the contemporary historical background. The BKA (Bundeskriminalamt – federal criminal police agency) conducted computer-assisted 'dragnet searches' to apprehend terrorists of the Red Army Faction, also known as the Baader–Meinhof Gang. 'Computerwelt's' lyrics state that the BKA is part of an international network of financial organisations and law enforcement agencies, correctly predicting that such institutions would be conducting their daily business digitally today. Similarly, it is hardly an exaggeration to claim that Kraftwerk anticipated the surveillance of digital privacy by state agencies such as the NSA or the British GCHQ.

With its obsessively repeated sequences of numerals in various languages, *Computerwelt*'s key track 'Nummern' (Numbers) fits perfectly into this context, simulating, as it were, the automated stock exchange deals and transnational financial transactions that characterise today's digital economy. The track foresaw the proliferating flow of numerical data that has replaced traditional language-based communication and cultural exchange.

In 'Nummern', even more importantly, Kraftwerk also found a new musical form, a radically minimalist aesthetic that combined a modernist approach with strict functionality inspired by the Bauhaus: a hypnotic piece of music that was almost brutal in its reduction to a mercilessly hammering beat, audibly anticipating techno. 'Numbers', according to

Joseph Toltz, 'is a striking work, not only in the general context of Kraftwerk's output, but also because it seems so different and more experimental than their other tracks'.[36] 'Nummern' encapsulates the radically new sound aesthetic of *Computerwelt*, which Kraftwerk had worked on for three years – longer than any previous album. It was true *Zukunftsmusik* (future music), considering its clinically pure sound and perfect musical realisation of an electronic aesthetic that proved eminently influential transnationally.

Computerwelt concludes and artistically crowns the sequence of five pioneering albums Kraftwerk had released in the seven years since *Autobahn*. In the 1980s, their electronic music inspired both British synth-pop musicians and African American producers who developed synth pop, disco, new wave, and funk into techno and house. Likewise, Kraftwerk's use of speech synthesis and electronic processing of vocals, for which Florian Schneider was primarily responsible, became a staple of music production today. With *Computerwelt*, Kraftwerk's mission as the avant-garde of electronic pop music had come to an end; from now on, they were competing with the multitude of musicians who pushed their *industrielle Volksmusik* in new directions.

Digitisation (1983–2003)

After *Computerwelt*, a paradigm shift set in. With the acquisition of a New England Digital Synclavier, Kraftwerk ushered in the era of digital music production. This, in turn, heralded a new *modus operandi*: a shift from the production of new tracks to the curation of existing work. Under the aegis of sound engineer Fritz Hilpert, all analogue tapes were painstakingly digitised. This groundwork not only laid the foundation for the 1991 compilation *The Mix*, on which new versions of Kraftwerk's most important songs were digitally reconstructed, but also for the transition to digital sound production at live performances.

The follow-up to *Computerwelt* was announced in 1983 under the title *Techno Pop* but then withdrawn, only to finally appear in 1986 as *Electric Cafe*. As the change of title indicates, the conceptual nature of the album was not particularly pronounced: *Electric Cafe* can be understood as

---

[36] J Toltz, Dragged into the Dance: The Role of Kraftwerk in the Development of Electro-Funk, in S Albiez & D Pattie (eds.), *Kraftwerk: Music Non-Stop* (London: Continuum, 2011), pp. 181–93 (185).

a record about communication or as a self-reflective album about electronic pop music.[37] The use of several, mostly European languages, explored for the first time in 'Numbers', also characterises the erstwhile title track 'Techno Pop', which celebrates the transnational omnipresence of 'synthetic electronic sounds / industrial rhythms all around' – in large part due to Kraftwerk – in German, French, English, and Spanish lyrics.

'Tour de France', which mirrored Hütter and Schneider's obsession with cycling[38] and was to have appeared on the withdrawn *Techno Pop*, was released as a single in 1983. Some twenty years later, this celebration of cycling turned out to be the basis for *Tour de France Soundtracks* (2003), Kraftwerk's final studio album. This often-underrated record features a clear concept and various thematic links to prior albums: it shares not only the motifs of movement und propulsion with *Autobahn* and *Trans Europa Express* but also the principle to musicalise sounds produced by modes of transportation, this time cycling. Furthermore, the pairing of cyclist and bicycle, in Hütter's view, also represents a configuration of a man-machine.[39] While the concept album *Autobahn*, which praised an ambivalent national symbol and featured German lyrics for the first time, served as their official debut, Kraftwerk's remarkable run of studio albums is concluded by a concept album sung (almost) entirely in French that celebrates the most sustainable way to travel.

This reflects a notion that already characterised *Trans Europa Express* and became increasingly manifest using multilingual lyrics on their albums during the 1980s. Given the country's fascist history, German identity in the post-war period involved a commitment to the idea of a European community of countries sharing the same culture and common values. Or to put it another way: Kraftwerk were always advocating a political utopia still unfulfilled today, namely, to move from a violent Nazi past into a European future characterised by peace, freedom of movement, and cooperation. On the occasion of seeing Kraftwerk in June 2017 at the Royal Albert Hall, Luke Turner succinctly remarked that 'an idealised sense of the European is distilled in every vibration of every note and tonight feels like another world'; and considering Brexit, Turner added the valid question: 'Do we Brits no longer deserve their European futurism?'[40]

---

[37] Compare S Nye, From Electric Cafe to Techno Pop: Versuch einer Kritik eingefahrener Rezeptionsmuster, in U Schütte (ed.), *Mensch-Maschinen-Musik: Das Gesamtkunstwerk Kraftwerk* (Düsseldorf: Leske, 2018), pp. 140–56.

[38] Compare K Bartos, *Der Klang der Maschine: Autobiographie* (Cologne: Eichborn, 2017), pp. 307–10.

[39] Hütter considers cycling as 'a dance of man and machine'. F Durst, Kraftwerk: Iedeeren houdt van herhaling, *Humo* 8 (2003), pp. 160–1.

[40] L Turner, Europe, Endless? On Watching Kraftwerk Live, A Year After Brexit, *The Quietus* (22 June 2017), https://thequietus.com/articles/22676-kraftwerk-live-review-brexit.

A Pop-Cultural *Gesamtkunstwerk?*

During the band's fifty-year existence, Kraftwerk's orientation towards a concept-based aesthetic led to a process in which image, sound, and text were increasingly synthesised to form a unified body of artistic work. This process, however, took place as a successive reaction to external circumstances along conceptual lines, some of which emerged only during the development process. It is further noteworthy that Kraftwerk's overall multimedia aesthetic not only concerns the audio-visual core of the œuvre (i.e. the officially released music and stage performances) but also such related marketing paraphernalia such as concert posters, tickets, the Kraftwerk website, and merchandise.

Following the release of *Tour de France Soundtracks,* the artistic activities of the project, now solely led by Hütter, shifted more and more towards the curation of the core work as well as the musealisation of Kraftwerk. With the help of the renowned Sprüth Magers gallery, Hütter moved Kraftwerk successfully from the context of pop music into the field of art. An important prerequisite for this undertaking was the remastered edition of the eight albums from *Autobahn* to *Tour de France* in the box set called *Der Katalog* (*The Catalogue*), released in 2009.

The now officially sanctioned corpus of albums formed the basis for the concert series *Retrospective 12345678* at the Museum of Modern Art in New York in April 2012. Further performances of musical retrospectives, each spanning eight evenings, took place at other symbolic venues such as the Sydney Opera House, Vienna's Burgtheater, the Tate Modern in London, the Arena in Verona, and Berlin's Neue Nationalgalerie. In autumn 2011, the stage visuals, which have been presented in 3D technology since 2009 and are billed by Kraftwerk as 'musical paintings',[41] were exhibited at Munich's renowned Lenbachhaus museum. Increasing recognition of Kraftwerk by the art scene as a performance art collective (rather than a mundane pop band) closed a circle insofar as many of the band's first public appearances had taken place in Düsseldorf galleries due to a lack of music venues in the early 1970s.

Hütter's curation activities in the twenty-first century have focused on updating and extending the visual component of the core works. In addition to the introduction of continuous 3D live projections, this involved the revision of all cover designs and a radical revision of the œuvre in the *3-D Der Katalog* boxset released in 2017. The first version of *Der Katalog* already featured some noticeable changes in the album artwork. For

---

[41] Rapp & Thadeusz, Maschinen sind einfach lockerer, p. 139.

example, the Nazi *Volksempfänger* on the sleeve of *Radio-Aktivität* was replaced by an intense yellow cover with the nuclear Trefoil symbol in bright red, and the photographs of the real musicians disappeared from the artwork of *Trans Europa Express* and *Mensch-Maschine*.

In the radical design overhaul of the 2017 version of *Der Katalog*, however, all cover designs have been replaced by monochrome record sleeves. This move towards abstraction was accentuated by substituting the numbers one to eight for the album titles, which made the records appear as segments of a coherent, eight-part work. Finally, all the tracks were re-recorded with current equipment – ostensibly during live performances from 2012 to 2016, but possibly in the Kling-Klang studio – and in several cases the original track sequence was altered.

Given the decidedly inter- as well as transmedial nature of the œuvre, one can argue that Kraftwerk firmly belong in the tradition of the modernist *Gesamtkunstwerk*. Many of their formative stylistic influences, especially Bauhaus and the theatre reform movement, point to modernist updates of Wagner's *Gesamtkunstwerk* model. For example, Erwin Piscator's vision of a 'total theatre' – in which he sought to unite the stage with the cinema – bears an evident resemblance to Kraftwerk's conceptual notion of moving, three-dimensional 'musical paintings'; similarly, Piscator's goal of an 'ecstatic overcoming of the "only-individual" in a communal experience'[42] in the theatre audience finds its counterpart in the immersive, audio-visual experience of a Kraftwerk concert. Anke Finger sees 'teleology as the central tenet' of the *Gesamtkunstwerk* aesthetics of modernism, which is why every *Gesamtkunstwerk* 'represents something which is in the process of emerging, something which may be perfectly conceived but is not perfectly executed and perhaps never can be'.[43]

Kraftwerk's astounding fifty-year body of work is a pop-cultural *Gesamtkunstwerk* that confirms Finger's theoretical assessment and, in accordance with the pop musical core strategy of 're-make, re-model',[44] Kraftwerk's œuvre remains in flux. Their live performances deliver an unprecedentedly immersive experience that fuses art, technology, and music and are a true 'Kunstwerk der Zukunft' (future work of art), to borrow a term from Wagner, which one should experience while it is still possible.

---

[42] G Hiß, *Synthetische Visionen: Theater als Gesamtkunstwerk von 1800 bis 2000* (Munich: Epodium, 2005), p. 259.

[43] A Finger, *Das Gesamtkunstwerk der Moderne* (Göttingen: Vandenhoeck & Ruprecht, 2006), p. 8.

[44] Compare E Schumacher, Re-Make/Re-Model. Kraftwerk international, in U Schütte (ed.), *Mensch-Maschinen-Musik: Das Gesamtkunstwerk Kraftwerk* (Düsseldorf: Leske, 2018), pp. 262–74.

Essential Listening

Kraftwerk, *Ralf & Florian* (Philips, 1973)
Kraftwerk, *Expo Remix* (EMI, 2001)
Kraftwerk, *Minimum–Maximum* (EMI, 2005)
Kraftwerk, *Der Katalog* (EMI, 2009)
Kraftwerk, *3–D Der Katalog* (EMI, 2017)

7 | Can

PATRICK GLEN

This chapter focuses on Can, a band who formed in Cologne around 1968 and remained active until 1979 – reforming to record a final album in 1986 and then a single song in 1999. It first considers the formation of the group, and contextualises their position in post-war West German culture as well as West German and international networks of music making. The chapter then surveys and analyses Can's musical practice, releases, tours, and relationship with the press and public in sections divided by who undertook lead vocals: Malcolm Mooney, Kenji 'Damo' Suzuki, and finally a revolving vocalist system (typically Michael Karoli and sometimes Irmin Schmidt). It concludes by providing an overview of Can's legacy in global music making since the 1970s.

Can and their collaborators fostered a remarkable camaraderie that lasted despite the pressures of the music industry, touring, and negotiating the politics of personalities, individual musical expression, and meaningful collective music-making. They made use of varied approaches to and styles of music, and developed connections and collaborations that left a mark enduring on modern music across the world. Ulrich Adelt noted that the band were uncommonly outward-looking, going 'beyond Germany's borders for musical influences', which enabled them to comment upon and distinguish themselves from 'the Nazi past and the influx of Anglo-American music into West Germany'.[1] This search for new influences – sometimes documented in their ironically-named 'ethnological forgery series' – extended to collaborating with musicians from different racial and cultural backgrounds. They worked with Malcolm Mooney, an African American sculptor, Damo Suzuki, a Japanese hippie found singing improvised tunes on the street in Munich when travelling through Europe, and, during the late 1970s, Rosko Gee, a bassist from Jamaica, and Anthony 'Rebop' Kwaku Baah, a Ghanaian percussionist.

As Beate Kutschke argued, Can represented an international network of 'politically engaged, New-Leftist' musicians who 'shuttled between cities in

---

[1] U Adelt, Machines with a Heart: German Identity in the Music of Can and Kraftwerk, *Popular Music and Society* 35:3 (2012), pp. 359–74 (360).

different countries and continents and exchanged knowledge of musical styles, aesthetics and socio-political issues'.[2] Can performed across Britain extensively, where they charmed music journalists and enraptured members of the emerging punk, post-punk, and electronic music scenes, and had enough of a following in France to play sporadic concerts and occasional short tours. The band even scored hits: 'Spoon' reached number six in the German charts in 1971 and the band skirted the British mainstream with a performance of their number twenty-eight hit 'I Want More' on *Top of the Pops*, a Friday night television institution. However, they are better remembered as a group who cultivated a devoted international cult audience, which included numerous musicians from a diverse range of genres.

Can before Can

Considering the musical training of two of Can's so-called founders, their place in the rock scene and on the margins of pop success is curious – perhaps only comparable to John Cale of the Velvet Underground, who was taught by the minimalist composer La Monte Young as a postgraduate student. Czukay and Schmidt were conservatoire-trained and studied under Karlheinz Stockhausen, Germany's most notable post-war composer and a pioneer of electronic music. This brought them into contact with several luminaries of post-1945 Western modern composition, including John Cage, the American composer known for his explorations of chance composition. In interviews, Czukay and Schmidt often characterised themselves as too playful and outward-looking towards the 1960s pop and counter-culture scenes for the rarefied world of composition. Czukay advocated a method that encouraged spontaneity over technique, and Stockhausen had been one of few in the academy who tolerated this approach. Speaking to Richard Cook in the *New Musical Express* in 1982, Czukay reminisced: 'I was always being thrown out of music colleges. Stockhausen took me in – he asked me if I was a composer and I had to reply I don't know. If you are an "artist" you can lie the music away in professionalism.'[3]

Liebezeit, on the other hand, was a jazz drummer before joining Can. He explained his pre-Can career to Jono Podmore, who has edited a book on

---

[2] B Kutschke, Protest Music, Urban Contexts and Global Perspectives, *International Review of the Aesthetics and Sociology of Music* 46:2 (2015), pp. 321–54.

[3] R Cook, Holger Czukay: Strangely Strange but Oddly Normal, *New Musical Express* (20 February 1982).

Liebezeit's life and approach to drumming.[4] Liebezeit began performing in high school bands but was picked up by semi-professional rock 'n' roll bands in Kassel. He soon became aware of American jazz, and jazz drummers Max Roach, Art Blakey, and Elvin Jones caught his ear. This led him to performing with Manfred Schoof's group. Liebezeit played with an impressive list of jazz stars during his twenties, which were spent between Cologne and Barcelona, including Art Blakey, Don Cherry (they shared a flat in Cologne), and Chet Baker. However, from 1964, Manfred Schoof's group had moved towards atonal and arrhythmic free jazz, whereas Liebezeit had developed an interest in 'Spanish, Arabic, Gypsy, North African and Afro-Cuban music'.[5] In 1968, Liebezeit began to work with Can as they were fellow devotees of his 'cyclical approach to rhythm'.[6]

Michael Karoli, Can's guitarist, was ten years younger than his bandmates – Holger Czukay was born in 1937, both Schmidt and Liebezeit were born in 1938. He had moved from Bavaria to St. Gallen in Switzerland as a schoolboy; Czukay had been his guitar teacher in high school. After Karoli had graduated and accepted a place to study law at the University of Lausanne (where he played in several amateur jazz and dance bands), Czukay convinced him to join Can instead. Wickström, Lücke, and Jóri have noted that most West German musicians in the post-1945 period were self-taught and generally first learnt from American GIs and catered to their tastes – few were schooled in the Western art music tradition like Can.[7] Indeed, even fewer were able to integrate aspects of the emerging pop sounds of the 1960s and free jazz into their approach.

As has been documented in Rob Young and Irmin Schmidt's comprehensive autobiography/biography, *Can: All Gates Open*, the band's initial successes were related to composing film soundtracks.[8] Schmidt had made waves as a solo film score composer alone but moved towards a collaborative approach when commissioned to provide accompaniment to Peter F. Schneider's film *Agilok & Blubbo* (released in 1969) in 1968 – a year of student uprisings, and social and political unrest in Germany and the wider world. They named the new band The Inner Space; it featured Schmidt alongside Czukay, Karoli, and Liebezeit, with a vocal turn from Rosemarie

[4] J Podmore, Biography, in J Podmore (ed.), *Jaki Liebezeit: the Life, Theory and Practice of a Master Drummer* (London: Unbound, 2020), pp. 5–46.

[5] Ibid., p. 18.   [6] Ibid., p. 21.

[7] D-E Wickström, M Lücke & A Jóri, Not without Music Business: The Higher Education of Musicians and Music Industry Workers in Germany, *International Journal of Music Business Research* 4:1 (2015), pp. 55–81 (61).

[8] R Young & I Schmidt, *Can: All Gates Open* (London: Faber, 2018).

Heinikel, an actor and counter-cultural figure, and accompaniment from David C. Johnson, an American composer who had assisted Stockhausen at *Westdeutscher Rundfunk's* (WDR) electronic studio in Cologne. The film attempted to capture and lampoon the politics of the moment; it was a satire of West German politics and the counter-culture that followed two young revolutionaries who conspired to kill an establishment figure until their plan was disrupted by a co-conspirator, Michaela, whom both of the film's protagonists fall for. Between 1968 and 1979, Can were credited with creating seventeen original film and television soundtracks – a selection of their early soundtrack recordings was released on the compilation *Soundtracks* (1970).

Can's success in the film industry was not universally well received. In what may be a case of envious revisionism, Chris Karrer, a member of Amon Düül II and labelmate on United Artists, claimed to Edwin Pouncey in the *Wire* that Can had knowingly undercut other bands competing for soundtrack work.[9] This animosity might stem from how, unlike Amon Düül and Amon Düül II, Can shied away from direct political commentary and tended not to play radical squats or communes – although they were generally of the left and anti-authoritarian. Can made their political points and represented the struggles of their generation through musical practice and sound.

The Malcolm Mooney Era: 1968–1969

Soundtrack composition paid for Can's equipment and recording space. Christoph Vohwinkel, an art collector with aspirations to host an artistic commune, rented them rooms within a castle near Cologne, Schloss Nörvenich. There they practiced in a group that included Malcolm Mooney, and recorded and made their initial live appearances – playing spontaneously composed music – in June 1968. Their first concert was later released as a tape in 1984 entitled *Prehistoric Future*. The band, as is documented on *Prehistoric Future*, improvised together extensively, developing, refining, and combining their own approach(es) to musical practice. During Mooney's time in the band, Can developed a distinctive sound as their rhythm section, Czukay and Liebezeit, played ostensibly simple but intricate, repetitive rhythms. The drums and bass complimented Schmidt's novel electronic approaches, which incorporated ambient textures and

---

[9] E Pouncey, Communing with Chaos: Amon Düül II, *Wire* (February 1996).

more abrasive sounds in tandem with Karoli's overdriven and expressive guitar lines and Mooney's impassioned vocals. Les Gillon suggests that Can's egalitarian football-based metaphor for improvisation – 'the collective and non-hierarchical nature of the band as a team' – could illustrate a broader point about social freedoms that diverged from concepts of freedom in a 'rational' capitalist society.[10] Till Krause and David Stubbs have each argued that the social meanings associated with this approach and the resulting music were powerful in creating new ideas of national identity in West Germany.[11]

Can's approach to musical practice was innovative and has been explored by journalists and authors both during and after the band effectively disbanded in 1979. They were keen listeners and drew from a broad array of reference points beyond their musical training. Each has spoken about the influence of American bands such as the Velvet Underground and the Mothers of Invention (Karoli is claimed to have introduced his older counterparts to Jimi Hendrix, the Beatles, and the Rolling Stones as well); Liebezeit introduced Czukay to the propulsive rhythm of James Brown's funk, and they shared enthusiasm for non-Western approaches to rhythm.[12] Can, in general, were open to non-Western music as documented in their 'ethnological forgeries' series, which set to tape their attempts to emulate a range of non-Western musics. Liebezeit and Czukay developed a system based upon painstakingly accurate repetitions and minor variations of drum and bass patterns, which was often understood as a reaction to Liebezeit's aversion to the unstructured clang and clatter of free jazz.

The band privileged intuition alongside repetition. Schmidt and Karoli often described this approach as telepathy, with Karoli going so far to claim a telepathic relationship with 'the green eye of the reverb machine'.[13] The intensity of their approach was described by Mooney when he recalled the recording of their first released album *Monster Movie* (1969):

Our first record, *Monster Movie*, to give an example, the A-side is completely controlled, planned. The B-side, 'You Doo Right', is a first take in the vocals. There

---

[10] L Gillon, Varieties of Freedom in Music Improvisation, *Open Cultural Studies* 2 (2018), pp. 788–9.

[11] T Krause, 'Amerrrika Ist Wunderrrbarrr': Promotion of Germnay through Radio Goethe's Cultural Export of German Popular Music to North America, *Popular Music* 27:2 (2008), pp. 225–42 (229–30); D Stubbs, *Future Days: Krautrock and the Building of Modern Germany* (London: Faber, 2014), pp. 458–68.

[12] R Chapman, No Borders Here: Holger Czukay's Movies and on the Way to Peak of Normal, *MOJO* (March 1998).

[13] A Gill, Can: Art Terrorism! Sensory Derangement! Holistic Vomiting! Available Weekends . . ., *MOJO* (April 1997).

were overdubs added, but the recording, which started at about 11 AM, ended around 11 PM. It was quite a session. I left the studio at one time for lunch, when I returned the band was still playing the tune and I resumed where I had left off and that is how we did 'You Doo Right'.[14]

What Mooney fails to mention is that the lengthy improvisations that made 'You Doo Right' were recorded to two tracks of tape later edited into pieces by Czukay. Throughout the existence of Can, Czukay would edit, cut, and recut two-track tape recordings of their sessions into coherent pieces, only moving to more conventional multi-track recording from the recording of *Soon Over Babaluma* (1974) onwards. Adelt argues that Can, and particularly Holger Czukay, used recording technology as a means to experiment with recorded sounds 'long before it became common practice'.[15] Kai Fikentscher similarly noted that Czukay was, like Phil Spector, George Martin, and Trevor Horn, a pioneer in using the studio as an instrument, demonstrating that 'recorded music could now be a product of illusionary performance'.[16] This approach had a bearing on the work of Brian Eno and Kraftwerk, among others, in their Kling-Klang studio.

Can independently released only 500 copies of *Monster Movie* at first. The first pressing was hoped to attract major label interest, and ultimately led to them signing a record deal with the American label United Artists. The album could be seen as one of the first templates for what would be deemed 'Krautrock' as it was codified and adapted into a recognisable sub-genre. Even though Krautrock is frequently questioned by its supposed creators, and its derogatory name misrepresents the work of musicians who were as outward-looking and aware of international music making as possible at the time, *Monster Movie* contains its hallmarks of repetitive, subtle rhythms and a free approach to guitar, synthesiser, and vocal embellishments. Mooney's lyrics were existential and surreal. He explored motifs from gospel songs and nursery rhymes, and vented thinly veiled anguish about relationships, sex, desire, reproductive anxiety, and hedonism. The album led to Can's first mention in the influential British music press (which was distributed across parts of Western Europe and the United States), when Richard Williams gave *Monster Movie* a positive

---

[14] A Patterson, Malcolm R. Mooney: An Interview, *Eurock 1983* (July 2019).

[15] U Adelt, *Krautrock: German Music in the Seventies* (Ann Arbour: University of Michigan Press, 2016), p. 23.

[16] K Fikentscher, 'There's Not a Problem I Can't Fix, 'Cause I Do the Mix': On the Performative Technology of 12-Inch Vinyl in R Lysloff (ed.), *Music and Technoculture* (Wesleyan: Middltown, 2013), pp. 290–315 (293).

review in *Melody Maker*.[17] The album's opening track, 'Father Cannot Yell', was played twice to a nationwide British audience on John Peel's BBC Radio One show 'Top Gear' on 16 May and 26 June 1970. Several tracks from this time were later rediscovered and released as *The Lost Tapes* (2012) – they are a testament to Mooney's importance to Can's early music.

Mooney left Can and West Germany in December 1969, having experienced heightened anxiety due to the possibility, as an American citizen, of being drafted into the Vietnam War or accused of avoiding the draft. A psychiatrist advised Mooney to return to the Untied States, where he used his experiences as a sculptor to teach art to socially and economically disadvantaged children in ethnically diverse neighbourhoods of New York City.

The Damo Suzuki Era: 1969–1973

Between 1969 and 1971, Can toured across West Germany despite losing Mooney. In 1970, as well as releasing their collection of film soundtracks, Can played numerous *Stadthallen* (municipal halls), youth centres, a few festivals, and Munich's trendy Beat Club. In 1970 their concerts were, however, predominantly clustered around Cologne, Essen, and Dortmund within the Rhine–Ruhr area, their home region. During their travels, Can met Damo Suzuki singing improvised songs outside a café in Munich for spare change. They asked him if he would like to perform in their band that evening and he agreed because he had nothing better to do.[18] Damo Suzuki was born in 1950 near Tokyo in the town of Ōiso. Teenage Kenji – before he was known as Damo, an affectation in honour of his favourite comic book character that he adopted in Europe – became enraptured with the post-war American trope of the romance of the open road, which inspired him to move to Europe. He certainly sought a free approach to lyrics and vocal delivery: Suzuki broadly continued the style pioneered by Mooney, but Can's new singer was more abstract lyrically and slightly less informed by the blues and rock 'n' roll canon.

The first album that Suzuki recorded with Can was *Tago Mago* (1971). The album's title refers to the Mediterranean island of Tagomago, which is near Ibiza and had putative links – arguably contrived by Can members to impishly mislead the British music press – with Aleister Crowley, the

---

[17] R Williams, Can: Monster Movie, *Melody Maker* (30 May 1970).
[18] D Suzuki & P Woods, *I Am Damo Suzuki* (London: Omnibus, 2019), p. 77.

Illustration 7.1 Irmin Schmidt, Holger Czukay, Damo Suzuki, Jaki Liebezeit, and Michael Karoli of Can, early 1970s. Courtesy of Spoon Recs.

English writer and occultist who was a practitioner of 'magick' and liber-tinism. Crowley, often reduced to his adage 'do as thou wilt', had provided inspiration to numerous hedonistic and sexually adventurous, if not rapist, rock musicians and their entourages during the late 1960s and 1970s. The album is remarkable on a sonic level as the lack of separation between each instrument when recording – only three microphones were used – caused sounds to bleed into each other creating unplanned harmonic characteristics and sounds to arise.

Typically, by the 1970s, when multi-track recording had become well established in the music industry, each instrument could be recorded with its own microphone or direct input cable and heard separately, even when recorded simultaneously (i.e. live). In a conventional recording, these multiple tracks could then be brought together as a balanced multi-instrumental whole once the volume levels were mixed and frequencies blended during mastering. In another departure from conventional recording techniques, Czukay also captured on tape what he termed 'in-between-recordings' – the sound of the band jamming but unaware that they were being recorded – and used them in the final mix.[19] The resulting sounds are

[19] H Czukay & A Short, History of the Can-Discography, *Perfect Sound Forever* (May 1997).

darker, and although some of the lyrical content shares themes with *Monster Movie* there are moments of greater intensity, such as 'Mushroom', which interprets the atomic bomb as a moment of symbolic rebirth.

By 1971, assisted by their manager Hildegard Schmidt and accompanied by Damo Suzuki, buoyed by an appearance on WDR Television in January, and with their new album *Tago Mago* ready for release in August, Can were booked to play most major West German cities and larger towns between March and the album's release date. At the same time, the band's appeal in Britain was beginning to grow. In January 1972, for instance, Mike Watts of *Melody Maker* wrote an effusive – if strewn with casual assumptions about Germans – review of *Tago Mago*. He teased the prospect of Can's forthcoming British tour: 'Can are coming to Britain soon. I'm looking forward to their visit with guarded interest. They sound a weird bunch of geezers.'[20] After a German tour in February and March, Can indeed toured Britain for the first time. They started at Imperial College on 28 April 1972, then played the university circuit and a few other small-to-medium-sized venues for a month, before returning to the continent to play festivals in France and Germany. They visited later in the year as well, to play a one-off headline concert at The Rainbow in Finsbury Park, London on 22 July, which was impressive considering the venue had a capacity of nearly 3,000 people, much larger and more prestigious than the stops on their tour earlier in the year.

Can's tours around Germany and Britain demonstrate a willingness to play venues large and small in both the usual cities on the touring circuit and smaller less frequently visited towns. In 1973, taking advantage of Britain's widespread infrastructure for live rock performances and entry into the Common Market, Can made a somewhat unusual move (for a non-British band of their profile) by visiting smaller towns including Penzance, Plymouth, Westcliffe-on-Sea, and Chatham as part of a concert tour with nineteen stops across Scotland, Wales, and England. They then played their longest French tour (six stops), which included concerts in Paris, Rennes, and Bordeaux. This persistence, alongside the release of two of their most well-loved albums, *Ege Bamyasi* (1972) and *Future Days* (1973), meant that despite Damo Suzuki's departure from the band in late 1973 the band was in a strong position commercially. Suzuki had left Can to become a Jehovah's Witness like his new wife, and saw life in a band as incompatible with his new faith and lifestyle (Liebezeit recalled that

---

[20] M Watts, Can: Tago Mago, *Melody Maker* (29 January 1972).

Suzuki 'left with no warning' and claimed that he was 'brainwashed').[21] Gitta Suzuki-Mouret, his then wife, has rejected Liebezeit's account; she claimed that the internal politics of the group left Suzuki feeling isolated and keen to move on.[22]

Thanks to *Ege Bamyasi* and *Future Days*, Suzuki's remaining time in Can was well documented. *Ege Bamyasi* was the first Can album recorded in a former cinema, soundproofed with army-issue mattresses in the town of Weilerswist (some fifteen miles south of Cologne), which they named Inner Space. The album included 'Spoon' which was Can's biggest hit in West Germany, reaching number six in the charts. Its success was mostly due to being the theme of *Das Messer* (*The Knife*), a West German crime thriller that appeared on television from November 1971. The album, which is less intense and more immediately alluring than *Tago Mago*, received critical acclaim. The lyrics are again existential and often not always clearly meaningful but evocative and filled with imagery.

Future Days was also well-received by critics (the *New Musical Express*'s eleventh best album of the year). It is punctuated by more prominent electronic sounds, ambient stretches, and Liebezeit's polyrhythmic drumming than its predecessor. If *Ege Bamyasi* provided a template for experimental rock, post-punk, and indie musicians, *Future Days* is perhaps more aligned with Can's contribution to electronic music – particularly the way that the album's final track 'Bel Air' cleverly progresses through different movements and variations. Suzuki's vocal approach is more understated, even marginal, but – when heard – he questions the meaning of life in a modern consumer society and interrogates the possibilities of personal freedom within such a society's constraints.

Can after Suzuki: 1974–1979 (and Beyond)

After Suzuki left, Karoli and Schmidt slightly reluctantly shared vocals. The change did not upset the band's popular momentum, and Can's growing profile on the British rock scene allowed them to undertake a twenty-two date tour, with two live sessions on BBC Radio 1 and a television appearance on *The Old Grey Whistle Test* to play 'Vernal Equinox' in 1974. With each of the four Can founders born either just before or just after World War II in Germany, an interesting dynamic emerged, as music fans in Britain, a society often obsessed with the war and prone to seeing Germany

[21] Suzuki & Woods, *I Am Damo Suzuki*, p. 122.   [22] Ibid., pp. 122–3.

and Germans through the lens of Nazism during the 1960s and 1970s, adopted Can most eagerly.[23] Can tended to get on with British journalists, particularly *Sounds'* Vivian Goldman, the daughter of German-Jewish refugees who had escaped the Holocaust to London, and were typically presented as disarmingly funny eccentrics.[24] Nevertheless, during interviews, the band often seemed compelled (and it is not clear if it was a personal compulsion or at the request of journalists) to describe moments of their youth in post-war West Germany in a way that constructed them as inherently predisposed to anti-fascism – few British or American artists were pressed on their political affiliations in the music press during the early and mid-1970s.

Can recorded six further albums after Damo Suzuki left. The first was *Soon Over Babaluma* (1974). Perhaps due to capriciousness of the British music press, the album had become somewhat of a joke. However, it has been reappraised since the 1970s and is now viewed as a development of *Future Days* that informed electronic music styles of the 1980s and 1990s. The line-up of Czukay, Karoli, Liebezeit, and Schmidt alone made two more albums, *Landed* (1975) and *Flow Motion* (1976), their first records recorded with a full sixteen-track recording set-up – a distinct move away from their sometimes muddy, if alluring and often unique-sounding, two-track records. *Flow Motion* is a more pop and disco influenced album in comparison to the more experimental sounds of *Landed*. It delivered Can's biggest hit in Britain when 'I Want More' reached number twenty-six in the singles chart. This gained them an invitation to *Top of the Pops*, with Karoli, who was on a safari holiday at the time, replaced by a friend for the performance. The song caught the public's ear and gained radio play, and between 1974 and 1977 Can seemed to have played almost every town in Britain, in addition to cities where they had a large following – like London and Manchester – where they performed on multiple occasions.

Can's later albums saw Holger Czukay take a lesser role, and this is often seen as precipitating the band's split. Czukay moved from bass to manipulating electronics such as transistor radios and tape recorders. He met his replacement on bass, Rosko Gee, when performing on the *The Old Grey Whistle Test* in 1974, when Gee had appeared backing Jim Capaldi, his former Traffic bandmate.[25] Can had also taken on an engineer, René Tinner, which marginalised Czukay's contribution even more. Rebop

---

[23] P Glen, NEU! Europe: Krautrock and British Representations of West German Countercultures during the 1970s, *Contemporary British History* 35:3 (2021), https://doi.org/10.1080/13619462.2021.1925551.

[24] Ibid.   [25] Young & Schmidt, *Can*, p. 256.

Kwaku Baah, another former member of Traffic and an accomplished percussionist, was brought in to enhance and embellish Liebezeit's poly-rhythms; however, he ultimately clashed with Czukay.[26] Notwithstanding an enhanced level of creative tension (Czukay did not contribute to *Out of Reach* and only edited tape on *Can*), their final (non-reunion) albums *Saw Delight* (1977), *Out of Reach* (1978), and *Can* (1979) have their merits even if they are less well appreciated than their predecessors by fans and journalists. On these albums, Can warped and explored pop sounds in a way that could be seen as a precursor to the approach taken in scenes such as the 1980s New York underground.

The band disbanded on good terms in 1979. However, in the summer of 1986, Malcolm Mooney temporarily returned to Can for a 'reunion' album entitled *Rite Time* (1989), which was recorded in the south of France. From 1979 onwards, Hildegard and Irmin Schmidt curated Can's re-releases, box sets, and remix albums through their label Spoon Records. On the band's thirtieth anniversary, Spoon also promoted the Can-Solo-Projects tour. The showcase exemplified the richness of the original Can members' solo work and collaborations: Holger Czukay and U-She performed alongside Jaki Liebezeit's Club Off Chaos; Irmin Schmidt played (with Jono Podmore); and Michael Karoli's Sofortkontakt! appeared. Many Can solo albums and remasters were released through a collaboration between Spoon and Mute Records – the latter label founded by Daniel Miller, one of the British post-punk musicians influenced by Can and other German musicians of the 1970s that used electronic instruments and employed studio-as-instrument techniques. Czukay's music arguably gained the most acclaim, perhaps due to high-profile collaborations with Jah Wobble of Public Image Limited, David Sylvian, formerly of the British group Japan, and the Edge, the guitarist in U2. Czukay released much of his later solo work and moments from his back catalogue on Grönland Records.

Can's Legacy

Can have been often cited by post-punk, indie, and electronic musicians as a key influence on their taste and musical practice. Perhaps their most prominent early advocates were British post-punk musicians like Julian Cope of The Teardrop Explodes (author of *Krautrocksampler*), Mark

[26] Ibid., pp. 281–2.

Illustration 7.2 Can live in Hamburg, 1972. © Heinrich Klaffs.

E. Smith of the Fall, Genesis P-Orridge of Throbbing Gristle and Psychic TV, and John Lydon of Public Image Ltd. Alex Carpenter's essay in this collection notes the influence of Krautrock – and to varying extents Can – on Siouxsie and the Banshees, Bauhaus, Killing Joke, Cabaret Voltaire, and Simple Minds as well. Smith wrote the song 'I am Damo Suzuki', which appeared on the *This Nation's Saving Grace* (1985), in homage to Can. The lyric refers to aspects of Suzuki's life and the band's history, and bemoans the later Can albums that were released on Virgin Records in Britain; the song's descending bassline has similarities with the Can track 'Oh Yeah' from *Tago Mago* and 'Cool in the Pool', a track from Holger Czukay solo album *Movies* (1979). The band's appeal to musicians from the north-west of England was also clear in the amalgamation of electronic and avant-garde rock found in bands on the Factory Records label based in Manchester.

Despite Can never visiting the United States, American musicians from the 1980s and 1990s alternative underground, such as Pavement's Stephen Malkmus and the members of Sonic Youth, have declared Can's influence on their music making. In 2012, as part of a celebration of the album's fortieth anniversary celebrations, Malkmus performed *Ege Bamyasi* in full with Von Spar – appropriately a band that came from Cologne with a singer from elsewhere. Several post-rock musicians and even mainstream rock artists such as the Red Hot Chilli Peppers and Radiohead have paid their respects. Local musicians from the underground, post-punk, indie, and alternative rock tradition, alongside improvisers and electronic musicians, have typically made up the nightly changing 'sound carriers' that accompany Suzuki's (almost) continual international tours since 1997.

The link between Can, other Krautrock artists, and the development of electronic music may be overplayed, considering the roots of electronic music can be drawn as far back as the 1920s and 1930s, but a certain form of 'danceable' electronic music has certainly taken cues. Simon Reynolds has argued that Can anticipated and inspired 'dance genres like trip hop, ethno-techno and ambient jungle'.[27] On a local level, Hans Nieswandt has argued that they popularised electronic music in Cologne by bringing the approaches and sounds pioneered by Stockhausen to a wider public.[28] Rob Young has noted that the band's legacy is kept intact by the Kompakt record label in Cologne, artists such as Mouse on Mars, and those involved with the Basic Channel/Chain Reaction/Rhythm and Sound labels in Berlin.[29] Can's position as forerunners of ambient music has been recognised by their peers, not least Brian Eno. Furthermore, Can's enticing beats and sounds have also been sampled by hip-hop producers. Kanye West, for instance, sampled 'Sing Swan Song' on his track 'Drunk & Hot Girls' (*Graduation*, 2007), on which he collaborated with Yasiin Bey (then known as Mos Def), and Q-Tip sampled 'A Spectacle' to create a backing for 'Manwomanboogie' (*The Renaissance*, 2008). There are few bands that could claim to have caught the ear of such diverse communities of musicians and compelled them to try to incorporate the sounds and approaches into their own work, with so many varied effects. To borrow a pun from Malcolm Mooney, it's all about a 'CAN DO' attitude.

Essential Listening

Can, *Monster Movie* (Music Factory, 1969)
Can, *Tago Mago* (United Artists, 1971)
Can, *Ege Bamyasi* (United Artists, 1972)
Can, *Future Days* (United Artists, 1973)

---

[27] S Reynolds, Krautrock, *Melody Maker* (11 July 1996).
[28] H Nieswandt, Concepts of Cologne, in M Ahlers & C Jacke (eds.), *Perspectives on German Popular Music* (Abingdon: Routledge, 2018), pp. 225–30.
[29] Young & Schmidt, *Can*, p. 336–7.

8 | Tangerine Dream

SEAN NYE AND MICHAEL KRIKORIAN

Tangerine Dream has long held an exceptional dual status as one of the most popular and productive bands to have emerged from the Krautrock scenes of the 1970s. With over 100 live or studio albums and over 60 soundtracks to its name, the task of covering Tangerine Dream's influence and legacy is formidable.[1] Initially part of the arts scene of West Berlin, the band were formed by Edgar Froese in 1967; their founding thus preceded the student revolutions by a year. However, Tangerine Dream's musical productivity has been unceasing since then, moving far beyond the classic 1970s era of Krautrock. After a turbulent and experimental early period, the band managed by the late 1970s to attain heights of popular status that stretched from Hollywood films to world tours. With respect to Krautrock's experimental aesthetics and countercultural ideals, this commercial success and the band's resulting shifts in musical approach have repeatedly drawn criticism.[2] And yet, as an originator of the 'Berlin School' of electronic music, Tangerine Dream have garnered high praise and a devoted fan following to this day.

Froese remained the bandleader until his passing in 2015, leaving an extraordinary legacy in his solo work and as the driving force behind Tangerine Dream. The band have also continued to perform, curating Froese's legacy as managed by Thorsten Quaeschning, with the guidance of Froese's widow, Bianca Froese-Acquaye.[3] Still, given such productivity in terms of musical releases and media presence, a critical ambivalence regarding Tangerine Dream is practically unavoidable. A tension resides within Tangerine Dream between such distinctions as Krautrock and New Age, ambient and cosmic rock, synthwave and trance, and electronic live-act and soundtrack. Listening for that tension, whether in terms of cultural

---

[1] www.tangerinedreammusic.com/en/music/index.asp.

[2] Compare, for example, U Adelt, *Krautrock: German Music in the Seventies* (Ann Arbor: University of Michigan Press, 2016); J Cope, *Krautrocksampler: One Head's Guide to the Great Kosmische Music –1968 Onwards* (Yatesbury: Head Heritage, 1996); and D Stubbs, *Future Days: Krautrock and the Building of Modern Germany* (London: Faber, 2014).

[3] Compare E Froese, *Tangerine Dream: Force Majeure - The Autobiography* (Berlin: Eastgate, 2017); and M Kreuzer (dir.), *Revolution of Sound: Tangerine Dream* (2017).

status, media, or musical style, can arguably be the most fruitful way of appreciating their achievements. The band's influence on these genres and practices has resulted in a unique cultural constellation that other Krautrock bands did not touch in the same way – with the exception of Kraftwerk.

In this over-arching respect, this chapter provides an account of Tangerine Dream that expands beyond the traditional focus of the Krautrock 1970s. To be sure, Tangerine Dream made their most compelling leaps in audio experimentation and production during this time, with four classic albums released by Ohr between 1970 and 1973, followed by *Phaedra* (1974) and *Rubycon* (1975) with the band's move to Virgin Records. We will first address Tangerine Dream's musical transformation in the context of the 1970s. Our account then moves beyond this classic Krautrock study in the following respects. First, Tangerine Dream's live career through the 1980s will be highlighted, involving multiple groundbreaking performances that had both geographic and political consequences: from iconic events at European cathedrals to concert spectacles across the United States, and landmark tours in the Eastern Bloc during the 1980s. A parallel tradition of live albums, inaugurated by the classic *Ricochet* (1975), demonstrates that the band maintained some of their better experimental traditions in the live context.

The final sections continue with this expanded frame by addressing Tangerine Dream's legacy in music for visual media. Tangerine Dream's numerous film scores, especially during the 1980s, have been as consequential as their live and studio albums. Far beyond a commercial footnote, this Hollywood career has helped to solidify the band's legacy while reaching new audiences. Such a perspective, which highlights the 1980s as much as the 1970s, requires a leap beyond orthodoxies that focus primarily on the early albums as the band's Golden Age. This original view was arguably cemented in Julian Cope's landmark *Krautrocksampler*, where he focused almost exclusively on the early albums. Indeed, Cope even omitted *Phaedra*, long seen as a definitive album, from his list of the top 50 Krautrock albums. He finished with *Atem* from 1973[4] – although in fairness, he gave some praise for the later albums of the 1970s. Regardless, the critical tension between freeform Krautrock and the sequenced future of Tangerine Dream's later albums is implied here.

To a certain extent, this desire to focus on early Tangerine Dream is related to the band's overwhelming productivity, which is matched only by Conrad

---

[4] Cope, *Krautrocksampler*, pp. 131–3.

Schnitzler and Klaus Schulze, coincidentally the original members on the debut album from 1970.[5] Indeed, Tangerine Dream's prolific discography can seem daunting, as though one is climbing a cosmic Mont Blanc. Reasonable concerns about a dilution of quality are also evident here. In this sense, if Kraftwerk achieved cult status on account of their minimalist approach, Tangerine Dream occupy the other extreme of abundant overload. And yet, this dive into discographic oceans of sound might also yield its own benefits, and not just for the most committed Tangerine Dream fans. While a canon of landmark albums exists for legitimate reasons, especially between 1972 and 1977 when the band established their definitive sound,[6] this wider discography should also be revisited. Some surprising outcomes can result, from the spectacle of live performances to a world of visual media.

The Ohr Years and *kosmische Musik*

This multi-decade career of Tangerine Dream was not foreseeable at the band's inception. With their initial years in the late 1960s as part of the Zodiak club scene in West Berlin, involving related bands such as Ash Ra Tempel and Kluster, Tangerine Dream initially had a constant turnover of members – It was a feat that Edgar Froese managed to keep the band active. Still, practices of professionalisation and productivity were established for the band early on by Froese. He was older than the other band members, as he was born on D-Day in 1944. Froese grew up in West Berlin playing piano as a teenager and initially focusing on sculpture and painting. His talents eventually led to a brief period of study at the Academy of Arts in Berlin. He experienced the 1960s Beat era and toured with his first band, The Ones, which resulted in a life-changing experience. In Spain, Froese met Salvador Dali and was inspired to devote his artistic efforts to the experimental Berlin scene, with a kind of sonic surrealism that combined psychedelic rock and Dali.[7]

After founding Tangerine Dream in 1967, the band went through a number of formations before recording their first album, *Electronic Meditation* (1970), on Rolf-Ulrich Kaiser's Ohr label. At this time, apparently in response to Kaiser, Froese also began using the term *kosmische Musik* to describe the band's musical vision.[8] With Schulze and Schnitzler,

---

[5] Ibid., pp. 28–9.   [6] Stump, *Digital Gothic*, pp. 7–9.

[7] Adelt, *Krautrock*, pp. 30–1; see also Stubbs, *Future Days*, pp. 302–4 and Froese, *Tangerine Dream*, pp. 1–7.

[8] J Papenburg, Kosmische Musik: On Krautrock's Takeoff, in M Ahlers & C Jacke (eds.), *Perspectives on German Popular Music* (Abingdon: Routledge, 2016), pp. 55–60 (57–8).

Tangerine Dream's freeform rock was already on full display on *Electronic Meditation,* though Cope astutely sums up this album as 'really neither electronic nor meditative'.[9] Kaiser himself offered elaborate esoteric descriptions in representing this new cosmic music of the Berlin School, stating at one point: '[K]osmische Musik more narrowly relates to the specific direction of musicians who, as a medium, realize life's molecular processes directly through their instrument of electronic vibrations.'[10] Tangerine Dream's audio experimentations also gradually involved more electronic equipment. Ulrich Adelt describes these ideas about the synthesiser and Kaiser's vision as aiming at a 'deterritorialized, postnational cosmological identity'.[11] While the origins of the term are unclear, it was Kaiser who popularised this idea by adapting it for one of his record labels, founded in 1973. However, Froese would later become dissatisfied with such psychedelic rhetoric and reject the idea of *kosmische Musik.* He decided to abstain from drugs and maintained an artistic discipline that ensured Tangerine Dream's prolific output, which included splitting from Kaiser and the Ohr label at the right time.

Still, the 1970s legacy of *kosmische Musik* has accompanied Tangerine Dream with associations of science fiction and space music. Following *Electronic Meditation,* the albums *Alpha Centauri* (1971), *Zeit* (*Time,* 1972), and *Atem* (*Breath,* 1973) all had distinct cosmic trappings, and eventually achieved marked success, especially in Britain and France. The influential British DJ John Peel named *Atem* his album of the year for 1973, placing it in heavy rotation on his radio show. Such reception would make Tangerine Dream one of the most internationally successful German acts of the decade. *Zeit* was a landmark release, the glacial outlier to the more rhythmically driven albums on Ohr. An extended double LP, *Zeit* explored outer space – and head space – to its sonic limits. Florian Fricke of Popol Vuh joined in with his Moog synthesiser on the opening movement, 'Birth of Liquid Plejades', and Tangerine Dream would carry cosmic electronica even further on such chilling tracks as 'Origin of Supernatural Possibilities'. With such titles and extended forms, Tangerine Dream became a kind of Berlin answer to Pink Floyd and other British progressive rock acts. The progressive scene in France was likewise devoted to Tangerine Dream's music.

This mix of psychedelic rock, German romantic tropes, and surrealism formed a compelling intersection of cultural references for fans of Tangerine Dream. As mentioned earlier, Froese did not partake in the

[9] Cope, *Krautrocksampler,* p. 34.   [10] Adelt, *Krautrock,* pp. 91–2.   [11] Ibid., p. 83.

mind-altering drugs of the sub-culture, but the psychedelic connection is undeniable. After all, the band's name comes from having misheard the lyric 'tangerine trees' in the Beatles' LSD-inspired song 'Lucy in the Sky with Diamonds'.[12] The band's custom of performing in cathedrals in the 1970s reinforced the spiritual, mystic aura around them and their music. The 1973 album *Atem* proved to be an extraordinary musical moment that represented the band at the pinnacle of their Krautrock phase, with free-form drumming and sonic experimentation that evoked the sublime, featured especially on the twenty-minute title track of the album.

The band line-up had also crystalised by this time. As mentioned, Edgar Froese had always been at the heart of Tangerine Dream, though most fans view the classic trio of Froese, Christopher Franke, and Peter Bauman as central to the band's sound. This trio worked together from 1971 through 1977 for most of Tangerine Dream's classic albums, from *Zeit* (1972) to *Sorcerer* (1977). Franke had been classically trained at the Berlin Conservatory before joining Froese in 1971 to record *Alpha Centauri*, and Baumann, an accomplished pianist who knew Franke and joined by the time that *Zeit* was recorded, completed the trio. Together, they also made the leap from Ohr to Virgin Records.

This trio of Froese, Franke, and Baumann is thus comparable to Kraftwerk's classic quartet formation from 1975 to 1987. While Baumann had already left by 1977, Franke stayed on as a key member to shape Tangerine Dream's sound in music and media of the 1980s until his departure in 1987. Between 1971 and the move to Virgin in 1973, the trio gradually acquired new equipment and, Franke especially, worked tirelessly in the studio to develop the definitive sound. The band's close association with Krautrock is also confirmed by the fact that *Alpha Centauri, Zeit,* and *Atem* were all recorded in Dieter Dierks's iconic studio near Cologne and released on Ohr. But with their extraordinary international success, a young label owner named Richard Branson would become interested in signing Tangerine Dream, which would result in some radical changes.

The Virgin Years: Sequenced Success

The album that most fans and critics view as Tangerine Dream's most influential release followed their move to Virgin Records – the aforementioned *Phaedra* (1974). It could practically be seen as Tangerine Dream's

---

[12] Ibid., p. 95.

equivalent to Kraftwerk's *Autobahn* – as its new sequenced patterns on the fully electronic title track, an electronic statement comparable to 'Autobahn', would mark a new definitive style for the band. By signing with Virgin, Tangerine Dream also gained access to the Manor Studio in Oxfordshire to record their next releases. The instruments the band would have had access to at the time were the Electronic Music Studios (EMS) VCS3 synthesiser, a Mellotron, the Minimoog, a phaser for achieving various effects, and a rhythm controller called the PRX-2. These were the instruments primarily used to record the band's LPs of this era, including *Atem* and *Phaedra,* followed by *Rubycon* (1975),[13] which had similar critical and commercial success. With this series of albums, the experimentation with synthesisers and the complete discarding of traditional instrumentation on *Phaedra*[14] became crucial to the new sound.

Musically, Tangerine Dream offer listeners a particular kind of experience – usually expansive with tracks regularly clocking in at ten to twenty minutes. These were sometimes more meditative, such as on *Zeit,* and sometimes propelled by rhythmic sequencer patterns. Froese described their compositional process as follows: 'We could start very simply, with a bass line, the function of which is like the old basso continuum [*sic*] in Bach, and then move into nearly a classical counterpoint structure with up to five or six independent voices . . . if you do this in popular music today, most people would not realize what really goes on.'[15] If Froese here is referring to the sequenced synthesiser bass line that appears in much of their music, it seems he mistook the term *basso continuo* for *ostinato,* which is a more fitting label in this context. When their music is not conjuring ambient cosmic soundscapes, the 'basso continuum', in Froese's terms, gives the music a dance-like momentum. Exotic melodies and atonal elements, from Mellotron choirs to white noise, were also distinctive marks of Tangerine Dream's signature sound, which would overlay the sequenced synthesisers.

The music at times became a pastiche of concert and art music echoes, such as Maurice Ravel's *Boléro,* which is practically quoted on part 1 of *Rubycon* (at 13:30–14:05), or György Ligeti's *Atmospheres,* evoked in the haunting choirs of the Mellotron on part 2.[16] The same year as *Rubycon,* Froese further cemented his reputation with the release of his second solo album, *Epsilon in Malaysian Pale* (1975). An ambient landmark, this solo album was listed by David Bowie as one of his favourites, and an important

---

[13] P Stump, *Digital Gothic: A Critical Discography of Tangerine Dream* (Wembley: SAF Publishing, 1997), pp. 41, 67.
[14] Ibid., pp. 48–52.   [15] Ibid., pp. 131–2.   [16] Ibid., p. 68.

influence especially on the B-sides of his own Berlin trilogy. Bowie and Froese would also meet and become good friends at the time of the English star's move from Los Angeles to West Berlin in 1976 – quite a new mark of recognition for the Berlin School.[17] Along with these new networks, Froese's own solo career would evolve in the coming years.

However, following Tangerine Dream's next landmark album, *Stratosfear* (1976), it must be admitted that the band's output gradually became uneven. In strictly compositional terms, Tangerine Dream lost some of their edge by the end of the 1970s, and particularly with the last major release on Virgin, *Hyperborea* (1983). New Age sounds and attempts at pop vocals and more standard structures gradually crept into these studio albums. In this context, in its most unfortunate examples the music descended from cosmic heights to planetarium 'Muzak', although still boasting standout moments that anticipated techno/trance. By taking on such an overwhelming number of projects in the late 1970s and 1980s, Tangerine Dream seemingly lost their experimental edge.

Franke comments: 'We did not have the time to explore our minds or the great computer instruments we had at our disposal ... I began to feel our quality was dropping.'[18] Moreover, by having so many projects, including major releases on other record labels, a split with Branson and Virgin occurred in the mid-1980s. Johannes Schmoelling, member of the band from 1979 to 1985, deeply regrets losing Branson's support and business acumen, as he felt that 'after Branson, it petered out'.[19] The efforts at record promotion by other labels and Froese himself could not match Virgin's support. Indeed, it is ironic here that such corporate trajectories would eventually make Branson – now famously – the first billionaire space-voyager in 2021 as head of Virgin Galactic. However, he certainly owes this partly to the success of Tangerine Dream's cosmic music in building his Virgin brand.

From Australia to Poland: Tangerine Dream on Tour

We do not have space to discuss the expanded discography in detail, although across the late 1970s and 1980s, as mentioned, Tangerine Dream continued to release a wide variety of studio albums, ranging from the initial adventures in song structures with Steve Jolliffe on

---

[17] Compare Froese, *Tangerine Dream*, pp. 70–94.   [18] Stump, *Digital Gothic*, p. 90.
[19] *Revolution of Sound: Tangerine Dream* (DVD).

Cyclone (1978), to the proto-trance pop of *Optical Race* (1988). To be sure, Froese maintained an excellent discipline in seeing these projects to fruition, while rapidly expanding Tangerine Dream's work on soundtracks and keeping the band on tour. However, following the split with Branson around 1985, the second major blow came, with Franke's departure in 1987. Froese thus had ever more challenges maintaining the band's studio innovations into the next decade. As Paul Stump states: 'The departure of Franke, the engine-room of the Tangerine Dream mothership ... was something else entirely. He was the man responsible for the trademark sequencer squiggle, chatter and thud that *was* the Tangerine Dream sound.'[20]

But that signature sound and Froese's own innovations, along with other key band members, left a major mark in two significant areas also during the 1980s: the realm of live performances and of film scores. Indeed, the parallel importance of Tangerine Dream's influence as a performing act is difficult to overstate. Tangerine Dream constantly toured at a level that had important social and cultural consequences, which reflected back on Krautrock. A tradition of live albums thus evolved in parallel with the studio albums. With *Phaedra*, a major UK tour took place in 1974, to be followed up by an additional UK tour and an Australian tour in 1975.

The most symbolic events at this time were a series of concerts in European cathedrals. These first occurred in Reims, France on 13 December, 1974, at the conclusion of the first UK tour, with a performance night also featuring Nico.[21] Though Tangerine Dream were later banned from playing additional Catholic churches, this event was a landmark success, attended by 6,000 people. It was followed by two performances in Anglican cathedrals, at Coventry Cathedral on 4 October 1975 and Liverpool Cathedral on 16 October 1975, both part of their second major UK tour.[22] These three events, along with additional performances at concert halls and arts venues, established the iconic imagery of Tangerine Dream as an electronic trio.

Ricochet brilliantly inaugurated their tradition of live albums, as it was based on the materials from these tours in Britain, Europe, and Australia. This album would also be used as the soundtrack to Tony Palmer's BBC film, *Live at Coventry Cathedral*, with vintage footage of Froese, Franke, and Baumann in performance.[23] To be sure, the performance at Coventry, a cathedral that had been bombed during World War II and now houses

---

[20] Stump, *Digital Gothic*, p. 89.   [21] www.voices-in-the-net.de/vitn_concerts.htm   [22] Ibid.
[23] www.voices-in-the-net.de/live_at_coventry_cathedral_1975.htm

Illustration 8.1 Tangerine Dream at Coventry Cathedral, 1975. © Michael Putland/ Getty Images.

an International Centre for Reconciliation, was also a symbolic moment of political transformation and the emergence of a new musical culture in the 1970s.

Ricochet would be followed by *Encore*, the live album based on Tangerine Dream's first major American tour of 1977. Of the Krautrock bands, Tangerine Dream and Kraftwerk had been receiving the most press in the United States at that time.[24] While the band's German identity remained a topic of fascination, this helped rather than hindered interest in America. Indeed, the tour represented Tangerine Dream's transatlantic success in popular music, and the tour appropriately took place in the same year as their crossover to Hollywood soundtracks. With a lightshow provided by Laserium, a pioneering technology launched by Ivan Dryer in 1973, the spectacle of Tangerine Dream live took on new dimensions of laser visuals accompanying the synthesiser consoles. It should be noted though that the stress of touring and production resulted in new friction, as Baumann famously split with the band in Colorado while on tour.[25]

[24] A Simmeth, *Krautrock Transnational. Die Neuerfindung der Popmusik in der BRD, 1968–1978* (Bielefeld: Transcript, 2016), pp. 264–7.

[25] Stump, *Digital Gothic*, pp. 58–9; and Froese, *Tangerine Dream*, pp. 122–5.

Along with such tours that crossed oceans, the other major influence that Tangerine Dream would have on live performance was their extensive Eastern European tours during the 1980s, singular among Krautrock bands. On 31 January 1980, this bridge across the Cold War divide was inaugurated with the iconic performance at the East Berlin *Palast der Republik* as part of the East German radio station DT40 'Youth Concert' series. Tangerine Dream were formally introduced with a practically diplomatic announcement, involving a discussion of the band's discography and new currents of 'electronic rock'.[26] East German concerts in cities such as Rostock and Karl-Marx-Stadt (now Chemnitz) followed in 1982, along with concerts in Hungary and Yugoslavia. An Eastern European tour in 1983 brought Tangerine Dream to new cities in East Germany and Poland. This last tour resulted in another landmark in their live discography, *Poland: The Warsaw Concert* (1984), and these tours made Tangerine Dream an important influence on East German and Eastern European electronica, foreshadowing the explosion of techno music and rave culture in the 1990s.

Tangerine Dream continued to tour extensively through 1988, though by the 1990s, the band's activities and musical innovations comparatively declined. Nevertheless, the band continued to tour in subsequent decades, and dozens of bootlegs of the live performances have been collected by fans under the Tangerine Trees and Tangerine Leaves bootleg series. Such recordings have also circulated online to invite listeners into new directions of Tangerine Dream's almost endless discography. This legacy also involves a performance schedule that continues to this day, involving a new generation of band members. The international networks of Tangerine Dream's formation and reception, as a perpetual work-in-progress, have thus extended to new dimensions in the context of their iconic live performances.

Hollywood Scores: 1977, 1981–1988

The influences of Tangerine Dream's film scores should likewise be seen as more than an addendum to the studio albums or live albums, even if the scores sometimes consisted of reworked sections of those albums. Through film music, just as with their live tours, Tangerine Dream have attracted

---

[26] Compare Tangerine Dream – Tangerine Tree - Volume 17 - East Berlin 1980, Discogs, www .discogs.com/Tangerine-Dream-Tangerine-Tree-Volume-17-East-Berlin-1980/release/11521229.

new audiences from multiple generations to the band, and to electronic music and Krautrock generally. In film music alone, the group were one of the key forces behind Hollywood's shift in the late 1970s and 1980s towards scores with driving synths and electronic textures. To be sure, Popol Vuh also had an extraordinary influence on film music history on account of their classic soundtracks for Werner Herzog's films.[27] However, these soundtracks were in the context of New German Cinema, whereas Tangerine Dream became the primary Krautrock influence in Hollywood itself.

No other Krautrock groups had such extensive careers in film music. The closest examples of German electronica in Hollywood at that time were the 'Munich Machine' producers Giorgio Moroder (*Midnight Express* (1978), *Flashdance* (1983)) and Harold Faltermeyer (*Beverly Hills Cop* (1984), *Fletch* (1985)). Their combined talents were then featured on the song hits and score for the blockbuster *Top Gun* (1986). Tangerine Dream, Moroder, and Faltermeyer thus became the primary examples of 1980s composers in Hollywood that crossed over between Krautrock, new wave, and Euro-disco. Tangerine Dream were also certainly part of the larger trend of electronic composers, most prominently Wendy Carlos and Vangelis, who transformed Hollywood film music during the 1970s and 1980s.

The band's career in Hollywood took place in stages. Tangerine Dream's opportunities were foreshadowed by their colleague at Virgin, Mike Oldfield, whose *Tubular Bells* (1973) became a massive hit following the use of its opening theme for William Friedkin's *The Exorcist* (1973). Friedkin likewise realised the possibilities of Tangerine Dream for Hollywood films. He met the band in 1974 when he was on tour in Europe to promote *The Exorcist,* having the luck to see a performance at an abandoned church in the Black Forest.[28] Friedkin states plainly: 'I was mesmerized. I met with them afterward and said I'd like to send them the script for my next film.'[29] The tradition of live performances thus helped to bring about the new leap to Hollywood. Friedkin's interest was understandable, as his musical experiences on *The Exorcist* were rocky. He had been dissatisfied with the score by Lalo Schifrin and chose a compiled soundtrack of music, which ranged from Penderecki to Oldfield. *The Exorcist* thus became a kind of horror-music answer to *2001: A Space Odyssey* (1968).

[27] Adelt, *Krautrock*, pp. 110–27.
[28] W Friedkin, *The Friedkin Connection* (New York: HarperCollins, 2013), p. 341.   [29] Ibid.

After this meeting in 1974, Friedkin followed through, and Tangerine Dream would eventually score *Sorcerer* (1977). He sent them the script after a second meeting in Paris, and late in the filming process, Friedkin received their musical impressions via tape. He purportedly edited the film 'around the group's music' as inspiration.[30] *Sorcerer* has also remained one of Friedkin's most critically acclaimed works, despite an initially disappointing box office performance. The film had the misfortune of being released in the same year as *Star Wars*. Indeed, there is a certain irony that the first major film scored by the pioneers of cosmic music would suffer because of the science-fiction epic of *Star Wars*. Still, despite these challenges, *Sorcerer* would be held in high regard. Tangerine Dream released the vinyl soundtrack to *Sorcerer* that year, inaugurating their new tradition of soundtrack albums. For the liner notes to the soundtrack, Friedkin would claim: 'Had I heard them sooner, I would have asked them to score [*The Exorcist*].'[31]

The story of *Sorcerer* is a fatalist tragedy about characters unable to escape the consequences of their life decisions. Tangerine Dream's ostinato figure, what you might call the main 'theme', musically symbolises the wheel of fate that carries the protagonists towards their demise. The climactic scenes of a terrifying truck haul through jungles and rough terrain also resemble a hallucinatory tripscape that is effectively underscored by Tangerine Dream's otherworldly music. At this time, the band's line-up still consisted of Froese, Franke, and Baumann, which would have consequences for all three artists.

As mentioned, Franke and Baumann contributed the most to shaping Tangerine Dream's sound, especially Franke,[32] who was also involved in the major scores of the 1980s. He went on to have a lucrative scoring career – most famously for the TV series *Babylon 5* (1993–7) and *The Amazing Race* (2003–19).[33] For Baumann, *Sorcerer* proved to be his only score with Tangerine Dream, though he would likewise develop a scoring career. Indeed, Franke and Baumann, as well as Paul Haslinger and Michael Hoenig, would all eventually relocate to Los Angeles and score numerous films and TV series. The Berlin School of electronic music thus seems partly to have evolved into a 'Berlin–LA School' of visual media composers.

Tangerine Dream were naturally the most prominent representatives here, as guided by Froese and Franke during the 1980s, along with Schmoelling and Haslinger. Following *Sorcerer*, the most active and successful years in Hollywood were between 1981 and 1988. One familiar with

---

[30] Ibid. [31] Tangerine Dream, *Sorcerer*, 1977. [32] Stump, *Digital Gothic*, p. 87.
[33] Compare www.imdb.com/name/nm0006081/.

Tangerine Dream's music, with its mind-bending cosmic flavours, might expect that they would be confined to science fiction or David-Lynchian psychological horror. However, the band's filmography boasts a surprising variety of genres, from neo-noir thrillers to teen comedies, and from action movies to sword and sorcery fantasies. Across this history, their sound became synonymous with a certain 1980s aesthetic, with its propulsive sequencer ostinati, dark ambient tones, and sustained Mellotron pads. With respect to the film industry, the band also took on all forms of projects, from major studio features to B-movie shlock to cult classics. Furthermore, they participated in some interesting shifts in the studio system, providing, for example, the music to *Flashpoint* (1984), the first theatrical release by HBO Films.

In addition to Friedkin, Tangerine Dream worked with several major Hollywood directors. The band's reputation in Hollywood became fully established by working with Michael Mann on his first two films, *Thief* (1981) and *The Keep* (1983). Also in 1983, Tangerine Dream scored the teen blockbuster *Risky Business*, which established Tom Cruise as a major star. *Firestarter* (1984), based on Stephen King's bestselling novel, prominently featured Tangerine Dream's score as a blend of horror sound effects, a method comparable to *The Keep*. Two additional films with major directors followed – Ridley Scott's *Legend* (1985) and Kathryn Bigelow's *Near Dark* (1987). While filmographies of Tangerine Dream tend to focus on these films, a few cult classics should be added to this legacy – the teen satire *Three O'clock High* (1987) and especially the apocalyptic sci-fi film *Miracle Mile* (1988), which features a Los Angeles fever dreamscape that is remarkably complemented by the score. Furthermore, Tangerine Dream developed a parallel career composing for West German film and TV, which had already begun in the early 1970s. During the 1980s, this included a number of episodes of the popular TV series *Tatort*, as well as Edgar Froese's score for *Kamikaze 89* (1982), which featured the final starring role for Rainer Werner Fassbinder.

As the band's Hollywood reputation grew, they earned many commissions, and their arsenal of gear and scoring techniques became more sophisticated. This slew of new commissions meant more disposable income for the band, which they invested in the acquisition of new instruments and recording equipment.[34] The Mellotron was still a favourite of theirs, but from the late 1970s onwards polyphonic synthesisers made it easier to layer sounds and achieve a more varied range of effects.[35] In the 1980s, digital sampling and the Musical Instrument Digital Interface

---

[34] Stump, *Digital Gothic*, p. 79.   [35] Ibid., p. 58.

(MIDI) made the compositional process even more efficient, but at the cost of the analogue grit that characterised their older material.

The lack of memorable tunes and the unyielding rhythmic ostinato also gave a homogenised feel to the overall sound, what Paul Haslinger describes as their 'monochromatic' scores, which all have 'the electronic-analog trademark sound that TD had become famous for'.[36] That is not to say their music fails in the context of film, or lacks quality of craft. Many of their scores certainly stand on their own purely as musical compositions. However, in comparing their music from this period to other electronic scores of the era, especially the monumental works by Wendy Carlos for *A Clockwork Orange* (1971) or Vangelis for *Blade Runner* (1982), Tangerine Dream does not achieve a commensurate level of musical depth or nuance in underscoring visuals and narrative.

Still, many of these soundtracks work so effectively because the music does not interfere melodically with the narrative. It consists primarily of rhythm and texture, which complements and enhances the tone, atmosphere, and pacing of the film. Haslinger, although he didn't join the band until later in their scoring career, shares the sentiment that a good score should not obstruct the narrative: '[I]t's not good if you notice a film's music. If you don't notice it and the effect is created, that's what we are striving for.'[37] The soundtrack to *Risky Business* (1983) is consistent with this philosophy, especially the track 'Love on a Real Train', which is a clear homage to Steve Reich's *Music for 18 Musicians* (1976). Their score for *Risky Business* also provides a compelling emotional contrast to the 1980s hit songs for the teen drama. As mentioned, Tangerine Dream's last major score could be said to be *Miracle Mile* from 1988. While the band's activities in major Hollywood studios ended at that time, Tangerine Dream left an impressive and often underestimated filmography to be added to the studio and live discography of a band that maintained an extraordinary pace across multiple decades.

Stranger Dreams: Legacies in Music and Media

Indeed, the legacies of Tangerine Dream's music have traversed popular culture in subsequent decades. Most prominently during the 1990s, the band became recognised as one of the forefathers of electronic dance

---

[36] M Bonzai & P Haslinger, From Tangerine Dream to the Big Screen: Paul Haslinger Scores Big in the World of Movie Music, *Electronic Musician* 22:3 (2006), pp. 55–63 (56).

[37] Ibid.

music, especially within the genre of trance music, but also techno and ambient chillout music. For example, on the 'Intro' to the 1991 album *Frequencies,* the British electronic duo LFO presented their own homage to house and rave culture, prominently including Tangerine Dream among 'the pioneers of the hypnotic groove'. Numerous techno artists, both German and international, as well as post-rock artists, have also listed Tangerine Dream as a major influence. To this day, the band are repeatedly reported on in such prominent venues as the website *Pitchfork,* introducing new fans to the music.

In related ways, Tangerine Dream's legacies in music and sound for visual media have been just as prominent. In concluding our account, this intriguingly returns us to Froese's original interest in visuals, but now in the form of TV and video games rather than modern painting. Froese's final major project with Tangerine Dream before he passed away in 2015 was an extraordinary opportunity to produce music for a major video game in the new era of visual media: *Grand Theft Auto V.* The influence of this game is difficult to overstate, as it was for a time the best-selling video game in history. The significant opportunity, but also the enormous task, for Tangerine Dream to contribute music to this compiled score is striking. Thorsten Quaeschning explains: 'For *GTA 5,* we composed and wrote 35 hours of music in 1.5 years. The deal was such that we had to upload 5.5 minutes of music every day, five days a week. The game mixes the music itself, so we upload the stems, the subgroups, layers, basses, rhythms, etc., separately.'[38] Thus, the prolific maximalism of Tangerine Dream practically concluded with electronic music as a kind of minimalist craft of stems, woven into the tapestry of sound design. *GTA 5* received numerous awards for innovations in video game design, and it can be presumed that many new listeners of Tangerine Dream were reached along the way.

Just as consequential to this legacy, Tangerine Dream also experienced a TV revival in the mid-2010s that has resulted in a re-evaluation of some of the group's film scores. This is most evident through the band's central influence on the Netflix smash-hit series *Stranger Things* (2016–present). An homage to the science fiction and horror genres of the 1980s, *Stranger Things* loops back to Tangerine Dream's scores in multiple ways. In a feature for MTV, '*Stranger Things* and How Tangerine Dream Soundtracked the '80s', Molly Lambert astutely observed these connections.[39] The series'

[38] *Revolution of Sound: Tangerine Dream* (DVD).
[39] M Lambert, *Stranger Things* and how Tangerine Dream Soundtracked the '80s, MTV (4 August 2016), www.mtv.com/news/2914736/molly-lambert-on-the-german-synthrock-bands-tv-moment/.

Emmy-winning composers, Kyle Dixon and Michael Stein, cited Tangerine Dream as arguably the most prominent influence on their original music for the series – another indication of a Berlin–LA School of soundtrack influence.

Dixon and Stein's score was a highly innovative expansion upon those synth soundtracks, since Tangerine Dream's music was sometimes used in the temp track.[40] Along with *Sorcerer* and *Thief* (1981), Dixon and Stein cite *The Keep* (1983) as a key influence. The music for the show's title theme provides evidence for this influence, since it resembles ominous synth tracks like 'Betrayal (Sorcerer Theme)'. Tangerine Dream's own tracks 'Exit', 'Green Desert', and 'Horizon' were also used on three episodes of the first season. Similarly, the plot of *Stranger Things* recalls *Firestarter* (1984), as it involves an escaped girl from a lab who has special powers. As mentioned, *Firestarter* innovatively used Tangerine Dream's cues as sound effects for psychic terror, with a blurring of diegetic and non-diegetic sound. Similar innovations helped make *Stranger Things* – with superior production values, acting, and writing compared to *Firestarter* – one of the most popular series that Netflix has released.

Stranger Things has thus confirmed that Tangerine Dream's sound is as inseparable from 1980s Hollywood scores as it is from Krautrock in the 1970s. It is appropriate here that the TV show highlighted this mix of science fiction and horror, to which Tangerine Dream's soundtracks were ultimately best suited. This TV revival of Tangerine Dream has continued with the use of 'Love on a Real Train' on multiple shows, such as *Mr. Robot* in 2016.[41] And finally, the 2018 film *Bandersnatch: Black Mirror,* related to the critically acclaimed British series *Black Mirror,* used *Phaedra* as a key record in its musical and video game narrative. The main character actually receives *Phaedra* as a recommendation from a co-worker, expanding his musical tastes while doing creative work on video games. In such a spirit, with the weaving of Tangerine Dream's legacy through new music and media, it does not seem that the band's influence will end anytime soon. As former band member Klaus Schulze said: 'It was Edgar and me who fought hard, who starved, who put our souls into electronic music . . . . Today, electronic music is a normal thing. We have won, if I may say so.'[42]

[40] F Cohen, How the *Stranger Things* Soundtrack Became the Show's Secret Weapon, *New York Times* (17 August 2016), www.nytimes.com/2016/08/17/arts/music/stranger-things-soundtrack-interview.html.

[41] Cf. Lambert, *Stranger Things*.

[42] D Stubbs, *Future Days: Krautrock and the Building of Modern Germany* (London: Faber, 2014), p. 310.

Essential Listening

Edgar Froese, *Epsilon in Malaysian Pale* (Virgin, 1975)
Tangerine Dream, *Zeit* (Ohr, 1972)
Tangerine Dream, *Phaedra* (Virgin, 1974)
Tangerine Dream, *Ricochet* (Virgin, 1975)
Tangerine Dream, *Sorcerer* (MCA, 1977)

9 | Neu!

DAVID STUBBS

The Düsseldorf duo Neu!, comprised of guitarist Michael Rother and drummer Klaus Dinger, are, particularly for many anglophones, emblematic of Krautrock. Their first three albums, released between 1972 and 1975, did not see them achieve the sort of international success enjoyed by Can, Kraftwerk, and Tangerine Dream. There were several factors for this lack of success: commercial failure, the duo's inability to sustain a working relationship, and a failed romance (Klaus Dinger and his estranged girlfriend) at the heart of their lyrical narrative. As with so much of West German music of the time, their success was posthumous.

Neu! cemented their own individual freeway of departure from the dominant orthodoxies of Anglo-American blues-based rock, which held such sway with West German youth in the 1960s and the 1970s. It was a lonely freeway back then, but it has since proved immensely influential on post-punk and subsequent experimental bands such as Joy Division, Sonic Youth, and Stereolab. A host of twenty-first century bands, including Britain's Toy and Now, were also fired by the velocity of Neu!'s trademark *motorik* beat, the deceptive simplicity of which had profound implications for the future shape and direction of rock music.

Rubble Music: Neu! and the German Past

As with their experimental contemporaries across West Germany, Neu! were not immune to the profound political upheavals that took place as they came of age in the late 1960s. On the one hand, it was hard for Rother and Dinger to feel patriotic pride: Dinger declared himself 'not a big fan of Germany'.[1] On the other hand, an inescapable sense of cultural pride –

---

[1] C Bohn, Unedited Klaus Dinger, *Wire* (March 2020), www.thewire.co.uk/in-writing/interviews/p=14780.

obligation even – impelled them to make a political point through the nature of their music-making, according to Rother:

You cannot separate the music from all of the political events, the student uprisings, the changes happening in film, art. We were all exposed to this virus of change and what you came up with depended on your own creative potential. Everyone might have the wish to do that but some just cannot.[2]

In both name and approach, Neu! strove for originality, or at least an escape from Anglo-American rock norms. However, as Lloyd Isaac Vayo observes, Neu! came into existence in a West Germany in which the debris of the past was still a feature of the 1970s urban environment, a reminder of unresolved issues: 'The material reproduction of the state lags well into the 1970s and beyond, with lots remaining clogged with the detritus of the bombs dropped so long ago, the rubble of shattered buildings merely pushed aside rather than removed.'[3]

Neu! falls short of the pristineness and serenity of Kraftwerk's new electronic architecture. There is a sense of a lack of resolution, an emotional undertow, a future that has not yet arrived, and a country still in the grips of a patriarchal past, against which Dinger rages. The inner sleeve of Neu! '75 features an image of Dinger with a black-and-white photo of his grandfather and great uncle from World War I. They remain, for Dinger, a presence in the 'new' Germany of the Federal Republic. The notion of motorik in relation to Neu! Is also helpful. Much as Kraftwerk were not a purely futurist concept, but also concerned with re-connecting with the tenets of the Bauhaus movement cut abruptly short by the Nazis in 1933, so motorik connects Neu! with the music of composer Paul Hindemith, for whom the term was previously used, and whose music was condemned as 'degenerate' by the Nazis.

In the context of Neu!, Vayo speaks of the 'record-as-mirror'.[4] The duo found it curiously difficult to recreate their records live, their subtle simplicity being too much for guest musicians such as Guru Guru's Uli Trepte and Eberhard Kranemann to grasp and carry out. They only played a handful of concerts in their lifetime, and as such were never able to manifest themselves effectively as a live spectacle. And so their records are all we have, their mirror surfaces inviting reflection by the listener on past,

---

[2] Quoted in D Stubbs, *Future Days: Krautrock and the Building of Modern Germany* (London: Faber, 2014), p. 248.
[3] LI Vayo, What's Old is NEU! Benjamin Meets Rother and Dinger, *Popular Music & Society* 32:5 (2009), pp. 617–34 (617).
[4] Ibid., p. 626.

present, and future, their forms offering the prospect of a new mode of rock practice drawn from West German origins, sources, and ingenuity.

Rock and Krautrock

Michael Rother and Klaus Dinger had enjoyed a liberation through imported rock music. In the 1960s, Dinger joined a group called The No, clearly influenced by the British art school rock of groups like The Who. Michael Rother, meanwhile, had been influenced by the surging dynamism of Little Richard and later fell in love with a Danish cover of pre-Beatles British group The Shadows' instrumental hit 'Apache'.

There was no Krautrock manifesto: the movement was too heterogenous to be reduced to a common denominator. While Neu!'s *motorik* beat is considered by some to be Krautrock's rhythmical signature, it is but one aspect of the new music produced in the late 1960s and early 1970s. While there is no distinctive Krautrock style, the groups assembled – albeit reluctantly – under its banner share some common properties, which make the term useful. These properties include: an understanding of twentieth-century avant-garde visual art that was often lacking in their Anglo-American contemporaries; an embrace of electronics as vital tools in the construction of any new music; a tendency towards instrumental music, reflecting the cultural 'implicitness' of the genre, which represented more of a 'formal' protest than one of content; and a rejection of the 'strong vocalist', the big, declarative character up front and centre stage.

Krautrock vocals, from Kraftwerk to Faust to Neu! themselves tend to be deliberately 'weak', deadpan, and understated. Krautrock also departs from orthodoxies such as the verse–chorus structure as well as the hierarchical format of the traditional rock group, with the rhythm section subordinate to the lead guitar. Arising as it did from the commune ethos, Krautrock regards all musical elements as equal, counterbalancing and complementing one another; and in Düsseldorf, Neu! would abide by most, if not all of these characteristics.

Kraftwerk and Neu!

Much as there was a rivalry of sorts between the flamboyant Liverpool and the more terse, severe Manchester in the post-punk years in Britain, so there was a contrast in character between the rival cities of Cologne and

Düsseldorf in the 1970s, with Can bearing some of the character of Cologne's anarchic sprawl, while Kraftwerk reflected the industrious, elegant efficiency of Düsseldorf. Rother and Dinger were briefly members of Kraftwerk during a short period in 1971 when Ralf Hütter temporarily left the band to focus on his architectural studies. It was the first time the pair met, and was a fortuitous meeting at that.

The 'Kraftwerk' that consisted of Rother, Dinger, and Florian Schneider represent a very different iteration of the group. This early era is one that the modern-day Kraftwerk seem almost anxious to suppress: their messy, organic, pre-*Autobahn* phase, none of which features in their live shows or has been reissued by them on CD. They have the sense of propulsion, of unremitting forward momentum one associates with Kraftwerk, but the most dominant feature is the flute of Florian Schneider, with which Kraftwerk would dispense entirely after *Autobahn*.

Rother and Dinger soon left Kraftwerk and do not appear on any of their recordings. There was a telling tension between Dinger, and Schneider and the returning Hütter. Dinger was very assertive of his working-class origins and was resentful of their more privileged family background. He also resented their reliance on electronic instruments. Dinger was horrified that such machines would displace skilled, artisanal manual labourers on the drumkit like himself, with Kraftwerk-like factory owners switching to automated techniques to put flesh-and-blood workers on the breadline. This disagreement marked the distinction between the two Düsseldorf groups.

As Rother said, 'I think an important element of the Neu! music – that along with the beauty there is a portion of dirt. And that's something that separates Neu! music from Kraftwerk, in my own understanding. There is a contradiction in our sound.'[5] It was here, then, that Neu! and Kraftwerk parted company. The sheer rhythmic regularity of Neu!'s sound and the layers of treated guitar make it seem 'electronic' in nature, but it is a new form of rock music, in which guitars and drums feature most prominently, and strong emotions, from melancholy to outright rage, are frequently evoked through Dinger in particular. Although Kraftwerk's music is subtly soulful – Ralf Hütter once explained that 'the "soul" of the machines has always been a part of our music'[6] – they would come to deal wholly in electronics, their emotional register serene, reflecting a symbiotic relationship between man and machine.

[5] Quoted in Stubbs, *Future Days*, p. 247.
[6] Quoted in P Bussy, *Kraftwerk: Man, Machine and Music* (London: SAF, 2001), p. 99.

Illustration 9.1 Klaus Dinger and Michael Rother of Neu! © Anton Corbijn.

Rother and Dinger

The contrasting, yin and yang characters who made up Neu!, and their differing upbringings, were both the reason for their artistic success and their ultimate break-up. Theirs was an unusual set-up by the standards of Krautrock, which tended to deal in more 'communal' line-ups of at least three or more members, reflecting the role of communes in the origin of groups like Amon Düül II. Neu!'s duality later become more commonplace, in groups like Suicide (who formed in 1970 but did not release their debut album until 1977), DAF, The Pet Shop Boys, Soft Cell, and others.

Rother brought to the group a pacific, ambient element, born out of his fondness for water. 'I always lived near water', said Michael Rother. 'In Pakistan at the seaside, Düsseldorf near the Rhine – I feel comfortable near water – it has an effect I can't quite explain. It has to do with the passage of time, it also moves along like music itself – there are some parallels.'[7] Having lived in Pakistan as a child, with his father employed by an airline

---

[7] Compare B Whalley (dir.), *Krautrock: The Rebirth Of Germany* (BBC 2009).

that operated in that region, Rother absorbed at first hand the particular strain of oriental music that emanated from the region. 'I do remember being completely fascinated by the strange sounds of Pakistani music as a child – snake charmers, local musicians playing at the gates to get some money. This music that seemed to go on and on with no structure that I could make out – just an endless stream of melody and rhythm, like a river.'[8] That fluidity is demonstrated on, for example, 'Weissensee' (White Lake) on Neu!'s self-titled debut album.

Dinger was always at loggerheads with his own father – a recurring theme in Krautrock and its rejection of rigid, patriarchal structures. His combative rage was lifelong, a 'permanent sense of opposition',[9] but provided the impetus for Neu!, the forward pulsation, whereas Rother provided the scenery, the blues, the greens, and the oranges: the full colour palette. Dinger studied for three years as a carpenter – work in which he took an immense pride – as well as in architecture. Like Can's Jaki Liebezeit, he rejected machines out of a pride in his own mechanical exactitude as a player. As Dinger's widow Miki Yui said: 'He knows what is "straight" and what is "not straight". You hear it on what people call his Hammerbeat – he did three years of carpentry training and learnt to be very good with his handwork and in using his tools. All of these things came together in his playing.'[10]

Neu! and Düsseldorf

Thanks to the regeneration of the Rhineland, and its proximity to the provincial town of Bonn, declared capital of West Germany in 1949, Düsseldorf prospered in the post-war years industrially and commercially. However, it wasn't merely a manufacturing base. From architecture to fashion to its many art galleries and the patronage of Joseph Beuys, it also had a strong aesthetic sense. Commerce and style met in its extensive advertising industry, of which the Neu! logo was a product.

Klaus Dinger himself founded an 'advertising agency' while living in a commune in Düsseldorf in 1971, though it existed on paper only. This was the impetus for him to strike upon the band name 'Neu!' (New!). 'Neu! at that time was the strongest word in advertising, everybody knew, and I think it still is, everybody knows, so I don't know why nobody else did that before.'[11]

---

[8] Ibid.   [9] Stubbs, *Future Days*, p. 249.   [10] Ibid.   [11] Bohn, Unedited Klaus Dinger.

The Neu! logo functions as a brilliantly acute piece of branding; the group were, after all, striving for absolute originality. It also satirises, however, the nakedly commercial imperative with which so much modern music making was bound up, an industry from which Rother and Dinger sought to set themselves apart. Although they welcomed any sales that came their way, their work was in no way dictated by pop ambition, but by artistic imperatives, the primary one being the rejection of the tried and tested, the formulaic, the dominant hegemony of Anglo-American rock and pop.

As with Kraftwerk, Neu! had a complex relationship with time. Kraftwerk are considered 'futurists' but in their often kitsch-like imagery and neo-Bauhaus aesthetic, their love of Schubert, they are conscious of the German past, its ruptured heritage. Neu! in their branding are making a play for originality rather than novelty; they want nothing to do with the commercial pop industry, whose concept of the 'new' is merely a series of short-lived trends, soon to be dated. They sought, successfully as it turns out, a timelessness in their music.

This timelessness is evoked through the natural, physical flow of their sound, and through an ambient sense of the natural, eternal elements – water in particular. Neu! do not 'fetishise' the future, as do Kraftwerk, with (often playful) dehumanising evocations of mechanisation, automation, and the effortless conquest of nature. Yes, they are *motorik*, but this represents a necessary moment of intensification in the 1970s, a fast-forward motion that is bound up with their cultural circumstances in the early 1970s.

The Role of Conny Plank

Neu! were fortunate in that they were produced by Conny Plank. He was fully sympathetic to the broad, non-commercial aims of the genre while being *au fait* with, and having access to, the most advanced technological means to realise the musical visions of, among others, Kraftwerk, Can, and Cluster. Unlike some producers, including Joy Division's Martin Hannett or ZTT label founder Trevor Horn, Plank did not have a signature style that he imposed on the artists with whom he worked.

Rather, he functioned as an enabler, spending considerable time with the artists he worked with. Only when he had gained a good sense of the character and musical ambitions of the artists would work begin. Using all the technologies at his disposal, as well as his improvisational ingenuity in the studio, he would assist Neu! in achieving their ideals with a stark clarity and impact that matched their striking logo.

Michael Rother recalled how struck he was by Plank's open mindedness. 'He was, in a way, crazy. He was open to everything. It couldn't be crazy enough.' And while he had advanced technical means, they were by no means the match of twenty-first century standards. He had at his disposal a tape machine to create delays and an echo chamber, but mostly he benefitted from his extraordinary sense of timing and memory, without the assistance of a computer.

They played 'Hallogallo' to him, over a twelve-minute period on an eight-track, and he was able to offer notes from memory as to which elements worked and which did not. His ability to organise sound, his selflessness in not imposing his own pre-set ideas, and his exploratory spirit and clarity of vision that exceeded the technology of his day were all vital to the development of Neu!'s design and momentum.

Birth of a New Sound: *Neu!* (1972)

Neu!'s eponymous debut was recorded in December 1971 and released in 1972. While Kraftwerk took a few years to arrive at what is considered their trademark sound, Neu!'s sound came fully formed on 'Hallogallo', track one of their first LP. The song proceeds at a steady, not breakneck speed, with a relentless disregard for the protocols of verse, chorus, and bridges. Dinger's 4/4 drumbeat (labelled 'Dingerbeat') is maintained without distraction, with Rother's guitars throwing up shapes and colours like scenery – streetlamps, fields, buildings – receding in a rear-view mirror, or creating a windscreen-wiper whiplash effect. The engine ticks over, the (instrumental) mood one of sustained excitement at what might lie beyond the horizon.

While Kraftwerk's 'Autobahn' is evidently a sonic simulation of an automobile journey, Neu!'s music is more open-ended, abstract. The images and narrative it conjures in the mind of the listener depend on one's individual perspective. Rother himself professed himself bemused at some of the impressions and feedback of fans and critics but did not deny their validity. As with 'Autobahn', however, there is a physical sense of landscape traversed, and here again is the West German landscape, an alternative topography to that of Route 66 rock 'n' roll Americana. Neu! travel hopefully, though 'arriving' will be another matter. There is a perpetual, existential sense of getting somewhere yet remaining in the same place, implied in the velocity and repetition of the 'Dingerbeat', a yearning that remains tantalisingly unfulfilled.

This momentum has already broken down by 'Sonderangebot' (Special Offer), with its rush of panning, its strange note of desolation – like a breakdown in the middle of nowhere. A high note pierces like the unforgiving sun. The weather of the album has taken a turn. As a result of this experience, 'Weissensee' proceeds at a much more thoughtful, slow pace, as if the landscape has run out and an uncertain seashore beckons, with Dinger's cymbals crashing like waves. These are not individual tracks but seem to follow on from one another, bleeding into each other in a narrative flow. There is a physical reflectiveness about Neu! thus far, a sense of the album as mirror-scape in which the listener is invited to contemplate themselves, to evaluate and reassess. 'Via the record-as-mirror, the listener aurally comprehends both their own literal individuality, as well as their emblematic status as German, therefore creating the individual as initial locus of and venue for action', according to Vayo.[12]

The album puts to water again with 'Im Glück' (Happiness), a grainy sample of a recording made while rowing with Dinger's girlfriend Anita Heedman. This is the beginning of a key thread in the Neu! saga: the recording is of Dinger with his then girlfriend, in a hazy, indistinct, brief moment of tranquillity. Rother's guitars lie like horizontal patterns on the slow, shifting water: distorted, shimmering. Following the violent, jack-hammer interlude of 'Negativland', which signals the past, in the form of a sample of applause of a Kraftwerk concert, and the future, in its prefiguration of the post-punk of Joy Division, romance resumes with 'Lieber Honig' (Dear Honey), in which Dinger serenades his girlfriend with the most affecting of vocals, as if so love-stricken and emotionally dependent he can barely muster the oxygen to sing. This is among the most effective deployments in the Krautrock canon of the 'weak' vocal, in which the individual is not all-dominant in vocal might, but just a small player subject to much larger forces.

Beginning Again: *Neu! 2* (1973)

Neu! 2 sees the duo follow a very similar arc to their debut, as if once again travelling hopefully. The Dingerbeat of the opening track 'Für immer' (Forever) varies only subtly from 'Hallogallo': it is less dreamlike,

---

[12] Vayo, What's Old Is Neu!, p. 626.

sharper – aggressive almost – with a stormier ambience. 'Für immer' implies the length of the journey undertaken, perhaps by a ghost-rider, condemned to live out the same loop of forward propulsion. Again, with 'Spitzenqualität' (Top Quality), a companion to 'Sonderangebot' and another title that might have been taken from an advertising hoarding, the album decelerates, traffic whooshing past as you stand by your broken-down vehicle. Once again, the sanguine spirit of the opening track suffers a puncture. By the end, it's as if Dinger is not so much drumming as hammering a dashboard in frustration.

'Lila Engel' (Lilac Angel) is a further paean to Dinger's girlfriend, a fevered dervish of a track in which his vocals feel like a desperate incantation. The remainder of the album is the result of simply having run out of money, a series of proto-'remixes' of their 'Neuschnee' (Fresh Snow) single, sped up, slowed down, distorted, stretched out. Such plasti-cine use of sonic matter would be commonplace thirty years on but in 1973 it was supposed that Neu! and producer Conny Plank had taken leave of their senses. 'I remember at the time, the critics hated us for the second side and many fans in Germany thought we had gone completely crazy. The idea of treating recorded music in an unusual way simply wasn't under-stood', recalled Michael Rother.[13]

Later critics were more forgiving. Simon Reynolds described the remixes as 'not as irritating as you'd expect, highly listenable, actually, and, sheer desperation aside, conceptually clever in a John-Cage-meets-turntablism style'.[14] Julian Cope, meanwhile, in his *Krautrocksampler*, described the album overall as more 'lush and fertile' than the 'short-grassed plains' of its predecessor. As for the budgetary mishap that resulted in the B-side, he writes: 'What's an experiment for if there is never a failure? And this failure is undoubtedly one of the most successful ever.'[15]

Artistically, however, in the cold reality of 1973, Neu! were in a lonely place, having arrived somewhere too soon. Their lack of chemistry saw them drift temporarily apart, with Rother hooking up with Dieter Moebius and Hans-Joachim Roedelius to form the 'supergroup' Harmonia, whose eventual liaison with the likeminded Brian Eno sowed the seed of the future high regard in which Neu! and others of their West German generation would be held. But not yet.

---

[13] Stubbs, *Future Days*, p. 261.   [14] S Reynolds, Neu!: Reissues, *Uncut* 5 (2001).
[15] J Cope, *Krautrocksampler: One Head's Guide to the Great Kosmische Music –1968 Onwards* (Yatesbury: Head Heritage, 1996), p. 126.

Famous Last Words: *Neu! '75*

After the release of the sophomore album, and the subsequent hiatus, the Rother–Dinger partnership would resume in 1975 with *Neu! '75*. The two members recorded across separate sides, and Dinger brought on personnel who would join him for his breakaway group La Düsseldorf, who would break away from the orthodoxies of Krautrock itself.

Once again (on the A-side, Rother's side), the album sets forth in determined *motorik* vein, with 'Isi': bathed in evening sunlight, blues-less, an anthemic instrumental. Once again, the mood breaks down, the vehicle slows as the sun sets on 'Seeland' (Sea Land), as Neu! arrive at those lonely waters with only their own reflections for company. Finally, with the melancholy of 'Leb Wohl' (Farewell) and its spare, ambling piano, mortality seems at hand. The waters have all but ceased to lap, and the image that comes to mind is that of Arnold Böcklin's portrait *Die Toteninsel* (*The Island of Death*, 1880/86). Rother's vocals are weak emissions, like a dying man trying to muster breath for a last testimony. It's as if, over the course of twenty minutes, we have gone through the three ages of a life.

Dinger takes the reins on the B-side, eschewing drums for a guitar. 'E-Musik' is perhaps the most advanced version of *motorik* to date: chromium-plated, swerving with abandon along a freeway regardless of destination, topped and tailed by the winds of desolation. It is preceded, however, by 'Hero', which is, in effect, Dinger's breakout track. In the posture he assumes – declamatory, explicit, guitar brandished, self at the forefront – he has abandoned Krautrock protocols, in which sublimation, implicitness, green investment in the musical future, laboratory avant-garde exploration, and the subjugation of excessive individuality are all pushed to the fore.

But the fabric has to be torn. In his sneering, lowing, nihilistic tone he prefigures John Lydon on the Public Image Ltd track 'Theme'. 'Just another hero, riding through the night', Dinger cries out. The reason for this despair? 'Honey went to Norway, to Norway', he laments. His girlfriend Anita has left him, pulled away by the malign force of her family, Dinger suspects, her businessman father having deemed the unkempt, lower-class Dinger an unsuitable mate.

Nazism may have ended in 1945 but the oppressively masculine values of the fascist era continued to thrive in the Federal Republic. The tyrannies of commerce, the snide, reactionary values of the monopolist tabloid *Bild Zeitung*, the persecution of 'longhairs' by a society still dominated by a former Nazi party faithful have all conspired against Dinger, it appears, robbing him of the love of his life. 'Fuck your business, fuck the press / Fuck the bourgeoisie!', Dinger screams. It is hard to blame him for breaking Krautrock's customary, meaningful silence on political matters, though having done so, there is no way back. Anita represents a romantic dream of what once was, flickering across these albums, tormenting Dinger in his own dreams: what was suppressed, what has been lost, perhaps for good, in Dinger's generation at least.

After Neu!, What Now?

Neu's first three albums are their essential trilogy. Neu! made a further, poorly received album, *Neu! 4*, made up of tentative but abandoned studio recordings, but the chemistry between the pair was not really there. Dinger did not approve of Rother's use of synthesisers in the sessions, while Rother was upset that Dinger went ahead and released the album without Rother's knowledge or consent in 1995, followed by the live album *Neu! '72 Live!* in 1996, again not having sought Rother's approval. This led to the final breakdown of relations between the two musicians.

Dinger's unauthorised actions may have been an attempt to resurrect the Neu! brand following the demise of his follow-on project La Düsseldorf, as well as multiple other attempts to return to the limelight through collaboration with various partners. La Düsseldorf, his only post-Neu! project worth mentioning in this context, enjoyed some success in the early 1980s, as leftfield West German music, though still formally innovative, became more brutally explicit than its Krautrock forbears: Einstürzende Neubauten and DAF (Deutsch-Amerikanische Freundschaft) in particular.

A trio comprising Dinger, his brother Thomas, and Hans Lampe, La Düsseldorf made three albums: *La Düsseldorf* (1976), *Viva* (1978), and *Individuellos* (1980). These were impressive records, bearing the fruit of the seeds of proto-punk embedded in Neu! They were in the spirit of the times. They departed, however, from the protocols of Krautrock in key ways, especially in Dinger's desire to be up front and centre stage. Predictably, the money that came with (relative) fame and fortune brought its own disputes and, as so often was the way with Dinger, personal recriminations with his fellow band members. Following a further project, Japandorf, Dinger passed away in 2008 while recording his last album, released posthumously in 2013 under the name Klaus Dinger + Japandorf. Dinger was only sixty-one years old when he died.

Herbert Grönemeyer, one of the most successful German musicians in German-language album-oriented rock, re-released the *Neu!* trilogy in 2001 on his label Grönland. This led to a renaissance of the band in Germany and renewed interest internationally. Michael Rother, meanwhile, has navigated the quiet, rewarding seas of his own solo career. He has released a total of ten albums since his 1977 solo debut *Flammende Herzen* (*Flaming Hearts*). His solo works reflect the aqueous, ambient element of Neu!, while never lapsing into the clichés of New Age music.

Comprehensive box sets called *Solo* (2019) and *Solo II* (2020) on Grönland collect Rother's solo oeuvre of nine studio albums between 1977 and 2004. His 2020 album *Dreaming* marked a triumphant return to form. He still performs regularly, playing tracks from Neu! and his own work, supported by a band including Hans Lampe – is the closest possible replacement for the ultimately irreplaceable Dinger.

Legacy

Back in the 1970s, Neu! benefitted from the blessing of Brian Eno – who described the Dingerbeat as being as important as those of James Brown and Fela Kuti[16] – and, by association, David Bowie. Bowie understood, not least from personal experience, that the momentum of Anglo-American rock was all washed up on the West Coast of the United States by 1975, and that decadent old dinosaurs like Led Zeppelin, The Who, and John Lennon were in every sense physically incapable of taking the music any further. It was time to look eastwards, to Europe; hence Bowie's relocation to Berlin. This led to a reconsideration of the value of West German experimental music among those who had not fully embraced it, and an understanding that its conceptual approach – as opposed to one based in mere technical aptitude, à la prog rock – lent it a kinship with the spirit of punk.

There was even the possibility, in 1977, that Bowie would recruit Michael Rother as his guitarist. As Rother himself explained on his website, he had been surprised to read Bowie's claim that Rother had declined to work with him. Rother had not; he had been told that Bowie no longer needed him. Rother suspected that wires had been deliberately crossed, possibly by someone at Bowie's record company anxious about the sluggish sales of his experimental 'Berlin trilogy'. As was his wont, Bowie feted the avant-garde – in this instance, Neu! and Kraftwerk – while prudently never travelling too far in that direction himself.

---

[16] Quoted in Vayo, What's Old Is Neu!, p. 621.

Ian Curtis was keen to educate his bandmates in Joy Division by bringing in LPs in his collection for them to listen to and absorb: Neu!'s albums were among them. Their spirit can be heard in the skittering, linear, reflective surfaces of 'Isolation' on *Closer*, for one. 'This was the first record where I thought, "I want to do this too! And I could do this!" Krautrock was like punk in that way', confessed Joy Division and New Order's Stephen Morris.[17]

For subsequent generations of musicians, Neu! would become emblematic of Krautrock cool – Sonic Youth in particular picked up on this from afar. Under their side moniker of Ciccone Youth, they cut 'Two Cool Rock Chicks Listening To Neu!' which featured on 1988's *The Whitey Album*, while Sonic Youth drummer Steve Shelley sat in as replacement for the late Klaus Dinger on the Michael Rother & Friends tour in 2010.

It may well have been the scarcity of Neu! that added to the group's widespread appeal beyond Sonic Youth. Certainly, for those aficionados for whom the esoteric nature of Krautrock was an attraction, Neu! developed a mythical status. As Julian Cope put it in *Krautrocksampler*: '[T]he music and story of Neu! is a legend with a great canon of work attached to it.'[18] For while contemporaries such as Can, Faust, Tangerine Dream, Cluster, and Kraftwerk either continued to perform or at least had their 1970s back catalogues available throughout the 1980s and 1990s, ongoing disputes ensured that Neu! had only circulated as vinyl rarities or on pirated cassettes up until the belated reissue of their first three albums in 2001.

In Neu!'s absence, Stereolab came to the fore, the relentless, 4/4 beat element of their music key to their overall Franco-German homage. This lent further grist to Klaus Dinger's sense of rage and injustice. Tim Gane of the group recalls Dinger being persuaded to come to one of their concerts to be assured they were not a mere rip-off, only for him to refuse to set foot in the hall once he got there.[19] Therefore, and maybe not surprisingly, Stereolab is missing on *Brand Neu!*, a compilation released in 2009, a year after Dinger's death. The tribute album reflected the esteem in which Neu! were held, as well as their influence, featuring as it did contributions of self-written material by, among others, Primal Scream, Cornelius, LCD Soundsystem, and even Oasis, as well as Michael Rother himself.

All of this meant that there was a significant delay of at least a quarter of a century before the albums of Neu!, reflective as they were of the early 1970s post-war condition in West Germany, were more widely

---

[17] Quoted in C Dallach, *Future Sounds: Wie ein paar 'Krautrocker' die Popwelt revolutionierten* (Berlin: Suhrkamp, 2021), p. 385.
[18] Cope, *Krautrocksampler*, p. 126.   [19] Compare Stubbs, *Future Days*, p. 271.

disseminated (and even then, not to a vast international audience). For while Neu!'s music aggressively, if sometimes implicitly, laid claim to a 'new' German identity, it must be admitted that if their mission, and that of Krautrock as a whole, was to remake German popular cultural identity and displace the old Anglo-American hegemony, the mission failed. Anglo-American music styles from rock to hip-hop continue to dominate the musical tastes of pop music listeners in Germany, and we can only talk about the emerging Krautrock renaissance in Germany happening some twenty years after anglophone audiences re-discovered the music.

The contrast between Krautrock's effect on the national mood and that of Britpop could not be starker. But then, 1990s Britpop was triumphalist, retrograde, and nostalgic in mood, as well as formally conservative. Krautrock was the very opposite of these things in every respect: no big chants to sing along to, silently haunted by past trauma and ruin, invested in future prospects, and musically difficult, which made it a tough sell to West Germans (like any other mainstream audience). This certainly applied to Neu!, whose innovations and departure from commercial musical norms inevitably cost them in terms of sales, not least domestically.

However, Neu! did help profoundly impact perceptions of West German identity as others in Europe and America saw it, working to break down ubiquitous stereotypes and aiding the healthy regeneration of the country's reputation internationally. At the same time, if not wholly at the behest of Neu! or Krautrock generally, post-war West Germany has undertaken civic acts of reparation and self-cleansing: it is not in the same place it was in 1968, and time alone has seen to that. Meanwhile, with each successive generation and the temporal distance West Germans put between themselves and World War II, the music of Neu! – its immaculate surfaces, rippling with underlying drama and emotion – remains, 'Für immer', forever, on offer as a paradigmatic product of West Germany.

Essential Listening

Neu!, *Neu!* (Brain, 1972)
Neu!, *Neu! 2* (Brain, 1973)
Neu!, *Neu! 75* (Brain, 1975)
La Düsseldorf, *La Düsseldorf* (Teldec, 1976)
Michael Rother, *Dreaming* (Grönland, 2020)

10 | Faust

ALEXANDER HENKLE

Listed among the handful of prominent Krautrock groups lies Faust, who were a self-described 'amalgam of eight people, and the only thing they had in common was the fact that they belonged to the male species'.[1] They are the first band after Can and Neu! on leading American online music publication Pitchfork's Best Krautrock list (an aggregate ranking compiled from reviews as far back as 2001).[2] Academic research on the band is non-existent prior to Arne Koch's 2009 article, and critical efforts before that, such as Julian Cope's *Krautrocksampler*, have disseminated either false or highly exaggerated information often perpetuated by the band members' elusive and contradictory responses to direct questions. It is therefore a challenge to academically assess the band based on any solid statement, researchers like Koch, Wilson, and Adelt having been left to speculate both Faust's history and intentions based on scattered anecdotes.

Furthermore, Faust's abrasive sound is unlike other Krautrock bands. Rather than the driving *motorik* beats and *kosmische* synthesiser soundscapes, Faust created experimental cut-ups incorporating any noise imaginable, reaching solipsistically for 'the sound of yourself listening'.[3] The reactions of listeners to Faust's dissonance range from surreal laughter to horrified confusion; Faust's music is not social music, and tracing the lineage of their influence creates a complicated path with no easily distinguished progenitors and inheritors.

While their acclaim was not immediately felt, Faust would be appreciated for decades to come. The band's legacy leaves a fractured gaze into a world of invention that reacted against the contemporary prevailing norms of Anglo-American rock music. Faust aimed to find a specifically German approach to inject the established rock mythos with avant-garde experimentation, mixing noise, and radical aesthetics within a Romantic-Dada spirit.

---

[1] J Péron, Arnulf Meifert, *The Faust List*, www.faust-pages.com/publications/jeanherve.arnulf.html.

[2] Pitchfork, Highest Rated Krautrock Albums of All Time, www.albumoftheyear.org/genre/97-krautrock/all/pitchfork/.

[3] Quoted in A Wilson, *Faust: Stretch Out Time 1970–1975* (London: Faust Pages, 2006), p. 156.

Chance Encounters: Formation, 1969

In 1969, Polydor approached journalist Uwe Nettelbeck to create a German rival to The Beatles. In Hamburg, Nettelbeck found Nukleus (Jean-Hervé Péron on bass, Rudolf Sosna on guitar, and Gunther Wüsthoff on saxophone) and suggested adding drums, contacting Campylognatus Citelli (Werner 'Zappi' Diermaier and Arnulf Meifert on drums and Hans-Joachim Irmler on organ).

For a name, Nettelbeck suggested Richard Wagner's Norse-influenced opera 'Götterdämmerung' (Twilight of the Gods). Band members rejected this by stabbing a note with the name onto Nettelbeck's front door.[4] Instead, they settled on Faust, which translates as 'fist' and references the Faust folk tale, their decision to sign a deal with a major label suggesting they 'sold their souls', much as Faust does to Mephistopheles as portrayed most famously in Johann Wolfgang von Goethe's 1808 play. These foundations, and Nettelbeck's love of Herman Melville's novel *Moby Dick*,[5] suggest a Romanticist mindset nestled within their musical experimentation.

In 1970, Faust recorded two tracks for a demo in an abandoned air-raid shelter: 'Baby', a psychedelic jam sung in falsetto, and 'Lieber Herr Deutschland' (Dear Mr Germany), a collage of protest shouts and improvised noise, followed by steady rock accompanying a mumbled recitation of a washing machine manual. The political reaction against consumerism targets the machine's destruction of conscious thought, comparing political organisation with mechanic automation and illustrating the necessity of individual autonomy.[6]

Polydor signed the group after hearing the demo, providing full studio equipment in a converted schoolhouse/commune in small-town Wümme in north Germany. Kurt Graupner (described as 'a straight mind'[7] when compared to the rest of the odd cohort) sat beside Uwe Nettelbeck and tinkered behind the production desk, finding new ways to process and organise the chaotic sounds. Equipment was wired through the house so members could record new sounds from the comfort of their beds. Television and radio were prohibited, blocking outside influences. Artists

---

[4] A Koch & S Harris, The Sound of Yourself Listening: Faust and the Politics of the Unpolitical, *Popular Music and Society* 32:5 (2009), pp. 579–94 (592).

[5] J Boyd, Uwe Nettelbeck Obituary, *The Guardian* (13 February 2007), www.theguardian.com /news/2007/feb/13/guardianobituaries.germany.

[6] U Adelt, *Krautrock: German Music in the Seventies* (Ann Arbor: University of Michigan, 2016), p. 61.

[7] M Dwyer, Life in the Faust Lane, *The Age* (21 May 2011), p. 25.

and girlfriends occasionally visited the site, which was a hotspot for 'hippie' living and far-left politics. Nevertheless, Faust's ethos could not easily be defined as 'hippie' or 'radical'. The music often attacked 'flower-power' sensibilities with claustrophobic noise, and Irmler claimed later that while 'you can't make music while being political', he felt that they 'were not really a political group'.[8] Even though the protest recordings and the clenched fist of their debut's cover art lampshade a flirtation with the political, ideological unity is erased in the large band's multiplicity of potential intentions and perspectives.

Their German heritage contributed to what commune frequenter (and later collaborator) Peter Blegvad described as 'a need for a radical exorcism of their [the German peoples'] recent past'.[9] Faust were of a generation shielded from the horrors of Nazism yet living in the shadow it had left over perceptions of German culture. Faust acknowledged the paradoxes of these cultural tensions but sought past it to discover new states of being. Critic Pierro Scaruffi stated, 'Faust had little or no interest in psychedelia, and even less interest in the universe. They were (morbidly) fascinated by the human psyche in the 20th century.'[10] Support for this claim runs deep, such as in a manifesto issued in 1972, wherein they claimed they were influenced by 'the Heisenberg principle, anti-matter, relativity, Hitler, relativity, cybernetics, D.N.A., game theory, etc.'.[11] While several 'influences' directly reference German identity, some are purely physical or biological, each reflecting an aspect of that over-arching nature from which the individual could never free itself, against which the individual is found helpless in the world.

The band's music comes out of the limitations of each member's socio-psychological states, but also resists these limits through collaboration, all in search of new frontiers of expression and being. Much like Dada and Fluxus artists, Faust acted on a need to eschew all authority and form, to react to the constraints of modernity and industrialised society with not only a recognition of but a commitment to the absurd. Indeed, this quest was always Romantic in nature. Tzara claimed: 'Dada was born of a moral need . . . that man, at the centre of all creations of the spirit, must affirm his primacy over notions emptied of all substance.'[12]

---

[8] A Wilson, Interview with Jochen, *The Faust Pages* (19 October 1998).
[9] Quoted in A Gill, Having a Smashing Time, *Mojo* (April 1997).
[10] P Scaruffi, A Brief Summary of German Rock Music, Scaruffi.com, www.scaruffi.com/history/german.html.
[11] Quoted in Wilson, *Faust*, p. 155.
[12] T Tzara, An Introduction to Dada, in R Motherwell (ed.), *The Dada Painters and Poets: An Anthology* (Boston: Hall, 1981), p. 394.

This relates to Northrop Frye's claim that the Romantic hero gains his individualist power from nature as separated from civilisation, a power that civilisation supposedly lacks.[13] Similarly, Faust wished to rediscover man's supposed primacy in reaction to modernist nihilism. Escaping to their commune and combining psychoactive drugs with 'hippie' spirituality, Faust were in search of thought at the edge of the eternally fleeting present, lacking essence and meaning, but embodying momentum and physicality. To explain, Faust wrote an English manifesto (with the help of fellow musician Peter Blegvad) on their 1973 tour, wherein they declared:

this is the time we are in love with. The Absurd was ushered in & seated in the place of honour ... [it] has medicinal properties, the Absurd, it is now discovered, decides! but that was now, learning to eat time with one's ears. savouring each moment – distinct as a dot of braille.[14]

The goal was not only to discover the enlightened state of present awareness and absurdity but to create music that destroys the constraints limiting the individual from achieving that state. A group consciousness takes hold both in the communal living style and introduction of mechanical 'black boxes' to the musical processes, whereby any musician could alter another's sound by the quick flip of a switch, with effects such as ring modulation and extreme echoes rendering instruments' timbre and performance unrecognisable.[15] Musicianship was purposefully removed from the performance, distorted and filtered through Graupner and Nettelbeck's chaotic mixes.

That said, the role of these overseers adds composition to the chaos. The futurist aesthetics of fascist spirit in the sounds of machinery and protest ('Why Don't You Eat Carrots?') clash with moments of pastoral folk ('Chère Chambre') and psychedelic improvisations ('Krautrock'), but nevertheless, the aesthetics function on their own logic outside the crutch of exploiting associative signs. Rather than create a spectacle of disorientation, Faust make music that functions, as if ideological, as a cohesive whole, composing noise to avoid pop music's repetition of timbres and forms. What monomania this 'wholeness' points to is without a singular rhetoric, instead opening itself up to multiplicities of differing meanings. Ian MacDonald, in his review in the *New Musical Express*, once described this paradoxical form by claiming:

Faust aren't, like Zappa, trying to piece together a jigsaw with the parts taken from several different jigsaw sets; they're taking a single picture (which may be extremely

---

[13] N Frye, *A Study of English Romanticism* (New York: Random House, 1968), p. 41.
[14] Quoted in Wilson, *Faust*, p. 155.   [15] Adelt, *Krautrock*, p. 62.

unorthodox in its virgin state), chopping it into jigsaw-pieces, and fitting it together again in a different way.[16]

This suggests an acousmatic process, blurring this original 'picture' to make sounds displaced with new states of reference. As Péron suggests, approaching the albums in chronological order both mirrors the development of 1970s upheaval and Faust's own philosophy and artistry.[17]

Experiments in Sound and Spirit: *Faust* (1971)

Polydor announced the band's debut as follows: 'Faust have taken the search for new sounds farther than any other group.'[18] As if in defence, Cope argued, 'Faust were brought up with middle-European dances and a staple of folk and tradition which was not 4/4 . . . German bands could get far more complex than U.S. and British bands would ever dare.'[19] While his description displays a tendency to exoticism, it aligns with the band's own postures, tapping into clichéd half-thoughts of Germanic pagan roots uncomfortably associated with Nazi imagery, reclaiming rather than abandoning their presence.

The opening song 'Why Don't You Eat Carrots?' fades in with a thick, distorted wall of radio hum, washing out hooks from The Beatles' 'All You Need is Love' and The Rolling Stones' 'Satisfaction', and reworking them into a fluid whole while ironically quoting them to contrast the mess of dissonant marches and foghorns to follow. Deranged, drunken voices join in, clapping and chanting or screaming into the torment of industrial hell. Analysing the lyrics here seems futile, the words forming an exquisite cadaver. Being mostly written in English, the album's lyrics were meant to be heard by English-speaking audiences abroad, creating a denied expectation for meaning and creating confusion. It is not the conscious semantics, but language's unconscious energy – the rhyme and meter – that end up possessing the listener.

The next two tracks carry the album's visceral, psychedelic flow through messy jams and abstract soundscapes, deconstructing the

---

[16] I MacDonald, The Sound of the Eighties, *New Music Express* (3 March 1973).

[17] Quoted in Koch & Harris, The Sound of Yourself Listening, p. 582.

[18] Polydor, Faust Press Release, http://faust-pages.com/publications/polydor.pressrelease.html.

[19] J Cope. *Krautrocksampler: One Head's Guide to the Great Kosmische Music – 1968 Onwards* (Yatesbury: Head Heritage, 1996), p. 115.

boundaries of music and noise in composition. Field recordings give attention to space, pairing 'private' sounds of creaking doors and clinking dishes with 'public' sounds of machinery, producing an indistinguishable mass that, as in Adelt's applied analysis of Lipsitz to Krautrock, creates a hybrid space that both offers revolution and creates culture anew.[20] Lyrics dismantle the supposed difference between the primitive and modern: for example, on 'Meadow Meal', Faust state that to avoid becoming 'a meadow meal' eaten by wild beasts, man industrialises, wherein he must 'stand in line, keep in line', only to 'lose [his] hand' in a red (i.e. blood-stained) accident. Faust suggests that industrialisation, rather than solving man's problems, simply rearranges them into new, obfuscated forms. Even these more serious moments are interrupted by humour, pitch-shifted voices, and jarring dynamic shifts, resisting even their own systems in a carnival of Bakhtinian-Dionysian gestures.

Most explanatory perhaps of the band's whole project are the closing lyrics of 'Miss Fortune', a deadpan manifesto bouncing across the stereo image, quipping 'Are we to be or not to be?' and 'Voltaire . . . told you to be free / and you obeyed'. In consequence of these questions and demands, Faust conclude: 'We have to decide which is important: . . . / A system and a theory, / or our wish to be free?'

Faust confronts the listener here, rhetorically pointing to a humanist liberation from disillusioning societal expectations, supporting inaction in the final line's attack on praxis, reaffirming the purpose of Faust's music: to liberate the listener from those contexts and expectations to which he is enslaved, and invent new values. To experience 'the sound of yourself listening' is to understand how to experience reality. This single proclamation does not explain the music in an all-too singular narrative, but it does invite the listener to participate in Faust's 'here and now'.

The album went up for sale in October 1971 and sold less than 1,000 copies in Germany. To promote their music, the group would play at Hamburg's Musikhalle, fifty speakers surrounding the audience as if geared to play Stockhausen. Critics and locals prepared for the show, but equipment malfunctioned, and the performance devolved into 'an improvised happening'.[21]

English sales of the record comparatively succeeded, mostly thanks to the unique packaging. Radio DJ John Peel fondly described his encounter: 'When

---

[20] Adelt, *Krautrock*, pp. 4–6.
[21] Klangbad, History of Faust, Faust Pages, www.faust-pages.com/publications/faust.history.html.

I saw their extraordinary first LP with its equally extraordinary sleeve and felt that, regardless of the music within, I had to acquire one.'[22] The sleeve and vinyl disc were transparent except for a black and white X-ray image of a hand clenched into a fist, communicating revolt or an industrial-zen look into man's (and, being an album cover, advertising's) emptiness, making the cover into one of Krautrock's definitive images.

Illustration 10.1 Faust in Wümme, 1971. © Jürgen D. Ensthaler.

[22] J Peel, Faust: So Far, *Disc and Music Echo* (10 June 1972), p. 17.

Stepping Backwards: *So Far* (1972)

In response to Polydor's dismay at the poor sales, Faust made quick changes, kicking out Meifert for being too 'conventionally con-scientious',[23] and making their second release far more accessible. In place of dizzying cut-ups and massive suites are songs with melodies and riff-focused, yet subversive jams. In the pastoral piece 'On the Way to Abamäe', listeners find they have been deceived by a flute revealing itself to be a synthesiser, complicating the boundary of mechanic and organic. Chord progressions throughout are complex, yet harmonious, comparable to Soft Machine's particular style of jazz-rock. But snuck into the B-Side where Polydor might not be listening as closely, 'Mamie is Blue' assaults the listener with metallic percussion, radio buzzes, and distorted guitar, fore-shadowing 1980s industrial and EBM.

The lyrics on *So Far* are naive and silly, yet subtly hint at their debut's themes of alienation. 'I've got my Car and my TV' echoes Zappa's critiques of consumerism, while 'Mamie is Blue' comments on Germany's gener-ational issues stemming from an inability to discuss denazification.[24] Most direct, lyrics from '. . . In the Spirit' read: 'It's never you / it must be others / sleeping tight / thinking of the past / I wonder how long / is this gonna last?' While some may ask this question in relation to the track's obnoxious, parodic *Schlager*-jazz, Faust attacks Germany's inability to reconcile with its past. The lyrics attack individuals living in blissful ignorance, further problematising German identity rather than addressing Nazi issues.

So Far contains the Krautrock hit 'It's a Rainy Day, Sunshine Girl'. For seven minutes, the track features Diermaier's monotonous quarter-note tom pattern, played on a deliberately dented drum,[25] before the introduc-tion of jangly guitar, keyboards, and a chanted repetition of the title lyric. The naturalist lyrics and mantra of 'A-Ohm' at the end of each line suggest an imitation of Native American music. Bluesy harmonica and saxophone, a shift from Wüsthoff's cacophonous, yet mathematically patterned free jazz ('typical of the dry humour and systematic thinking of the northern German',[26] said Péron) to a pastiche of Afro-jazz, are heard partway through the track, transporting listeners to an America of Faust's making.

---

[23] D Stubbs, *Future Days: Krautrock and the Building of Modern Germany* (London: Faber, 2014), p. 221.

[24] Koch & Harris, The Sound of Yourself Listening, p. 587.

[25] K Micallef, What Do You Know About . . . ? Werner "Zappi" Diermaier, *Modern Drummer* 36:3 (2012), pp. 98–100 (99).

[26] Stubbs, *Future Days*, p. 219.

This is not the only example of Krautrock's fetishistic interest in Native Americans, most recognisable when Gila named their 1973 album *Bury My Heart at Wounded Knee* after Dee Brown's 1970 book. While motivations vary, one that held appeal for these German bands was the discovery of a common identity in 'primal man', idealising a connection between America's Natives and Germany's pagans. The reference brings awareness to the horrors of British and American colonialism, horrors that Brits and Americans supposed their own culture to have avoided – and are still less acknowledged than the Holocaust – and horrors that were topical to the unrest leading up to 1973's Wounded Knee massacre. Recognition of this controversial appropriation is fundamental to understanding Krautrock's goals and cultural context.

Perhaps due to the song's length, Polydor didn't think 'Rainy Day' would be a hit, instead releasing the album's title track as a single. The album and single hit the press and, even with favourable reviews, sold worse than the debut.

The Eternal Now: *Outside the Dream Syndicate* (1973)

With tensions rising, the band distanced themselves from the label and sought to collaborate. Tony Conrad was in New York, playing violin in La Monte Young's renowned minimalist band The Dream Syndicate. However, he was disillusioned, stating the scene was 'too boring'.[27] By this time, he had gained some notoriety for his 1966 short film *The Flicker*, which consisted of strobing black-and-white frames for thirty minutes. The movie often made viewers sick, even giving them seizures, so Conrad justified: 'I had felt that my own experience with flicker was a transporting experience in the way that movies affect the imagination at their best by sweeping one away from reality into a completely different psychic environment.'[28] This transcendental minimalism informed Faust's jam-oriented aesthetics in their collaboration.

Outside the Dream Syndicate was recorded over three days in semi-improvised sessions led by Conrad, who found time to visit Wümme between showing his films and helping La Monte Young perform in Berlin. The songs were basic in construction, the first starting with a steady, monotonous drum and bass paired with long, buzzing drones.

---

[27] Tony Conrad, in T Oursler, *Synesthesia: Interviews on Rock & Art* (New York: Electronic Arts Intermix, 2001), www.eai.org/titles/synesthesia-tony-conrad/ordering-fees#terms.

[28] Quoted in Tate Modern, Sue Tompkins, and Tony Conrad, Tate, www.tate.org.uk/whats-on /tate-britain/film/sue-tompkins-and-tony-conrad.

These drones would hardly change throughout the song, but Péron played 'a deep bass note tuned to the tonic on Conrad's violin and ... the drummer "tuned" to a rhythm that corresponded to the vibrations',[29] invoking the kind of harmonic and rhythmic interplay that would inform the Totalist-rock of Glenn Branca and Rhys Chrystham. The B-side is more energetic, but the harmonic content never shifts from the initial tonic key, the composition driven by atmosphere rather than any melody or riff.

Many listeners and critics argue the album expresses Conrad's creative voice louder than Faust's, but said evaluation fails to recognise in it Faust's ethos: the embodiment of an eternal present. *Outside the Dream Syndicate* is The Velvet Underground's drone-rock taken to a transcendental extreme, melody denied and exchanged for a complete focus on sound-scape. The effect is a joined expression of Faust's and Conrad's ethos, pushing art's boundaries to transform the mind.

Surprising Success: *The Faust Tapes* (1973)

With Polydor refusing to support Faust any longer, Uwe Nettelbeck reached out to Simon Draper and Richard Branson of the up-and-coming Virgin Records in London. The label started as a shop and mailing service importing Krautrock releases, but after finding success, became a professional label.[30] Mike Oldfield's classic *Tubular Bells* was released alongside records by Gong, Tangerine Dream, and the new Faust release, which sold for forty-eight pence, the price of a seven-inch single. The radical idea: Nettelbeck would offer the tapes 'for nothing' if the label would sell the record for no profit.[31] The price would be just enough for the label to cover pressing costs, and the action would not increase profit, but notoriety for the band and label.

Part of the record deal allowed Faust to record at Virgin's studio in Oxfordshire, forcing the band to leave for England. While the liner notes claim the tapes were compiled from Wümme recording sessions, Irmler claimed the collection 'was not old material'.[32] Songs interrupt each other constantly, tracks often less than thirty seconds in length earmarking

---

[29] B Sirota, Tony Conrad/Faust – Outside The Dream Syndicate, *Pitchfork*, https://pitchfork.com/reviews/albums/1582-outside-the-dream-syndicate/.

[30] S Reynolds, Shaping the '70s: Simon Draper and the Story of Virgin Records, Red Bull Music Academy, https://daily.redbullmusicacademy.com/2017/10/simon-draper-virgin-records.

[31] Gill, Having a Smashing Time.

[32] J Irmler, Interview, in *The Wümme Years 1970–73* (Recommended Records, 2000).

lengthier ones. This approach allowed Faust to introduce musical moments without concern for an over-arching continuity, compiling a barrage of experimental feats not to be reproduced until a decade later by post-punk bands like Swell Maps and This Heat.

The Faust Tapes' longer songs are among Faust's most lyrical. The laid-back psychedelia of *So Far* returns with the mature balladry of 'Flashback Caruso' and the softly plucked chanson of 'Chère Chambre', while 'J'ai Mal Aux Dents' screeches and noisily stumbles along. Lyrics beckon to a counter-cultural hope for peace and love, inviting listeners 'bring our minds together' and 'stretch out time / dive into my mind'. A dichotomy forms between nature and industry. Nature evokes sensuality, as in the 'rainbow bridge' and 'dancing girls' of 'Flashback Caruso', or, in 'Der Baum' (The Tree), the description of a woman's 'bum' ('see her lying on the grass / must be a nice feeling for her ass') and winter's cold winds leading said 'bum' to bed. It is notable that 'Baum' translates to the phallic 'tree', the title's pun joining the 'bum' with the 'tree'.

Meanwhile, industry awakens an individualist apathy, as in the 'man hard working song' on 'J'ai Mal Aux Dents', the singer imitating a factory manager, snarling 'If it means money / this is time ... because you are crying and I don't listen / because you are dying and I just whistle', all behind the lamentation of pained teeth and feet. This is Faust's strongest anti-capitalist statement, the singer mocking working-class listeners buying into an alienating, middle-class ideal.

The song's refrain seems to change with repetition's desensitisation, with Cope proposing the alternative interpretation 'Chet-vah Buddha, Cherr-loopiz' before Faust accepted another fan's 'Schempal Buddah, ship on a better sea!'[33] Phrases are de-territorialised from meaning and re-territorialised into idyllic nonsense, as if to suggest, even in the subtext of a joke, a hidden liberation in industry's mechanical repetition only if its meanings can be reclaimed from selfishness and exploitation. *The Faust Tapes* concludes with 'Chère Chambre'. Its French poetic prose suggests that – as society's limits fail at the whim of human will – rather than to rely on empty promises of an easy life of creature comforts, we have to connect our pasts, both socio-culturally, and introspectively, to the changes that make up our selves.

Bearing a sleeve of reviews and a note claiming it was 'not intended for release' with 'no post-production work', the record was released in May 1973. Owing to the cheap price, the record was a hit, reaching number

---

[33] Wilson, *Faust*, p. 91.

eighteen on *Melody Maker's* chart before controversially being removed. Virgin Records did not calculate taxes into the cost of production, and 60,000 records lost the label and band 2,000 pounds.[34] Not all the listeners enjoyed the strange music, but many did, and with rave reviews and a (pre-recorded) performance on John Peel's radio programme in March,[35] Faust toured England and France to promote the album.

The reputation of these live performances is legendary. Following the academic-inclined opener Henry Cow, Faust would clutter the stage with machinery, TVs, and pinball machines, upon which members might contribute a barrage of balls and bells into the soundscape. Sets would shift from written songs to more improvised, playful material, and would often stretch to over two hours in length, with varying sound quality. Members were noted to have been shy and nervous at times, perhaps owing to their history of fault-ridden shows, but were nevertheless a hit. Some shows were still a disaster, with hydraulic drills dangerously firing cement chips into an unsuspecting audience,[36] but these incidents only added to the band's rising prominence.

Under Pressure: *Faust IV* (1973)

Faust's fourth and final 1970s album was created out of demand for a new release to market with the band's fresh surge in popularity. Members of Faust felt alienated, living in England and facing the stress of their first tour, contributing to a notable departure from their previous work's abrasive experiments into conventional song structures, at least by Faust's standards. This change in sound estranged Faust's fans, who considered *Faust IV* a 'sell-out'.[37]

The album was recorded in June 1973, only one month after the last album's release. Richard Branson invited the band to The Manor in Oxfordshire, his residential studio for the label. But all was not well, as band members disagreed with Branson's desire for a marketable product, and recordings stretched further beyond the intended schedule. Nettelbeck dismissed the band to finish the album himself. Making up

[34] The Raver, Deleted: LP that was TOO Popular, *Melody Maker* (July 1973).

[35] K Roberts & J Blaiburg, BBC Sessions, Faust Pages, www.faust-pages.com/records/bbcsessions.html.

[36] D Keenan, Kings of the Stone Age, *Wire* (22 March 2003).

[37] D Leone, Faust – IV, *Pitchfork* (3 October 2007), https://pitchfork.com/reviews/albums/10728-iv/.

for lost time, 'Picnic on a Frozen River' from *So Far* was reworked with an increased tempo and intricate multitracking, and the previously performed 'Krautrock' and previously released 'It's a Bit of Pain' bookend the album.

'Krautrock' opens with walls of pulsing fuzz, mixing various instruments into an indecipherable sound-mass. After a timeless seven minutes, the drums kick in, and the song, like Neu! before it, creates a simultaneous feeling of motion and stillness. Contrastingly, 'Krautrock' is neither meditative nor utopian, but violent and noisy. As Irmler said of the song, 'We are not those "krauts" that you think we are and who you hate so much but we also don't play that "rock" that you want to force upon us. So we said, let's play a really heavy song and then we'll call it "Krautrock".'[38]

The album continues with the dreamy 'Jennifer'. Lyrics describe the titular woman with 'burning hair' and 'yellow jokes', while the bass follows with a laid-back, two-note jam. The sparse repetition creates a sense of unease, which collapses into cacophony. The Summer of Love has died, and in its wake grows a claustrophobic ennui, tension without the release of a cadence. Noise floods the composition before disappearing in a mess of detuned piano. The song is a bridge between the naïveté of the 1960s and the moody introspection of the 1990s.

The rest of the album consists of focused, energetic jams. Gone are the cut-ups, replaced instead by cohesive, melodic riffs interspersed by clouds of atmosphere. 'Run' (mistitled 'Läuft ... Läuft') reminds one of Terry Riley's minimalist synths, while anticipating Eno's ambience, while 'Läuft ... Läuft' (mistitled 'Giggy Smile') anticipates the orchestration of 2000s indie-folk. It's hard to say the music is inventive, but Faust's unique, playful style distinguishes these jams from blander jazz-rock stylings. The closer, 'It's a Bit of Pain', incorporates a painful screeching noise to comically interrupt what sounds like The Byrds' psychedelic country rock over a Swedish reading of Germaine Greer's feminist manifesto *The Female Eunuch*.

Released with a cover of empty musical staffs, *Faust IV* was a commercial failure, Faust's reputation and change in sound inhibiting new listeners and discouraging old fans respectively from buying the album. But to quote Pitchfork's retroactive review, 'the record's rep has mostly recouped ... it's an easy starting point [into the band's music]'.[39]

---

[38] Quoted in Adelt, *Krautrock*, p. 69.   [39] D Leone, Faust IV.

Epilogue, or: The Death and *Return of a Legend* (1986) and Other Releases

After *Faust IV*'s commercial failure, Virgin Records was not happy with Faust's refusal to create a marketable product. Some band members were bitter with Nettelbeck's musical and packaging decisions, made without consulting the band. This caused Irmler and Sosna to quit and Nettelbeck to return to Hamburg. The remaining members replaced the missing musicians to tour again and, sensing their demise, returned to Germany.

Without Nettelbeck, Faust attempted one last recording and entered Musicland Studios in Munich, where Irmler recounts meeting the owner Giorgio Moroder, who had recently produced and co-written Donna Summer's international disco hit 'Love to Love You Baby'.[40] The band claimed to be from Virgin, directing any hotel and recording costs to the label, and recorded for a couple weeks. When Virgin received the bill, the band attempted to escape with the tapes, but were arrested by police and bailed out by their parents. A low-quality promotional cassette later surfaced as a bootleg.

Faust subsequently disappeared. Chris Cutler (Henry Cow) opted to re-release several Faust records on his Recommended Records label along with unreleased material, compiling *71 Minutes of Faust*. The compilation is a notable addition to the band's legacy, documenting quality songs from their demo up to their initial demise. Cutler also released *Return of a Legend* (1986) and *The Last LP* (1988), each repurposing material released through bootlegs or to be released on the *BBC Sessions* (2001).

Interest in Faust grew as more popular musicians (i.e. Merzbow, Joy Division, Radiohead etc.) cited them as an influence. Some members returned to record 1994's *Rien*, an industrial-tinged take on their older material. The band have released albums since then, touring in two separate configurations and often collaborating with guest musicians. They have resumed elaborate live shows, providing a soundtrack for *Nosferatu*, or droning while separated by miles of desert in Death Valley, California.[41]

It appears the band are not trying to surpass the historical impact their old material has had, nor repackage the music for a new generation, but are simply, as they always have done, making music for themselves. Indeed, if anything, the band are often attempting to solidify the legacy of their old

---

[40] Quoted in C Dallach, *Future Sounds: Wie ein paar Krautrocker die Popwelt revolutionierten* (Berlin: Suhrkamp 2021), p. 311.
[41] Klangbad, History of Faust.

material, playing fan favourites and keeping the music in circulation. Independent record label Bureau B has re-released nearly all 1970s Faust releases in 2021 in one box set, including the original Polydor demo, higher-quality and more complete recordings of the fifth album, and previously unreleased tracks from the original Wümme tapes, displaying the band's obfuscated penchant for the space-rock jams of Pink Floyd or Gong. The release will prove essential to any efforts, scholastic or fan-driven, to understand the band's explorations.

Throughout their career, Faust have functioned within the constraints of the contemporary popular rock band's mythos, mirroring The Beatles' studio experimentation, Jimi Hendrix's use of noise, and The Beach Boys' symphonic approach to composition. But Faust are remembered not for meeting the paradigms established by these bands, but by creating a new syntax that extended these paradigms, creating something recognisable, yet extreme and disruptive, a new space where the Romantic hero flourishes in poetic expression divorced from civilisation's rigid repetitions and where a new identity, both German and international, can thrive. While not as technological as Kraftwerk, as professional as Can, or as cosmic as Ash Ra Tempel, Faust pushed a playfully experimental, yet existential edge into the fringes of experimental rock music.

Essential Listening

Faust, *Faust* (Polydor, 1971)
Faust, *Outside the Dream Syndicate* (Caroline, 1973)
Faust, *The Faust Tapes* (Virgin, 1973)
Faust, *Faust IV* (Virgin, 1973)

11 | Cluster/Harmonia

DAVID PATTIE

The track 'By This River', on the Brian Eno album *Before and After Science* (1977), is structured very simply; a repeated keyboard figure, placed against a descending bassline which ends on the track's relative minor. The track captures a moment of absolute serenity – a moment where any sense of a past or a future collapses into an eternal present. The instrumentation contains no drums; indeed, there is no percussion on the track at all. The time is kept by the metronomic keyboard bassline; above this, a piano, an electric piano, a synthesiser, and what sounds like a celeste weave simple harmonic and melodic patterns around the keyboard figure.

'By This River', however, is not a solo track. It is a collaboration with the musicians Hans-Joachim Roedelius and Dieter Moebius of the avant-garde electronic group Cluster. It grew from a specific moment in Eno's and Cluster's careers. Roedelius, Moebius, and the guitarist Michael Rother (a former short-term member of Kraftwerk, and one half of the influential duo Neu!) had come together to form the group Harmonia, and by the time that Eno came to record with them both Cluster and Harmonia had released albums that were to prove very influential in the development of ambient music and electronica more generally. Cluster's *Zuckerzeit* (1974) and *Sowiesoso* (1976), and Harmonia's *Musik von Harmonia* (1974) and *Deluxe* (1975), had no impact on either the German music scene of the time or the kind of European and American audiences that Kraftwerk could command; but crucially for the future reputation of the musicians, they attracted the attention of tastemakers such as David Bowie, who contemplated asking Rother to play on the sessions for *'Heroes'* (1977), and Eno, who was going through a period of accelerated artistic transformation, from the louche experimental songwriter of his first two albums to the ambient artist of *Another Green World* (1975), and beyond.

Eno's fame means that, in most publications about the group(s) in English, the relatively short time he spent working with Roedelius, Moebius, and Rother in Germany has tended to dominate discussions of their work. In this chapter, I would like to reverse that narrative, and to look, not at the relation between Cluster, Harmonia, Eno, and the wider history of electronica, but at the way that Cluster's music itself changed during the 1970s. This was part of a wider transformation in Krautrock. It was also related to the setting in which the bands produced their music. I will argue that the changes in Cluster's music (and Harmonia's) is intimately related to the fact that the musicians settled in an out-of-the-way part of rural Germany – Forst, in Lower Saxony, on the banks of the river Weser.

From the City to the Country

The musicians who went on to form Cluster first came together in a setting that was as remote as possible from the rural idyll captured in 'By This River'. The motive force for their collaboration came at first, not from either Moebius or Roedelius, but from Conrad Schnitzler, an avant-garde musician and artist who was based, in the late 1960s and early 1970s, in Berlin. Unlike other Krautrock groups (Can, for example, or Kraftwerk), neither Moebius nor Roedelius had much formal training in music. Moebius (born in Switzerland in 1944), had received some instrumental instruction when he was growing up (at this point, his main instrument was piano). However, his formal musical training was set to one side when he encountered popular American music, and rather than pursuing his instrumental studies he went on to train as an artist in Berlin. Roedelius (born in 1934) had an especially complex history. A native of Berlin, he had been at various times a child actor, an unwilling member of the Hitlerjugend, a prisoner of the Stasi, a postman, a refuse collector, and a masseur. Their collaboration began at the Zodiak Arts Lab in Berlin, a music venue co-founded by Roedelius and Conrad Schnitzler in 1968.

The Arts Lab did not exist for long but during its brief life the loose collection of musicians and artists who used the venue became influential figures in the development of some of the styles associated with Krautrock. It provided a venue for the agit prop rock group, Ton Steine Scherben, the jazz saxophonist Peter Brötzmann, and the psychedelic music of the early Ash Ra Tempel.[1] In particular, though, the venue was crucial in the formation of Tangerine Dream, one of the earliest of the Krautrock bands to become both widely known and successful. The very earliest version of the group (captured on their first album, *Electronic Meditation* (1970)) is, in retrospect, a fascinating mixture of the two most influential

[1] For more info on the Zodiak as a catalyst, compare C Dallach, *Future Sounds: Wie ein paar Krautrocker die Popwelt revolutionierten* (Berlin: Suhrkamp 2021), pp. 153–62.

musical styles that would grow from the work of the Arts Lab. Two of Tangerine Dream's founder members – Edgar Froese and Klaus Schulze – were drawn to the expansive soundscapes of what would come to be known as *kosmische Musik*. The third, Conrad Schnitzler, was by his own admission drafted in as a non-musician, on the understanding that he would disrupt the harmonic structure of the music. The resulting album is best described as a collision between Pink Floyd's early cosmic improvisations, and Pierre Schaeffer's musique concrète. Froese and Schulze went on to develop long-form electronic music, making heavy use of synths, sequencers, and the latest musical and studio technologies; Schnitzler formed the trio Kluster with Moebius and Roedelius, and set off in a very different direction.

The beginning of Moebius' and Roedelius' musical collaboration was, significantly, as spontaneous as the music they were to create. They met in a bar in Berlin's Charlottenburg area; according to Moebius, Roedelius and Schnitzler simply asked: 'Hey, Moebius, do you want to play with us in our band?'[2] It is not simply that there is a neat correlation between the musicians' first meeting and the style of music they produced. From the outset, the onus was placed on the act of spontaneous creation, rather than on the careful preparation of previously composed music. This was, at times, problematic – Harmonia proved unsustainable largely because Michael Rother wished to rehearse and perform material the band had previously released. On the other hand, it gave Kluster (the name adopted by the original trio), Cluster, and Harmonia a way of working that enabled them to create music that was, as it proved, uniquely responsive to the interaction of musicians within a specific environment.

However, this is not to say that they automatically moved into territory that Eno would later occupy. The music produced by Kluster, in the first instance, was if anything the antithesis of the kind of music that Eno, Moebius, and Roedelius would go on to create. Schnitzler was affiliated to Fluxus, a loosely organised group of artists whose goal was the disruption of the outcomes and practices of art. For Schnitzler, this tended in practice to take the form of an assault on the conventional markers of acceptable music: tone, rhythm, harmony, and above all melody. As a result, the first Kluster albums, *Klopfzeichen* (1970); *Zwei-Osterei* (1971), and *Eruption* (1971), are rather challenging listens – made even more challenging by the spoken text that was imposed on much of the music by their label (the Catholic Schwann-Verlag).

---

[2] A Sweeting, Dieter Moebius Obituary, *The Guardian* (22 July 2015).

Kluster was an unstable grouping. Schnitzler, by his own admission, was a 'harsh guy',[3] and his approach proved to be incompatible with that of the other two musicians. However, the trio prefigured Cluster in three very important ways. Firstly, the music was created spontaneously; the first three albums were recorded (with the exception of the unwanted vocal samples) in the same amount of time it takes to play the tracks. Secondly, the music was made from whatever elements were to hand. Synthesiser technology was too expensive for Kluster to afford; or, and they thought of themselves as non-musicians, so they improvised, using what instruments and effects they had at their disposal.

Thirdly (and most significantly) the trio left their base in Berlin, and started to tour. In doing so, they removed themselves from the emerging musical framework that groups like Tangerine Dream and artists like Klaus Schulze were beginning to map out. West Berlin, as much as any place could be in the dispersed musical systems that constituted Krautrock, was the home of *kosmische Musik*; in divorcing themselves from the city, Kluster, and then Cluster, began to mark out a different musical territory – one that, as it happened, led them to create work that musicians like Brian Eno would find particularly congenial. The ensuing collaboration between the German musicians and the British music conceptualist hence exemplified Krautrock's transnational quality: Cluster's de-territorialisation from its original context made it particularly suitable to travel across cultural borders and enter into exchange processes of hybridisation.

Shorn of Schnitzler, Moebius' and Roedelius' music began to change. The first album they released as a duo, *Cluster 71* (1971), was markedly less assaultive than anything released by Kluster, although it could not be said to have embraced any conventional notions of musical harmony. The music does now have structuring elements, in particular a series of low electronic pulses that run behind each one of the album's three tracks. *Cluster II* (1972) moves closer to the kind of music that later came to be associated with the band. In particular, the track 'Im Süden' (In the South) is based on two simple repeated melodic fragments – a four-note rising guitar arpeggio, and a contrasting, angular four-note figure, also played on guitar. Shortened, and with a rhythm track behind it, 'Im Süden' could fit neatly on *Zuckerzeit* (1974), *Sowiesoso* (1976), or *Musik von Harmonia* (1974).

The change discernible on record was mirrored in the duo's live performances. Gradually, they moved away from the kind of abrasive

---

[3] D Stubbs, *Future Days: Krautrock and the Building of Modern Germany* (London: Faber, 2014), p. 291.

soundscapes of Kluster and Cluster's first album, towards music that showed an emerging interest in rather more conventional ideas of harmony (if not of structure). When asked, Moebius was dismissive of the idea that this change was born of a desire to be more commercially successful; rather, he saw it as an understandable outcome, when two self-declared non-musicians found themselves involved in creating music. Partly, then, the progression from *Cluster II* to *Zuckerzeit* is explicable in terms of simple competence; however, it is also at least partly attributable to a change in the band's location and lifestyle.

In 1971, Roedelius and Moebius were given the chance to live and to set up a studio in Forst, in the Lower Saxony region of north Germany. An antiques dealer had been given the lease on buildings hard by the river Weser. The buildings themselves were historically significant, having been in place since the Renaissance; as part of the condition of the lease, the dealer promised to develop a cultural centre on the site. Forst did more than give the musicians a secure base. As Roedelius put it, in a 2010 interview with *The Quietus*: 'Cluster without Forst is unthinkable.'[4] Fixing and maintaining the properties in Forst required a great deal of hard work, but according to Roedelius, the site itself had an impact on the band's music. A clear difference can be seen when one compares the music that Cluster and Harmonia produced in the mid-1970s, with the music produced by Tangerine Dream, Schulze, Ash Ra Tempel, and early Popol Vuh – the kind of music loosely described as *kosmische Musik*. Harden has identified some of the key features as follows:

the creation of large, unrealistic, and non-static acoustical spaces; the manipulation or generation of sounds with little or no correlation with acoustic instrumentation; and, an increased emphasis on timbral shaping of sounds, which correspond in several cases with greater use of technology to trigger them.[5]

These features could be realised in a number of ways; there are discernible musical differences between the monumental synth chords of Popol Vuh's *Affenstunde* (1970) and Klaus Schulze's propulsive, sequencer-driven *Timewind* (1975). However, Harden is right to point out that the general *kosmische* soundscape has a number of recurring features, which together aim to create a sense of limitless space, free of the taint of the human. Cluster's – and Harmonia's – music sounded rather different. Produced on

---

[4] A Bliss, Cluster Interviewed: Nobility in the Blood, *The Quietus* (14 April 2010).
[5] A Harden, Kosmische Musik and Its Techno-Social Context, *IASPM Journal* 16:2 (2016), pp. 154–73 (160).

the kind of amended instruments and cheap technology that had been used on earlier albums, the music Cluster/Harmonia produced from *Zuckerzeit* onwards has, for the most part, a rather more lo-fi quality than the music produced by contemporaries such as Tangerine Dream. This was, as the band admitted, because they had no money; the rhythm machine used on *Zuckerzeit*, for example, was a cheap, basic Italian model made by Elka.

Their manipulation of this basic piece of technology was, first of all, an economic necessity. The band were never commercially successful. This meant that necessarily, the band found themselves working with simple synths and other instruments (a flute, a cello, and two organs) that they could manipulate. From *Phaedra* (1974) onwards, Tangerine Dream's

Illustration 11.1 Hans-Joachim Roedelius and Dieter Möbius of Cluster, 1970. © Cluster Archive/Bureau B.

music had the kind of sheen associated with the professional production standards of the time. Cluster's and Harmonia's music sounds different; a track like 'Es war einmal' (There Once Was) on *Sowiesoso* has a rather more indistinct production, with the different musical elements seeming to bleed into each other. More than this, the tones employed across the range of Cluster's and Harmonia's recordings frequently sound as though they come from manipulated acoustic instruments – and rather than being placed within the soundscape of the production in a fashion that suggests space, they sound as though they have been crowded in together, growing organically around each other. If Schulze's 'Echoes of Time' sounds as though it soundtracks the limitless depths of space, 'Es war einmal' sounds as though it comes from the tangled undergrowth of the German countryside.

Cluster, Harmonia, Landscape, and Germany

German musicians of the post-1968 generation responded to the complex problems of national identity in various ways; by mocking it (as Amon Düül II did on the album *Made in Germany* (1975)); by reconnecting with those German cultural traditions interrupted and destroyed by Nazism (as Kraftwerk did); by embracing world music (as Can did); by heading off into space (as the *kosmische* musicians did); or simply heading away, as fast as the music would allow (Klaus Dinger, the drummer for Neu! and La Düsseldorf, described the *motorik* beat he pioneered as the rhythm of endless movement).[6] In general, the most common impulse felt by musicians associated with Krautrock, was to escape the idea of Germany as it currently existed. This could be said even of Kraftwerk, whose escape was both into the future and the past.

Cluster/Harmonia's escape route was different. The environment of Forst, the Weser, and the surrounding woods was, for Roedelius especially, a crucial influence on the music the band produced. Moebius, by his own admission rather less romantic in outlook than his collaborator, also admitted that Forst had 'some kind of influence'[7] on their music. Going to the countryside for inspiration was a common trope in the popular music culture of the late 1960s and early 1970s; Rob Young's *Electric Eden*

---

[6] Compare U Adelt, *Krautrock: German Music in the Seventies* (Ann Arbor: University of Michigan Press, 2016), p. 33.
[7] Bliss, Cluster Interviewed.

(2010) captures the relation between the resurgence of folk music in England between 1968 and 1972, and an idea of the English landscape as simultaneously profoundly familiar and unknowable. American psychedelia was, by 1968, overtaken by musicians who drew on folk and country (such as Gram Parsons, The Byrds, The Band, and The Eagles). A strong strain of pastoral, folk-influenced music ran through British progressive rock, and even, through Led Zeppelin, into early hard rock and heavy metal. For musicians in post-war West Germany, going to the German landscape for inspiration was a rather more overtly problematic idea. From the nation's formation in 1945, the German countryside functioned as a timeless backdrop to the tumultuous and violent development of the nation.

Such evidence of national longevity was especially important to Germany, the so-called belated nation, which had been unified only since 1871 and whose pathway to modernity was punctuated by political instability ... [Preservationists] offered a stable and supposedly apolitical vision of German nationhood that was rooted in the natural landscape.[8]

After the war, this paradoxical relation to the German countryside (as both unchanging and part of a restless, protean nation) was no longer sustainable. After an interim period of four years, the country was split into East and West; the *Heimat* was no longer whole. Moreover, the country had been conquered as armies had swept over the inviolable German soil from both the East and the West.

Michael Imort, in an essay collected in T. M. Lekan's 2005 volume *Germany's Nature: Cultural Landscapes and Environmental History*, argues that the forest occupies a special place in the German cultural imagination. It is seen as something primeval, something that is tied into the formation of German identity, and, as with so much in the representation of German culture in the twentieth century, this link was used by those who wished to make claims for the ethnic unity and rootedness of the German people:

During the first half of the twentieth century, however, German public discourses were replete with ethnic or *völkisch* interpretations that presented forest-mindedness not as a learned cultural pattern, but as a national characteristic of Germans that was supposedly the result of two thousand years of coevolution between forest and people.[9]

---

[8] T Lekan, *Imagining the Nation in Nature: Landscape Preservation and German Identity 1885–1945* (Cambridge: Harvard University Press, 2004), p. 5.

[9] M Imort, A Sylvian People: Wilhelmine Forestry and the Forest as a Symbol of Germandom, in T Lekan & T Zeller (eds.), *Germany's Nature: Cultural Landscapes and Environmental History* (New Brunswick: Rutgers University Press, 2005), pp. 55–80 (55).

English musicians like Traffic and early Genesis could retreat to the archetypal English rural location (cottages in the rural home counties) and be sure that, in doing so, they were acting in line with the *Zeitgeist*. For musicians such as Roedelius and Moebius, in the cultural context of post-war West Germany, the retreat to a rural idyll (the river and woods of their base at Forst) did not carry the same automatically positive implications. It is not that the musicians, and Rother when he came to work with them, improvised music that was imbued by an innate distrust of the German countryside, and the uses to which the idea of an archetypal German landscape had been put. Rather, one of the main musical differences between Krautrock and British prog rock is that progressive musicians in Britain found it very easy to include pastoral elements in their work; Krautrock musicians, almost unanimously, did not. When the countryside figures, it does so as a source of disturbing imagery (compare the front cover of Amon Düül II's *Yeti* (1970)) or as something that is tamed, and orderly. The landscape described in passing in Kraftwerk's 'Autobahn' is ordered, designed, and mapped out in poster colours, as though designed at the Bauhaus: the green of the verges, the glittering sun, the road stretching out in front of the car.

The musician whose work comes closest to the type of pastoral compositions common in prog rock is Florian Fricke of Popol Vuh. Fricke's work, from *Hosianna Mantra* (1972) onwards, makes greater use of acoustic instruments than is the norm for Krautrock; and especially in the soundtracks he composed for Werner Herzog, his music is strongly linked to the representation of primordial, untamed landscape. However, these landscapes are, sometimes, not German; perhaps the most striking marriage of Fricke's music and Herzog's images comes in the opening shots of *Aguirre, der Zorn Gottes* (1972), as monumental block synth chords play over footage of the Spanish expedition and their bearers traversing the narrow mountain paths of the Andes. Where the films are set in Germany and middle Europe, Fricke's music helps to delineate a landscape that is profoundly *unheimlich* – the haunted settings of *Nosferatu* (1979) or the uncanny, disintegrating Alpine landscapes of *Heart of Glass* (1976).

The musical approach of Cluster/Harmonia was rather different. For one thing, as the quotes from Imort and Lekan might suggest, they were rooted in the German countryside in a way that few other musicians of the time could match. Other groups, such as the Amon Düül collectives, also had rural retreats in Bavaria, but the music produced by Moebius, Roedelius, and the other musicians who came to Forst came into being within a particular landscape, and could not be reproduced outside of the setting in which it was spontaneously composed. Also, as Roedelius pointed out, music was produced at Forst as one part of a cycle of activities necessary to keeping the small commune going. Even Eno, who had a far higher international profile than any of the German musicians at Forst, was expected to play his part. Lastly, for Roedelius at least, the idea of being surrounded by natural sound was itself an inspiration. As Roedelius put it in 2015: 'Listening to the richness of sound in nature is something you should be aware of, to select what you really want to do, to find your own tone language.'[10]

In practice, given the comparatively low-tech instruments the musicians worked with, the music produced at Forst suggests a landscape completely different to that created by the *kosmische* groups. To go through Harden's typology point by point: whereas *kosmische* musicians oversaw the creation of large, unrealistic, and non-static acoustical spaces, Cluster/Harmonia created acoustical spaces that were smaller, and crowded with detail. *Kosmische* musicians focused on the manipulation or generation of sounds with little or no correlation with acoustic instrumentation. In Cluster's and Harmonia's work, manipulated acoustic instruments take their place beside electronically generated sounds, and as for timbre, all are given a production that emphasises the roughness and the grain of the music, rather than the sheen of *kosmische Musik*. It is not so much that there is a direct connection between the implied subject matter of Cluster's and Harmonia's music and the countryside around Forst; rather, it is that the soundscape the music creates is far more earthbound than that of Tangerine Dream – closer to Eno's idea of music as landscape, than to music as cosmic journey. In the last section of this chapter, I will examine two contrasting pieces of music – one from Cluster and one from Harmonia – in order to suggest the soundscape the musicians working at Forst created, and its relation to the natural world in which they worked.

Tangled in the Landscape

First, I want to look at 'Rosa' from *Zuckerzeit*, Cluster's third album and the first to be recorded after the band took up residence in Forst. The duo's way of working was by this stage very well established, but the tracks on *Zuckerzeit* demonstrate a more considered, more structured approach to

---

[10] Red Bull Music Academy, Cluster on Brain Records, Brian Eno and Harmonia, YouTube video (3 June 2015), www.youtube.com/watch?v=vBeujTXtzxA.

music. The compositions were short by the standard of other Krautrock bands; 'Rote Riki' (Red Riki), the longest, was six minutes long; the shortest, 'Heiße Lippen' (Hot Lips), under two and a half. Their titles were also playful, some of them suggesting the sweetness implied in the album title ('Caramel', 'Marzipan'). 'Rosa' is a typical example of the music Moebius and Roedelius found themselves creating. As Ulrich Adelt notes, the track and the album as a whole seem to be cut from the same cloth as the music of Neu!:[11] It is minimalist, and is built on the secure foundation of a rhythm track that stays constant throughout. However, this beat cannot really be termed *motorik*. *Motorik* as a style is uncomplicated. 'Rosa', however, has a definite rhythm, but on the bassline, rather than on the rhythm track. The other rhythmic elements on the track play against the insistent bassline rhythm; none of them stick to a particular pattern. The effect, as is often the case on *Zuckerzeit*, is of a track with a rhythm that doubles back on itself, never achieving the propulsive forward momentum of *motorik*.

Over this, Roedelius plays a repeated descending pattern in A minor against a repeated chord pattern. This starts simply, suggesting a definite melody. However, as the track progresses, the melodic elements stated at the beginning form the basis for two extemporised keyboard lines; these lines periodically return to the descending melody stated at the beginning, but they never do so completely, and they never do so in sync. At 2:01, after what sounds like an edit, the main theme recurs for a moment. Beneath it, however, the chords and bass are accompanied by a repetitious, processed sound, which recalls nothing so much as the end of the Roxy Music track 'For Your Pleasure'. On that track, Eno processed the tape, blending all the instruments together into an indistinct blur. Cluster's track never quite reaches that point, but musically the last two minutes of 'Rosa' sound as though the music is deliquescing, and that if the track continued for much longer it would melt away entirely.

The idea of *motorik* is of an endless journey into the future, with nothing to impede the relentless forward motion. It calls to mind man-made forms of transport (the car, the train) and the man-made landscapes they travel through. 'Rosa' suggests, on the other hand, not so much a forward journey as a progressive entanglement in a landscape whose elements evolve together in a mesh of musical ideas that grow together as the track progresses. The term 'organic' is used, sometimes very loosely, to describe various types of music, usually those that are produced on acoustic instruments and that fall within the broad parameters of folk music. What 'Rosa'

---

[11] Adelt, *Krautrock*, p. 40.

suggests is another way of using the term; in this case, it describes a track and a type of music that progresses by filling in the spaces in the sound-scape, as melodic lines develop and divide, and as the musical texture of the track works to blend separate elements together into one, much in the same way as plants colonise and cover areas of soil.

Next, I want to examine 'Sonnenschein' (Sunshine) on *Musik von Harmonia*. Michael Rother first came to Forst in 1973, initially to ask whether Moebius and Roedelius would be prepared to act as backing musicians when his current group, Neu!, played live. He stayed at Forst, in the first instance, largely because he found the experience of playing with Moebius and Roedelius instantly congenial. Rother was aware of Cluster's music; in particular, he liked 'Im Süden' from *Cluster II* (perhaps the piece that came closest to the kind of music he had released as part of Neu!). Given this, it is no surprise that the music he made with Roedelius and Moebius represented something of a compromise, between the straight-ahead rhythms of his previous band and entangled, interwoven compos-itions such as 'Rosa'. 'Sonnenschein' is a good example of the music the trio produced, and the compromises that emerged as they improvised together. For one thing, compared to the tracks on *Zuckerzeit* (which was recorded in the same year, and released after the first Harmonia album), the rhythm is far closer to *motorik*: an invariant 4/4, with an emphasis on the second and fourth beats.

The track also contains a low but persistent drone effect, the volume of which rises and falls as the music develops. In other words, the track uses some of the same musical components as 'Hallogallo', 'Für immer', or any of the longform *motorik* instrumentals on *Neu!* or *Neu! 2*. Over the top of this *motorik* structure, however, we find musical elements that derive from the work Moebius and Roedelius had already done as Cluster. The produc-tion, in comparison to the smoothly blended sound of a Neu! album, is lo-fi, characterised by timbres that suggest the instruments and amplification have been pushed almost to the point of distortion. As the track fades up (in common with 'Rosa', the music does not have a definite starting point), we hear an insistent, repeated six-note melodic pattern, played against a lower keyboard line that develops into a set of syncopated arpeggios. Neither of these elements is exactly rhythmically fixed, however – both drift in and out of sync with the insistent driving rhythm of the track.

One of the things that makes *motorik* such a compelling, driving musical force is the fact that the other musical elements either match and comple-ment its rhythm, or seem to have no connection to rhythm at all (compare 'Für immer' (Forever), the first track on *Neu! 2* (1973)). 'Sonnenschein' does not work like this; the various musical elements never lock together with the rhythm. Rather, although the beat insistently drives forward, the other components of the track either impede the smooth forward progress of the music, or threaten to take the music in a different, less rhythmically sure direction. In other words, just as with 'Rosa', the soundscape is completely different to those created by the *kosmische* musicians; and in this case it is also different to the clean, technological landscapes conjured up by *motorik*. Even though the beat is more insistent, the soundscape is the same; closed in, entangled, organic, in the sense used earlier. 'Sonnenschein' maps a journey: but in this case, we are not driving down an autobahn. We are on a track through the landscape, one that is close to being entirely overgrown.

Conclusion: 'Sowiesoso' by the Weser

'Sowiesoso' (Anyways) is the title track of Cluster's fourth album. The front cover of the album catches the duo leaning against trees, silhouetted against the sky and the Weser. The album bears the imprint both of Rother and Eno. It is more rhythmically exact than previous work, and it has the same carefully worked out, evocative musical textures that one might find on Eno's work of the period (the sonic template of the album can be thought of as a mixture of two Eno albums, both from roughly the same time – *Another Green World* (1975) and *Music for Films* (1978: recorded 1975–78). 'Sowiesoso' however, even though it has a secure rhythm, does not have the same sense of forward momentum as 'Sonnenschein'. The pace is slower, the musical timbres are softer, and although the track develops in the way as 'Rosa' and 'Sonnenschein' it does so by accruing those elements far more gradually than in the earlier tracks. 'Sonnenschein' suggests a journey down an overgrown track; 'Sowiesoso', in contrast, is a gentle drift downriver, through a landscape constantly various and at the same time unchanging.

The landscapes implied in 'By This River', 'Sowiesoso', 'Rosa', 'Sonnenschein', and the other tracks produced at Forst are, therefore, very close to each other. They exist at some distance, both to the idealised landscape of German cultural memory, and to the implied landscapes (variously haunted, exotic, technological, or unearthly) created by other Krautrock musicians. Even before Eno came to influence their work, the music produced by Cluster and Harmonia fulfilled two of the criteria that Eno came to use in creating his own music. First of all, it made use of the technologies available, even if (as was the case), those technologies were homemade or dated. Secondly, it was immanent in that it was founded on an immediate response to the situation within which it was recorded. In terms that Eno would later come to use, Cluster/Harmonia composed by, in effect, setting themselves a series of musical heuristics (or simple instructions that, taken together, lead to complex outcomes).[12] Those heuristics were embedded both in the technologies the musicians had available; and, for each of them, in Forst as a location and a source of musical inspiration. What resulted from the interaction of these elements was a unique response to the German landscape, and to the idea of the pastoral in music. Cluster and Harmonia created music that did not hymn the archetypal German countryside; rather, they created sonic landscapes formed from the organic entanglement of blurred, imprecise musical elements; landscapes formed as an immanent response, not to the cultural representation of landscape, but to the complex, entangled, immanent environment in which they lived and worked.

Essential Listening

Cluster, *Zuckerzeit* (Brain, 1974)
Cluster, *Sowiesoso* (Sky, 1976)
Harmonia, *Musik von Harmonia* (Brain, 1974)
Harmonia & Eno '76, *Tracks and Traces* (Grönland, 2007)

---

[12]   For more on Eno's use of heuristics, see S Albiez & D Pattie, *Brian Eno: Oblique Music* (London: Bloomsbury, 2016).

12 | Popol Vuh

SASCHA SEILER

Discussing one of Krautrock's most remarkable and spiritual acts, Frank Fiedler, long-time creative partner of Popol Vuh mastermind Florian Fricke, states:

Popol Vuh wasn't a band in the traditional sense and only rarely gave concerts. Popol Vuh was actually more of a studio project by Florian. Even if different people joined the project for a while, some a little longer, the impetus for the music always came from Florian.[1]

Florian Fricke, who like many Krautrockers came from an affluent background, was the sole creative force behind the musical project he named Popol Vuh. While he gratefully accepted the moniker of *kosmische Musik* being applied to his mostly instrumental compositions, Fricke from very early on regarded his music as fundamentally different from the drug-induced space sounds that many of his contemporaries favoured. Rolf-Ulrich Kaiser, founder of labels Ohr Records and its subsidiary Pilz, was a key figure in the Krautrock scene which he also helped to define as the author of countercultural books such as *Das Buch der Neuen Pop-Musik* (1969). In *Rock-Zeit* (1972) he wrote on Popol Vuh:

The wind, the thunder, strong, weak sound that gives way to new births, transformed sound. The human soul has an inkling of the 'cosmic', of light, darkness, limitlessness, death, resurrection. The knowledge of the soul is a gateway to heaven, a departure into the cosmos. A music that is able to express these inner things, the free flight out of the connection to time into something eternal: that could be '*kosmische Musik*'. We would call this music dreamlike, ecstatic or blissful.[2]

Fricke developed a far more spiritual approach to music than most of his *kosmische Musik* colleagues due to his intensive studies of the five world religions as well as spiritual cults, which had led him on his quest for meaning from the Marxist world view he cultivated in the late 1960s to

---

[1] C Dallach, *Future Sounds: Wie ein paar Krautrocker die Welt revolutionierten* (Berlin: Suhrkamp, 2021), p. 219.

[2] R-U Kaiser, *Rock-Zeit: Stars, Geschäft und Geschichte der neuen Pop-Musik* (Düsseldorf: Econ, 1972), p. 308.

a highly religious understanding of spirituality, with music as its highest form of expression.

In *Krautrocksampler*, Julian Cope mentions as many as four albums by Popol Vuh in his list of 'the 50 indispensable Krautrock records': *Affenstunde* (*The Hour of the Ape*, 1970), *In den Gärten Pharaos* (*In the Pharaoh's Gardens*, 1972), *Einsjäger und Siebenjäger* (*Onehunter and Sevenhunter*,[3] 1975), as well as *Hosianna Mantra* (1972) – though surprisingly he omits the soundtrack to Werner Herzog's film *Aguirre, der Zorn Gottes* (1975).

A Spiritual Journey with the Moog

While debut album *Affenstunde* is a pure Moog album, Popol Vuh's second offering, *In den Gärten Pharaos*, begins to digress from sole use of the technically complex synthesiser. While being perfectly able to produce what might be regarded as 'cosmic sounds', synthesisers sounded too artificial and were therefore counter-productive in creating a spiritual atmosphere. Fricke began to understand that his vision of a transcendental, celestial sound could only be achieved with analogue instruments. He therefore made greater use of them on his albums following *Affenstunde*. In addition to the records listed by Cope, *Seligpreisung* (*Beatitude*, 1973) and the soundtrack to *Aguirre* should also be considered to constitute what might be called Popol Vuh's classic phase.

The band name derives from the holy book of the Quiché-Maya, the *Popol Vuh*, which also contains the Mayan creation myth, studied by Fricke in detail in the 1960s. His first album's title, *Affenstunde*, was taken from a chapter of the *Popol Vuh* that deals with the creation of mankind. This chapter describes how the 'Creator, Heart-From-Heaven', attempts to bring man into being as a perfect creature but in the end is only able to create a monkey-like animal. One day, Fricke commented, all the men who have evolved from this ape would mature into true human beings who would bear no resemblance to it anymore.[4]

Through the *Popol Vuh*, Fricke was introduced to other writings from different cultures that helped him on his quest for the very essence of

---

[3] The names are taken from a German translation of Popol Vuh, the originals being Hun Hunaphu (Einsjäger) and Vucub Hunaphu (Siebenjäger), Hun and Vucub meaning 'one' and 'seven', respectively, whereas 'hunter' is a possible translation (among others) of 'Hunaphu'.

[4] P Bebergal, *Season of the Witch: How the Occult saved Rock and Roll* (New York: Random House, 2014), p. 189.

religion and spirituality, as he recalled in one of his earliest interviews.[5] In fact, the quest for a connection between the unconscious and spirituality, which he thought to have first found in the *Popol Vuh*, was to exclude every type of cultural imperialism. He did not, as a Westerner, intend to appropriate Indigenous culture and spirituality. Rather, he was looking for his own form of meditation that could relate to these cultural influences and at the same time be rooted in Fricke's own cultural environment. It is hence only consistent that the photograph inside the gatefold cover of *Affenstunde* shows a Bavarian alpine panorama, which stands in harsh contrast to the music played on the album, carefully augmented by Indian tablas and tympanums.

A former Marxist, Fricke also claimed that, strangely enough, he had come to religion partly through synthesisers and partly through the physical theory of oscillations. He believed in touching people emotionally with the help of electronic devices in order to set free their hidden energies in a way that political activism – at least from his own point of view – could not.[6] With this approach he tried to find personal inspiration in Western as well as eastern spirituality and its sacral traditions. At first, Fricke firmly believed in being able to document his own spiritual journey by using the Moog as a means of musical communication, to combine sound and spirituality through this very instrument – an instrument that he thought would enable him to find access to his own subconscious to finally unfold his full spiritual potential. This way Fricke would arrive at his utopia in a way that he did not consider possible with Marxism.[7]

Such assessment of the Moog was not unusual at the end of the 1960s. In fact, Herbert Deutsch, who alongside Robert Moog invented the synthesiser, saw it as the result of a long search for the expansion of consciousness; a cultural quest that had started with the use of LSD together with the mainstream success of mysticism that developed in the second half of the 1960s. There was only one more step to take, announced Deutsch, to reach the next level, although this could only be done with the help of technology.[8] At the beginning of the 1970s Fricke explained:

For us the Moog synthesizer is the ability to create sounds that we have never heard or have only suspected. You can make about seven billion different sounds, and

---

[5] D Mulder, Liner Notes, *Popol Vuh – The Essential Album Collection*, vol. 1 (2019), p. 2.
[6] A Simmeth, *Krautrock Transnational. Die Neuerfindung der Popmusik in der BRD, 1968–1978* (Bielefeld: Transcript, 2016), p. 76.
[7] R Langhans, Musik ist für mich eine Form des Gebets, *Sounds*, 3 (1973), pp. 35–7 (36).
[8] Bebergal, *Season of the Witch*, p. 182.

each sound represents a different feeling you might have. The music that can be made with the Moog simply encompasses the possibilities of human sensation.[9]

Furthermore, the machine offered Fricke ways to 'experience myself in all my possibilities', and so he took to calling the sounds he got 'mind-expanding music'.[10] For him, spirituality meant being one with earth. Fricke believed that, if we live in unison with Mother Earth, heaven would automatically open above us as well as inside us. But if we live in dissonance with Mother Earth, heaven will close upon us and inside us: 'When heart and head have lost their way, it's good to return to our roots at the base, surrendering our despair, aware of Earth's despair, as our first step to reconciliation.'[11]

Fricke was only the second German to own a Moog synthesiser, the first one being the avant-garde composer Eberhard Schoener, who lived just 300 feet away from Fricke's house in the small Bavarian town of Miesbach. Incidentally, Schoener had acquired his instrument from none other than John Lennon. In 1970, Fricke, then in his early twenties, was working as a film critic for the national paper *Süddeutsche Zeitung* and news magazine *Der Spiegel*, among others, when he heard about his neighbour's miracle music machine. He was a major talent on the piano, having studied it at the conservatory in Munich, but soon realised classical music was not for him. After testing it at Schoener's house, Fricke was fascinated by the surreal soundscapes and the endless possibilities the Moog had to offer. Thanks to his wife's wealthy family,[12] he was able to buy one of the expensive instruments – he paid 60,000 deutsche marks for the Moog III, which was the equivalent of a small property at the time – after Schoener had used his contacts with Robert Moog himself.

Sadly, Schoener and Fricke never co-operated musically. 'Since no user's manual came with the instrument,' Jan Reetze writes in *Times & Sounds*, 'Schoener as well as Robby Wedel tried to explain to Fricke how this thing worked. This was not an easy job; Fricke's understanding of technology was limited.'[13] After Fricke and his wife had relocated to a 'picturesque former parsonage at Peterskirchen near Wasserburg'[14] to enjoy the communal living typical at the time with fellow Popol Vuh musician Holger Trülzsch, his girlfriend, and a changing cast of artists, filmmakers, and musicians,

---

[9] Kaiser, *Rock-Zeit*, pp. 300–1.   [10] Simmeth, *Krautrock Transnational*, p. 273.
[11] Mulder, Liner Notes, p. 2.   [12] Dallach, *Future Sounds*, p. 218.
[13] J Reetze, *Time & Sounds: Germany's Journey from Jazz and Pop to Krautrock and Beyond* (Bremen: Halvmall, 2020), p. 307.
[14] Ibid.

Fricke was approached by Gerhard Augustin of Liberty Records (which later became part of United Artists). The label manager was looking for a German artist able to record an album of electronic music based on the Moog. The 'Moog-based act' Augustin was looking for was intended to be a German version of Wendy Carlos (born Walter Carlos), who had been very successful with her otherworldly interpretations of compositions by Johann Sebastian Bach on the album *Switched-On Bach* (1968).

Fricke, along with his now wife, Trülzsch, and Frank Fiedler on 'Synthesizer-Mixdown' recorded *Affenstunde* at the Bavaria Studios in Munich. The back of the record sleeve later very fittingly would show 'Fricke in a sleeveless sheepskin top, attending to his Moog like a radio ham, as percussionist Holger Trülzsch sits swaddled in Afghan coating astride his drumskins, while Bettina Fricke, Florian's wife, who coproduced the album and designed the cover, attends to her tabla'.[15] However, when Augustin played the final mix to the record company executives, they first opted not to release the album, claiming it was 'terrible'.[16] It took a lot of convincing on Augustin's side to change their minds, although the company immediately decided not to release a second Popol Vuh album.[17]

'The idea of *Affenstunde*', recalls Trülzsch, 'was to imagine a marketplace where people meet, talk, and make music.'[18] Mutual friends in the music scene made sure that copies of the record found their way into the hands of John Lennon and Bob Dylan and – according to Trülzsch – the superstars were amazed.[19] The photographer Jim Avignon was said to have played the album in his studio continuously for six months.[20] Still, despite the pioneering spirit of this album and the positive reviews it received (the most important German music magazine of the time, *Sounds*, calling it 'the best and most satisfying LP with German pop music yet'[21]), it only sold around 3,000 copies at the time. Reetze partly blames this poor performance on what he conceives as being the sound of an artist still on the 'search for something', the compositions sounding unfinished and somehow erratic.[22] In spite of Reetze's concerns about an artist well aware of his spirituality but still unsure how to transform it into music, Cope calls Fricke a musician,

---

[15] D Stubbs : *Future Days. Krautrock and the Building of Modern Germany* (London: Faber, 2014), p. 359.

[16] Dallach, *Future Sounds*, p. 220.   [17] Ibid.   [18] Reetze, *Time & Sounds*, p. 307.

[19] Ibid., p. 308.   [20] Ibid.

[21] J Legath (ed.), *Sounds. Platten 66–77* (Frankfurt: Zweitausendeins, 1979), p. 183.

[22] It is interesting to note that Reetze points to two appearances of Popol Vuh on German TV in 1971, one of them on the famous show *Beat Club*. In both, Fricke has allegedly 'no coherent idea of what to do with his synthesizer' and is seen 'more or less cluelessly twisting the knobs of his Moog'. Reetze, *Time & Sounds*, p. 308.

who 'was never so much ahead of time as out of time: that is, he appeared as an avant-gardist but was really a traditionalist-hearted visionary'.[23]

This might also be the reason why *Affenstunde* ended up being such a hermetic, strange album that is difficult to appreciate on an intellectual level. The friction caused by the avant-garde sound aesthetics stands at the centre of the listening experience, not least because at the same time it was marketed as 'pop music' by the record company. In between these two different labels – avant-garde and pop – was Florian Fricke's longing to strive for what Mark Goodall characterises as 'Heavy Consciousness',[24] but what in his own words he delineates as 'sacral'. As a result, Peter Bebergal sees Popol Vuh as outsiders even within a heterogeneous musical genre such as Krautrock, particularly because Fricke was primarily led by his religious vision.[25]

The cosmic sounds produced by the Moog would be paired with the tribal percussion played by Holger Trülzsch, which caused further friction within the sound structures Popol Vuh created. While the album's A-side includes three fragments improvised on the Moog and referred to as 'Dream Parts' that make up a composition called 'Ich mache einen Spiegel' (I Am Making a Mirror), the B-side consists of the title track, running to nearly twenty minutes – the Moog sounds and Trülzsch's tribal percussion being augmented with distant voices, real as well as synthetic-ally produced, that attempt to take the lead amid a billowing mass of sound. Suddenly a 'low tone begins, a hanging bouncing pulse behind it, the hell-tone dips and melodically forms into a Keltic mantra of some great beauty'[26] – only for it to disappear again quite suddenly and make way for atonal sonic experimentations and pulsating rhythms. In his essay that accompanied the re-release of the album in 2019, music critic Mike Barnes claims that this track consists of 'a strange eerie tone and there was an undulating serpentine flow to the melodies pitched somewhere between signalling and singing, its rhythmic complexity enhanced by the use of sequence and echo and delay'.[27] Fricke was said to have used an electronic soprano part, then tried to eliminate the electronic element with the help of filter effects in order to make the music sound more human though electronically generated. In hindsight, these ideas made Trülzsch recognise

[23] J Cope, *Krautrocksampler: One Head's Guide to the Great Kosmische Musik – 1968 Onwards* (Yatesbury: Head Heritage, 1996), p. 128.

[24] M Goodall, *Gathering of the Tribe: Music and Heavy Conscious Creation* (London: Headpress, 2012), p. 1.

[25] Bebergal, *Season of the Witch*, p. 189.   [26] Cope, *Krautrocksampler*, p. 128.

[27] M Barnes, The Song of Songs, *Prog* 99 (2019), pp. 89–91 (90).

the enormous complexity of the project, not least because it took a lot of time simply to permanently filter the sound to achieve the result the musicians had in mind.[28]

A New Path

Affenstunde represented a possible avenue to approach *kosmische Musik*, but strangely, Fricke himself was far from convinced. He understood something had to change and that the best way to achieve this would be to slowly move away from the dominance of the Moog. Popol Vuh's second album *In den Gärten Pharaos* – which quite fittingly appeared on Kaiser's Pilz label – only consists of two long pieces, each of them taking up one side of the original vinyl record. The title track recalls the electronic experiments on *Affenstunde*, but according to Trülzsch, the musical possibilities offered by the Moog to create the envisioned sacral sounds were exhausted at that point, not least because Fricke was none too tech-savvy and therefore had problems with electronic devices.[29]

Fricke's new objective was further emulation of the human voice by technical means, only to realise he had failed this task while still in the middle of recording the title track. He therefore decided to embark on an altogether new direction with the second track on the album simply called 'Vuh', which makes up the whole of B-side: 'It is all too obvious that one of the great meditational holy works has been captured on tape',[30] Cope boldly states. In fact, Fricke opted for an unconventional method: he recorded 'Vuh' with a church organ located in a former monastery in the Upper Bavarian village of Baumburg. The piece is based on a single chord, which is only slightly varied throughout the composition and augmented with restrained percussion work.

As the picture of a Bavarian alpine landscape on the gatefold sleeve of *Affenstunde* already indicated, Fricke certainly saw himself committed to a German cultural tradition and therefore (in the press notes to *In den Gärten Pharaos*) refers to the influence German poetry, classical music, and philosophy have had on him and his music, while at the same time distancing himself from his country's recent fascist past. So it comes as no surprise that, on this album in particular, Fricke acts out the conflict between his German and his international influences by embracing the upcoming electronic music scene and German classical music he had

---

[28] Ibid.   [29] Reetze, *Time & Sounds*, p. 309.   [30] Cope, *Krautrocksampler*, p. 129.

studied at conservatory while at the same time opening up to the more organic, archaic sounds of African and Indian instruments.[31]

At that time, Fricke already saw Popol Vuh as 'a group of people who make music, but are not a music group',[32] a factor that, according to Reetze, increasingly led to tensions among the musicians:

In a certain way, this statement shows that Fricke saw himself not so much as the leader of a band but as an individual working with other musicians under a project name. He undoubtedly saw the project Popol Vuh as his own.[33]

Despite Fricke playing his Moog on Tangerine Dream's *Zeit* (1972), the album that comes closest to attaining the vision of a *kosmische Musik* on record, he was determined to follow through with his own ideas on 'Vuh', and thus dispensed with the instrument he increasingly saw as an electronic shackle. Fricke sold it to another leading keyboard player in the Krautrock cosmos, Klaus Schulze. Fricke radically rejected the very notion of *kosmische Musik* and claimed that a 'more beautiful and honest way' would be to free your mind without the help of technology.

Over the years, music has increasingly become a form of prayer for me. With electronics you can first reach the depth, the unconscious, the timelessness of the human being more than with other natural sounds. I am aware of that, and it has fascinated me for a long time. These days, a more beautiful and honest way seems to me to purify and internalize oneself without technical aids and then to touch these spaces of darkness or light, the inner man, with simple, human music.[34]

For his next album *Hosianna Mantra*, Fricke makes use of acoustic instruments only and incorporates a true soprano with the Korean singer Djong Yun, rendering a very human element to his music. Years later, his widow Bettina von Waldthausen would explain Fricke's repudiation of the Moog by claiming that electronic sounds were in clear opposition to the natural beat of the human heart.[35] What was new for Fricke here was that he increasingly broke away from abstract structures and opened to pop music to continue his spiritual journey. He described his newfound creative process as follows:

The path to creation is like walking on a small path. It begins without intention, purposeless, yet a goal arises. I say YES and approach the goal. I forget it again, but

---

[31] U Adelt, *Krautrock: German Music in the Seventies* (Ann Arbor: University of Michigan Press, 2016), p. 107.

[32] N Odorinsky, Popol Vuh: In den Gärten Pharaos, in J Legath (ed.), *Sounds*, p. 294.

[33] Reetze, *Times & Sounds*, p. 309.

[34] Langhans, Musik ist für mich eine Form des Gebets, p. 36.

[35] Bebergal, *Season of the Witch*, p. 19.

the goal starts to be more and more alive in me and I move steadily towards it, to receive it. It is me, who is moving. This is my collaboration, my devotion, which fills my person totally with an undivided attention. And I feel the power within, focused on the goal. This is the path to a small path.[36]

Fricke saw himself as a representative of an anti-capitalist, universalist, and anti-consumerist variant of Christianity, which he pays homage to on *Hosianna Mantra*. This title already gives an indication of Fricke's conception of a non-denominational form of Christianity by combining Christian and Hindu terminology. Music had become his very own form of prayer;[37] by cutting his ties to electronic music,[38] Fricke aimed to achieve immediate access to his own spirituality. Unlike many of his contemporaries, he did not claim to possess inner wisdom relating to Eastern religions. Rather, Fricke aimed to understand Eastern spiritual essence through his own Christian culture, as expressed through the album's title.[39]

The Cinematographic View

Thanks to their rewarding co-operation with German director Werner Herzog, Popol Vuh succeeded not only in making their music known to a larger audience, but also, more importantly, in enhancing their spiritual vision through the association with Herzog's grandiose visual aesthetics. Fricke had met Herzog in 1967 and made a short appearance as a piano player in Herzog's debut *Lebenszeichen*, which was released in 1968. They stayed in contact, so Popol Vuh were approached to do the soundtrack of Herzog's Amazonian adventure film *Aguirre* in 1971, starring Klaus Kinski in the leading role. The soundtrack, however, would not be released until 1975.

Herzog's approach was to wait for the audio track to complement the visual experience, so that the full effect was only ignited by the intermedial connection of image and sound. The director once explained[40] that there is no such thing as 'background music' in any of his films as they constituted a synthesis of images and music. For a long time, Popol Vuh were responsible for soundtracking the films of the internationally acclaimed German director and one of the main protagonists of the New German Cinema

---

[36] Mulder, Liner Notes, p. 2.   [37] Adelt, *Krautrock*, p. 108.

[38] Adelt points out somewhat sarcastically that the loosening of the electronic fetters did not imply modern recording technology, especially the use of microphones, in the recording studio. Adelt, *Krautrock*, p. 108.

[39] Langhans, Musik ist für mich eine Form des Gebets, p. 36.   [40] Adelt, *Krautrock*, p. 113.

movement in the 1970s (which comprised such directors as Edgar Reitz, Wim Wenders, and Alexander Kluge). Fricke worked with Herzog on *Aguirre, der Zorn Gottes* (1972), *Herz aus Glas* (1976), *Nosferatu, Phantom der Nacht* (1979), and *Fitzcarraldo* (1982) as well as on two documentaries. Later, Herzog used some of Fricke's compositions for parts of his soundtracks. *Cobra Verde* (1987) was completely soundtracked again with Popol Vuh's music.

The director described his relationship with Fricke's music as follows:

Popol Vuh is a stroke of luck for me because there is always something hidden in the images themselves, which lies and slumbers deep in the darkness of our soul and is made visible through the music of Florian Fricke. That is, the images suddenly have a completely new and unique and strange quality. There is something puzzling about this music.[41]

It is particularly the fusion of sound and image in *Aguirre* that illustrates Fricke's own spiritual quest. In the film's opening scene, a long shot shows hundreds of people painfully descending a narrow mountain trail in the blurred Andes. The accompanying music is reminiscent of a religious chorale – a celestial, exhilarating aural setting, which at the same time carries a reminder of the actual agony dominating the scene. This effect is due to the way Fricke created the chorale: what we hear are not actual human voices but electronic emulations that range between the human voice and synthetic sounds. To achieve this effect, the musician used a 'choir organ', an instrument reminiscent of a Mellotron, in which pre-produced tape loops were played or called up via a keyboard, and thus conjured up sounds and choirs.[42] The camera moves closer to the people who seem to be in harmony with the music consisting of otherworldly sounds, taking on a godlike perspective of the mountain. Then, however, the camera descends from its bird's eye position to reveal a series of shocking close-ups, showing the immense suffering on the faces of the expeditioners and their porters. The soundscape can be seen as a harbinger of the catastrophes that will haunt the expedition as its leader Aguirre gradually descends into madness and drives his companions ever deeper into the Amazonian jungle and thus into the very heart of darkness.

The overwhelming elemental force of nature that Herzog is trying to depict in his film is staged in an impressive way by merging long shots and the soundtrack. The naturalistic focus on the faces of suffering people,

---

[41] Simmeth, *Krautrock Transnational*, p. 77.
[42] G Augustin, *Der Pate des Krautrock* (Berlin: Bosworth, 2005), p. 236.

meanwhile, reveals an uncanny connection between man and nature that reaches its full effect only with the help of the soundtrack. Adelt points out that the circularity of the main chorale theme underscores the central character's lack of progress and is in turn supported by the camera moving in circles around Aguirre at the end of the film.[43] But the music not only reflects the disturbed psyche of the figure, but also the simultaneously sublime and oppressive soundtrack. As Herzog stated in an interview in the 1970s:

[The music] can reveal qualities and characteristics and rhythms in images, especially in the movie theatre, which would otherwise never come across. For example, when I filmed the jungle in *Aguirre*, then the jungle is first of all a landscape. Thanks to Popol Vuh's music, this landscape suddenly becomes something different. It becomes, so to speak, a quality of the soul, a human quality.[44]

David Stubbs even sees a deliberate contradiction between Fricke's music, which 'aspires cleanly heavenward',[45] and the fate of Herzog's hero, who embarks on a quite literal descent. This paradox will be repeated in their later co-operation on *Fitzcarraldo*, which features yet another anti-hero played by Klaus Kinski, once more fighting his fate accompanied by the spiritual sounds of Popol Vuh.

Many of the celestial sounds on Popol Vuh's recordings, especially on the soundtracks for Herzog, were accomplished with the 'choir organ', a custom-made instrument Fricke commissioned in the 1970s, based on the then popular Mellotron but able to produce sounds that came closer to Fricke's spiritual vision. It is not clear where exactly this instrument was made and where it ended up, although it can be heard on several other Krautrock albums such as *Tanz der Lemminge* (*Dance of the Lemmings*, 1971) by Amon Düül II. In 2019, Frank Fiedler describes this extraordinary instrument:

Unfortunately, we never took a photo – today it would look crazy. It was 60 or 80 tape loops with a keyboard; two big plywood boxes with all of his machinery in it, and it was very noisy when it was running because of its electric motors. We had to use speakers so you could hear the music over the noise.[46]

Though *Aguirre*, their first collaboration, might at the same time be seen as the pinnacle of their work together, Herzog and Fricke collaborated on

---

[43] Adelt, *Krautrock*, p. 116.   [44] Simmeth, *Krautrock Transnational*, p. 77.

[45] Stubbs, *Future Days*, p. 367.

[46] F Fiedler, Q&A: Florian Fricke's former collaborator Frank Fiedler talks to Uncut, *Uncut* 265 (2019), p. 41.

most of the films made with Klaus Kinski in the leading role, namely *Nosferatu, Fitzcarraldo,* and *Cobra Verde.* The soundtrack to *Nosferatu* was even released as a regular Popol Vuh album entitled *Brüder des Schattens – Söhne des Lichts* (*Brothers of Shadow – Sons of Light,* 1978).

But Herzog and Fricke fell out after their last collaboration, for reasons the director cited years later as follows: 'He was always too much into drugs, which I never liked ... Secondly, he drifted away into his idiotic, new-age-pseudo-philosophy babble, and I could not really communicate with him.'[47] These complaints, however, did not come only from Herzog. It can be argued that Popol Vuh's reputation has long suffered from Fricke's later musical attempts.

The Later Years: Celestial Music and New Age

Nevertheless, Popol Vuh's collaboration with Werner Herzog for his 1982 film *Fitzcarraldo,* now regarded a cinematic classic, marks a turning point in Fricke's work because the experience saw him turn into a filmmaker himself. Fricke understood his films made with long-term creative partner turned cameraman Frank Fiedler as a continuation and an extension of his spiritual search. They created the films during their travels that took both men to different regions of the world, with Fricke eagerly enriching Fiedler's images with his music as he had learned from his work with Herzog. This can be most impressively seen in the CD/DVD-Edition of *Kailash – Pilgrimage to the Throne of the Gods* (2015), released fourteen years after Fricke's death and showing their journey to Tibet. Equally impressive was *Messa di Orfeo,* a multimedia performance premiered in the labyrinth of Molfetta/Italy in 1998, the music being issued on CD in 1999.

Fricke continued to record albums under the Popol Vuh moniker until his untimely death in 2001, albeit at considerable intervals and sometimes, as Herzog pointed out, dangerously close to the popular New Age movement in the 1980s and 1990s. According to Reetze, he had turned into an alcoholic, and following his divorce from Bettina von Waldthausen had begun the life of a recluse.[48] A large-scale reissue campaign of his work on CD, started in 2004 by SPV Recordings, brought Popol Vuh's albums not only back into record stores but also into the public eye. A vinyl boxset

---

[47] J Wirth, Popol Vuh: The Essential Album Collection Volume 1, *Uncut 265* (2019), p. 38.
[48] Reetze, *Times & Sounds,* pp. 311–12.

released in 2019 called *The Essential Album Collection Vol. 1*, containing five albums from the early days, was not only enthusiastically received by music critics but also led to a series of feature stories on the band's history. A second box set with four LPs was released in November 2021 under the name *Vol. 2: Acoustic and Ambient Spheres*.

In his liner notes to *The Essential Album Collection Vol. 1*, Dolf Mulder praises Fricke's music as visionary, consisting of 'many styles and influences such as electronica, ambient, progressive rock and music of the eastern tradition. They were musical pre-cursors in many ways: ambient, trance, electronica, ethno-fusion, psychedelic-rock, raga-rock.'[49] His role within the Krautrock community – if one can speak of this at all – was always that of an outsider who wanted to go his own, spiritual way. Still, Popol Vuh is a musical project that – also in an intermedial context – can be seen as symptomatic of a certain strand of development in the 1970s and 1980s. Born out of the electronic pioneering spirit of Krautrock, Fricke soon sought new paths and broke away from what he saw as technological shackles.

The connection to Werner Herzog is by no means a coincidence, as the filmmakers of the 'New German Cinema' were looking for new forms of subjective expression. Although this was based on the ideals of the 1968 movement, it said goodbye to the idealisation of the collective that both Krautrock bands like Amon Düül and political rock groups like Ton Steine Scherben claimed for themselves. For Fricke, the path to the inwardness he envisaged led via his own, individually composed form of global spirituality. This connects him not only with Herzog, but also with authors such as Peter Handke or Hubert Fichte, as well as with that literary movement that is somewhat generalised under the term *Neue Innerlichkeit* (new inwardness). The music that emerged from this was quite hermetic in its approach but opened to the listener when he or she was ready to engage in the spiritual journey that Fricke envisaged.

It is therefore possible that Fricke's development towards New Age realms in the 1980s can be explained by disillusionment with the perception of his work, since New Age can generally be seen as a commercial decline of the spiritual. For although Popol Vuh's music sounds unique even in a Krautrock context, it never – even retrospectively – gained the recognition of a wider audience. And without the collaborations with Herzog, Fricke and his music would possibly only be a footnote in German rock history.

---

[49] Mulder, Liner Notes, p. 3.

Essential Listening

Popol Vuh, *Affenstunde* (Liberty, 1970)
Popol Vuh, *In den Gärten Pharaos* (Pilz, 1972)
Popol Vuh, *Hosianna Mantra* (Pilz, 1973)
Popol Vuh, *Aguirre* (PDU, 1975)

13 | Ash Ra Tempel, Manuel Göttsching, and Klaus Schulze

PERTTI GRÖNHOLM

Ash Ra Tempel represent an archetypal *kosmische Musik* and psychedelic rock group, an ensemble who became strongly associated with the desire for musical experimentation and detachment from the Anglo-American rock of the 1960s. The original band and later solo projects have gained a cult following over five decades. Their music has inspired musicians in space rock as well as electronic ambient, techno, and trance. This chapter focuses on the original line-up of the band Ash Ra Tempel (1970–73), and Ashra, who have continued their legacy. In addition, the essay offers an overview of the solo production and collaborations of two founding members of the band, Manuel Göttsching and Klaus Schulze (1947–2022).

Manuel Göttsching, who studied classical guitar for years as a youngster,[1] grew up with rock music in the late 1960s, listening to Jimi Hendrix and Eric Clapton. With his friend Hartmut Enke (1952–2005), Göttsching played in various school bands, later the Steeple Chase Blues Band, which was inspired by blues but played more 'free' self-expression and psychedelic rock.[2]

In 1969–70, a Swiss composer, Thomas Kessler, who had his own electronic music studio in Berlin, mentored Göttsching. Beat Studio was located on Pfalzburger Strasse, in the premises of a publicly funded music school. From Kessler, Göttsching received both a spark for electronic music and the basic skills of improvising and composing.

Another musician who wished to escape from Anglo-American formulas was Klaus Schulze, who had played drums in several rock bands in the late 1960s. The most notable of these was Tangerine Dream, in whose early line-up Schulze played until summer 1970, then joining

---

[1] T Gatward, The Story of E2–E4: Manuel Göttsching's Accidental Masterpiece, *Loud and Quiet* 6 (2019), www.loudandquiet.com/interview/the-story-of-e2-e4-manuel-gottschings-accidental-masterpiece.

[2] T Baumgärtel, Ganz simpel, *Tageszeitung* (12 December 2006); D Stubbs, *Future Sounds: Krautrock and the Building of Modern Germany* (London: Faber, 2014), p. 297; C Wheeldon, *Deep Distance: The Musical Life of Manuel Göttsching* (King's Lynn: Waveform, 2015), p. 5.

Ash Ra Tempel. Like Göttsching, Schulze was also interested in electronics, sound manipulation, and recording.[3]

Kessler's guidance strongly affected the emergence of the 'Berlin School'.[4] Although Kessler was not so enthusiastic about the bands' aspirations to abandon the idea of composition, he continued channelling the musicians' youthful energies. By autumn 1970, Ash Ra Tempel had already existed for three months, and Göttsching and Schulze joined the live sessions of Eruption, formed by Conrad Schnitzler and Klaus Freudigmann. The experience gave them extra confidence since Eruption's goal was to create music completely free of the hierarchies and conventions of existing styles.[5]

Already in summer 1970, Enke had travelled to London to look for inexpensive used music equipment that was hard to find in Germany. He returned to Berlin with four large WEM amplifiers, which had been touring with Pink Floyd. Only the wealthiest bands and biggest festivals in Britain used similar cabinets. Schulze, who had just parted from Tangerine Dream, saw the towering amplifier set in the Beat Studio and suggested to Enke and Göttsching that they should form a band with him. Two weeks later, the band played their first gig.[6] Enke and Göttsching were only seventeen at the time.

Göttsching (guitar), Schulze (drums), and Enke (bass) formed a trio with the outlandish name Ash Ra Tempel, which translates as 'the remnants of the temple of Ra' (the sun god in ancient Egyptian mythology). The group positioned themselves in the emerging scene of new German rock as a band of psychedelia and experimental music. According to Göttsching, the activities of the band were intensive, creative, and free, but rather unprofessional.[7]

In the latter half of the 1970s, Ash Ra Tempel performed regularly in Berlin, two or three times a week. The band gained a reputation as musicians who were able to improvise in front of an audience for several hours, communicating with each other only through their instruments.[8] In

---

[3] Stubbs, *Future Sounds*, pp. 297, 399; Wheeldon, *Deep Distance*, p. 5.

[4] J Reetze, *Times & Sounds: Germany's Journey from Jazz and Pop to Krautrock and Beyond* (Bremen: Halvmall, 2020), pp. 250–1.

[5] Stubbs, *Future Sounds*, p. 291.

[6] R Barry, Everything Was in the Moment: An Interview with Manuel Göttsching, *The Quietus* (7 March 2017), www.thequietus.com/articles/21928-manuel-gottsching-interview-ash-ra-tempel-e2-e4.

[7] Red Bull Music Academy [RBMA], Manuel Göttsching Talks Ash Ra Tempel and E2–E4, YouTube video (17 September 2018), www.youtube.com/watch?v=wqVxw7x1urg, 22:20–25:10.

[8] Wheeldon, *Deep Distance*, p. 7; Barry, Everything was in the moment; Gatward, The Story of E2–E4.

Illustration 13.1　Hartmut Enke, Manuel Göttsching, and Klaus Schulze of Ash Ra Tempel, 1971. © MG.ART Archive.

addition, they played at exceptionally high volume. According to Göttsching, the performances of Ash Ra Tempel were always long – from forty-five minutes to three hours – and purely improvisational. The only thing the members agreed on in advance was who would start playing. The band performed in restaurants as well as at community centres, galleries, and the Academy of Arts: 'The audience liked that. We didn't have any big advertisements, word got around. Perhaps the actual music was not that important at our first concerts. There were a lot of people and something happened, that's why you went there.'[9]

Entering the Empire of Kaiser

Overall, the music circles in Berlin were remarkably informal; jazz and rock musicians as well as experimental sound artists met and formed short-lived gig ensembles.[10] In his subsequent interviews, Göttsching has emphasised that from the beginning, Ash Ra Tempel were one of the bands who tried to

[9] Baumgärtel, Ganz simpel; compare also Barry, Everything Was in the Moment.
[10] Stubbs, *Future Sounds*, pp. 299–300.

get rid of the influence of Anglo-American blues structures and create new sounds and music.[11]

With the help of label manager Rolf-Ulrich Kaiser, who was seeking out new bands in Berlin, Ash Ra Tempel were able to record their debut album for the Ohr label, founded in 1970 by Kaiser.[12] In early 1971, after overcoming many obstacles, sound engineer Konrad 'Conny' Plank helped Ash Ra Tempel in a recording studio in Hamburg. Göttsching remembers that Plank was very excited and proposed all sorts of technical experiments.[13]

The self-titled *Ash Ra Tempel* album, released in June 1971, consisted of two improvised instrumental tracks.[14] Both 'Amboss' (Anvil) and 'Traummaschine' (Dream Machine) are intense but distinct works that transport the listener into the post-rock world. 'Amboss' progresses with Schulze's hectic rhythm and Göttsching's guitar playing, which distances the listener from rock and blues conventions. 'Traummaschine' is a twenty-five-minute jam that initially pulsates very softly, soothing the listener with gentle sounds and the ethereal vocals of Göttsching. After that, the trio cautiously wake up the listener while the rhythm becomes stronger. Supported by bongos and bass, the rhythm finally reaches a timeless cosmic sphere. Plank managed to create a strong sense of space for the whole album. Inspired by ancient Egyptian culture, the cover art of the LP's very special folded front cover attracted attention.

Ash Ra Tempel continued playing to full venues in Berlin and elsewhere. The band also toured in Switzerland.[15] Their performances were much more intense than the studio sessions, as can be heard in a few surviving concert recordings from summer 1971, which Göttsching released in the 1990s. They used to immerse themselves in extended improvisations, based on Schulze's fast drumming and Enke's distorted bass-playing. On top of those, Göttsching played solos, roaring feedback, and rhythmic parts with the help of delay effects.[16] Schulze left Ash Ra Tempel right after the Swiss Tour in September 1971 and was replaced by drummer Wolfgang Müller. In interviews, Schulze stated that he would rather create music than play as a member of a band. However, his relationship with the other members remained close.[17]

Ash Ra Tempel's second album *Schwingungen* (1972) was recorded with a different line-up. Wolfgang Müller, a partner of Göttsching and Enke

[11] Ibid., 2014, p. 399; Wheeldon, *Deep Distance*, p. 8.
[12] For more on Ohr and Kaiser, compare Reetze, *Times & Sounds*, pp. 267–86.
[13] Wheeldon, *Deep Distance*, p. 9; RBMA, Manuel Göttsching Talks, 20:20–22:30.
[14] Gatward, The Story of E2–E4.   [15] Wheeldon, *Deep Distance*, p. 12.   [16] Ibid., p. 11.
[17] Ibid., p. 12.

from the Steeple Chase Blues Band, joined the core group on drums and percussion. The change is particularly noticeable in the album's first track, 'Light: Look at Your Sun', which introduced Manfred Peter Brück (a.k.a. John L.) as a guest vocalist. He was a former member of Agitation Free and a famous figure in the rock circles of Berlin. 'Darkness: Flowers Must Die' takes the listener into psychedelic despair and aggression, where both Göttsching's guitar and John L.'s roaring vocals are processed with a heavy phaser effect. Additional guest musicians Matthias Wehler (saxophones) and Uli Popp (bongos) bring fresh overtones to an increasingly chaotic song.

The B-side of the album is very different. The seamlessly segued songs 'Suche' (Search) and 'Liebe' (Love) fill the entire side with cosmic ambiance. 'Suche' begins with Müller's low-key vibraphone. Gradually rising from the background, Göttsching's organ and guitar complement the band's gauze-like weaving, slightly reminiscent of 'Traummaschine'. The ethereal atmosphere is broken by Müller's drum beat, which rises from the distance in the front, restlessly wandering and then fading again. Göttsching's occasional glissandos on guitar and his whining organ, as well as Müller's cymbals, suggest an ascent such as in 'Traummaschine', but the album ends with a melodic ballad flavoured by Göttsching's wordless singing and Müller's cymbals. Kaiser's trusted engineer Dieter Dierks[18] recorded the album.

Psychedelic Encounters and Collaborations

In 1972, Kaiser and his partner Gerlinde 'Gille' Lettmann commercialised the concept of *kosmische Musik* and associated it with German electronic rock. The concept smoothly mixed the escapism and esotericism of psychedelic rock with the dreams of the space age, science fiction, and the soundscapes of electronic music. In particular, Ash Ra Tempel, Klaus Schulze and Popul Vuh, Wallenstein, and Mythos were labelled as cosmic music, through the marketing efforts of Ohr.[19]

According to Harald Grosskopf, a drummer from Wallenstein who later played with both Göttsching and Schulze, the musicians involved in Kaiser's projects were people who, instead of radical political activism, chose to withdraw from society and focus instead on philosophy, drugs,

---

[18] On Dierks, compare Reetze, *Times & Sounds*, pp. 256–8.
[19] Stubbs, *Future Sounds*, pp. 373–5.

and esotericism.[20] Hence, it was not a big surprise that in 1972, Ash Ra Tempel ended up in one of the most peculiar ventures in the history of German rock.

The band had dreamed of collaborating with Allen Ginsberg, but their attempts at establishing contact had not succeeded.[21] In 1972, Timothy Leary, a former professor of psychology at Harvard University and an evangelist for LSD, had ended up in Switzerland after escaping from prison in the United States. He had to hide and change his whereabouts to remain free, but he received help from the Swiss author and esotericist Sergius Golowin. Leary's travelling companion included the British writer Brian Barritt, who considered himself a forerunner of the psychedelic counterculture.[22]

Enke travelled to Switzerland to give Leary and Barritt the album *Schwingungen*. Neither of them knew of the band before, but they considered the music appropriate to advance their agenda and outlined the concept of the release with Enke. The goal was an album built on Leary's theory of the seven steps of consciousness. Leary felt that Ash Ra Tempel could produce an appropriate soundtrack for his lyrics. Klaus D. Müller, the road manager of Ash Ra Tempel and a later collaborator with Göttsching, recalled that throughout the recording project, everything but the music was chaotic. A wide variety of people gathered around Leary and Barritt, and drug-driven parties and general unrest disrupted the project. Neither Leary nor Kaiser knew how the album would be structured and produced. At some point, Edgar Froese made an offer to Kaiser to step in for Ash Ra Tempel.[23]

However, Göttsching and Enke had ideas about the music and their own role. With the help of Dierks, they managed to finish the recordings in three days at the Sinus Studio in Bern. Appropriately titled *Seven-Up*, the album featured various guest musicians. Micki Duwe took the lead vocals. Göttsching and Enke created the songs on A-side ('Space') in response to Leary's recitations, but gradually the players got a grip, and the B-side of the album ('Time') sounds like the more familiar Ash Ra Tempel.[24] According to Göttsching, Leary was initially only supposed to write the text and recite a little on tape, but eventually he emerged as the leading vocalist.[25]

[20] K Breznikar, Harald Grosskopf Interview, *It's Psychedelic Baby Magazine* (28 December 2013), www.psychedelicbabymag.com/2013/12/harald-grosskopf-interview.html/.

[21] Wheeldon, *Deep Distance*, 15; RBMA, Manuel Göttsching Talks, 30:00–31:00.

[22] Stubbs, *Future Sounds*, pp. 381–3; Wheeldon, *Deep Distance*, p. 15.

[23] Email from Manuel Göttsching (30 November 2021).

[24] Stubbs, *Future Sounds*, pp. 384–7. Compare also Reetze, *Times & Sounds*, pp. 276–7.

[25] Wheeldon, *Deep Distance*, pp. 17–18; RBMA, Manuel Göttsching Talks, 37:15–37:35.

At his studio near Cologne, Dierks mixed in some new instrument and vocal parts with various session musicians and singers and added electronic effects. Göttsching and Enke, along with lead vocalist Duwe, finalised the album with the help of several session musicians. In the end, as many as thirteen musicians and singers appeared on the album.[26] Released in 1973 under the Kosmische Kuriere sub-label, *Seven-Up* gained a reputation as a somewhat failed project the ideas of which looked better on paper than the music actually sounded. Furthermore, Leary's desire to harness rock music as a vehicle of the LSD revolution, as was to be expected, did not lead to a societal breakthrough.[27]

Reunion, the End of the Original Line-Up, and Schulze Solo

In 1972, Göttsching, Schulze, and Enke also became involved in Kaiser's second collaborative project, where they, along with other musicians including Schulze, made music for Walter Wegmüller's *Tarot* (1973) album. The Swiss-born artist drew inspiration from Tarot cards, and the album contained plenty of spoken words.[28] Released in 1973, *Tarot* remains Wegmüller's only album, and many commentators, such as Julian Cope and David Stubbs, have valued its jam sessions.[29]

Ash Ra Tempel's fourth album, *Join Inn*, was released in 1973 and grew out of the hazy sessions of *Tarot*. Schulze played not only the drums but brought also his Farfisa organ and EMS Synthi A synthesiser to the studio. The album again consisted of a pair of long tracks. 'Freak and Roll' begins with wild jamming. Schulze's hyperactive drumbeat is both dynamic and precise. Göttsching's guitar moves seamlessly from blues solos to ethereal moods. Enke's bass mourns mostly in the lowest register. Electronic glissandos and noises from the synthesiser pop up here and there.

The contrast with the song 'Jenseits' (Beyond) on the first side is enormous. The band take listeners into a dream space filled with vibrating guitar, organ, and synthesiser sounds, all coloured with tremolo, wah-wah, phaser, and delay effects. Enke joins the sonic landscaping with very slow

---

[26] Wheeldon, *Deep Distance*, pp. 17–18.

[27] J Cope, *Krautrocksampler: One Head's Guide to the Great Kosmische Music – 1968 Onwards* (Yatesbury: Head Heritage, 1996), pp. 75–6; Stubbs, *Future Sounds*, p. 388, Wheeldon, *Deep Distance*, p. 19; J Littlejohn, Krautrock: The Development of the Movement, in U Schütte (ed.), *German Pop Music: A Companion* (Berlin: De Gruyter, 2017), pp. 63–84 (73).

[28] Wheeldon, *Deep Distance*, pp. 21–2.

[29] Cope, *Krautrocksampler*, pp. 80–2; Stubbs, *Future Sounds*, pp. 398–9.

bass patterns. On top of it all, Rosi Müller, Göttsching's partner and muse at the time, slowly recites her text: 'Let us dance on the wet grass. Look at me, please. Do you believe in peace? Sometimes it is so incredibly beautiful. Take me with you. Far away, you hear? The road is so long. Do you know the way – a little?'[30] *Join Inn* epitomises both sides of Ash Ra Tempel, with psychedelic visions and distressing bursts of energy, as well as serene sound spaces that invite the listener's own imagination and emotions.

In February 1973, Ash Ra Tempel performed three concerts in West Germany and France. At these concerts, Schulze's synthesisers seasoned the overall sound of the band and Göttsching's playing was more sophisticated than earlier.[31] However, these concerts also marked the end of the original line-up. In the middle of the last concert in Cologne, Enke gave up his bass guitar and sat down on the edge of the stage. Afterwards, Enke stated: 'Yeah, the music you played was just so beautiful I didn't know what to play. I preferred listen to it.'[32] Troubled by many personal problems, Enke resigned from Ash Ra Tempel and never played again. He died in 2005 at the age of fifty-three.[33]

Klaus Schulze embarked on a solo career at about the same time. His solo works allowed him to transcend the role of a drummer in a way that set free his creativity, which was not quite possible in his former bands.[34] *Irrlicht: Quadrophonische Symphonie für Orchester und E-Maschinen (Will-o'-the-Wisp: Quadrophonic Symphony for Orchestra and E-Machines*, 1972) is a dark pseudo-classical album, populated by treated orchestral recordings, organ sounds, and electronic droning. His music is both restless and static and manages to escape the conventions of musical time. *Irrlicht* somewhat approaches to Tangerine Dream's *Zeit* (1972) but is even more alienating. *Cyborg* (1973) is perhaps his most radical work. It introduces the EMS VCS 3 synthesiser, which Schulze elaborates on intensively, creating soundscapes and pulses. *Cyborg*, which takes up the man-machine trope later to be developed by Kraftwerk, consists of four tracks, all exceeding twenty minutes in length. As in *Irrlicht*, the strongly meditative organ parts and the orchestral sections create a strong sense of murky cosmic ambience.[35]

In these two albums, Schulze's distinctive musical qualities began to take shape. Both build on soundscapes and moods created at the mixing desk. Obtrusive electronic sounds and a mysterious atmosphere distinguish

---

[30] Wheeldon, *Deep Distance*, p. 24. Müller later collaborated with Claudia Skoda in the Dominas project.
[31] Ibid., pp. 24–6.   [32] Ibid., p. 26.   [33] Stubbs, *Future Sounds*, p. 394.   [34] Ibid., pp. 298–9.
[35] For more, compare Littlejohn, Krautrock, p. 74.

Schulze's early releases from the later ambient. Carefully created panning, delays, and echoes build Schulze's space in an exceptionally vivid manner for the time. However, his early records still strongly divide opinions among his fans; some see them as experimental masterpieces, while others find them too extreme and challenging.

Cosmic Superfluity and the Departure from Ohr

In spring 1973, Schulze and Göttsching took part in recording sessions organised by Kaiser and Lettmann. The all-night, drug-driven jam sessions produced about sixty hours of recorded music for the future releases of the Kosmische Kuriere sub-label.[36] In 1972, Kaiser had run into trouble with his early Ohr partners, Bruno Wendel and Günter Körber, who, after leaving the company, had formed a competing record label, Brain Records. Kaiser and Lettmann sought to raise the profile of their releases with glaring slogans and marketing, merging psychedelia and LSD culture into music. Schulze and Tangerine Dream's Edgar Froese especially disliked Kaiser's marketing style.[37]

Despite that, Schulze and Göttsching, and a few other musicians, such as Wallenstein's Grosskopf and Jürgen Dollase, surrendered their jam sessions to Ohr. In 1974, Kaiser and Lettmann released some parts of the sessions on a series of albums entitled *Cosmic Jokers, Galactic Supermarket, Planeten Sit In*, and *Sci-Fi Party*.[38] After Kaiser edited the session tapes to a proper length, Lettmann added her own vocal parts to some of the songs. Despite receiving monetary compensation for the sales, many of the musicians, and Schulze in particular, protested against Kaiser and Lettmann's arbitrary actions.[39] Flamboyant words and sci-fi tropes became a routine in the marketing. For example: 'The time ship floats through the Galaxy of Joy. In the sounds of electronics. In the flashes of light. Here you will discover Science Fiction, the planet of COSMIC JOKERS, the GALACTIC SUPERMARKET and the SCI FI PARTY: That is the new sound, Space. Telepathy. Melodies, Joy.'[40]

Such verbally overbearing marketing of Ash Ra Tempel's music put the band in a strange light. Even their musician friends began to worry. For

---

[36] Wheeldon, *Deep Distance*, pp. 26–7; Reetze, *Times & Sounds*, p. 275.

[37] Stubbs, *Future Sounds*, p. 389; Wheeldon, *Deep Distance*, p. 27; Reetze, *Times & Sounds*, pp. 275–6.

[38] For more on these albums, compare Wheeldon, *Deep Distance*, pp. 31–4; Reetze, *Times & Sounds*, pp. 281–3.

[39] Stubbs, *Future Sounds*, pp. 390–2; Wheeldon, *Deep Distance*, p. 27.

[40] Stubbs, *Future Sounds*, p. 390.

Illustration 13.2 Manuel Göttsching, 1973. © MG.ART, Photo: Marcel Fugère.

example, Froese thought Ash Ra Tempel lived 'in a dream world': 'They think that everything will turn out okay, that the explosion of consciousness will conquer the world and all the problems will solve themselves.'[41] Göttsching had no problems with Kaiser, but he did not appreciate the idea about the mind-expanding effect of musical awareness, while Enke kept tirelessly explaining the matter to outsiders. Later, Göttsching associated the talk about a higher consciousness as part of the West German music culture of the early 1970s, where all rock music had to have some political content or social purpose. Göttsching himself just wanted to play his guitar.[42] Eventually, he also began to disassociate himself from the influence of Kaiser and Lettmann.

The Final Band Album and Innovations with Tape Machines

The last Ash Ra Tempel album on Ohr was *Starring Rosi* (1973). Featuring Göttsching on vocals, guitars, bass, mellotron, synthesiser, electric piano, and congas and Rosi Müller on vocals, speech, vibraphone, and concert

[41] Ibid., pp. 392–3, 395; Wheeldon, *Deep Distance*, p. 28.
[42] RBMA, Manuel Göttsching Talks, 22:30–23:00.

harp, the album also featured Grosskopf on drums. In addition, Dierks played bass and percussion on a few tracks. This relaxed-sounding album is closer to New Age-inspired folk rock and light progressive rock than the band's previous recordings.[43]

In 1974, Kaiser's cosmic empire was collapsing because of debts, lawsuits, and the departure of bands. Göttsching's first solo album, *Inventions for Electric Guitar* (1975), remains one of the last releases by Ohr, which initially marketed the album as Ash Ra Tempel's sixth album.[44] Later, it was re-released as Göttsching's solo album. He recorded the album at home using only his electric guitar, a few pedals, and two open-reel tape recorders. The tape machine became a revolutionary musical instrument for Göttsching; with a two-track recorder and a guitar, he could create rhythmic delays, while a four-tracker captured his playing one track at a time.[45] This is how Göttsching made use of the skills of tape manipulation that he had learned from Kessler. Pulsating guitar playing and harmonious interaction of melodies layered on top of the rhythmic parts revealed the inspiration Göttsching took from minimalist composers, especially Steve Reich and Terry Riley.[46]

Filling the entire A-side of the album, the track 'Echo Waves' is quite experimental with its rhythmic patterns and panning guitars. Still, it is unobtrusively captivating. The only guitar part that is classifiable as a proper solo only emerges at the end of a nearly eighteen-minute piece. The second track, 'Quasarsphere', is a subtle, melodic recollection of the early years of Ash Ra Tempel. On the B-side, 'Pluralis' weaves a swinging, discreetly evolving pattern of delayed rhythm guitars. The album features many of the elements upon which Göttsching has created music, especially in his solo career. These elements include repetitive patterns and theme variations, as well as melodic and rhythmic loops.[47]

In December 1974, Göttsching and guitarist-keyboardist Lutz 'Lüül' Ulbrich from Agitation Free began to perform together as Ash Ra Tempel. In 1975, the duo played in West Germany, France, and Britain to audiences of up to several thousand people.[48] Especially in France, the band was still very popular. Contrary to *Starring Rosi*, the music of these concerts sprouted from the band's earlier style. This especially applies to the songs that Göttsching and Ulbrich composed for the soundtrack of Philippe Garrel's *Le berceau de Cristal* (*The Crystal Cradle*, 1976), a French

---

[43] For more, compare Wheeldon, *Deep Distance*, pp. 36–7.   [44] Ibid., p. 29.
[45] Ibid., p. 40; RBMA, Manuel Göttsching Talks, 43:00–50:00.
[46] Wheeldon, *Deep Distance*, p. 45.   [47] Baumgärtel, Ganz simpel.
[48] Wheeldon, *Deep Distance*, pp. 46–9.

experimental film that featured Nico, Dominique Sanda, and Anita Pallenberg.[49]

The base of the soundtrack consisted of ethereal guitar patterns that cruise between organ and synthesiser sounds, sometimes merging into a harmonic aural environment. The overall sound is rather electronic, as the duo also played guitar synthesiser and a programmable rhythm machine. The film music remarkably resembles the style that Göttsching, Ulbrich, and Grosskopf adopted later in Ashra. The recording was issued only in 1993 as an Ash Ra Tempel release.

The Electronic Minimalism of Ashra

From 1974 onwards, the music of both Göttsching and Schulze is impossible to associate with the Krautrock of the early 1970s. Both artists moved further away from psychedelic rock and found inspiration in synthesisers and various genres of music. However, if we understand Krautrock not as a style category but rather as a quest for new means of expression, the same desire to experiment and discover still drove both musicians in the latter part of the decade.

Göttsching continued making music at his Berlin-based Studio Roma and began collecting ARP, Moog, and EMS synthesisers and sequencers. His first distinctively electronic album was *New Age of Earth*, released by French label Isadora in 1976. For this album, Göttsching played all synthesiser parts by hand.[50] However, at his 1976 solo concerts in France, he performed with pre-programmed sequencers and synthesisers.[51] The initial release was credited to Ash Ra Tempel, but after Göttsching obtained a record deal with Virgin in 1977, he shortened the band name to Ashra to avoid confusion. The new moniker was intended to serve all future projects, both solo and band efforts.

New Age of Earth and the following *Blackouts* (1977) were both solo albums, but for *Correlations* (1979) and *Belle Alliance* (1980), Göttsching invited his former partners Ulbrich (guitar and synthesiser) and Grosskopf (drums and synthesiser) to form a trio. Initially, the Ashra trio only assembled for a concert in London in August 1977. However, they would remain the heart of the band until the first decade of the twenty-first century.[52] *New Age of Earth* combined Göttsching's interest in minimalism and the use of

---

[49] Ibid., p. 50.
[50] Wheeldon, *Deep Distance*, p. 40, pp. 53–4; Barry, Everything Was in the Moment.
[51] Baumgärtel, Ganz simpel.   [52] Wheeldon, *Deep Distance*, p. 61.

synthesisers. His arpeggios, chord progression, shimmering chords, and propulsive rhythms created an uplifting atmosphere. Songs such as 'Sunrise' and 'Deep Distance' push the listener forward. In 'Ocean of Tenderness', he created an ethereal sphere upon which the sound of guitar was able to float freely. The difference from *Inventions for Electric Guitar* is significant, as the guitars now played only a minor role. The album received a lot of praise from the music reviewers.[53]

Göttsching has said that he wanted to get rid of the limitations of guitars.[54] However, in *Blackouts*, his guitar returned to the forefront and the synthesisers were to create a base for Göttsching's long solos and other guitar parts. His playing not only echoed the Krautrock era, but it had also elements of jazz and funk. The side-long 'Lotus Parts 1–4' initially resembles the slowly evolving melodies and hypnotic groove of *Inventions for Electric Guitar*, but in the middle of the piece, electronic sounds are set free and tonal harmonies become supressed by sudden distortions and dissonance. Many reviewers also welcomed *Blackouts*.[55] These two albums started Göttsching's intense home studio period. In addition, he toured with Schulze and Ashra and made music with Michael Hoenig (Agitation Free).[56] With the help of sequencers, Göttsching began to play long improvisations at concerts as well as at fashion shows.[57]

Ashra fused pop elements into *Correlations* and *Belle Alliance* yet did not forget their psychedelic roots. Electronic instruments still played an important role in Ashra's music, but in balance with the band's playing. Many of the songs relied on funk and disco rhythms and bass lines, which Göttsching became mesmerised with while visiting the United States in the late seventies. Good examples of this are the tracks 'Club Cannibal' and 'Phantasus' from *Correlations*. The tracks 'Screamer' and 'Aerogen' from *Belle Alliance* are faster and more rocking. Not surprisingly, Virgin requested more material that could attract the pop audiences.[58]

An Ambassador from the Synthetic Spheres: Klaus Schulze

In the mid-1970s, Klaus Schulze released many albums such as *Blackdance* (1974), *Timewind* (1974), *Picture Music* (1974), and *Moondawn* (1976). His music evolved to be more rhythmic and structured than his earlier output,

---

[53] Ibid., p. 54. [54] RBMA, Manuel Göttsching Talks, 59:30–1:00:00.
[55] Wheeldon, *Deep Distance*, p. 64.
[56] Barry, Everything Was in the Moment; Wheeldon, *Deep Distance*, p. 55.
[57] Wheeldon, *Deep Distance*, p. 90. [58] Ibid., pp. 70–1.

and to some extent, it also began to resemble Tangerine Dream's style in their early Virgin era. In the media, his music – along with Ashra's and Tangerine Dream's production – became labelled the Berlin School, which also referred to their common background as the apprentices of Thomas Kessler's Beat Studio. From 1974 onwards, Brain and Virgin started to release Schulze's works.[59] Gradually, his sound palette expanded to include acoustic instruments, such as flute, trumpet, acoustic guitar, drums, piano, and percussion, as well as the human voice.

For *Blackdance*, Schulze used a rhythm machine and a guest singer for the first time. On *Timewind*, he introduced a Synthanorma sequencer, an ELKA string machine, and EMS Synthi A and ARP 2600 synthesisers. *Picture Music* and *Moondawn* were coloured by the then-famous Minimoog synthesiser. As a live performer, Schulze was very conscious about the power of electronic instruments as visual and material attractors and used them extensively; he became famous for piling the stage set with synthesisers, string machines, and sequencers.[60]

Schulze dedicated *Timewind* to his favourite composer, Richard Wagner. Later, Schulze returned many times to Wagner's music with his electronic interpretations and compositions inspired by Wagner. The role of melodies, harmonies, and rhythm in Schulze's music grew larger. However, a certain structural inertia and rhythmic immobilism remained his musical hallmarks through the seventies. The casting of vast sonic layers and building tensions without surrendering to a cathartic climax was typical of his musical language.

In the late seventies, Schulze expanded his repertoire to soundtracks in erotic films (*Body Love*, vols. 1 and 2 (1977)), historical figures (*X* (1978)), and works drawing on scientific fiction and fantasy (*Dune* (1979)). *Mirage* (1978) strongly manifested the liberating force of electronic music. For Schulze, the synthesiser represented a universal music machine that could overcome all restrictions of time, place, and social limitations. Schulze assured that electronic music could bridge the mind and the universe in a way that is neither a dream nor a hallucination. In the late seventies, Schulze achieved fame as a proponent of both electronic music and New Age music, which allowed him to build a relatively large and enduring fan base. In 1979, Schulze began releasing albums under the pseudonym Richard Wahnfried. With *Time Actor* (1979), he joined forces with the eccentric singer-musician Arthur Brown. In the 1990s, Wahnfried's style

[59] Stubbs, *Future Sounds*, pp. 301–2; Littlejohn, Krautrock, p. 74.
[60] Reetze, *Times & Sounds*, pp. 322–3.

began to resemble the electronic ambient and trance music of the time, and since then Schulze has gained recognition as one of the pioneers of trance.

From a New Opening to the Second Coming of Ashra

Göttsching's first solo offering *New Age Of Earth* (1976) proved commercially successful upon initial release in France. This led Virgin to offer a lucrative nine-album deal and release the album worldwide in 1977. *Blackouts* (1978), too, sold very well. It was only with *Correlations* (1979) that sales figures stagnated, causing Virgin to release *Belle Alliance* (1979) in Germany only.

Göttsching's home sessions did lead to an unpredictable and far-reaching acclaim. In December 1981, he recorded a piece in which a couple of synthesiser sequences revolved around two chords and a drum computer set the pace for the other machines. On top of that, Göttsching played guitar solos and riffs. He recorded a nearly hour-long piece directly on a tape without any doubling, mixing, or editing. A few years later, Göttsching offered the recording to Schulze's Inteam label, which released *E2–E4* in 1984.[61] Named after a typical opening move in chess and the droid R2–D2 of the *Star Wars* franchise, the release anticipated the rise of electronic dance music and influenced its evolution.

In 1984, German newspapers downplayed the release as an example of the inability of the vintage Krautrockers to regenerate.[62] Coincidentally or not, *E2–E4* became a small hit on a radio, trendy stores, and DJs playlists in Europe and the United States. Surprised by the success, Göttsching assured that he had never thought of it as a dance piece.[63] Ultimately, *Sueño Latino* (1989), an album two Italian producers built upon the 'E2–E4' sample, established the song's status as one of the early cornerstones of house and trance. Despite that, Göttsching, like many other Krautrockers, found himself on the margins, playing as a guest on other artists' records and making soundtracks for fashion shows and television. Only in the late 1990s did the legacy and influence of the German electronic musicians of the 1970s became widely acknowledged.[64]

In the 1980s, Ashra recorded only two albums. On *Walkin' the Desert* (1989), Göttsching and Ulbrich revived their minimalist ambitions. The

---

[61] Baumgärtel, Ganz simpel; Barry, Everything Was in the Moment; Littlejohn, Krautrock, pp. 73–4.
[62] Gatward, The Story of E2–E4; Wheeldon, *Deep Distance*, pp. 84–5.
[63] Barry, Everything Was in the Moment.
[64] RBMA, Manuel Göttsching Talks, 1:10:00–1:13:00.

release of the exotica-style pop album *Tropical Heat* (1991) was delayed for five years. In the mid-1990s, a handful of companies began to reissue Krautrock albums, which by then had become rarities but increasingly attracted young fans of techno, ambient, and progressive rock. Interestingly, it was a French label that showed interest in the branch of the Berlin School under discussion here, with Spalax re-releasing the majority of the albums by Ash Ra Tempel, Ashra, and Manuel Göttsching.

Ashra's second coming began in 1996, when Steve Baltes joined the line-up and helped to update the band's sounds and live performances. Ashra updated their rhythms with electronic dance beats that brought plenty of new fans, for example in Japan where the quartet toured in 1997. Concerts in Germany and the Netherlands re-mobilised thousands of Ashra's older fans.[65] Ashra released three concert albums between 1998 and 2002, as well as a compilation in 1996.

Göttsching has been active throughout the last three decades. In 1991, he released a previously unreleased solo album, *Dream & Desire*, recorded in 1977. Since the early 2000s, samplers and music software have allowed Göttsching to perform solo concerts with a guitar, portable computer, and keyboards.[66] In 2000, Schulze and Göttsching reunited to play in London at the Cornucopia Festival. The duo performed as Ash Ra Tempel and released a live recording, *Gin Rosé* (2000). In addition, they made even more music together and released an album entitled *Friendship* (2000). Also worth noting is the live DVD *Ashra: Correlations in Concert* from 2013. Göttsching remains very much active today, with several albums released in 2019 and 2021.

Conclusion

Ash Ra Tempel have gained their place in the history of rock music as a group of three musicians who did not compromise their vision but challenged many of the rock conventions of their time. Since the break-up of the original line-up, both Manuel Göttsching and Klaus Schulze have proved that the most intense and chaotic years of Krautrock in 1970–73 were eventually a fertile breeding ground for experimental and ambitious musicians – despite the volatility of the rock music trends, conflicting ideas, and disappointments in the music business.

[65] Wheeldon, *Deep Distance*, pp. 116–17.
[66] RBMA, Manuel Göttsching Talks, 1:17:30–1:18:00.

In the music of Ash Ra Tempel, the influence of electronic music has especially manifested itself as an innovative mind-set and experimentalism. Exploration of new sounds and musical structures started even before actual synthesisers entered the studios and stage. Göttsching's and Schulze's solo careers have also introduced their earliest musical output to new generations of fans. Ash Ra Tempel's fame as acclaimed pioneers of psychedelic and experimental rock has remained among musicians, rock journalists, and reviewers.

Essential Listening

Ash Ra Tempel, *Ash Ra Tempel* (Ohr, 1971)
Ashra, *New Age of Earth* (Isadora, 1976)
Manuel Göttsching, *Inventions for Electric Guitar* (Kosmische Musik, 1975)
Manuel Göttsching, *E2–E4* (Inteam, 1984)
Klaus Schulze, *Irrlicht* (Ohr, 1972)
Klaus Schulze, *Mirage* (Brain, 1978)

14 | Amon Düül II

RYAN ISEPPI

Within the realm of Krautrock, a number of notable artists – Can, Faust, Neu!, Cluster, Harmonia, Tangerine Dream, and a few others – are frequently heralded for providing 'a sonic template for younger musicians'[1] with their ground-breaking approaches to music-making that have proven influential to successive generations of both avant-garde and mainstream musicians. Somewhat outside of this sphere of musical futurists are two interconnected bands – Amon Düül and Amon Düül II – whose stature and influence within Krautrock derive more from their conceptual underpinnings as a commune-based musical project and their recontextualization of rock music as a mechanism for examining a German cultural identity than from any particular musical innovation. Julian Cope, who used the artwork of their album *Yeti* for the cover of his *Krautrocksampler*, identifies Amon Düül II as 'the group whose music continued to feel the pain of post-war Europe',[2] while Ulrich Adelt describes their music as 'a deterritorialized musical hybrid, challenging essentialized Germanness through its cosmopolitanism'.[3]

Amon Düül II were also one of the Krautrock groups most able to transmit their ideals to an international audience – Lester Bangs declared their album *Yeti* 'one of the finest recordings of psychedelic music in all of human history'[4] at a time when the prevailing critical attitude in the Anglosphere towards Krautrock was one of mild condescension. Yet Amon Düül (both I and II) were not significant merely for their reception abroad, for they were also highly public representatives of trends and legitimate social movements of the post-1968 West German counterculture, particularly the commune movement, while also engaging in

---

[1] J Littlejohn, Krautrock: The Development of a Movement, in U Schütte (ed.), *German Pop Music: A Companion* (Berlin: De Gruyter, 2017), pp. 63–84 (63).

[2] J Cope, *Krautrocksampler: One Head's Guide to the Great Kosmische Musik – 1968 Onwards* (Yatesbury: Head Heritage, 1996), p. 59.

[3] U Adelt, *Krautrock: German Music in the Seventies* (Ann Arbor: University of Michigan Press, 2016), p. 54.

[4] L Bangs, Amon Düül: A Science Fiction Rock Spectacle, in A Patterson (ed.), *Eurock: European Rock and the Second Culture* (Portland: Eurock, 2002), p. 5.

Illustration 14.1 Cover of *Krautrocksampler* by Julian Cope. © Julian Cope.

alternative lifestyle practices collectively described as 'the alternative concept of the politics of the self'.[5]

Simultaneously, they engaged with their German cultural identity in
ways both clever and problematic, embodying 'both [the] promise and
failure of the communal as a counter-model to the nationalist'.[6]
Throughout the initial run of their career, from 1967 to 1981, Amon
Düül and Amon Düül II typified each phase of the Krautrock movement,
starting with the highly conceptual avant-gardism of the early days, the
innovative and influential 'classic' period of 1969 to 1972, and the genre's

[5] S Dirke, *All Power to the Imagination!: The West German Counterculture from the Student
    Movement to the Greens* (Lincoln: University of Nebraska Press, 1997), passim.
[6] Adelt, *Krautrock*, p. 58.

slow subsumption into the mainstream of modern rock music from 1972 onwards.

The Founding of a Musical Commune: 1967

Amon Düül was formed in a flat on Munich's Klopstockstraße in 1967. The core founding members included brothers Peter and Uli Leopold, Chris Karrer, Falk Rogner, and Christian 'Shrat' Thiele, all of whom came from affluent families and were acquainted from their boarding school days. They also shared an interest in the popular rock and beat music of the day as well as avant-garde jazz and traditional music from various cultures. By the end of 1967, this core group of flatmates moved into a stately house on Prinzregentenstraße, a location that would provide an expanded sense of communal possibilities. By April of 1968, the loose collection of amateur musicians living in the house had begun performing under the name 'Amon Düül'.

Munich in the late 1960's was not particularly receptive to radical musical happenings, and the members of the Prinzregentenstraße commune frequently found themselves at odds with the suffocating conservatism of the region. Band members were disturbed by the hostility they faced in their home city, with Shrat recalling people screaming 'you ought to be gassed!' from open windows.[7] Guitarist John Weinzierl explains how this stark cultural divide informed the politics of a musical commune: 'In those days, there were bloody Nazis around all over the place. . . . We didn't have guns or the tools to chase them away, but we could make music, and we could draw audiences, we could draw people, with the same understanding, with the same desires.'[8] These desires corresponded to 'a violent catharsis' in the musical expression of the German counterculture, 'a sometimes unacknowledged sense of wanting to purge the past and to establish a new youth cultural formation through experimental music'.[9]

Amon Düül was not conceived as a rock band as such, but as an alternative lifestyle in and of itself, with the earliest Amon Düül performances taking the form of multimedia exhibitions involving all members of the commune, even the handful of children living there. Peter Leopold

---

[7] I Schober, *Tanz der Lemminge: Amon Düül – eine Musikkommune in der Protestbewegung der 60er Jahre* (Reinbek: Rowohlt, 1979), p. 27.

[8] B Whalley (dir.), *Krautrock: The Rebirth of Germany* (BBC 2009).

[9] D Buckley, Krautrock, in *Grove Music Online* (2001), www.oxfordmusiconline.com /grovemusic/view/10.1093/gmo/9781561592630.001.0001/omo-9781561592630-e-0000049687

recalls, not entirely fondly, the concept's genesis: 'The ideologues [in the commune] came and said "now everyone has to make music". . . . That was at first a social requirement. . . . Then we tried to transpose it to the stage.'[10] The concept of a commune of like-minded individuals who lived and made art together proved an attractive alternative for young people seeking to escape a staid traditionalism. Even the name Amon Düül demonstrates the group's desire to shatter conventions: 'Amon' derives from the ancient Egyptian deity, while the band had this to say about 'Düül' in a 1969 interview with *Underground* magazine: '"Düül", well, that's a word that's never existed before, with two ü's – not in German, nor English or Japanese or anywhere else.'[11]

Amon Düül's riotous and shockingly loud early performances immediately brought them notoriety in their home city of Munich. The presence of supermodel and underground sex symbol Uschi Obermaier, who sang and played maracas in the group's early days, also boosted their fame, and established perhaps the first link between Amon Düül and some of the more politically engaged communes in West Germany. Obermaier and her boyfriend Rainer Langhans were the public faces of Kommune 1, originally founded in Berlin, which engaged in both serious-minded political actions as well as provocative pranks. Kommune 1 shared some members as well as a certain political impetus with the Amon Düül commune.

Kommune 1 favoured attention-grabbing demonstrations and performances over direct armed engagement with the establishment. Similarly, Amon Düül commune member and occasional band manager Peter Kaiser describes the political leanings of the band as 'anarchists, but only verbally'.[12] Kaiser, a member of the left-wing Sozialistischer Deutscher Studentenbund (Socialist German Student Union, or SDS), also claims that Amon Düül's first public performance took place at a demonstration in which the SDS occupied Munich's Academy of Fine Arts, and that the band's performance in particular served as a catalysing moment for the nascent commune movement.

Sabine von Dirke's analysis of the unified personal-political approach that characterized the West German counterculture at this time proves apt in explaining Amon Düül's appeal as a uniquely multifaceted musical, political, and cultural entity: The counterculture

combined a revolution of lifestyles with new cultural and aesthetic paradigms as well as with political demands. . . . Mainstream culture viewed even explicitly non-political

---

[10] Schober, *Tanz der Lemminge*, p. 28.
[11] *Underground*, 1969, quoted in Schober, *Tanz der Lemminge*, p. 29.
[12] Schober, *Tanz der Lemminge*, p. 28.

aspects of this middle-class counterculture – for example, a hippie lifestyle – as political and potentially dangerous for the hegemony.[13]

Peter Kaiser's comment about Amon Düül's 'verbal' anarchism overlooks the band's desire and ability to transmit a political ideology, albeit a vague one, through their music itself. Alexander Simmeth describes this as 'a political self-conception, expressed through the breaking of established musical structures',[14] while the band members themselves explain in a 1971 press release: 'We were able to achieve an articulation of a fundamental critique of the existing system because we had set out a model of the counterculture with the music.'[15] While this model overlaps with that of Kommune 1 or the SDS, who similarly promoted alternative lifestyles, the arts, and engagement in political demonstrations as the most pragmatic and effective courses for effecting social change, Amon Düül's standing as Germany's most famous commune band (perhaps barring Berlin's Ton Steine Scherben) and their wide network of occasional members and fellow travellers sometimes brought the band into contact with the armed terrorists at the extremist end of the West German counterculture.

Like Kommune 1, whose co-founder Dieter Kunzelmann eventually tired of non-violent pranks and actions and joined the militant Tupamaros West-Berlin,[16] members of Amon Düül held political beliefs spanning the spectrum of radicalisation. Chris Karrer was once arrested for something as innocent as throwing bonbons during a university demonstration, while producer Olaf Kübler once remarked of Peter Leopold, 'If he hadn't been a drummer, he probably would have become a terrorist.'[17] It is unclear to what extent any members of Amon Düül held militant views or sympathised with the 'Rote Armee Fraktion' (Red Army Faction, or RAF), a radical left-wing terrorist faction also known as the Baader-Meinhof Group, but the band was, at the very least, acquainted with the leaders of the RAF. Singer Renate Knaup recalls an incident from 1969, when RAF leaders Andreas Baader, Gudrun Ensslin, and Ulrike Meinhof attempted to hide out with the band while on the run following an arson conviction.[18]

---

[13] Dirke, *All Power to the Imagination*, p. 29.

[14] A Simmeth, *Krautrock Transnational: Die Neuerfindung der Popmusik in der BRD, 1968–1978* (Bielefeld: Transcript, 2016), p. 76.

[15] Schober, *Tanz der Lemminge*, p. 130.

[16] D Hauser, Terrorism, in M Klimke & J Scharloth (eds.), *1968 in Europe: A History of Protest and Activism, 1956–1977* (New York: Palgrave Macmillan, 2008), pp. 271–2.

[17] G Augustin, *Der Pate des Krautrock* (Berlin: Bosworth, 2005), pp. 134–5.

[18] Whalley (dir.), *Krautrock*.

She angrily ejected them from the property, suggesting that the band's radicalism stopped short of abetting accused terrorists.

Two Bands, Two Concepts: 1968

Band logistics and varying levels of musical proficiency determined that most of the members of the early incarnations of Amon Düül wound up playing some kind of percussion instrument, and it is a distorted wave of crashing, clattering percussion that dominates the early Düül sound. The consistently jagged and abrasive nature of the music reflected the chaos of the band members' lifestyles and personal relationships, and by the time the group was ready to enter the recording studio, it had split into two acrimonious factions. Uli Leopold became the de facto leader of Amon Düül, while Karrer, Rogner, Shrat, and a handful of other members were ejected from the commune just before the group was set to record the jam session that would provide the material for four of the five albums released under the Amon Düül name. Those members also missed out on the group's performance at the Internationale Essener Songtage, a landmark festival that served as a major catalyst for Krautrock and the West German counterculture in general. Peter Leopold, one of the most tempestuous personalities in a group filled with them, was the only member to keep one foot in both camps.

Rather than embarking on a different musical project altogether, the cast-off Düüls decided to continue to expand and refine the concept of commune-based rock music. Though the names Amon Düül and Amon Düül II suggest two distinct eras of a single group, the two formations actually recorded and performed concurrently, and pursued two different conceptual goals. The original Amon Düül was conceived of first and foremost as a commune, and to prohibit certain unmusical communards from participating in the music-making would have violated the commune ethos: as biographer and friend of the band, Ingeborg Schober explains, 'That was the story of Amon Düül – that the people who made music there really couldn't [make music] at all, but they had the desire to do so.'[19] It is questionable whether one can even definitively categorise Amon Düül as rock music, given that typical verse–chorus–verse song structures are entirely absent, the largely wordless vocals are shrieking and wailing, and the rhythms are pounding and monotonous.

[19] Schober, *Tanz der Lemminge*, p. 31.

Amon Düül's first album, *Psychedelic Underground*, was released in 1969, though the recordings date from 1968, just after the departure of the future members of Amon Düül II. The album's rhythmic monotony and loose-yet-controlled sense of propulsive energy puts it in contention for the title of first true Krautrock album. Schober asserts that the very term 'Krautrock' originated in the German rock scene and derived from the album's track 'Mama Düül und ihre Sauerkrautband spielt auf' (Mama Düül and her Sauerkraut-Band Start to Play),[20] though surviving band members like John Weinzierl vigorously reject the notion that the band's music ought to be included under this label.[21] The recordings from that single 1968 jam would later be edited and spliced together for three more Amon Düül albums – *Collapsing Singvögel Rückwärts & Co.* (1969), *Disaster* (1972), and *Experimente* (1982). This musique concrète-like reassembly of disparate bits of music aligns Amon Düül with other significant studio tinkerers of the era, such as Can and Faust.

The Amon Düül commune continued to exist in varying configurations until the mid-1970s, but the group would record only once more, in 1970, and this session would form the basis of *Paradieswärts Düül*, released in 1971 by Ohr. This album finds the band in a somewhat more subdued mood than on the 1968 session, with a largely acoustic psychedelic folk sound. Shrat and Weinzierl of Amon Düül II are credited as guest musicians on the album, while Leopold appears as a guest on Amon Düül II's album *Yeti* from the same year, suggesting that the initial prickliness between the two Düüls following their split did not take long to soften. By 1973, the original Amon Düül had splintered even further, and only Amon Düül II remained to carry forwards the musical impetus engendered in the flat on Klopstockstraße in 1967.

Emblemising the Counterculture: 1969–1972

While the original Amon Düül was a resolutely avant-garde musical project and would never have been likely to attain much mainstream attention or credibility in any music scene of the late 1960s and early 1970s, Amon Düül II's sheer countercultural force of personality and visceral 'acid rock' sound engaged a record-buying public far outside the worlds of political communes and academic avant-gardism. The release of their first LP, *Phallus Dei*, in 1969 immediately established them as one of the forerunners in the

---

[20] Ibid., p. 42.   [21] Email by Weinzierl to Uwe Schütte (12 November 2021).

wave of young German musicians exploring 'a new legacy in sound that reconnected with older German traditions'[22] – a sound that would soon come to be known as Krautrock.

Phallus Dei, with its incendiary title (*God's Penis* in Latin) seeming especially galling for a band from the heart of Catholic Bavaria, was an act of musical provocation that thrilled increasingly agitated countercultural types throughout Germany. That the album was warmly received in these circles speaks to a growing pessimism and paranoia in the German counterculture – the lyrics, album artwork, and overall tone of the album are decidedly violent and forbidding. Though by 1969 many rock artists had moved on from the simple pleasures and lysergic silliness of the Summer of Love's first wave of psychedelic rock and begun to plumb darker sounds and lyrical themes, Amon Düül II's complete indulgence of these trends in their lyrics sets them apart from their peers. From 'Phallus Dei': 'The raper he is raping / The victim is crying still / The priest he is escaping / He's creeping 'round the mill.'

That these lyrics appear on the title track of the first album ever released under the Amon Düül II name is no fluke. The band's fascination with scenes of violence and the macabre prevails throughout their discography, though it is rarely articulated as audaciously as on *Phallus Dei*. Another track on the album, 'Dem Guten, Schönen, Wahren' (Dedicated to the Good, the Beautiful, the True) is narrated from the perspective of a child rapist and murderer, and pointedly features German lyrics, 'recalling traditions of German murder ballads'.[23]

It is not only the lyrics that mark *Phallus Dei* as a conspicuously sinister outing for a late 1960s rock group. The music itself is ferocious, challenging, and much like the sound of Amon Düül, vaguely ritualistic. Percussion still figures heavily in shaping the Düül sound, with frantic tablas and bongos augmenting Peter Leopold's propulsive fills, with which he shapes lengthy cycles of riffing and improvisation into something raga-like. Meanwhile, melodies are carried by an array of electric and acoustic guitars, violins, twelve-string bass, and organ, sometimes all played in unison in moments of stormy intensity. The album's occult mood and sense of mystery is taken further by producer Olaf Kübler's studio manipulations – isolated vocal and instrumental tracks echo and slice through the mix, inducing a feeling of creeping paranoia.

---

[22] D Stubbs, *Future Days: Krautrock and the Building of Modern Germany* (London: Faber, 2014), p. 4.
[23] Adelt, *Krautrock*, p. 54.

By the recording of *Phallus Dei*, Peter Leopold, Chris Karrer, Shrat, and Falk Rogner had been joined by a number of additional members who would be influential parts of Amon Düül II's creative nucleus on-and-off throughout the band's career. Guitarist John Weinzierl would prove a stalwart, if occasionally combative, contributor across most of the band's albums, while Olaf Kübler, a more polished and professional musician than most of the other members, would make his presence felt as a producer and occasional saxophonist for years to come. However, it was the introduction of Renate Knaup, vocalist and the closest thing Amon Düül II ever had to a frontperson, that would perhaps most distinctively shape the future Düül sound.

Her ability to marry her operatic tendencies to rock's power lent the band a grandiosity that the former Amon Düül never could have, nor would have, attained. Knaup's influence also had a hand in gradually pushing the band closer to the rock mainstream during the 1970s: 'I had really beautiful songs in my head, but "beautiful" in the sense of normal, not this freak stuff we produced in the beginning.'[24] Her talents are under-utilized on the band's early, more experimental albums, where she is largely constrained to wordless whooping and shrieking, though on later albums she stands out as a commanding vocalist in the context of a somewhat less avant-garde rock group.

Since the split between the two Düüls had occurred, most of the core members of Amon Düül II had been half-heartedly pursuing another attempt at a communal coexistence in a run-down villa in Herrsching am Ammersee, a posh lake resort town outside Munich. Visitors to Herrsching noted that any pretence of unity and oneness had gone out of the band, and explosive arguments became more and more frequent as garbage and filth accumulated in the villa. Eventually, the band decided to abandon Herrsching for the tiny village of Kronwinkl near Landshut, also on the outskirts of Munich, a pastoral setting that would acquire an almost legendary reputation as the location where Amon Düül II would ensconce themselves to produce some of their finest work, including their second album, *Yeti*, released in March 1970.

Yeti opens with the thundering riffs of 'Soap Shop Rock', one of Amon Düül II's most iconic tracks, and an encapsulation of the band's cataclysmic energy during this period. Once again, the listener is treated/subjected to a scene of disarming violence: 'Down on the football place / I saw my sister burning / They tied her on a railroad track / And made her blue eyes burning.'

---

[24] C Dallach, *Future Sounds: Wie ein paar Krautrocker die Popwelt revolutionierten* (Berlin: Suhrkamp, 2021), p. 233.

'Soap Shop Rock' runs to nearly fourteen minutes, spans several movements and codas, and could well function as a primer on everything that characterises Amon Düül II: phantasmagorical lyrical scenes, a blend of passages of free improvisation and operatic structure, a richly textured and varied auditory experience, and simply rocking out. *Yeti* showcases a guitar-driven hard rock sound akin to that of British space rock pioneers Hawkwind, with whom Amon Düül II shared a bassist – Englishman Dave Anderson played on both *Phallus Dei* and *Yeti* – as well as Black Sabbath and some of the lesser-known groups in the nascent heavy metal scene, who also toyed with similarly macabre lyrical themes. Indeed, while various Krautrock groups are regularly cited as influences on electronica and indie rock, Amon Düül II is one of the few that also left a significant mark on heavy metal. Weinzierl recalls his pleasant surprise at a festival with Slayer in Sweden in recent years, when 'all these metal guys . . . just wanted to say, "You inspired me!"'[25]

'Soap Shop Rock' is an imposing set piece, but the rest of *Yeti* is no less impressive – it contains all of the same components as *Phallus Dei*, but they are tighter, more coherent, and more accomplished than before. The album also gave the band their first single, 'Archangels Thunderbird', the most conventional rock track on the album, but a masterful piece of expression-istic hard rock nonetheless, thanks to Renate Knaup's commanding vocals (comparing Knaup's vocals with the bizarrely electronically processed vocals on 'Eye-Shaking King' three tracks later, the two polarities of Amon Düül II become apparent). Tracks like 'Archangels Thunderbird' also helped the band garner attention outside of West Germany – write-ups about the band had already appeared in *Melody Maker* by 1970,[26] and American rock critic Lester Bangs wrote about them as early as 1971.[27] Though Amon Düül II were one of the first groups pasted with the faintly condescending 'Krautrock' label in Britain, they drew a devoted following there and shared a fanbase with similarly avant-garde-leaning progressive rock groups such as Hawkwind and Van der Graaf Generator.

Over the next two years, Amon Düül II would release three studio albums in quick succession – *Tanz der Lemminge* (*Dance of the Lem-mings*) in 1971, and *Carnival in Babylon* as well as *Wolf City* in 1972. This run of albums would solidify the band's reputation as one of the premier progressive rock groups in continental Europe. Meanwhile, chaos continued to reign behind the scenes, as interpersonal conflicts at the

[25] Stubbs, *Future Days*, p. 108.
[26] R Williams, Amon Duul II: Phallus Dei, *Melody Maker* (21 March 1970).
[27] Bangs, Amon Düül, p. 5.

Kronwinkl house led to yet another series of personnel changes – producer and DJ Gerhard Augustin estimates that over 120 different members passed through the two Amon Düüls over the years[28] – and arguments about songwriter credits and copyrights persisted throughout those years.

A number of unsettling events further exacerbated the turmoil: in March 1971, a fire broke out during an Amon Düül II concert in the Cologne nightclub KEKS. Two concert-goers were killed, another 500 were injured, and almost all the band's instruments and equipment were destroyed. In December of the same year, several band members were held at gunpoint by police under suspicion of being members of the RAF. Only days after the run-in with the police, Amon Düül II shared a bill with Hawkwind at the Olympia in Paris. Following Hawkwind's set, a spontaneous political demonstration in the crowd rapidly turned into a riot, which culminated in Amon Düül II bassist Lothar Meid hurling a drum at some unruly audience members. The band then launched into one of the most well-reviewed sets of their career, prompting Ingeborg Schober to note that: '[O]ne is inclined to believe that as long as chaos existed around the band, they were instantaneously able to reach soaring heights, and as long as order and calm reigned around them, the chaos broke out amongst themselves.'[29]

Schober's assertion is proven correct by the excellent run of albums Amon Düül II put out around this time. *Tanz der Lemminge* is more varied, more proficient, and more representative of trends in progressive rock than the two albums that preceded it. The double album features three extended suites, which are further divided into seventeen movements ranging in length from under one minute to over eighteen minutes. The suite taking up the first side, 'Syntelman's March of the Roaring Seventies', was composed primarily by Karrer, and his appreciation for folk music shines through more buoyantly than on previous recordings. The B-side, 'Restless Skylight-Transistor-Child', composed mainly by Weinzierl, finds the band exploring new territory, as electronically processed organs and a Mellotron – listed in the album notes simply as 'electronics' – introduces a new layer of the Amon Düül II sound that they would embrace more fully on future albums. This side also blends hard rock guitars, sitar, and droning violins into the heady mix, marking the nearly twenty-minute suite as one of the most creative and inspired moments of the band's career. The C- and D-sides are taken up by 'Chamsin Soundtrack', a largely improvised thirty-three-minute feast of psychedelic indulgence that serves as a signpost moment for the band: this is essentially the band's last dalliance with

[28] Dallach, *Future Sounds*, p. 235.   [29] Schober, *Tanz der Lemminge*, p. 147.

'acid rock'. That is to say, the raw, untutored, largely improvisational sound of the first two albums would now come to be replaced by more polished, progressive and compositionally bound structures, as heard on the band's next two albums, *Carnival in Babylon* and *Wolf City*.

Due to one of the band's countless personnel shakeups, Renate Knaup is credited only as a guest vocalist on one brief track on *Tanz der Lemminge*, but she would return as a full member on *Carnival in Babylon* and *Wolf City* and become an essential part of the band's sound and identity from then on. So too would bassist and vocalist Lothar Meid, who first appeared as a full member on *Tanz der Lemminge*, though he had previously toured with the band. Meid was an experienced musician who had played with jazz musician Klaus Doldinger and co-founded Embryo, the jazz- and world music-inspired Krautrock ensemble from Munich. Meid's compositions tended to be somewhat more pop-oriented than those of the founding members, as evidenced by his later work with mainstream German classic rockers Peter Maffay and Marius Müller-Westernhagen.

Carnival in Babylon, released in January 1972, is a transitional album with some satisfying moments, though it feels like a relatively minor entry in the Amon Düül II catalogue. It does, however, set the stage for the shimmering progressive elegance of *Wolf City*, an inspired synthesis of the laissez-faire experimentation of earlier albums and the tighter, more song-oriented path the band was starting to tread. 'Wie der Wind am Ende einer Straße' (Like the Wind at the End of a Street), an instrumental from the second side, is a mellifluously layered blend of proto–New Age *kosmische Musik* and Indian influences, and, according to Falk Rogner, represents the only time that the band actually recorded while under the influence of LSD.[30] The album closes with the serene 'Sleepwalker's Timeless Bridge', a minor masterpiece of progressive rock, spanning several movements within just five minutes, with Mellotron textures that single this out as one of Amon Düül II's gentlest and most forward-looking compositions.

Exploring National and International Identities: 1973 until Today

Wolf City is not the last notable Amon Düül II album – their next three studio albums, *Vive la Trance* (1973), *Hijack* (1974), and *Made in Germany* (1975), all have strong moments. *Vive la Trance* gloomily

---

[30] Stubbs, *Future Days*, p. 102.

predicts a sci-fi apocalypse and describes horrific bloodshed in the Mozambican War of Independence on the fearsome 'Mozambique', perhaps the band's most obviously political track, with lyrical depictions of 'the white beast . . . in the villages, dealing only in death', and an exhortation to 'unite and fight'. *Hijack*, on the other hand, is upbeat and accessible for an Amon Düül II record and is clearly inspired by Roxy Music and Ziggy Stardust–era David Bowie. Meid's influence is apparent throughout the album, which bears similarities with his side projects Utopia and 18 Karat Gold from 1973, both of which also feature a number of other Amon Düül II members.

One release from this era that satisfyingly captures some of the visceral energy of the old Düül is the band's first live album, *Live in London* (1973). Consisting of spirited adaptations of fan favourites from *Yeti* and *Tanz der Lemminge*, it draws a stark contrast between the psychedelic freak-outs of the band's earlier work and their more polished contemporary studio work. The album is also significant for its provocative cover art: a militarized, *Stahlhelm*-clad demon looms threateningly over Big Ben and the Tower Bridge. Such an obvious reference to the Third Reich seems uncharacteristic of a band as outspokenly opposed to Nazism as Amon Düül II, though the satirical intent of the artwork is made clearer in the context of a disagreeable incident from 1972: the band's first ever performance in Britain was marred by an attendee who loudly shouted 'Heil Hitler!' and gave a Nazi salute during every song break.[31] Recent reissues of *Live in London* have featured different, less incendiary cover art.

It may have been this incident that started the group contemplating their identity as a German band and the stereotypes and ignorant jokes they could expect to face from international audiences. Their last notable album, *Made in Germany*, is an odd, amusing exercise in grappling with German national pride and shame. Originally intended as a concept album based on German history, it was aimed mainly at the American market, an audience for whom Amon Düül II and Krautrock in general were still largely unknown. Olaf Kübler claims to have previously presented the Düül side project Utopia to some American record label executives under the name Olaf & His Electric Nazis.[32] That idea was ultimately canned, but it seems that the band had fixated on a satirical embrace of German history as the way to reach a broader international audience.

---

[31] Schober, *Tanz der Lemminge*, p. 157.   [32] Ibid., p. 160.

Made in Germany features humorous songs about Kaiser Wilhelm II, Ludwig II of Bavaria, and Fritz Lang, along with many playful references to the 'kraut' label – 'the krauts are coming to the USA' – as the band gleefully exclaims on the country-tinged 'Emigrant Song'. The album is musically diverse, drawing heavily from glam rock and musical theatre, with a sense of whimsy that is dampened somewhat by the inclusion of a skit featuring a mock 'interview' with Adolf Hitler. Ironically, the edgy double concept album the band was sure would pique the interest of American audiences was trimmed to a single LP for the American release, with the Hitler skit being removed altogether.

Following *Made in Germany*, Amon Düül II released four more largely lacklustre albums before disbanding in 1981. The final album of the band's original run, *Vortex* (1981), is somewhat of a return to the sinister Düül sound of yore, though it sounds overproduced and rather lifeless. Two years later, in 1983, the album *Experimente* appeared under the original Amon Düül name, featuring the last of the studio floor cuttings from the 1968 session that spawned four of their five albums. Comparing *Vortex* and *Experimente* is jarring in that the chaotic, amateurish jamming of the early Amon Düül actually sounds timelier and more ground-breaking in the context of post-punk and early industrial music in 1983 than the bloated prog pop of latter-period Amon Düül II.

After the band's initial breakup in 1981, Weinzierl forged onward with a new incarnation of Amon Düül II, often referred to as Amon Düül UK, featuring members of Hawkwind, Van der Graaf Generator, and Ozric Tentacles, while a more complete version of the band has reunited from time to time for short tours and two new studio albums in 1995 and 2010. Karrer, Weinzierl, and Knaup all remain involved with the group and perform occasionally to this day.

As a Liberty Records press release for *Phallus Dei* explained in 1969: 'Amon Düül II understands itself as a community. . . . The music of Amon Düül II is inseparable from the history of the group, their sociological basis, and their societal experiences.'[33] Or, as the members themselves put it in a later press release for *Tanz der Lemminge*:

We want to show with our group that it's possible to live together, work together, and overcome difficulties together and nevertheless remain an autonomous individual. We want this truth, which dictates our conscious and collective action, to be conveyed through the music and to reach the public.[34]

[33] Ibid., p. 69.   [34] Ibid., p. 131.

Judging by the successive generations of fans and musicians who continue to rediscover this music, the message has been received.

Essential Listening

Amon Düül, *Psychedelic Underground* (Metronome, 1969)
Amon Düül II, *Phallus Dei* (Liberty, 1969)
Amon Düül II, *Yeti* (Liberty, 1970)
Amon Düül II, *Wolf City* (United Artists, 1972)

15 | The Flip Side of Krautrock

JENS BALZER

This chapter will look at what I call the 'flip side' of Krautrock. That is to say I will focus on the political, social, economic, and cultural developments in 1970s West Germany that this music genre did *not* reflect, rather than those it did. The protagonists of Krautrock posed as the cultural avant-garde of their era, a stance that is often uncritically adopted by commentators.[1] In fact, as I will show here, Krautrock was essentially a highly conservative music movement. There are three good reasons for this.

First, Krautrock was almost exclusively dominated by heterosexual men. Consequently, it had no links to the women's rights movement of the time. In the first part of this chapter, I will show that feminist values were reflected in German pop and rock music made during the decade of Krautrock – but only in genres outside of Krautrock itself. A connection between Krautrock and women's liberation only took place in the transition period to Neue Deutsche Welle, or NDW (German New Wave) at the beginning of the 1980s.

Second, Krautrock was almost exclusively the domain of white, German men, who often came from wealthy, upper-middle-class backgrounds. Despite this, Krautrock presented itself as an international, cosmopolitan movement. Apart from Can's two vocalists – Malcolm Mooney and Damo Suzuki – musicians from diverse ethnic backgrounds were rare on this scene. West Germany's gradual transition from an ethnically homogeneous to a multicultural society in the 1970s is therefore not reflected in Krautrock. For this reason, I will mention the migrant community most prominently represented in Krautrock – the Turkish labour migrant community or *Gastarbeiter* (guest workers).

Third, despite its emphasis on cosmopolitanism, Krautrock also featured a group of bands that aimed to rediscover and preserve German cultural traditions. These bands took their names from famous Romantic poets, set medieval poetry to music, or sang in the regional dialects of north

---

[1] Compare P Felkel, Die kosmischen Kuriere, in A Koch (ed.), *Made in Germany: Die hundert besten deutschen Platten* (Höfen: Koch, 2001), pp. 59–63; or C Wagner, *Der Klang der Revolte: Die magischen Jahre des westdeutschen Musik-Untergrund* (Mainz: Schott, 2013).

and south Germany. While canonised, cosmopolitan Krautrock is regarded outside Germany as the most important, formative, influential music to emerge from post-war West Germany, within Germany the impact of this traditionalist movement has been far greater: it continues in *Mittelalter Rock* (medieval metal) bands who have enjoyed commercial success since the early 1990s in a reunified Germany.

Feminist Approaches: Inga Rumpf, Juliane Werding, Schneewittchen, and Claudia Skoda

Krautrock, as the genre has been canonised in recent decades, remained a purely male affair. Apart from Renate Knaup, the singer from Amon Düül II and, briefly, Popol Vuh, there were no prominent women in this music genre. For this reason, its political impact was limited. Krautrock had no connections to the German feminist movement of the 1970s. Women's sexual emancipation played no role in Krautrock – in fact, the entire subject of sexuality was strangely absent. This is even more astonishing in a decade that was essentially all about sexual liberation.

The first female rock band in Germany, The Rag Dolls, from Duisburg,[2] were founded in 1965 and oriented on American rhythm and blues and British beat music. They named themselves after a song by the Four Seasons; the only single they recorded was a cover version of 'Yakety-Yak' by The Coasters. Despite numerous performances, The Rag Dolls failed to produce another single, let alone an entire album. They disbanded in 1969.

The most prominent German female rock singer at the beginning of the 1970s was Inga Rumpf. She started her career in 1965 in the folk band City Preachers, from which the rock band Frumpy emerged in 1970. In 1972, Rumpf founded Atlantis with former Frumpy members Jean-Jacques Kravetz and Karl-Heinz Schott. Their name and the psychedelic design of their album cover art were inspired by the burgeoning style of Krautrock, yet they remained strongly rooted in blues, jazz, and soul. Not least due to their English song lyrics, the leading German music magazine *Sounds* described them as 'the "most English" of German groups'.[3] Rumpf was

---

[2] Compare I Jung, *RuhrgeBEATgirls: Die Geschichte der Mädchen-Beatband The Rag Dolls 1965–1969* (Hamburg: Marta Press, 2016).

[3] Quoted in G Ehnert, *Rock in Deutschland: Lexikon deutscher Rockgruppen und Interpreten* (Hamburg: Taurus, 1979), p. 23; I Rumpf, *Darf ich was vorsingen? Eine autobiografische Zeitreise* (Hamburg: Ellert & Richter, 2021).

Illustration 15.1 Inga Rumpf. © Jacques Schumacher.

soon considered a female role model. On her first solo album, *Second-Hand Mädchen* (*Second-Hand Girl,* 1975), she sang in German for the first time. The title track is one of the first female empowerment songs written in German. Defying male expectations, her lyrics encouraged young women to refuse to dress in 'glitter jackets' or wear 'sequins' to get ahead in their careers, proudly stating 'meine Nähte sitzen schief und krumm' (the seams on my clothes are crooked).

In 1975, a hit feminist anthem was also released: 'Wenn du denkst du denkst dann denkst du nur du denkst' (When You Think You Think, Then Only You Think You Think) by Juliane Werding, written by Gunter Gabriel. The lyrics of this hit single encouraged women to behave 'like men': to drink as much as they could in the pub without falling over, and to win at cards. Werding started her career as a political pop and folk singer in 1972. Her first hit 'Am Tag, als Conny Kramer starb' (The Day Conny Kramer Died) was a cover version of 'The Night They Drove Old Dixie Down' by The Band, but with different, German lyrics: Werding's version mourns a friend who has died of a drug overdose. She was also one of the first singers to focus on environmental pollution and ecological disaster in 'Der letzte Kranich vom Angerburger Moor' (The Last Crane on Angerburg Moor).

In 1976, the first group formed who explicitly saw themselves as a mouthpiece for second-wave feminism, the all-female Schneewittchen. They were led by the folk singer, guitarist, and flute player Angi Domdey. She had previously played in a jazz band. Schneewittchen, however, combined German folk songs and blues ballads with feminist messages. Their debut album *Zerschlag deinen gläsernen Sarg (Frauenmusik – Frauenlieder)* (*Smash your Glass Coffin (Female music – Female songs)*) was released in 1978. For example, on 'Der Mann ist ein Lustobjekt' (The Male is an Object of Lust), Domdey critiques the sexualised male gaze on women by reversing it, while on the title track of the album she demands:

Schneewittchen, glaub nicht,
Was das Märchen verspricht
Das Happy-End kann nur dein eignes sein.
Es gibt noch viele andere Schneewittchen, drum wandere
Zu ihnen, hilf sie befrei'n.

Snow White, don't believe
What the fairy tale promises
The happy ending can only be your own.
There are many other Snow Whites, so wander
To them, set them free.

These are some of the few feminist voices in German pop music in the mid-to-late 1970s. However, they developed independently of Krautrock or were even – in the case of Inga Rumpf, Frumpy, and Atlantis – diametrically opposed to its musical style. There was, nevertheless, one exception: Die Dominas (The Dominatrices) emerged in West Berlin in the early 1980s, consisting of fashion designer Claudia Skoda and her model Rosi Müller. Their first and only single was produced by Ash Ra Tempel's founder Manuel Göttsching, while the cover was designed by Kraftwerk members Ralf Hütter and Karl Bartos.

Claudia Skoda was one of the defining figures of West Berlin's underground scene in the early 1970s and beyond. She designed avant-garde knitwear, combining wool with polyester yarn and tape from music cassettes. In 1972, Skoda moved into a factory floor in Berlin with artist friends who named their headquarters 'fabrikneu' (mint condition, or literally: 'factory-new') in an allusion to Andy Warhol's Factory. Klaus Krüger, who experimented with homemade drums and later worked with Iggy Pop and Tangerine Dream, belonged to this community.

The fabrikneu family maintained close relations to the Krautrock scene. Amon Düül II often stayed at fabrikneu when he was in Berlin, and Göttsching wrote music for Claudia Skoda's fashion shows in 1976. The highlight of their collaboration was the 1979 fashion show 'Big Birds':

There was no longer any catwalk in the classical sense. . . . The team of acrobats consisted of Salomé and Luciano Castelli, who would later become famous as painters and performers with the 'Junge Wilde' tendency, along with the Australian duo Emu, who hatched out of a large egg at the start of the performance. Screened concurrently was a film of penguins in the Antarctic.[4]

Göttsching provided electronic music. 'He began with a simple heartbeat, which immediately drew the public into his narrative, at the same time providing a foretaste of the never-ending tracks, characterised by repetition and phrase displacement, that would become so formative for the sound of the time.'[5] Göttsching started working with computers in 1979, first with the Apple II, then with early Commodore and Atari models. In 1981, his first solo album, *E2–E4*, recorded exclusively with electronic instruments, was released. It inspired Claudia Skoda to store her knitting patterns on punch cards and in the early 1980s she also began to make her knitwear with the help of Atari computers.

Together with Rosi Müller in the duo Die Dominas, Skoda sang about sadomasochism to Göttsching's minimalist beats: 'Schlag mich / schlag mich nicht / Schmerz, wo bist du?' (Hit me / don't hit me / pain, where are you?). Minimalism and sadomasochism were also echoed in the music of the first successful album by Deutsch-Amerikanische Freundschaft, *Alles ist gut* (*Everything is Fine*), released in 1981. It was not until the 1980s that Krautrock music became sexualised, and the first women performers staked their claim, but this transition occurred when Krautrock was already giving way to post-punk and Neue Deutsche Welle.

Krautrock was therefore blind to German society's feminist awakening. Despite its avant-garde aspirations, its line-up had a highly conservative character, especially on the topic of sexual politics. Feminist expression was more likely to be found in music genres maligned by Krautrockers and their supporters, such as German *Schlager* or in rock

[4] F McGovern, From Improvised Catwalk to Dressater, in B Bommert (ed.), *Claudia Skoda: Dressed to Thrill* (Dortmund: Kettler, 2020), pp. 109–15 (111).
[5] Ibid.

based on Anglo-American models. Strong indications of feminist tendencies only featured on the West German underground scene when the era
of Krautrock was over.

Migrant Voices: Türküola, Metin Türkoz, Cem Karaca, and Ozan Ata Canani

Krautrock was not only almost exclusively a male domain: the men who
dominated the scene were almost all white Germans. Musicians with
diverse ethnic backgrounds were few and hard to find, with the notable
exceptions of Malcolm Mooney and Damo Suzuki, vocalists with Can, and
the female Korean singer Djong Yun, who featured on records by Popol
Vuh. These exceptions were evidently made for the singers' 'exotic' appeal.
Diverse voices were not represented in Krautrock as a matter of course,
which once again shows its political failings. From 1968 to 1980, the
number of ethnic migrants in West Germany increased from 3.2 to
7.2 per cent, or from just under 2 million to roughly 4.5 million.[6] This
influx profoundly changed West German society, but the increasing visi-
bility of migrants was barely reflected in Krautrock.

In the 1960s, however, a flourishing music scene developed among
Turkish migrants living in Germany. They were the largest migrant
group from 1961 onwards. Following a government drive to recruit
Gastarbeiter, by 1973, some 867,000 workers from Turkey alone had
come to live in West Germany.[7] The Turkish music scene was just as
strictly segregated from the German cultural scene as its people were
from German society. Significantly, Germany's best-selling independent
record company in the 1960s and 1970s was one that produced Turkish-
language music for migrants living in Germany.

The record label Türküola was founded in Cologne in 1964 and still
exists with a catalogue that comprises more than 1,000 albums, singles, and
compilations. Its vinyl records and, later, compact cassettes were not
distributed through regular record shops but in corner grocery shops and
other stores that were part of the German-Turkish community. Türküola's
most successful artist, Yüksel Özkasap, nicknamed Köln'ün Bülbülü (The
Cologne Nightingale), sold 800,000 copies of her 1975 album *Beyaz Atli*

---

[6] U Herbert, *Geschichte der Ausländerpolitik in Deutschland: Saisonarbeiter, Zwangsarbeiter, Gastarbeiter, Flüchtlinge* (Munich: Beck, 2001), p. 233.

[7] S Luft, Die Anwerbung türkischer Arbeitnehmer und ihre Folgen, BPB, www.bpb.de/internationales/europa/tuerkei/184981/gastarbeit.

(White Horseman). But that went unnoticed by German society; Özkasap did not appear on any TV shows, nor were her immense sales reflected in the official album charts because of the label's unconventional distribution channels.[8]

Another prominent Türküola artist was Metin Türkoz, who started his career in Germany as an assembly line worker in Cologne's Ford factories. From the late 1960s to the early 1980s, he sang about his own experiences and everyday problems, and the longings and dreams of first-generation migrants. For example, in 'Guten Morgen, Mayestero'[9] (Good Morning, Mayistero), Türkoz switches back and forth between German and Turkish, in a slightly mocking conversation with his line manager. At the turn of the 1980s – because of Germany's economic crisis and the resulting rise in unemployment – Türkoz also incorporated racist slogans such as 'Ausländer raus!' (Foreigners out!) into his lyrics as these were now heard more and more often in real life. He was the first singer to systematically mix German and Turkish slang words, a technique that became a key stylistic device in the next generation of German-Turkish music rappers like Microphone Mafia and Eko Fresh or, most recently, Haftbefehl.

From the end of the 1960s, the Türküola label also released albums by Cem Karaca, one of Turkey's best-known musicians. He combined Anatolian folk style with elaborate soundscapes and elements of progressive rock and psychedelic music, coming surprisingly close to the aesthetics of Krautrock. Karaca's lyrics took up the theme of social revolution as well as calls to resist Turkish nationalism. *Yoksulluk kader olamaz* (*Poverty Need Not Be Fate*) is the title of his 1977 album. 'Safinaz', released the following year, was a rock symphony inspired by Queen's 'Bohemian Rhapsody' on the difficult fate of a working-class girl. When political tensions in Turkey intensified – culminating in the military coup in September 1980 when a military junta seized power, imposing martial law and banning all political parties – Karaca emigrated to Germany and remained there until 1987. He founded a German-language band called Die Kanaken (The Kanaks, a derogatory German expression for Turks) and released his first eponymous German-language album in 1984.

The songs on this album are musically far less ambitious than Karaca's songs from the 1970s, though they too alternate between rock and folk themes, and between Western and Anatolian music styles. The opening

---

[8] Compare J Balzer, *High Energy: Die Achtziger – das pulsierende Jahrzehnt* (Berlin: Rowohlt, 2021), pp. 92–107; N Hazar, *Deutschlandlieder. Almanya Türküleri: Zur Kultur der türkeistämmigen Community seit dem Anwerbeabkommen 1961* (Berlin: Rotbuch, 2021).

[9] Mayistero is a Turkish slang word for German *Meister*, meaning shift supervisor or overseer.

track of the album 'Mein deutscher Freund' (My German Friend) is particularly succinct in showing how Turkish guest workers hope to be seen by Germans as more than just cheap labour: 'Er glaubt so fest daran, oh, so fest daran / Freund ist jeder deutsche Mann' (He believes so firmly, oh, so firmly / That every German is his friend). But the social barriers remain insurmountable: 'Gastfreundschaft war zugesagt / Und jetzt heißt es: "Türken raus!"' (They promised to welcome us / And now it's: 'Turks out!'). The song still ends with a euphoric verse promising reconciliation between people of future generations: 'Da wo jetzt noch Schranken sind / Reißt sie nieder, stampft sie ein' (Where there are now barriers / Tear them down, stamp on them).

Ozan Ata Canani, born in 1963, was one of Die Kanaken's musicians. He came to Germany from Turkey in 1975 and taught himself to play the Turkish long-necked lute, the *bağlama*, while still at school. He performed at Turkish wedding parties and began to compose his own songs, soon also in German. 'Deutsche Freunde' (German Friends) is the name of his first German-language song. 'Arbeitskräfte wurden gerufen / ... Aber Menschen sind gekommen' (Labourers were called for / ... but human beings turned up). 'Deutsche Freunde' is a song about the fate of the people who eke out an existence in Germany as welders, unskilled workers, and bin collectors, as well as about the fate of their children: 'Sie sind geteilt in zwei Welten / Ich ... frage Euch / Wo wir jetzt hingehören?' (They are divided into two worlds / I ... ask you all / Where do we belong?).

It was already clear to Canani as a teenager that he would spend his life in Germany.[10] But it was just as clear to him that Germans would like him sent 'home', sooner rather than later. His songs about split identities tried to mend this rift through music. But despite his best efforts, success escaped him. Turkish audiences in Germany did not want to hear songs in German; and Germans were not interested in the problems or music of their fellow citizens. The same applied to fans of alternative and countercultures: at the beginning of the 1980s, these groups were open to Afro-American sounds, hip-hop, and Jamaican reggae as well as the emancipatory struggles they reflected. But the music of the large Turkish minority living in their own country was ignored in the same way as everyday racism.

After Cem Karaca went back to Turkey, for a while Canani led the follow-up project, Die Kanaken 2, but again with little success. He finished

---

[10] Compare J Balzer, Das Alterswerk als Debüt: Mehr als 30 Jahre nach seinen ersten Auftritten veröffentlicht der bedeutende Rock-Künstler Ozan Ata Canani endlich ein Album: 'Warte mein Land, warte', *Die Zeit* (2 June 2021).

his musical career in the late 1980s and it took almost three decades before he was rediscovered when he re-recorded 'Deutsche Freunde' in 2013 for a compilation with the title *Songs of Gastarbeiter*. Now he regularly plays concerts with the Munich-based neo-Krautrock band Karaba. In spring 2021, his long-delayed debut album *Warte mein Land, warte* (*Wait, My Country, Wait*) was released. He plays his intricate, melodic *bağlama* over a solid machine-like rhythm section, reminiscent of Can and Neu! No less than forty years after their first performances, the sound of German-Turkish migrants joined that of Krautrock.

Krautrock and the German Nation: Hölderlin, Novalis, Ougenweide, and Achim Reichel

Krautrock is often labelled as iconoclastic, hostile to tradition and trail-blazing. Krautrock's goal to make a decisive break with the tainted musical traditions of post-war West Germany is often described as its most significant political impetus. Holger Czukay of Can put it as follows: 'In the end, music has only two options: either to outperform music history or to start from scratch. Can decided on the latter.'[11] But apart from those who sought to break with tradition, various bands also dedicated themselves to cultivating and reappropriating German cultural traditions. German Romantic literature and philosophy played a role, as did medieval poetry; historical and regional forms of German such as Old and Middle High German, as well as Low German and Frisian, were also included.

One of the first acts to be released on the Krautrock label Spiegelei was Hölderlin, named after the poet Friedrich Hölderlin (1770–1843). Initially, the band mainly played cover versions of British folk revival bands like Fairport Convention, Traffic, and Pentangle. On their debut album *Hölderlins Traum* (*Hölderlin's Dream*, 1972), their lyrics were political as well as ecstatically romantic. Later, Hölderlin's arrangements were more sophisticated and featured extensive organ and guitar solos. The musicians also set texts to music by political writers such as Bertolt Brecht, Erich Fried, and H. C. Artmann. Touring with their third album *Rare Birds* (1977), singer Christian Noppeney appeared in costume as a giant bird, inspired by Peter Gabriel and the stage shows of early Genesis.

---

[11] J Balzer, Musical Materialism, in C Tannert (ed.), *Halleluwah! Hommage à Can* (Stuttgart: Abtart, 2011), pp. 125–9 (126).

Another German Romantic poet, Georg Philipp Friedrich von Hardenberg (alias Novalis; 1772–1801), lent his pen name to the group Novalis, which formed in Wuppertal in 1971. Their 1973 debut album *Banished Bridge,* released on the Krautrock label Brain, was an exercise in 'Romantic rock music',[12] as they put it. Novalis dispensed with the electric guitar and opted for expansive organ solos and English lyrics. For their eponymous second LP in 1975, Novalis used German lyrics. They also set poems by their namesake to music, such as 'Wunderschätze' (Wondrous Treasures) or 'Wenn nicht mehr Zahlen und Figuren' (When Numbers and Figures Are No More) from his unfinished novel *Heinrich von Ofterdingen* (1802). These poems convey a deeply Romantic mistrust against the rationalisation of the world.[13] Some centuries after the poet Novalis, the twentieth-century band of the same name belatedly brought hippie mysticism to German rock music. And they did so very successfully: with sales of 300,000 albums, Novalis were one of the most successful West German rock bands of the 1970s.[14]

The formation with the most long-term, decisive impact in the cultivation of German tradition was Ougenweide, founded in 1971 and named after a poem by the Middle High German minstrel Neidhart von Reuenthal (1210–45). In modern German, their name translates as *Augenweide* (a sight to behold). Using the xylophone, guitars, slide whistle, flute, cymbals, and other rare instruments, they set medieval German poetry to music. Lyrics included, among others, poems by the first great German minstrel from that epoch, Walther von der Vogelweide (ca. 1170–1230) as well as his lesser-known contemporaries like Burkhard von Hohenfels (thirteenth century) or Dietmar von Aist (1115–1171). Ougenweide singers Minne Graw and Renee Kollmorgen chanted German from centuries yore with great vigour. On their second album, *All die weil ich mag* (*All Those Because I Like*) from 1974, Ougenweide even set an Old High German poem to music, the 'Merseburger Zaubersprüche' (Merseburg Incantations) from the ninth century, probably the oldest surviving literary text in the German language.

Ougenweide's producer was the Hamburg musician Achim Reichel; on their debut album, he can also be heard on timpani and bass. Reichel's career was one of the most interesting at this time because it spanned all

---

[12] Quoted in Ehnert, *Rock in Deutschland*, p. 187.

[13] Compare Herbert Uerlings (ed.), *Novalis und die Wissenschaften* (Tübingen: Niemeyer, 1997).

[14] Compare M Eggers, 'Unsere Sprache – sie muß wieder Gesang werden.' Sprachliche und musikalische Romantik im deutschen Progressive Rock: Novalis, in U Schütte (ed.), *German Pop Music in Literary and Transmedial Perspectives* (Oxford: Lang, 2021), pp. 135–56.

Illustration 15.2 Achim Reichel (with A.R. & Machines), Hamburg, 1971. © Heinrich Klaffs.

areas of German rock music.[15] In 1961 he was one of the co-founders of The Rattles, the first successful English-language beat band in West Germany. In 1971, under the moniker A.R. & Machines, he released *Die grüne Reise* (*The Green Journey*), which consists of looped guitar improvisations recorded on an Akai 330D tape machine, allowing Reichel to create an entire guitar orchestra by himself. He continued to pursue this concept – in parallel to his collaboration with the traditionalists of Ougenweide – until 1976 when his career took another surprising turn.

He completely reinvented himself as an interpreter of sea shanties sung in Low German. His debut *Dat Shanty Alb'm* (*The Shanty Album*) from 1976 opens with the track 'Rolling Home' and features the chorus: 'Rolling home, rolling home / Rolling home across the sea / Rolling home to di old Hamborg / Rolling home, mien Deern to di!' (Rolling home to you, old Hamburg / Rolling home, my girl, to you!). Mixing English and Low German, the song tells of a sea journey from Hamburg to a foreign country and the return to the woman who is at home waiting for him. Reichel's lyrics skilfully exploit the linguistic similarities between Low German and

[15] Compare A Reichel, *Ich hab das Paradies gesehen: Mein Leben* (Hamburg: Rowohlt, 2020).

English while the chorus openly alludes to his role models in rock music, The Rolling Stones.

Just as Ougenweide revived obscure forms of German, Reichel rejuvenated *Plattdeutsch* (Low German), a dialect that had almost completely disappeared in the 1970s. In northern Germany in the 1970s, Low German was widely used by older generations in rural areas; towards the end of the twentieth century, however, it had largely disappeared first from public, then from private use. This trend of decline was a development that equally affected other dialects and minor languages. The gradual disappearance of Low German was also reinforced by the standardisation of language promoted by the media and culture industries, and therefore also by pop culture. For this reason, a recourse to Low German could be seen both as an act of resistance against standardisation and as an attempt by musicians to promote 'the language of the people'. Reichel attempted to reach an audience who felt disowned both the political music by songwriters of the 1960s and the 'avant-garde' sounds of Krautrock.

Achim Reichel singing in Low German was considered by many followers of Krautrock in the 1970s to be a regression to outdated nationalist traditions. In fact, his recourse to a dialect could have been seen as an anti-nationalist reappropriation of a repressed (language) tradition. So his intention was closer to the Krautrockers' will to radically break with tradition than it might first appear. In the same year as *Dat Shanty Alb'm*, 1976, the album *Leeder vun mien Fresenhof* (*Songs from My Frisian Farm*) by the northern German songwriter Knut Kiesewetter, the former producer of communist songwriter Hannes Wader, was released. It sold over 500,000 copies in a short period, featuring new compositions by Kiesewetter with lyrics in Low German and Frisian.

The opening track is called: 'Mien Gott, he kann keen Plattdüütsch mehr un he versteiht uns nich' (Dear God, He Can't speak Low German Anymore and Doesn't Understand Us'). The lyrics address a young man who can no longer speak the language of his ancestors and is therefore cut off from his traditional origins. In his song, Kiesewetter laments the young man's cultural impoverishment and alienation from his rural, peasant, proletarian background: forgetting your own language is tantamount to forgetting your social class.

In the 1980s, lyrics in dialect underwent another astonishing revival. This time, however, the scene was not so much dominated by northern German artists: the Spider Murphy Gang from Munich wrote in Bavarian dialect while BAP from Cologne used local dialect *kölsch*, which until then had been mainly limited to German carnival songs. Now, it served as a tool for protest songs – for example, 'Kristallnaach' (Night of Broken Glass, referring to the anti-Semitic pogrom of November 1938) whose subject was the resurgence of right-wing radicalism in West Germany in the 1980s. The Austrian singer Falco also mixed Austrian dialect with English into a kind of early hip-hop hybrid in hit songs like 'Der Kommissar' (1982).

Shanty Bands and Beyond

The interest in German language and tradition found in groups such as Ougenweide, Hölderlin, and Novalis finally waned in the 1980s only to experience a remarkable revival in the 1990s. Following German reunification, a renaissance of political and cultural nationalism took place that led to a flare-up of nationalist violence. Especially in the East German federal states, there were repeated, violent riots against migrant workers as well as arson attacks on homes of asylum seekers. The most successful German rock band of the 1990s, Rammstein, dangerously and irresponsibly toyed with symbols of nationalism and national socialism that attracted attention and provoked outrage.[16]

Such recourse to patriotism and nationalism in German pop culture and politics from the 1990s[17] also found a less aggressive expression in many groups that emerged in this period. They drew their inspiration, music, lyrics, and instruments, once more, from the Middle Ages, resulting in the genre of medieval metal. Its most important proponents were bands like Corvus Corax, Schandmaul, Subway to Sally, Saltatio Mortis, and In Extremo; the latter explicitly referred in their music to the Krautrock of the 1970s as well as Ougenweide. These neo-medieval rockers combined electric guitars with bagpipes, hurdy-gurdies, harps, shawms, and many other kinds of historic instruments.

The *Shanty Album* by Achim Reichel, in turn, inspired the most successful northern German rock band of the 2010s: Santiano saw themselves as a 'shanty rock band' and posed as weathered mariners at their concerts. Their songs were mostly about seafaring and pirates. They both ironically ruptured tradition and raised it to a new, non-ironic level with their masculinist rock-music performance style. With Santiano, nostalgia for one's roots merges with a nostalgia for the perceived authenticity of 'good

---

[16] For a critical assessment of Rammstein, compare J Littlejohn & M Putnam (eds.), *Rammstein on Fire: New Perspectives on the Music and Performances* (Jefferson: McFarland, 2013).

[17] Compare J Balzer, *Pop und Populismus: Über Verantwortung in der Musik* (Hamburg: Edition Körber, 2019).

old rock music', all in the service of re-enacting a fake past that serves as an escapist fantasy from confusing, globalised culture.

Conclusion

By looking at the 'flip-side' of Krautrock, a counter-narrative emerges that puts into question its prevailing status as a modern movement of the 1970s. On the one hand, Krautrock was disconnected from the modernising forces of 1970s West Germany, such as feminism and Germany's shift towards multiculturalism. On the other, the legacy of the 1970s – one that reaches well into the pop-cultural scene today – springs from music traditions connected to this 'flip-side' of Krautrock. And these run counter to its claims of cosmopolitanism, anti-traditionalism, and internationalism. What's more, due to their immense commercial success, medieval rock and shanty rock were formative for German-language rock music of the 2010s. Albums by the bands mentioned consistently enter number one in the German album charts, although these genres do not feature in music-journalist discourses that critique artistically and/or politically relevant releases. So, the most powerful legacy of 1970s Krautrock is not a forward-looking, cosmopolitan music genre, but rather one that fulfils a nostalgia for old times when life seemed clearer and simpler.

Essential Listening

Ozan Ata Canani, *Warte mein Land, warte* (Staatsakt, 2021)
Die Dominas, *Die Dominas* (Fabrikneu, 1981)
Cem Karaca, *Die Kanaken* (Pläne, 1984)
Knut Kiesewetter, *Leeder Vun Mien Fresenhof* (Polydor, 1976)
Ougenweide, *Ougenweide* (Polydor, 1973)

PART III

Legacy

16 | Krautrock and German Punk

JEFF HAYTON

In a 2014 book documenting the history of electronic music in Düsseldorf, Germany, Gabi Delgado-Lopez, singer for electro-punk innovators Deutsch-Amerikanische Freundschaft (German-American Friendship, DAF), discussed the band's sonic antecedents. Explaining how DAF sought to chart a new musical path forward, he boldly asserted that the band had eschewed all previous influences: 'We didn't want to sound as if we were "historically aware"; we didn't want to follow traditions.'[1] Yet, as with much else that Delgado-Lopez has intimated over the years, his comments must be taken with a grain of salt: in that very same book he also expressed considerable admiration for Conny Plank, the Krautrock sound engineer par excellence, who recorded DAF's best albums: 'Conny was a real hippie,' he conceded, 'a hippie in the best sense.'[2] Delgado-Lopez is not alone in this, as German punk pioneers have frequently acknowledged how influential Krautrock has been for their own music.

While Delgado-Lopez is a notoriously suspect source, his claim nonetheless reflects one of punk's most enduring myths: that punk was a visceral rejection of 1970s rock 'n' roll, a radical agenda of musical rupture. As critics have long contended, punk music, fashion, and lifestyle constituted perhaps the biggest musical departure since Elvis.[3] With its fast tempos, distorted guitars, and snotty vocals, punk disdain for all that came before ostensibly freed the genre from the conventions of history and imbued artists and fans with a restless search for fresh musical vistas. Certainly, as punk evolved in the 1970s and 1980s across the globe, countless musicians and bands experimented with myriad forms of new sounds, styles, and behaviours as they sought to actualise musical rupture. This myth is thus deeply embedded in many of the practices and purposes that have guided the genre since its birth; myths, after all, usually contain at least some kernels of truth.

---

[1] R Esch, *Electri_City: The Düsseldorf School of Electronic Music, 1970–1986* (London: Omnibus, 2016), p. 205. The German original appeared in 2014.

[2] Ibid., p. 227.

[3] Compare G Marcus, *Lipstick Traces: A Secret History of the Twentieth Century* (Cambridge: Belknap, 2009).

Krautrock too, like every music genre, has its own set of myths. As Ulrich Adelt has noted, the genre's musical eclecticism makes it hard to categorise what is or is not Krautrock with definitive precision.[4] Nevertheless, Krautrock certainly had a time and a place, emerging in the late 1960s in West Germany and reaching its musical apex in the following decade. Krautrock bands often combined a host of at times competing musical influences – electronic minimalism, jazzy leads, layered soundscapes, noisy sounds, groovy basslines, syncopated drumming, and even German-language lyrics – to create some of the most experimental sonic tapestries of the decade. Yet, scholars of Krautrock tell us that these musical innovations made scant impressions upon their fellow Germans, and only found slight resonance abroad in Britain, especially among the music press. Indeed, it is only recently that Krautrock has enjoyed a certain belated recognition for its musical originality, having been discovered (again) by British critics and celebrated as an indigenous German musical tradition. As this obscure history suggests, one of Krautrock's myths is its mystery, a hidden repository of wisdom and sound whose innovations remained unrecognised at the time, only to be rediscovered by future generations.

Myths, however, for all their simplifying structures and oftentimes common-sense logic – or rather, because of them – usually do not stand up to even mild interrogation. Indeed, when considering the relationship between Krautrock and punk, as Delgado-Lopez's appreciation of Plank indicates, the suggestion that the genre was lost to Germans only to be recuperated by foreigners years later is belied by the tremendous influence that Krautrock had on subsequent musical developments. Of all the musical antecedents that came together to create punk, Krautrock seems to be the most unlikely. Yet as we will see, Krautrock and punk shared tremendous similarities as punk developed in West Germany during the 1970s and 1980s. While certainly not every musical influence informing punk can be traced to Krautrock – breaks are just as prominent as continuities as even a cursory listen to the two genres attests – enough exist to make us question punk's foundational myth of musical rupture.

In what follows, I track the evolution of punk as it developed in West Germany during the late 1970s and early 1980s and explore its connections to Krautrock. Doing so shows not only how punk's claims of musical rupture are more fiction than fact, but also that Krautrock, despite the near unanimity about its absent legacy, was not quite as unknown in its home country as

---

[4] U Adelt, *Krautrock: German Music in the Seventies* (Ann Arbor: University of Michigan Press, 2016).

commentators often suggest. And what above all unites Krautrock and punk were efforts at developing an indigenous popular music culture, although as we will see, both genres tried to do so in radically different ways.

Foreign Sounds, Domestic Appropriation: Punk in West Germany

While there is no space to recount the story of punk's origins again, suffice to say, punk did not originate in West Germany, but rather in Britain and the United States. In the 1970s, bands playing fast, aggressive sounds, singing raw, provocative lyrics, and engaging in confrontational stage shows emerged across the United States. Offering a stark alternative to the peace and love of 1960s psychedelia, critics and artists saw in this music a means of making rock 'n' roll dangerous again. Inspired by these developments, scenes soon dotted the urban areas of the country and by mid-decade, punk was ready for export overseas. In 1975, British fashion designer Malcolm McLaren put together a group of local delinquents as The Sex Pistols to sell his clothing through outrage and rudimentary rock 'n' roll. A shambolic musical outfit, the band courted controversy everywhere they went. But they also inspired a wave of similar acts whose belligerent sounds, sneering lyrics, and shocking performances upended musical customs. Within a year, punk had washed over the British Isles to the glee of a small if devoted fanbase and to the angst of the population at large.

Young West Germans followed these events with rapt attention. Long-accustomed to monitoring trends via the foreign press and visits abroad, Germans were always on the look-out for new sounds. With a few exceptions, music culture in mid-1970s West Germany was an assortment of indigenous *Schlager*, homegrown imitations, and imported rock. However, punk turned the heads of those looking for something different. The antagonism, insolence, and cheek embedded in punk praxis was attractive to youths fed up with the boring workaday present. As elsewhere, punk's celebration of musical amateurism and its DIY attitude was appealing to youth: instead of countless hours practicing, punk encouraged kids to just get up and play. After some early concerts and tours by British acts, bands and scenes began to form in the big cities of the Federal Republic: Düsseldorf, Hamburg, Hanover, and West Berlin.[5]

---

[5] On German punk, compare J Hayton, *Culture from the Slums: Punk Rock in East and West Germany* (Oxford: Oxford University Press, 2022).

At first, German punks mostly imitated their English forerunners, blaring distorted chords and singing about the banalities of daily life. By 1978, youths had begun establishing the spaces and networks that were growing the subculture: clubs where bands could play like the Ratinger Hof in Düsseldorf or SO36 in West Berlin; fanzines to promote the genre to wider audiences like *The Ostrich*, *No Fun*, or *Pretty Vacant*; record labels to release punk music like Konnekschen or No Fun Records; and independent shops to supply youths with punk wares like the Zensor in West Berlin or Rip Off in Hamburg. And the mainstream media began to take notice: in early 1978, *Der Spiegel*, Germany's leading liberal news magazine, ran a sensational article about punk ('Punk: Culture from the Slums'), depicting the subculture as a social menace and its adherents duped by the music industry's perpetual search for profit.

But quickly, West German punk came into its own. Especially in the more middle-class milieus of Düsseldorf and West Berlin, artists began to experiment with sounds and lyrics as they moved from imitation to innovation. By late 1978, several bands had started singing in German, an invention heralding a tectonic shift in the ability of bands to express themselves in their native tongue. Others began experimenting with new sounds and instruments as they groped towards music that would better reflect their surroundings. Bands as diverse as Mittagspause, S.Y.P.H., Einstürzende Neubauten, and Malaria! used these advances to better connect with audiences: no longer alienated by emulating Anglo-American originals, punks began to map out a new world of sonic possibilities for German listeners.

The next year, *Sounds*, the leading music magazine in the Federal Republic, threw its weight behind the genre as several journalists, especially Alfred Hilsberg, saw in punk the beginnings of a new national popular music culture. In 1979, the first recordings were released, and the first large festivals were staged, products and events suturing together the various scenes into a national collective. But already the scene started to fragment as different understandings of punk began splitting the subculture: for some, punk was a platform for individuality and experimentation, while for others, punk was a vehicle of social revolution and leftist politics.

Despite the growing divide, by the 1980s, the punk subculture had exploded across West Germany. Countless cities featured thriving scenes. Concerts were nightly affairs and tours criss-crossed the country. Albums poured forth from independent record labels and began to make their mark on the charts. As punk's popularity increased, the music industry awoke to the sonic and monetary possibilities of the new German sounds. By 1981, major labels had signed countless new acts and begun releasing music from some of the more commercial sounding ones, marketed as the Neue Deutsche Welle (German New Wave, NDW). Driven by the success of bands such as Ideal, Trio, Nena, and many more, German-language artists dominated the musical and cultural landscape of the Federal Republic in the early 1980s.[6]

Such growth, however, fuelled a widening divide within the underground scene. Aghast at the blatant profiteering and trite absurdity which characterised some of the NDW – especially as latecomers jumped on the bandwagon with little or no connection to the earlier scene – the subculture split. Slowly but surely, the more sonically adventurous artists abandoned the scene as conformity settled over the subculture. With an emphasis on fast rhythms, political lyrics, and hostile attitudes, the subtle nuances that had characterised punk initially began to disappear as hardcore – as this subgenre of punk came to be called – soon dominated the scene. Indeed, by 1983 at the latest, punk in West Germany was defined almost exclusively by the hardcore variant and has been ever since.

Continuities and Similarities: Musical Innovations and Generational Revolt

This short history of punk in West Germany, on its surface, seems to deny any continuities with Krautrock. Yet by exploring the ideological imperatives, musical elements, and subcultural praxis guiding punk, we can see how the genre mined Krautrock in various ways. Not only do these echoes suggest tremendous continuities between the genres, but they also point to the direct legacy of Krautrock on later German popular music genres. Above all, we can see is how both Krautrock and later punk sought – in their own ways – to use music as a form of emancipation.

Yet even on the surface there existed considerable similarities and connections between Krautrock and punk. Despite bombastic claims to the contrary, many punks acknowledged not only a debt to Krautrock but a genuine admiration for their musical ancestors. Figures as diverse as Blixa Bargeld from Einstürzende Neubauten, Harry Rag from S.Y.P.H., Jürgen Engler from Die Krupps, or Ralf Dörper from Propaganda have all expressed at one time or another their appreciation for bands like Faust,

---

[6] On German New Wave, compare B Hornberger, *Geschichte wird gemacht. Die Neue Deutsche Welle. Eine Epoche deutscher Popmusik* (Würzburg: Königshausen & Neumann, 2011).

Can, Cluster, Kraftwerk, and others: Rag went so far as to suggest his musical objective was to mix punk with Can.[7] Nor were these parallels a one-way street either as several Krautrock musicians – Holger Czukay from Can, for example – have hinted that Krautrock behaviours, such as their atypical stage shows, prefigured punk.[8] While others reject such insinuations as anachronistic – Michael Rother dismisses the suggestion by Julian Cope that Neu! invented punk *avant-la-lettre* – nonetheless, many continuities connect Krautrock to punk.[9]

Indeed, there were significant personnel links between Krautrock and punk. Czukay, much to Rag's delight, helped produce several S.Y.P.H. albums, while Klaus Schulze from Tangerine Dream and Ash Ra Tempel released Ideal's breakthrough debut on his IC label. Alfred Hilsberg, the *Sounds* journalist whose independent record label ZickZack released records from many of the most experimental punk bands, began his career organising Krautrock shows in his hometown of Wolfsburg. And Conny Plank, the Krautrock audio engineer, collaborated with DAF, Die Krupps, and others as he gravitated towards electronic pop in the 1980s: indeed, his production of DAF's *Alles ist gut* (1981) won the top record award of the Deutsche Phono-Akademie.[10]

Of course, not all punk or NDW musicians received Krautrock quite so favourably: if one can find compliments, one can equally find condemnations. Delgado-Lopez, despite his praise for Plank, also dismissed bands like Kraftwerk for their arrogant behaviour and languid stage shows.[11] Meikel Clauss, guitarist for the hardcore outfit KFC and later NDW act Nichts, likewise spoke generally about a distrust the younger generation felt for those with long hair.[12] In fact, long hair – the body – was a critical location where punk and Krautrock diverged: Peter Hein, the Mittagspause and Fehlfarben singer, spoke for many when he observed that Krautrockers looked just as ridiculous as punks, but unlike the former, for the latter, that 'was our job'.[13]

Even those who could appreciate Krautrock music had difficulty accepting the cultural baggage accompanying the 1960s generation. Diedrich Diederichsen, former editor of *Sounds* and *Spex*, for example, has

---

[7] J Teipel, *Verschwende Deine Jugend: Ein Doku-Roman über den deutschen Punk und New Wave* (Frankfurt: Suhrkamp, 2001), pp. 45–6. Compare also D Stubbs, *Future Days: Krautrock and the Building of Modern Germany* (London: Faber, 2014), p. 416; and Teipel, *Verschwende Deine Jugend*, p. 191.

[8] Teipel, *Verschwende Deine Jugend*, pp. 14–15.   [9] Esch, *Electri_City*, p. 96.

[10] M Spies & R Esch, *Das ist DAF: Deutsch Amerikanische Freundschaft. Die autorisierte Biografie* (Berlin: Schwarzkopf, 2017), pp. 162–3.

[11] Teipel, *Verschwende Deine Jugend*, p. 96–7.   [12] Esch, *Electri_City*, p. 134.   [13] Ibid., p. 244.

elaborated how, back then, hippies unproblematically recuperated German romanticism in their fascination with Eastern esotericism, an assemblage informing their musical productions that, for a younger generation, was precisely the kind of *naïveté* that had led to Nazism in the 1930s.[14] Although we should perhaps be sceptical of Diederichsen's analysis of Nazism, nevertheless, for punks, such sentiments were common currency and fuelled their contempt for Krautrock: indeed, there are numerous accounts of confrontations occurring between youths and their elders, conflicts even involving physical violence.[15] Yet for all the invective some punks spewed toward Krautrock, such engagement nonetheless speaks to connection whereby the latter functioned as an 'Other' for the former to rage against in their musical constructions.

Nevertheless, despite such antagonism, continuity was the dominant relationship between Krautrock and punk. These connections are quite explicit in the impulses driving both genres. One of Krautrock's ideological imperatives was the creation of a new cultural heritage, freed from the historical legacies that seemed to plague West German society in the 1960s. On the one hand, this meant divorcing German cultural production and expression from any hint of a nationalist or fascist past. On the other hand, it meant establishing indigenous musical forms rooted in German experiences rather than Anglo-American pop traditions.

Punks too saw their endeavours in such terms, as both a repudiation of the past and as a means of forging an alternative future. At the heart of their ambition was a commitment to radical experimentation in pursuit of cultural renewal. For many youths, the 1970s was a bleak decade full of stultifying conformity and deadening boredom, a period when 'Germany felt like an upholstered living room with a fat, cigarette-smoking old Nazi boss in it', as Frank Bielmeier from Mittagspause has evocatively described.[16] While not all youths felt burdened by the past to such an extent, for those who did, music was one way to break from such temporal claustrophobia.

To escape this living room of a bygone era, punk authorised radical musical rupture. Like Krautrock a decade prior, punk offered youths the freedom to pursue alternative models of identity and community through different sounds, rhythms, instruments, and more. As Bielmeier put it, while punk was developing in the late 1970s, there was ample space 'to try different things' as youths sought to remake rock 'n' roll's sonic catalogue.[17]

---

[14] Stubbs, *Future Days*, p. 409.   [15] Esch, *Electri_City*, p. 261.
[16] Teipel, *Verschwende Deine Jugend*, p. 42.   [17] Ibid., pp. 33–4.

In its initial phase before conformity took over the subculture in the 1980s, punk was a plethora of diverse music and unconventional sounds. For some, this meant composing songs around feelings. For others, it meant jettisoning verses, choruses, or refrains. Some tried introducing strange instruments or noises into the musical line-up: the construction of drums out of scraps of metal by Einstürzende Neubauten, for example, was an effort at expanding rock's rhythmic timbres.

But irrespective of tone or rhythm or lyrics or style, the purpose was clear: break with tradition and forge a new path forwards. Bernward Malaka, bassist for Male and later Die Krupps, put punk striving well when he remarked: 'We had the feeling that we could break with every-thing. Traditions: who gives a shit! They didn't mean anything. And certainly not to us.'[18] Comparing such statements with Rother's claim that Neu! 'simply wanted to play and strive forward, align ourselves to the horizon' illustrates the parallels between Krautrock and punk: both sought to radically revise musical expression and break with prior concep-tions of music-making.[19] Thus, even though many punks rejected Kraftwerk's techno-modernity or disparaged Ash Ra Tempel's sonic anarchy (their musical contents), the impulses driving the search for new sounds and styles (their musical intentions) were analogous.

As the comments about old Nazis and the discovery of new sounds suggest, punk – like Krautrock before it – was motivated at least in part by generational revolt. As observers have noted, Krautrock was intimately linked to the youth revolts taking place in the late 1960s and the alternative milieu of the 1970s.[20] Rebuffing a world considered to be synthetic and illegitimate, bands as diverse as Faust or Popol Vuh scorned the main-stream conventions of then popular German music. Instead, ethereal soundscapes merged with frenetic saxophones as Krautrock bands experi-mented with new sounds and rhythms and tones and more.

Punk too was motivated by a rejection of prior musical authorities, and rebelled against the principles governing mainstream musical expression and production. Denial of convention thus motivated the hunt for new musical possibilities in both the 1960s and the 1970s. These resemblances point to how punks were pursuing a similar strategy of musical refusal. Some have even commented upon these connections quite explicitly: Margitta Haberland, singer and violinist for Abwärts, who participated in

---

[18] Esch, Electri_City, p. 266.   [19] Ibid., p. 53.

[20] T Brown, In Search of Space: The Trope of Escape in German Electronic Music around 1968, Contemporary European History 26:2 (2017), pp. 339–52.

both the hippie and the punk revolts a decade apart, has noted how both had 'a similar approach' to cultural reinvention.[21]

Of course, the generation punks were revolting against was the '68ers: in other words, against the Krautrock generation. Countless statements by countless punks over the years attest to youth disgust with their elders. Punk hatred of hippies was complex. For some, the earnestness and seriousness of '68ers was off-putting. Others complained that hippie dogmatism was equally fascist as any Nazi. Most could not stand the endless conversations that hippies wanted to have or the probing for psychological trauma. Punks especially chaffed at the restrictions on thought or speech that they felt the Krautrock generation imposed upon others: Moritz Reichelt from Der Plan speaks for many when he describes how 'unfree' he felt back then, how there were 'many subjects' that were off-limits because to admit liking skyscrapers or concrete or plastic meant your progressive credentials were now in doubt.[22] In the late 1960s, Krautrockers were rejecting a society that had failed to come to terms with its past and seemed to be slipping into another authoritarian nightmare. Yet as Reichelt's comments suggest, punks were tilting at a similar windmill as these one-time rebels – a mere decade later – had become the reactionaries.

And in their rejection of hippies, punks condemned them for the same hypocrisies that '68ers had directed at their parents. The indictments punks lobbed at hippies were endless. Punks snorted derisively at hippies' romantic adoration of nature as nothing but escapist pandering.[23] They dismissed their ideological assumptions that saw workers as the revolutionary subject.[24] They hated the over-emphasis on politics; indeed, some youths were attracted to punk by its lack of politics.[25] They condemned the smug arrogance of '68ers who had supposedly liberated society through sit-ins and demonstrations: as Xao Seffcheque has insightfully observed, just as hippies had once grown their hair long to assert independence from their elders, so too did punks chop their long hair off to reject theirs.[26]

Crucially, the utopianism that motivated the 1960s generation was denied by punks, who were overjoyed that 'Die Welt ist schlecht, das Leben ist schön' (The World Is Terrible, but Life Is Grand) as a Der Plan song put it.[27] Indeed, the realism coursing through punk, the beauty that

---

[21] Teipel, *Verschwende Deine Jugend*, p. 62   [22] Ibid., p. 83.   [23] Ibid., p. 89.   [24] Ibid., p. 110
[25] Ibid., p. 66.
[26] X Seffcheque, Umgeschichtet wird die Macht!, in X Seffcheque & E Labonté (eds.), *Geschichte wird gemacht: Deutscher Underground in den Achtzigern* (Munich: Heyne, 2018), pp. 227, 230.
[27] Teipel, *Verschwende Deine Jugend*, pp. 38–9.

punks felt for a world of advertising and stoplights, was a posture intended to contrast themselves with their ancestors: when S.Y.P.H. sang 'Zurück zum Beton' (Back to Concrete), they did so to antagonise hippies, much as '68ers had once done through a celebration of nature with their parents.[28] Certainly, the contents of punk criticisms were different, but the forms were similar, a continuousness speaking to the limits of generational revolt, or perhaps even an innate repetitiousness of music culture critique.

Ruptures and Differences: Music-Making and the Politics of Emancipation

Yet intriguingly, haircuts and a love of cement also points to how, just as Krautrock had sought to restore agency and independence to German music culture years prior, so too did punk. The creation of the legendary institutions and infrastructure surrounding Krautrock – from the Zodiak Free Arts Lab in West Berlin to the independent record labels like Ohr and Brain – were efforts by '68ers to overcome the constraints of conventional youth culture and the hegemony of the music industry. These spaces and structures sought to construct alternative sites of musical production and to free artists and audiences from socio-economic dependency. The push for artistic autonomy was similarly a major objective informing punk. The DIY impulse, so crucial to the alternative milieu and to punk, was front and centre in this endeavour.[29]

As both a necessity and an ethos, youths attracted to punk had been compelled to create their own music culture because the music industry had no interest in it, at least initially. Before the subculture burst into the mainstream in the 1980s, punks had stapled together photocopies to make fanzines, rented out rooms to create clubs, and painted the tops of beer caps to fashion buttons. These activities sought to emancipate punk from influences in society that controlled music culture, whether the fashion industry or the mainstream media. Hilsberg's ZickZack record label, for example, just like Rolf-Ulrich Kaiser's Ohr, was created to release music that the major labels were ignoring.[30]

---

[28] Ibid., pp. 262, 89.

[29] On DIY, compare R Kreis, *Selbermachen: Eine andere Geschichte des Konsumzeitalters* (Frankfurt: Campus, 2020).

[30] On Hilsberg, compare C Meueler, *Das ZickZack Prinzip: Alfred Hilsberg – ein Leben für den Untergrund* (Munich: Heyne, 2016).

The label's slogan, 'Lieber zu viel als zu wenig' (Better too much than too little) was intended literally, to flood the market with punk music, and towards this end, Hilsberg released hundreds of records over the years. For youths in both the 1960s and 1970s, these drives towards independence were part and parcel of their musical rebellion as they sought to transform the production and consumption of music both spiritually and materially.

Indeed, DIY was a crucial continuity connecting punk with Krautrock as a vehicle of emancipation. More than anything, punk DIY freed music from professionalism and returned art to the hands of amateurs. One of the biggest complaints by punks was how contemporary music-making had been robbed of spontaneity and accessibility through virtuosity and pro-fessionalism. Considering such emphases alienating and inhibiting, punks instead sought to return music to the masses through dilettantism whereby sound was subordinate to expression, and talent secondary to effort.

In this respect, punk amateurism sought to democratise rock 'n' roll, an objective many Krautrock artists had sought as well.[31] In discussing how punks made music, Padeluun, a performance artist and sporadic member of Minus Delta t, explained: 'With punk, it didn't matter what came out. It wasn't about having any form of perfection . . . rather, it was about showing other people: "You can do this too."'[32] Such inspiration was also reflective of the incomplete nature of punk sound – the idea that music must not be perfect, that failure was an essential element of creation – a sentiment that encouraged people to get involved. These emancipatory attitudes, which hark back to earlier genres, unbound music-making and helped expand composition and performance beyond a narrow circle of professionals.

When punks made music, they often endeavoured to invent new sounds and new tones as part of their musical insurgency. And one of the driving impetuses behind these struggles was a rejection of foreign musical tradi-tions. For many youths, punk was an explicit means of freeing Germans from Anglo-American musical hegemony. As numerous artists have articulated, both at the time and since, they were frustrated that Anglo-Americans held 'a monopoly' over modern music, that Anglo-American conventions ruled musical production.[33] Harry Rag, for instance, was annoyed that in the 1970s, every song had to have a beginning and an end, while Delgado-Lopez hated harmony, verses, and refrains.[34] Nor was this monopoly simply a matter of sounds or composition, as they linked such hegemony to a loss of voice and identity.

---

[31] Compare Stubbs, *Future Days*, pp. 89–90.   [32] Teipel, *Verschwende Deine Jugend*, p. 87.
[33] Ibid., p. 177.   [34] Ibid., pp. 91, 292.

Delgado-Lopez, for instance, told *Sounds* at the time about the cognitive dissonance experienced by German bands as they made music: 'It's so funny to be in an all-German band playing for a German audience and singing in English!'[35] But as punks began to sing in German, and to make 'German music' they sought to broaden the space available for new forms of identifications, community, and culture. In this sense, punk represented a mode of resistance, defiance against musical dominion as artists wrested control over sonic expression that allowed youths the opportunity to create music that was modern, stylish, and 'German'.

Punk distaste for Anglo-American conventions was of course already prefigured a decade earlier by Krautrock musicians. As they sought to expand the conventions of musical possibility, they too had often pushed back against foreign impositions en route to developing their own musical and cultural identities. Amon Düül II guitarist John Weinzierl, for example, has related how the band did not imitate American rock and instead sought to discover a new path forward musically: 'It was about listening, seeing what comes, what could be done, what could be done differently.'[36] Schulze too has insisted that Tangerine Dream refused to copy Anglo-American music, how they deliberately played with new forms of musical expression, while Can sought to reject any blues-based formulations, which were deemed inappropriate for West German acts.[37]

Of course, how to create 'German music' was an open question and my use of scare quotes points to the concept's fundamental instability. For punks, creating 'German music' was similarly embedded in a rejection of Anglo-American pop traditions. But unlike Krautrockers, many punks located Germanness in their native tongue. Indeed, what separates punk above all from Krautrock is the former's emphasis on lyrics and singing in German. While a few bands had experimented with German lyrics – notably Kraftwerk's nursery rhyme repetitions and the occasional word by Can vocalist Damo Suzuki – sound-dominated Krautrock.

For punks, however, vocals quickly became paramount. When punk first emerged in West Germany, bands copied Anglo-American acts and sang in English. But already by 1978, especially in the Ruhr region, bands started to experiment with German-language lyrics. That hippies had rejected German as a continuity with the fascist past meant the native tongue was available for punk's generational revolt. However, the move to German lyrics was more than simply a Pavlovian reaction. Songs were crafted to reflect everyday life

---

[35] Quoted in Spies & Esch, *Das ist DAF*, p. 67   [36] Stubbs, *Future Days*, pp. 96–7.
[37] Ibid., pp. 122, 288.

as artists penned songs that could articulate contemporary concerns. Certainly, in the initial late-1970s burst of German-language songwriting, punk songs thematised many of the most pressing issues of the day: the Cold War, terrorism, deindustrialisation, etc. And critics hearing punk at the time understood how revolutionary the turn to German-language lyrics was: Hilsberg, writing in *Sounds* about Mittagspause's classic anthem 'Militürk', gushed that the song 'tells us more about Germany in 1979 than many pages of analysis'.[38] As Hilsberg's review recognised, German lyrics suddenly gave youth a new vocabulary of expression to vocalise the present after decades of remaining voiceless.

To sing in German, however, was challenging. As many commentators have observed, singing in German in the post-war era was considered taboo. Associated with *Schlager* or the Third Reich, German lyrics were deemed provincial or xenophobic.[39] They were also judged inappropriate for rock 'n' roll rhythms; that Anglo-American music became the lingua franca of 1960s youth culture only solidified these prejudices. For youths growing up in the 1970s, these biases were common: as Moritz Reichelt put it: 'In my hippie days, I didn't listen to Kraftwerk because it was German. And German was above all embarrassing.'[40] To sing in German meant to compose songs that would reflect German syntax and grammar, to write music accentuating alternative rhythms and irregular tempos. In the *New Musical Express*, for example, Delgado-Lopez outlined many of the considerations that needed to be pondered when pairing German-language texts with the electronica that DAF was pioneering in the early 1980s:

[German] is a very good language to sing in. It has a very complicated rhythm, a very good precise rhythm, and for the music we do, mainly with sequencers, it fits very well together. There are so many syllables in the German language, and the rhythm of the language fits very well into the sequencer rhythms. It is better than what you can with English. English is so relaxed.[41]

DAF saw this development as the culmination of their attempts to free German popular music from what they and others at the time called 'English pop imperialism'.[42] They were not alone: as Bob Giddens from *ZigZag* put it: 'For me, being a Brit, DAF was the only band – aside from

[38] A Hilsberg, Review: Mittagspause, *Sounds* 8 (1979), p. 52.
[39] E Larkey, Just for Fun? Language Choice in German Popular Music, in H Berger & M Carroll (eds.), *Global Pop, Local Language* (Jackson: University of Mississippi Press, 2003), pp. 131–51.
[40] Teipel, *Verschwende Deine Jugend*, p. 85.   [41] Quoted in Spies & Esch, *Das ist DAF*, p. 69.
[42] A Hilsberg, Punk Emigration, *Sounds* 11 (1979), p. 7. Compare also A Hilsberg, Rodenkirchen Is Burning – Krautpunk, *Sounds* 3 (1978), p. 24.

Kraftwerk – who managed to form a unit out of German lyrics and music, reflecting German culture without any Anglo-American influences.'[43]

Conclusion

The connection between Kraftwerk and DAF by an outside observer speaks to the continuities existing within German popular music. Of course, to listen to a Krautrock song and a punk song side-by-side is to immediately note the incredibly sonic dissimilarities: one does not need to be a musicologist to understand these are vastly different musical genres. Yet peeling back the surface to look at some of the underlying ideologies and impulses guiding these musical creations is to recognise tremendous continuities. Whether in the search for new musical innovations, the generational revolt, the emphasis on independence, or the attempts to create 'German music', punk and Krautrock share a surprising number of similarities.

For these reasons, the myth of musical rupture, which often informs our understanding of punk, demands greater scrutiny, as does the myth of Krautrock's absent presence: Krautrock was an influential spectre haunting German punk. As punk and Krautrock become increasingly incorporated into German cultural heritage, exploring the ways in which these genres respond to and interrogate with each other over time can illuminate the ways in which past echoes help direct future sounds.

Recommended Reading

R Esch, *Electri_City: The Düsseldorf School of Electronic Music, 1970–1986* (London: Omnibus, 2016).

M Hall, S Howes & C Shahan (eds.), *Beyond No Future: Cultures of German Punk* (London: Bloomsbury, 2016).

J Hayton, *Culture from the Slums: Punk Rock in East and West Germany* (Oxford: Oxford University Press, 2022).

B Hornberger, *Geschichte wird gemacht: Die Neue Deutsche Welle – Eine Epoche deutscher Popmusik* (Würzburg: Königshausen & Neumann, 2011).

C Shahan, *Punk Rock and German Crisis: Adaption and Resistance after 1977* (New York: Palgrave Macmillan, 2013).

J Teipel, *Verschwende Deine Jugend: Ein Doku-Roman über den deutschen Punk und New Wave* (Frankfurt: Suhrkamp, 2001).

[43] Esch, *Electri_City*, p. 219.

17 | Krautrock and British Post-Punk

ALEXANDER CARPENTER

The experimental aesthetic and anti-rock ethos of Krautrock played a key role in shaping the sound of British post-punk music. The term 'post-punk' is generally applied to the avant-garde popular music that arose in the immediate aftermath of the punk scene in the late 1970s and into the early 1980s. Well-known musicians who had been central to punk in Britain – perhaps most notably singer Johnny Rotten (John Lydon) of the Sex Pistols – drew upon Krautrock as a means to escape the strictures of their own legacy. Other bands that had been catalysed by punk's energy – like Siouxsie and the Banshees and Bauhaus – channelled Krautrock's 'Teutonic coolness' into new subgenres, such as gothic rock.

Still others, like Manchester's Joy Division, took David Bowie's Krautrock-inspired Berlin albums as a cue to experiment with songwriting, production, and expression; and post-punk cult band The Fall, also from Manchester, used Krautrock as the foundation for their potpourri of stylistic influences. Indeed, it was ultimately the post-punk rocker, Julian Cope, singer of The Teardrop Explodes, who would serve as Krautrock's most important and vocal advocate in Britain, publishing his now-(in)famous compendium, *Krautrocksampler*, in 1995.[1]

This essay focusses on several main issues. First, it addresses the question of how to define 'post-punk' in the first place, a vague term often simply used as a catch-all for the creative explosion and intermingling of genres that occurred in alternative British popular music, as punk was on the wane. Second, it considers how Krautrock contributed to the aesthetic of post-punk music. Finally, it reflects upon Krautrock as part of a broader and arguably constitutive Germanophilic impulse in the British post-punk movement.

---

[1] Ironically, little of Cope's music reflects the influence of Krautrock. The Teardrop Explodes' song 'Sleeping Gas', from the 1980 album *Kilimanjaro* is a notable exception.

The End of Punk and the Birth of Post-Punk

The historiography of popular music tends to privilege the punk era in Britain, focusing narrowly on the years 1976–77 as a period of musical revolution during which youth culture, driven by a general feeling of nihilism and ennui over socio-economic conditions, sought to challenge – if not overturn – the musical status quo via angry, irreverent, and often amateurish stripped-down rock. Epitomised by the Sex Pistols, whose proclamation of 'no future' and clarion calls for 'anarchy in the UK' characterised the genre, punk rejected much of what it saw in the popular music of the early 1970s – the self-indulgent virtuosity of progressive rock, the worn-out leftovers of blues-based hard rock, the banality of disco – in favour of the raw authenticity found in the simple, loud, sped-up garage rock already popularised in the United States by bands like MC5, Iggy and The Stooges, and The Ramones. Punk in Britain inspired a youth fashion movement comprised of ripped clothes and spiked hair, a club scene that featured primitive and punitive dancing, and a DIY approach to music that gave birth to a host of bands that could barely play their instruments as they noisily antagonised their audiences.[2]

Punk is well-known for its 'back-to-basics' aesthetic, focusing on rudimentary rock beats, a limited harmonic palette, self-produced recordings and a loose approach to pitch, rhythm, and ensemble playing. But rather than being a revolutionary movement, from a musical perspective punk was a decisive regression: in effect, it was something of a revivalist movement, its primary elements based firmly in the roots of rock. It was arguably the years immediately after punk that were truly radical and transformative, with young British musicians orienting themselves towards experimentation, hybridisation and, in sharp contrast to punk's nihilism, the future.

What Is Post-Punk?

The primary challenge presented by the concept of 'post-punk' as a genre is the stylistic diversity – or rather, the stylistic 'inconsistency', as musicologist Mimi Haddon insists[3] – of the music associated with it. The label

---

[2] On the history of punk, compare R Sabin (ed.), *Punk Rock: So What? The Cultural Legacy of Punk* (Abingdon: Routledge, 1999).

[3] M Haddon, *What Is Post-Punk? Genre and Identity in Avant-Garde Popular Music, 1977–1982* (Ann Arbor: University of Michigan Press, 2020), p. 2.

'post-punk' denotes a time period after punk, spanning roughly 1978–85, but also suggests a surpassing of punk with respect to its aesthetic characteristics. Haddon offers the following summary of post-punk, as it is commonly described in scholarly and journalistic discourses:

The music is oriented toward the radical, the new, and the experimental. It is not as mainstream as punk … And the genre displayed more 'musicianship' than punk, and assumed a kind of 'mature theatricality'. In addition to these tendencies, we might also think of post-punk in terms of its sonic characteristics … dour (male) vocals with erudite or self-conscious lyrics, accompanied by metallic-sounding, distorted electric guitars playing texturally, not melodically; an accelerated disco beat or dance groove; a melodic bass line; and echoing sound effects borrowed from dub-reggae.[4]

While this by no means encapsulates the totality of the post-punk move-ment, it provides a place to start. A key point – and directly applicable to Krautrock as well – is the paradoxical identity of the genre as diverse yet somehow coherent: post-punk is a recognisable genre that is at the same time highly fragmented and diasporic, comprising a kaleidoscope of sub-genres emerging out of the rubble of punk. Also paradoxical is post-punk's supposed modernist turn towards radical newness, in which moving for-wards to reject punk's conservativism – a rejection in fact catalysed by punk's energy and attitude – also meant looking backwards to the music of the pre-punk era, to borrow from the genres that punk had rejected, including disco, funk, and progressive rock. In so doing, post-punk was at once anti-punk even as it was saving punk from itself, allowing it to expand and diversify.[5]

Post-punk is a genre too large and too diverse to survey here, but there is a handful of representative bands that will be the focus of this chapter and will serve to demonstrate the affinities between post-punk and Krautrock, including Public Image Ltd., Joy Division, Siouxsie and the Banshees, and Bauhaus.

One Path to Post-Punk: David Bowie and Krautrock in Berlin

Post-punk owes an enormous debt to David Bowie, who was in turn indebted to Krautrock during a key moment of artistic crisis and change. As Simon Reynolds observes, Bowie's propensity for reinventing himself, for

---

[4] Ibid., p. 4.   [5] I Ellis, Post-Punk: The Cerebral Genre, *PopMatters* (17 April 2019).

'always chasing the next edge' made him the primary 'inspiration for post-punk's ethos of perpetual change'.[6] In addition to a penchant for black music styles – especially reggae, ska, and dub – post-punk bands drew heavily from Bowie's personae and musical style. Bowie's glam era inspired many post-punk musicians and groups, including early goth bands like Bauhaus and Siouxsie and the Banshees, which whole-heartedly adopted his early 1970s theatricality and playful androgyny as a means to both transcend the musical limitations of punk and to imaginatively explore the possibilities of popular music as a kind of gender-fluid, transmedial art form. But it was arguably Bowie's radical musical shift during his time in Berlin in the later 1970s – a shift strongly marked by the influence of Krautrock – that most significantly shaped the aesthetic of British post-punk.

Bowie moved from Los Angeles to Berlin in 1976 with Iggy Pop, in part to overcome a debilitating drug habit but also to flee the American music scene. Between 1976 and 1978, Bowie wrote and recorded his so-called 'Berlin trilogy' – the albums *Low*, *'Heroes'*, and *Lodger* – and produced Iggy Pop's album *The Idiot*. These albums are celebrated for their experimental ethos, formal variety, and sonic richness, in sharp contrast to the contemporaneous back-to-basics monochrome of punk in Britain. Indeed, the sound of the revolutionary drum production on *Low* (which is also clearly audible on some tracks on *The Idiot*, such as 'Funtime') – facilitated by experimentation with processing the drums through an Eventide Harmoniser – has been characterised as almost single-handedly helping to sonically shape the post-punk aesthetic, and was sought after by drummers in seminal post-punk bands.[7] While in Germany, Bowie became enamoured with Krautrock: during the Berlin period, Bowie recounts being 'a big fan' of Kraftwerk, Cluster, Can, Neu!, and Harmonia – regarding Krautrock as 'where the future of music was going' – and he actively sought collaborations with Krautrock musicians, perhaps most notably (if unsuccessfully), Michael Rother from Neu!.[8]

Bowie chronicler Nicholas Pegg suggests that the singer's interest in new German music is already evident on the title track of the 1975 album *Station to Station*, with its 'chilly Teutonic beat'.[9] But the Krautrock

---

[6] S Reynolds, *Rip It Up and Start Again: Postpunk 1978–1984* (London: Faber, 2005), xxi.

[7] Compare W Hermes, How David Bowie, Brian Eno Revolutionized Rock on 'Low', *Rolling Stone* (13 January 2017); H Wilcken, *David Bowie's Low* (New York: Continuum, 2011), p. 71.

[8] Quoted in S Albiez, Europe Non-Stop: West Germany, Britain, and the Rise of Synth-Pop, 1975–1981, in S Albiez & D Pattie (eds.), *Kraftwerk: Music Non-Stop* (New York: Continuum, 2011), pp. 139–62 (150).

[9] N Pegg, *The Complete David Bowie* (London: Titan, 2016), p. 382.

influence on Bowie becomes fully manifest on 1979's *Lodger*, the final album in the Berlin trilogy: tracks like the galloping 'Move On', and especially 'Red Sails', with its droning harmonies and brisk *motorik* beat, was immediately identified by critics like Jon Savage as derived from Neu!; Bowie himself acknowledged his debt to 'that Neu! sound', and also seems to have borrowed heavily from Harmonia's song 'Monza' for the chords and beat of 'Red Sails'.[10]

Bowie also connected with Krautrock via composer and producer Brian Eno, his main collaborator for the Berlin albums. Eno was influenced by the experimental techniques of German art music composer Karlheinz Stockhausen, as were a number of Krautrock musicians (including Irmin Schmidt and Holger Czukay of Can, both of whom studied composition with Stockhausen in the early 1960s). Drawing on Stockhausen, Eno – like Schmidt and Czukay – helped to build bridges between avant-garde art music and pop music. But Eno also worked directly with the Krautrock 'supergroup' Harmonia – comprised of members of Cluster and Neu! – in the early autumn of 1976, immediately before joining Bowie in Berlin to record *Low* at Hansa Studios (Eno would go on to record another 'Krautrock' album, *Cluster & Eno*, in 1977).

The influence of Krautrock, via Bowie's personal affinity for Kraftwerk's electronic experimentation and Eno's immediate experience composing and performing with important Krautrock musicians, is readily apparent on *Low*, through its emphasis on moody ambient sound, long instrumental tracks, heavy reliance on electronics, and a shift towards more abstract and intermittent lyrics. As Sean Albiez has observed, Bowie's Berlin albums were 'a crucial conduit through which travelled Krautrock and pre-war hedonistic and post-war geopolitical German myths and memes that fascinated British fans and musicians'.[11]

Musical Teutonism? A 'German Sound'?

Bowie's move to Berlin and the attendant Krautrock-inspired aesthetic changes in his music can be seen as reflecting a rather un-British Germanophilia, which, I argue, is an essential element of British post-punk: even as punk was still in full swing as of 1977, the music Bowie and Iggy Pop

---

[10] J Savage, David Bowie: Lodger, *Melody Maker* (26 May 1979); Pegg, *Complete David Bowie*, p. 223.

[11] Albiez, Europe Non-Stop, p. 152.

were recording in Berlin was already poised to cast a huge shadow over the alternative popular music scene in Britain. As Bowie's producer Tony Visconti has recounted, the Berlin albums were positively imbued with a 'Teutonic ambience', derived in part from the atmosphere and acoustics of the Hansa studio, but also, he insists, from simply being present in Germany and absorbing Berlin's 'manic energy [and] . . . manic aggression', which he associates with the city's (Nazi) history.[12] Simon Reynolds likewise has remarked on Bowie's shift away from American rock 'n' roll towards a Germanic aesthetic characterised as 'a cool and controlled sound modelled on the Teutonic *motorik* rhythms of Kraftwerk and Neu!'.[13]

Reviews of Krautrock albums in the British music press in the early 1970s – many of which were decidedly ambivalent – first inscribed many of these tropes. Bands like Can are commonly described as 'spare and stark', possessing a 'German sound' and 'Teutonic heaviness' that is 'often frighteningly cold'.[14] Kraftwerk, presumably because they foregrounded the use of electronic instruments, were especially singled out by the press for their perceived Germanic peccadillos, including austerity, emotionlessness, repetition, and regimentation in their music.[15]

These tropes of coolness and detached Teutonism shape much of the discourse surrounding post-punk music: influential post-punk and proto-goth bands like Siouxsie and the Banshees, Bauhaus, and Joy Division are sometimes given the generic designation 'coldwave',[16] with the heavy use of reverb, trebly and dissonant guitar sound effects, bass-dominated textures, and mechanistic rhythms contributing to the notion of a somehow cold, innately German sound.

Punk to Post-Punk: From Germanophobia to Germanophilia

Post-punk musicians, looking further afield for influences and inspiration, turned not only to Bowie but to Krautrock directly. It is now certainly becoming more common for contemporary mainstream bands

---

[12] Quoted in C Young, Producing David Bowie's Berlin Trilogy, *Prosound News* (6 April 2018).

[13] Reynolds, *Rip It Up and Start Again*, p. xxi.

[14] M Watts, Can: Tago Mago, *Melody Maker* (29 January 1972); J Johnson, Can Can . . . And They Will, *New Musical Express* (5 February 1972).

[15] Compare U Schütte, From Defamation to Adoration: The Reception of Kraftwerk in the British Music Press, 1974–1981, *Angermion* 31:1 (2020), pp. 1–24.

[16] Compare V Goldman, Siouxsie and the Banshees, *Sounds* (3 December 1977). Goldman uses the term 'cold wave' repeatedly to describe the music of Siouxsie and the Banshees; J Savage, Taxi zum Klo's Berlin Is a Sexual Playground, *The Guardian* (21 April 2011).

to name-check Krautrock as a formative influence – U2 and Coldplay, for example – and for pop and hip-hop artists to sample from Krautrock songs – in recent years, Jay-Z, Kanye West, Daft Punk, and A Tribe Called Quest, among others. However, in the 1970s Krautrock was, as David Stubbs notes, overshadowed by disco and punk, and 'marginal' at a time when, especially in Britain, 'Germanophobia still held sway, though now it took the shape of condescending amusement, rather than outright hostility'.[17] The very appellation 'Krautrock' makes this quite clear: it is a dismissive, if not outright offensive sobriquet, invented by British music journalists to denigrate German music.

The historian Patrick Major observes that 'British identity in the late twentieth century appeared to have been profoundly and negatively informed by its encounter with Germany', and that Germany 'was the nation Britons apparently loved to hate'. He links anti-German sentiment to post-war animosity but also sees it as the core of a more generalised Euroscepticism fostered by Cold War and reunification anxieties.[18] Furthermore, as Uwe Schütte has argued, 'perceptions of Germans and German culture in the UK continue to be dogged by old stereotypes'.[19] Today, the perpetuation of these 'old stereotypes' are made possible, according to Schütte, by contemporary German bands such as Rammstein, 'who peddle silly Teutonic clichés about Germany' and turn the German language in which they sing 'into the parodic representation of the Nazi Germans seen in war films'.[20]

In the mid-1970s, the punk movement in Britain traded directly on Nazi-themed Germanophobia, thanks in large part to the efforts of punk impresario and Sex Pistols' manager Malcolm McLaren, whose infamous London boutique Sex sold Nazi regalia. Swastikas became de rigeur fashion for controversy-seeking punk rockers, notably Siouxsie Sioux and Sid Vicious of The Sex Pistols. The Pistols would also flirt with Nazi history by writing and recording songs that blended clumsy social critique with provocative references to the Holocaust, including 'Holiday in the Sun' and 'Belsen Was a Gas'.

As a fashion statement, punk's use of Nazi symbolism and paraphernalia hinted at Susan Sontag's fascinating fascism – the aesthetic allure of totalitarianism, which she described in the *New York Review of Books* in

---

[17] D Stubbs, *Future Days: Krautrock and the Building of Modern Germany* (London: Faber, 2014), p. 3.

[18] P Major, Britain and Germany: A Love-Hate Relationship?, *German History* 26:4 (2008), pp. 457–68 (457).

[19] U Schütte, *Kraftwerk: Future Music from Germany* (London: Penguin, 2020), p. 6.   [20] Ibid.

1975[21] – but much of it was merely tasteless, anti-establishment provocation, trading in part on reflexive anti-German sentiment in Britain and, in
the case of McLaren and The Sex Pistols, simply 'us[ing] the swastika as an
instrument of boorishness and to profess total ignorance about the events
and political movements referenced by their clothing'.[22] Indeed, McLaren
himself was Jewish, as was Sid Vicious' girlfriend Nancy Spungen.[23] John
Lydon has since disavowed 'Belsen Was a Gas' as a nasty song that never
should have been released. In the immediate wake of punk, much of the
music that sprung to life was, though catalysed by punk, in fact
Germanophilic: while Stubbs characterises this impulse more generically
as 'Europhilia', part of a turning away from the strictures of British culture,
I would argue that it is clearly German music that is attractive to the early
generation of post-punk groups, who are ultimately responsible for
Krautrock's resurrection in the late 1970s as a 'legend, a posthumous
phenomenon'.[24]

Punk Rock versus Krautrock, I: Public Image Ltd.

The shift from punk to post-punk as a shift underwritten by Krautrock-
inspired Germanophilia can readily be seen in the music of Siouxsie and
the Banshees and Public Image Ltd. (or PIL, John Lydon's post-Sex Pistols
project). PIL is perhaps the UK post-punk band most often directly linked
with Krautrock. Lydon left the Sex Pistols in 1978, forming a new band with
bassist Jah Wobble, guitarist Keith Levene, and drummer Jim Walker. PIL
eschewed the controversy and increasing commercialism of punk, focusing
instead on music-making, bringing to the fore two of Lydon's great musical
interests: dub reggae and Krautrock (Stubbs calls Lydon a 'Krautrock
fanatic'[25]).

   The band's first album, *First Issue* (1978), is rough, with the band's
direction clearly not yet certain. The second album, however, *Metal Box*
(1979), saw the band take a decisive turn towards the avant-garde. The
group's sound is bass-dominated, reflecting the influence of dub, but also
drawing from Krautrock: bassist Jah Wobble was, along with Lydon,

[21] S Sontag, Fascinating Fascism, *New York Review of Books* (6 February 1975).
[22] M Boswell, *Holocaust Impiety in Literature, Popular Music and Film* (London: Palgrave
   Macmillan, 2012), p. 105.
[23] V Goldman, Never Mind the Swastikas: The Secret History of the UK's 'Punky Jews, *The
   Guardian* (27 February 2014).
[24] Stubbs, *Future Days*, p. 429.   [25] Ibid., p. 265.

a Krautrock enthusiast whose bass playing was directly inspired by Can bassist Holger Czukay. Wobble would indeed leave PIL after recording *Metal Box*, and would go on to collaborate with Czukay and Jaki Liebezeit on the 1982 record *Full Circle*.[26]

The utopian ethos of PIL – a band determined to improve the world with their emphasis on a liberal worldview and democratic creative processes – was well aligned with Krautrock's political optimism, desire for social change, and emphasis on self-expression. In his desire to experiment with unconstrained creativity – and especially, in pursuit of a freedom from rules and what Albiez describes as an 'avant-garde noise aesthetic' that The Sex Pistols failed to achieve – Lydon negotiated a path through a disparate array of stylistic influences, chief among them Krautrock, looking especially to Can and Neu!.[27] Lydon's other key collaborator, guitarist Keith Levene, was likewise a Krautrock devotee, developing anti-rock, quasi-improvisational, noise-based guitar techniques derived from both prog rock and Krautrock; moreover, as Albiez notes, 'Levene also had an interest in technical innovation, synthesisers and, with Lydon, new studio recording strategies and techniques antithetical to punk notions of immediacy (but sharing much in common with progressive Krautrock).'[28]

The first song on *Metal Box*, 'Albatross', reflects the shared aesthetic vision of Lydon, Wobble, and Levene while pointing towards Krautrock with its repetitive, droning bass line, strict four-on-the-floor drums, Lydon's cryptic, doomily intoned lyrics, and metallic, ambient guitar noise. It is the antithesis of punk in many ways, especially with respect to its length: it is nearly eleven minutes long, with virtually no formal changes, similar to many Krautrock tracks. Other songs, like 'No Birds', drive forward rhythmically, hinting strongly at Neu!, while 'Socialist' recalls some of the proto-punk freneticism of Can. 'Memories' and 'Graveyard' sound like a bizarre merger of Krautrock, dub, and disco. Julian Cope tacitly suggests an organic link between PIL and Krautrock, citing Lydon's gnosticism and unconstrained creativity and self-exploration: Cope ultimately proposes a compelling counterfactual, namely that 'Krautrock is what Punk would have been if Johnny Rotten alone would have been in charge.'[29]

---

[26] M Matos, Mapping the Influence of Holder Czukay, Alchemist of Krautrock Legends Can, *NPR Music* (6 September 2017).

[27] S Albiez, Know History!: John Lydon, Cultural Capital and the Prog/Punk Dialectic, *Popular Music* 22:3 (2003), pp. 357–74 (369).

[28] Ibid., p. 370.   [29] Ibid., p. 368.

Punk Rock versus Krautrock, II: Siouxsie and the Banshees

Siouxsie Sioux's rise to fame began with her membership in the so-called 'Bromley Contingent', a group of die-hard Sex Pistols fans and early leaders of the British punk movement. Siouxsie (née Susan Janet Ballion) formed Siouxsie and the Banshees in late 1976, with bassist Steve Severin, drummer Kenny Morris, and guitarist Peter Fenton (soon replaced by John McKay). The group began gigging in early 1977, and released their first album, the critically-acclaimed *The Scream,* in late 1978. Early on, Siouxsie rode the punk wave of Germanophobia as a self-confessed proponent of Nazi chic: in 1976, she could be seen dressed as a Nazi dominatrix, wearing leather bondage gear with a swastika armband, admitting: 'I have to be honest but I do like the Nazi uniform. I shouldn't say it but I think it's a very good-looking uniform.'[30] In addition, as the cultural historian Roger Sabin recounts, Sioux's 'goose-stepping and right-arm salutes on stage' likewise brought a Nazi-inspired aesthetic to the fore.[31] She had originally included the line 'Too many Jews for my liking' in the Banshees song 'Love in a Void' before the lyrics were changed so it could be recorded for Polydor and released as a single in 1979. Like John Lydon, Sioux would later minimise her – and punk's – flirtation with Nazism, asserting:

It was always very much an anti-mums-and-dads thing . . . We hated older people. Not across the board, but generally the suburban thing, always harping on about Hitler, and 'We showed him', and that smug pride. It was a way of saying, 'Well, I think Hitler was very good, actually'; a way of watching someone like that go completely red-faced.[32]

Turning away from Nazi symbolism as a means to provoke, Banshees bassist Steve Severin would insist that the band's musical aesthetic was in fact derived in large part from the influence of 1970s German popular culture, and specifically from Kraftwerk, Can, and Neu![33] The band would further eschew their earlier promotion of Germanophobia by recording songs like 'Israel', which seems rather like a hymn of atonement and a disavowal of Nazi chic (Siouxsie took to wearing a Star of David around

---

[30] Quoted in L Kidd, Goose Stepping Fashion: Nazi Inspiration, *Paideusis* 5 (2011), p. C5.

[31] R Sabin, 'I Won't Let That Dago By': Rethinking Punk and Racism, in R Sabin (ed.), *Punk Rock: So What?* (Abingdon: Routledge, 1999), p. 208.

[32] Quoted in J Savage, *The England's Dreaming Tapes* (Minneapolis: University of Minnesota Press, 2010), p. 340.

[33] L Ohanesian, The Guide to Getting into Siouxsie and the Banshees, Dark Pop Outsiders, *Vice* (7 December 2018).

this time), and 'Metal Postcard (Mittageisen)', which was inspired by and celebrated the anti-Nazi German cartoonist John Heartfield.

'Metal Postcard (Mittageisen)', which is included on *The Scream* but was first heard in December 1977, recorded for the BBC's John Peel radio show, points musically at Krautrock roots through its metronomic – if not *motorik* – drumming, and drone-like oscillation between two chords. Other songs on *The Scream*, like the opening track, 'Pure', is a haunting instrumental, strongly reminiscent of some of Harmonia's ambient tracks, with dissonant guitar effects and glissandi, some rattling percussion, and a repetitive, melodic bass line. An early review of *The Scream* in the *New Musical Express* immediately recognised Krautrock's influence on the Banshees, identifying its 'anti-rock 'n' roll' ethos, and drawing a direct line to Can's 1971 *Tago Mago* album, with some Velvet Underground mixed in for good measure.[34]

The slow-building song 'Tenant', from the 1980 Banshees' album *Kaleidoscope,* sounds unmistakably like Neu!, with Siouxsie Sioux intoning lyrics over a drone-like bass line, a tinny guitar part repeating muted chords, and a steady, unembellished medium-tempo drum track that seems haunted by a *motorik* pattern that almost, but never quite fully emerges. 'Lunar Camel', from the same album, uses a drum machine and synthesiser, creating a spare and icy sonic landscape suggesting an admixture of Tangerine Dream and Kraftwerk. The Banshees' anti-rock ethos and signature sound from this period – tribal drumming featuring steady eighth note patterns on the tom-toms, a guitar sound moving away from standard chording to thinner, atmospheric, increasingly dissonant parts, and the bass guitar shifting into the foreground to become a melodic instrument – was a key element of the sonic paradigm shift of post-punk, and of the nascent gothic rock movement, discussed in the next section (though the Banshees insist they were never a goth band). This shift was shaped by Krautrock.

Joy Division and Bauhaus: From Krautrock to Goth Rock?

An additional example of a Krautrock-inspired Germanophilic shift in post-punk music can be seen and heard in the evolution of the Manchester band Joy Division, arguably one of the most influential

---

[34] N Kent, Siouxsie and the Banshees: Bansheed! What's in an Image?, *New Musical Express* (26 August 1976).

bands of the post-punk era.[35] Inspired by The Sex Pistols and David Bowie, the group began performing as Warsaw in 1977, later adapting the name Joy Division – a reference to Nazi concentration camp brothels – from the pulp novel *House of Dolls*.[36] The band's Germanness/Germanophobia-via-Nazism was initially very provocative, clearly intending to shock, in the punk vein: the band not only adopted gratuitous umlauts on their early albums, but infamously invoked Rudolf Heß at gigs and in songs (as in the early single 'Warsaw'), adopted a fascistic style of dress, and used Nazi-inspired imagery for the cover of their first EP as Joy Division, *An Ideal for Living*.[37]

But the band's final album, *Closer*, reflected a much subtler 'Holocaust piety . . . rather than the more impious approach to Holocaust representation that characterised early punk bands', in the form of a powerful expression of empathy for the victims of the Nazi genocide, abstracted into the band's signature general suffering and existential angst, which served in part to emphasise the necessity of an historical reckoning with the atrocities of the past in order to confront violence in contemporary society.[38]

In terms of Joy Divison's musical sound and style, the band's former drummer, Stephen Morris, avers that, like many young musicians in the mid-1970s, he was excited by American proto-punk, and was actively seeking alternatives to shop-worn, blues-based rock. Ultimately, however, he turned to Krautrock, and bands like Can, Neu!, and Amon Düül for inspiration.[39] Indeed, Morris's playing with Joy Division represents perhaps one of the strongest examples of Krautrock's influence on the aesthetic of post-punk, as it blends looping *motorik* patterns with the cool, detached sound of a drum machine (achieved in part by recording each drum in the kit separately).

Tracks like 'She's Lost Control' and 'Isolation' exemplify this: quasi-*motorik* beats are played on a drum kit that includes Synare synthesiser drum pads and heavily effected acoustic drums, with Morris effectively becoming a human drum machine, his rigid rhythmic patterns underpinning repetitive, harmonically static melodic bass lines. The first three minutes of the early track 'No Love Lost' from the *An Ideal for Living* EP,

[35] Compare M Power, E Devereux & A Dillane (eds.), *Heart and Soul: Critical Essays on Joy Division* (London: Rowan and Littlefield, 2018).

[36] Compare U Schütte, Possessed by a Fury That Burns from Inside: On Ian Curtis's Lyrics, in M Power, E Devereux & A Dillane (eds.), *Heart and Soul: Critical Essays on Joy Division* (London: Rowan and Littlefield, 2018), pp. 63–79.

[37] Compare cover of *An Ideal for Living* (Enigma, 1978).

[38] Boswell, *Holocaust Impiety*, p. 119.

[39] J Savage, 'I Still Don't Know Where Joy Division Came From', *Literary Hub* (17 May 2019).

comprising a noisy, one-chord vamp over a clear *motorik* beat, could easily be mistaken for Neu! Moreover, one of Joy Division's best-known tracks, 'Atmosphere', sounds uncannily like Neu!'s 'Seeland', with its washy synthesisers and droning harmonies oscillating between tonic and subdominant chords. As the music journalist Chris O'Leary has noted, Bowie and Iggy Pop provide here a key link in the chain between Krautrock and post-punk: 'Atmosphere' is itself a distillation of the 1977 Pop/Bowie song 'Mass Production', which obviously takes its structural, harmonic, and textural cues from Neu!'s 'Seeland.' As O'Leary asserts, 'Joy Division, and others, starts here.'[40]

Joy Division are sometimes credited with the advent of gothic rock, due in large part to the band's lyrics and sound: through performance and production, the group, along with producer Martin Hannett, organically blended lyrics about alienation, isolation, and suicidal ideation with musical analogues created through experimental production effects. However, the Northampton band Bauhaus, formed in 1978, would become famous as the originary goth band – the 'godfathers of goth' – courtesy of their first single, the vampire rock anthem 'Bela Lugosi's Dead', which combines clattering drums, heavily treated with dub-inspired echo, chilly, reverberant vocals, and swirling guitar effects, held together by a lugubrious descending bass line.

While the band's singer, Peter Murphy, along with guitarist Daniel Ash were openly channelling glam-era Bowie, the influence of Krautrock is also clearly audible: Bauhaus' drummer, Kevin Haskins, took his cue directly from Krautrock-inspired post-punk drummers like Joy Division's Stephen Morris and Kenny Morris, the original drummer of Siouxsie and the Banshees. Haskins, like Morris, incorporated Synare pads in his drum kit, and emulated Krautrock's patterned loops and mechanistic rhythms and tempi. Bauhaus – again, evidently seeking to channel Bowie – also looked to Brian Eno, recording a cover of his song 'Third Uncle', itself audibly Krautrock-inspired, with its up-tempo *motorik* drum track, nonsensical droning vocals, echoing bass guitar, and repeating two-chord vamp.

Bauhaus may be one of the most Germanophilic bands of the post-punk era – as the group's name suggests; the band also drew heavily on German Expressionist cinema for their visual aesthetic – but perhaps also best exemplify the Krautrock ethos in the post-punk scene, insisting on the

---

[40] C O'Leary, *Ashes to Ashes: The Songs of David Bowie 1976–2016* (London: Repeater, 2019), p. 35.

primacy of simple musical ideas, the purity of improvisational and collaborative composition, and the ideals of newness, of starting with a blank page and eschewing rock traditions; or, as Bauhaus bassist David Haskins insisted, making future music from out of the 'void'.[41]

Conclusion

I have argued here that post-punk clearly owes a debt to Krautrock, but it is also obviously the case that Krautrock owes something to post-punk: namely, to the raft of British post-punk bands – the ones I have discussed in this chapter, but also other important post-punk groups like Killing Joke, Cabaret Voltaire, The Fall, Simple Minds, and U2, and perhaps especially Julian Cope via his *Krautrocksampler* book – that helped to bring Krautrock to the ears of anglophone audiences. There is, moreover, a powerful synergy that exists between Krautrock and post-punk, which manifests itself in the stylistic diversity that characterises both genres. It is also clear that both genres have in common a strange and enduring influence, as they continue to shape the sound of popular music well into the twenty-first century.

Essential Listening

Bauhaus, *In the Flat Field* (Beggar's Banquet, 1980)
David Bowie, *Lodger* (RCA, 1979)
Joy Division, *An Ideal for Living* (Enigma, 1978)
Public Image Ltd, *Metal Box* (Virgin, 1979)
Siouxsie and the Banshees, *The Scream* (Polydor, 1978)

Recommended Reading

S Albiez, Know History!: John Lydon, Cultural Capital and the Prog/Punk Dialectic, *Popular Music* 22:3 (2003), pp. 357–74.
A Carpenter, The 'Ground Zero' of Goth: Bauhaus, 'Bela Lugosi's Dead' and the Origins of Gothic Rock, *Popular Music and Society* 35:1 (2012), pp. 25–52.

---

[41] Quoted in A Carpenter, The 'Ground Zero' of Goth: Bauhaus, 'Bela Lugosi's Dead' and the Origins of Gothic Rock, *Popular Music and Society* 35:1 (2012), pp. 25–52 (32).

I Ellis, Post-Punk: The Cerebral Genre, *PopMatters* (17 April 2019).

M Haddon, *What Is Post-Punk? Genre and Identity in Avant-Garde Popular Music, 1977–1982* (Ann Arbor: University of Michigan Press, 2020).

N Pegg, *The Complete David Bowie* (London: Titan, 2016).

S Reynolds, *Rip It Up and Start Again: Postpunk 1978–1984* (London: Faber, 2005).

18 | Krautrock and German Free Jazz, Kraut Fusion, and Detroit Techno

MARCUS BARNES

Under the umbrella of the Krautrock movement, young German bands looked outside the nation's borders for inspiration. They incorporated a wide range of musical influences into their studio experimentations, which cultivated a remarkable diversity and eclecticism within the genre. This desire to uncover hitherto unheard sounds, as it were, resulted in the emergence of many innovative musical styles. Furthermore, the experimental spirit of the Krautrock era led both rock and jazz musicians to merge the two styles, resulting in homegrown free jazz and kraut fusion movements.

This injection of black music into Krautrock left a noticeable imprint on Krautrock and resulted in one particularly impactful line of development, namely the emergence of the automated machine funk of Kraftwerk. The band's electronic sound eventually fed back into black communities in the United States, triggering the conception of electro and Detroit techno. This chapter explores the legacy of Krautrock through the aforementioned genres, and the intersection of German experimentation with black American musicians and communities. It hence tells a paradigmatic story of the mutual interchangeability of musical forms that travel transnationally between nations, cultures, social groups, undergoing processes of adaptation and hybridisations that in turn spark the development of new musical genres.

Krautrock: The 4×4 Beat and Funk's Seedlings

As Krautrock transcended Germany's borders, its widespread transnational reception influenced the conception and development of new genres to varying degrees. Krautrock's fusion of electronic equipment with more traditional acoustic instruments broke new ground in the way that bands performed and recorded. The audacious experimentation by early Krautrock bands began to evolve, with key elements distilled into new variations encompassing folk, politically charged lyrics, unorthodox arrangement, minimalism, the integration of electronic synthesisers, and much more.

Of particular significance is the impactful cultural influence exerted by Krautrock on the conception of styles of electronic dance music developed by African American communities in the early-to-mid-1980s. This particularly concerns house and techno music. House emerged in the Chicago area in the post-disco era, named after the city's Warehouse nightclub – a popular nightclub among Chicago's black gay community – where DJ Frankie Knuckles was musical director. Later, the Warehouse closed and the venue was renamed Music Box. Ron Hardy became the nightclub's resident DJ, continuing the progressive music policy established by Frankie Knuckles. Among the key producers of the era were Larry Heard, Chip E, Farley 'Jackmaster' Funk, Steve 'Silk' Hurley, and Phuture. The group Phuture included DJ Pierre, who pioneered the 'acid' sound, using Roland's TR-303 synthesiser to create the distinct squelchy effect that defines acid house.[1]

Techno, meanwhile, had its origins in post-industrial Detroit and, parallel to house music, was also developed by young black artists. Juan Atkins and his high-school friends Kevin Saunderson and Derrick May (known as the Belleville Three) experimented with electronic synthesisers. Atkins had already had local and international success with his Cybotron project, which preceded his solo project as Model 500. Under this alias, he shifted from electro into what he defined as 'techno', or 'technology music', setting up the Metroplex label to self-release his music. A key venue for Atkins and his cohorts to showcase their music was the Detroit Music Institute.[2]

It is specifically this channel of transnational migration of music that will be explored here. How did the influence of German bands from the Krautrock era permeate into Detroit and connect with black communities? As hinted, a line can be traced right back to the early years of Krautrock, with free jazz among a number of – often overlooked – influences that lie at the genre's foundations. Free jazz, a radical subsection within the United States' jazz movement, emerged in the late 1950s as a form of music conceived and developed by African Americans. Musicians like Ornette Coleman and Cecil Taylor, an improvisation virtuoso who pioneered a radical piano playing technique, were at its forefront. Similarly, Coleman's progressive (and controversial at the time) saxophone playing

---

[1] H Rietveld, *This Is Our House: House Music, Cultural Spaces and Technologies* (Abingdon: Routledge, 2018), p. 17.

[2] D Sicko, *Techno Rebels: The Renegades of Electro Funk* (Detroit: Wayne State University Press, 2010), p. 62.

inspired the free jazz movement. Of particular note was his open-ended approach to melody and harmony.[3]

Members of several prominent Krautrock bands had experience of playing and performing free jazz prior to forming their respective groups. Jaki Liebezeit and Michael Karoli of Can both came from a free jazz background.[4] Drummer Klaus Dinger of duo Neu! performed free jazz. His *motorik* drumbeat proved an essential component of the automated nature of the music that came out of Düsseldorf.[5] Mani Neumeier was also a free jazz drummer before he joined Guru Guru.

As can be seen, the German free jazz scene – which orbited around key proponents such as saxophonist Peter Brötzmann, trumpet player Manfred Schoof, and pianist Alexander von Schlippenbach – constituted an important pool of musical innovators feeding the subsequent Krautrock scene. Drums were an intrinsic component of Krautrock, following on from their rise to prominence in free jazz. Drumming came to the fore thanks to free jazz, where the instrument was given more credence, beyond a mere timekeeping component, as it had been up until the conception of free jazz. In German free jazz and Krautrock, drums have equal standing with the rest of the instruments in the ensemble.

But German free jazz, being an imitation, or adoption, of a style originated by black Americans, was not the only source of influence for Krautrock. Black music was also enmeshed in the shift into kraut fusion, led by bands like Embryo, Xhol Caravan, and Kraan. Each of these groups incorporated a distinctly black influence into their music. Embryo are considered pioneers of kraut fusion, an offshoot that fused other styles of music onto the Krautrock framework, most commonly jazz and funk. Their album *Steig aus* (*Get off*, 1973) featured American jazz pianist Mal Waldron on electric piano. Embryo explored musical styles from outside their home nation, paying visits to Africa and India to get first-hand experience of music from those countries.[6]

Xhol Caravan featured three Americans among its line-up,[7] including African American Gilbert 'Skip' van Wyck on drums. The group initially played covers of artists like Otis Redding and James Brown – as heard on their *Soul Caravan – Live* LP from 1969 – before they moved in a more psychedelic direction and incorporated jazz into their rock-inspired

---

[3] I Anderson, *This Is Our Music: Free Jazz, the Sixties, and American Culture* (Philadelphia: University of Pennsylvania Press, 2016), p. 59.

[4] U Adelt, *Krautrock: German Music in the Seventies* (Ann Arbour: Michigan University Press, 2016), p. 61.

[5] Ibid., p. 101.   [6] Ibid., p. 78.   [7] Ibid.

compositions. This demonstrates how black music merged with German influences, with the aid of players with African American heritage, and the key musical touchpoints for these pioneering bands. Simultaneously, these bands rejected standardised Anglo-American structures, which had come to dominate the musical landscape in the 1960s, when they first began performing.[8] In doing so, they sketched out an entirely new rock template, which allowed for freeform expression and the hybridisation of styles, evident throughout their work.

As well as jazz, Ulm-based band Kraan also began to imbue their compositions with elements of funk. This can be heard on their LP *Wintrup* (1972), where songs such as 'Mind Quake' and 'Backs' feature funk-influenced basslines. James Brown and his peers developed funk in the United States during the mid to late 1960s. By the 1970s, it had been popularised and reached European shores, with hits like Brown's 'Sex Machine (Get On Up)' (1970) charting in Britain and Germany.

Kraftwerk, too, took inspiration from James Brown's funk rhythms.[9] In keeping with the ethos of Krautrock, the Düsseldorf group experimented with a variety of outside influences, including Tamla/Motown, and Detroit rock bands MC5 and The Stooges. Most pertinent to their connection to Detroit, though, is the underlying notion of funk. The black music styles that were present in the roots of Krautrock feed into the conception of techno in the mid-1980s, through the music of Kraftwerk. As one of the key acts name-checked by the foremost architects of Detroit techno, Kraftwerk are the bridge between Krautrock and the city's innovative form of electronic music.

The Socio-economic Background to the Evolution of Home Technology

The emergence of new, pioneering forms of black music based more on technology than conventional musicianship, is closely linked to the socio-economic background of 1980s Detroit. The city was amid huge social and economic upheaval as its automotive industry was in a state of collapse. An economic depression across the city, especially for its black population, created a need for escapism. Detroit's automotive industry, which gave it its nickname 'Motor City', started to decline in the 1950s. Thousands of

---

[8] U Schütte, Pop Music as the Soundtrack of German Post-War History in U Schütte (ed.), *German Pop Music. A Companion* (Berlin: De Gruyter, 2017), pp. 1–24 (13).
[9] D Sicko, *Techno Rebels: The Renegades of Electronic Funk* (Detroit: Wayne State University Press, 2010), p. 10.

employees were laid off, and the city suffered from rising crime rates, a low tax base, and what has been termed 'white flight', as many of the city's white occupants either fled to the suburbs or left the city altogether.[10] The result was a ghettoisation of parts of Detroit.[11]

Black unemployment in the United States has consistently been twice as high as that of its white population, going as far back as the 1960s, reaching a peak of 19.5 per cent for black people and 8.4 per cent for white people in 1983. In 2013, it was still 13.4 and 6.7 per cent, respectively.[12] Detroit's 'depression' of the 1970s and 1980s led to mass unemployment and a decaying city, where abandoned buildings and high crime rates became the norm. The dire economic circumstances in which many people lived was the catalyst behind a need for escapism. Creativity, imagination, and looking to the future for hope and optimism became important factors in the drive to develop new cultural expressions based on music and dancing.

Detroit techno emerged as a counter to the city's post-industrial collapse. The impact of the collapse of the city's automotive industry led to action in various tiers of Detroit's administration to portray it in a more positive light. Similarly, Detroit techno gave the city cause to celebrate, through events like the Detroit Electronic Music Festival (now known as Movement Detroit).[13]

Disco had its reign in the United States during the mid-1970s but a nationwide commercial backlash against the music, using the slogan 'Disco Sucks', led to its downfall. However, the popularity of the music primed the listening public for the arrival of electronic dance music, with its structured 4 × 4 beats, hypnotic arrangements, and pioneering electro-disco artists such as Giorgio Moroder and Cerrone. Both producers fused influences from soul and disco with synthesisers to cultivate a fresh new sound that arrived a few years after Kraftwerk were laying the groundwork for their own purely electronic sound from the mid-1970s onwards.

In Detroit, the post-disco era heralded a highly fertile and eclectic period, where DJs such as Ken Collier blended a range of sounds from Eurodisco and Italo disco to new wave, industrial, synth pop, and more. A melting pot of sounds was absorbed into the consciousness of the city's

[10] S Albiez, Post-soul Futurama: African American Cultural Politics and Early Detroit Techno, *European Journal of American Culture* 24:2 (2005), pp. 131–52 (134).

[11] Cf. M Binelli, *The Last Days of Detroit: Motor Cars, Motown and the Collapse of an Industrial Giant* (New York: Random House, 2013).

[12] D Desilver, Black Unemployment Rate Is Consistently Twice That of Whites, Pew Research (21 August 2013), www.pewresearch.org/fact-tank/2013/08/21/through-good-times-and-bad-black-unemployment-is-consistently-double-that-of-whites/.

[13] H Rietveld & A Kolioulis, Detroit: Techno City, in B Lashua, S Wagg, K Spracklen & M Yavuz (eds.), *Sounds and the City* (Basingstoke: Palgrave Macmillan, 2019), p. 5.

party communities at parties like Gables, run by Todd Johnson. These parties were mostly attended by middle-class high-school kids who coveted European fashion and music – a rejection of 'ghetto' styles.[14]

Globally, advances in technology were rapidly revolutionising the way that society operated, with post-war science-fiction fantasies gradually becoming reality. Neil Armstrong stepping foot on the moon on 20 July 1969 was a historic moment that united the world. Microchips offered a glimpse into the next phase of technological evolution: smaller gadgets and devices, portability, and the potential for humans to be augmented. Technology not only offered hope and safety, but it also presented the possibility of a democratised society, where equal opportunities could become a reality.

In the area of music production, the synthesiser became emblematic of the potential offered by new technology. Though hugely expensive at first, affluent German bands such as Popol Vuh and Tangerine Dream used them to create their otherworldly *kosmische Musik*. Ralf Hütter and Florian Schneider from Kraftwerk adopted the new technology most eagerly, evolving from their Krautrock roots into a conceptual art project. Though Kraftwerk took a critical stance in reflecting the new technological age by envisioning how machines would shape the future, their firm hope – not least in view of the nation's Nazi past – was that technology would help to build a better, equal society.

Such hope mirrored the situation of socially and economically deprived African Americans in Detroit. Amid a depression, the cultural movement of Afro-Futurism, which harks back in its musical component to the pioneering 'space jazz' of Sun Ra and his Arkestra, provided the opportunity to envision a better future thanks to technology.[15] Accordingly, science-fiction fantasies involving a future offering a clean slate, and a chance to rebuild the world anew, devoid of racial and social barriers, abounded, and served as a cultural interface to the 'future music' originating from Germany.

Hip-Hop and Electro: First Contact with The Robots

Hip-hop had been steadily developing since the early 1970s, with block parties, graffiti writing, and breakdancing flourishing in New York's ghettos and, by the beginning of the 1980s, it was a fully formed

---

[14] Sicko, *Techno Rebels*, p. 14.

[15] For an overview of the heterogenous movement, compare Ytasha Womack, *Afrofuturism: The World of Black Sci-Fi and Fantasy Culture* (Chicago: Chicago Review Press, 2013).

culture.[16] Preceding the development of techno, electro – a branch of hip-hop – encompassed the 'future funk' that emanated from the electronic music-producing machines operated by Kraftwerk, Tangerine Dream, and other German bands. Employing the TR-808 drum machine, manufactured by Japanese company Roland, electro (or electro-funk, as it was also known) utilised its science-fiction sounds and effects to cultivate futuristic sonics.

Hip-hop culture comprises 'four pillars': rapping/MCing, DJing, breakdancing, and graffiti. Each of the four pillars evolved prior to the development of electro. However, when the music emerged, breakdancers invented moves that complemented the music – the robot, which mimicked the mechanical movements associated with robots, and the electric boogaloo, which was a much smoother, flowing style of movement, and body popping/locking, where the dancer's make stiff, purposeful movements, while other parts of the body remain still. The notion of rigid robotic funk connects back to Kraftwerk's concept of artistic harmony between musicians and the electronic equipment they are using, or in other words: to musically merge humans and machines. According to Uwe Schütte, 'Robots, as mechanical doppelgängers of the band, and the conceptual notion of the man-machine are of course closely linked. . . . Clearly, the notion of the robot is deeply futuristic, as it epitomizes the potential moment of evolution at which man and technology would merge.'[17]

The most widely acknowledged connection between Kraftwerk and the roots of electro comes via 'Planet Rock' (1982) by Afrika Bambaataa and Arthur Baker. Baker was hugely influential in the development of electro in the 1980s, channelling his knowledge and expertise into a myriad production and engineering endeavours. His key releases of the time include 'I.O. U' by Freeez (1983), 'Play At Your Own Risk' by Planet Patrol (1982) and, his most famous work, 'Planet Rock' with Afrika Bambaataa and the Soul Sonic Force.

The seminal release is a direct link to Kraftwerk, using the beats from their single 'Nummern' (Numbers, 1981) and the eerie synthesiser melody from 'Trans Europa Express' (1977). Bambaataa was DJing at block parties in the Bronx, presenting his audiences with an eclectic selection of music, which included funk, soul, and early hip-hop, alongside pioneering electronic music artists such as Gary Numan, Yellow Magic Orchestra, and

[16] J Chang, *Can't Stop Won't Stop: A History of the Hip-Hop Generation* (London: Picador, 2005), p. 280.
[17] U Schütte, *Kraftwerk: Future Music from Germany* (London: Penguin, 2020), p. 187.

Kraftwerk. Highly influential New York radio DJ Frankie Crocker played Kraftwerk records on his WBLS show, which also helped popularise the group with his largely black listenership. Similarly, the radio show by Detroit's Electrifying Mojo also featured the German group on regular rotation.

Baker grew up in Boston, Massachusetts, becoming a DJ in the 1970s, and discovered Kraftwerk while digging for records.[18] Both Baker and Bambaataa were enamoured with Kraftwerk's ability to combine funk and soul with futurism. They worked with multi-instrumentalist John Robie, who interpolated Kraftwerk's music so well that many people mistakenly thought Baker and Bambaataa had sampled the German group. At the time, sampling – copying parts of a song and repurposing them in your own productions – was still very much in its infancy, but soon after became a key component in hip-hop, and the wider electronic music industry. In any case, Kraftwerk made legal demands and received royalties.

'Planet Rock' was a big hit when it was released in 1982 and remains an all-time hip-hop/electro classic, its influence reaching beyond New York's hip-hop scene to inspire artists around the world. The song was also the first hip-hop record to utilise Roland's TR-808 drum machine. In a 2012 interview Bambaataa stated:

To me, Kraftwerk always sounded European. *Trans-Europe Express* especially. But I understood the train and travel as a metaphor for transporting the sound through the whole universe, and so was their influence and power. . . . This is the music for the future and for space travels – along with the funk of what was happening with James Brown and Sly Stone and George Clinton.[19]

Cybotron: Architects of Techno Funk

Electro precedes techno by a few years. Its inception in the early 1980s would lead to the birth of techno, with the artist credited with coining the term 'techno', Juan Atkins, originally producing electro music himself. Born and raised in Detroit, Juan Atkins adopted the Cybotron moniker

---

[18] J Toltz, Dragged into the Dance: The Role of Kraftwerk in the Development of Electro-Funk, in S Albiez & D Pattie (eds.), *Kraftwerk: Music Non-Stop* (London: Continuum, 2011), pp. 181–93 (188).

[19] Afrika Bambaataa on Kraftwerk, Electronic Beats (13 November 2012), www.electronicbeats.net /afrika-bambaataa-about-kraftwerk/.

with his friend Richard Davis in 1981. The duo released several records that employed synthesisers creating music with similar tropes to the electro sound coming out of New York, but with their own darker twist.

In 1981, they released 'Alleys Of Your Mind' (1981) on their label Deep Space. This was followed by 'Cosmic Cars' (1982) and their biggest hit 'Clear' (1983), an all-time electro classic. 'Clear' features a rising and falling melody lifted straight from Kraftwerk's 'Spiegelsaal' (Hall of Mirrors). Again, like 'Planet Rock', Atkins played the riff himself, rather than sample it: 'I recreated it. I think that at the time, samples weren't even in existence.'[20] Atkins's philosophy had its grounding in futurism, with Alvin Toffler's books *Future Shock* (1984) and *The Third Wave* (1981) key influences in his outlook. Davis, also an outlier, created the terminology connected to their project: the name Cybotron for instance, a combination of the words cyborg and cyclotron.

Fellow Detroit pioneer, Jeff Mills, characterised the popularity of futurist thinking in the black community in Detroit thus:

All my friends were into futurism. Not Afro-futurism but in a technological way. We were interested in how we were going to live tomorrow. . . . People were much more open back then. Technology had a lot to do with that – for Black people, so long as it was funky . . . it wasn't just Kraftwerk, it was Visage, it was Gary Numan. . . . It was Kraftwerk's track 'Numbers' that sealed the deal, followed by 'Tour de France'.[21]

Mills is one of the exponents of techno who has pushed it furthest into the future. He aimed to express a sense of futurism in his music, realised in numerous conceptual productions and performances. Mills even composed a soundtrack to Fritz Lang's 1927 classic *Metropolis* in 2000, a film that also greatly inspired Kraftwerk, in the visual direction of the video for 'Trans Europa Express', for example, and the band's fascination with retro-futurism.[22]

Automation and the Universal Appeal of Machine-Funk

The metronomic beat used by Krautrock bands set it apart from more traditional rock, which commonly used a backbeat. This rhythm was referred to as *motorik*.[23] Neu!'s drummer Klaus Dinger pioneered this

[20] V Brown, Techno's Godfather Speaks, Reverb (26 March 2021), https://reverb.com/fr/news/interview-juan-atkins.

[21] Quoted in D Stubbs, *Future Days: Krautrock and the Building of Modern Germany* (London: Faber, 2014), p. 201.

[22] Compare Schütte, *Kraftwerk*, p. 183.   [23] Adelt, *Krautrock*, p. 47.

'machine-like' 4 × 4 beat. His work with the Düsseldorf band radically reinvented the rock template, discarding unnecessary flourishes and focusing on a more minimalistic approach to drum patterns. Automation, or industrial rhythm, is the language that binds Kraftwerk's music to Motor City and it has been at the core of a sonic dialogue that has been occurring since the group's early stages.

Both Detroit and Düsseldorf have histories that have been deeply impacted by their industrial nature. Automation, monotony, and the hypnotic power of repetition were core characteristics of Kraftwerk's compositions. Their synthesisers afforded them the ability to programme beats and repeat them perfectly for as long as they wanted, something that is virtually impossible for humans. This repetition was present in the industrial belt of Düsseldorf and Detroit's factories, where mechanised sounds were prevalent – robots and machines programmed to perform monotonous actions as part of the automated manufacturing process. As Hütter explained: 'It has always interested us to make industrial music. Assembly line music. Production processes, which are all around us in the industrial world.'[24] Within this rigid, robotic monotony was an innate, hypnotic 'funk'. This trance-inducing repetition forms the blueprint of modern dance music; disco, house, techno, drum 'n' bass, dubstep, trance, and many of their offshoots.

According to Hütter: 'The dynamism of the machines, the "soul" of the machines, has always been part of our music. Trance always belong to repetition, and everybody is looking for trance in life etc., in sex, in the emotional, in pleasure, in anything ... Machines produce an absolutely perfect trance.'[25] Finding soul, groove, and funk in apparently soulless machines is one of Kraftwerk's great achievements.

What must also be considered when speaking about the connection between the United States' black communities and Kraftwerk is the way in which the German group's music transcended racial categorisation. It balanced American rhythms and European melody, as epitomised in Kraftwerk's conceptual notion of electronic pop music and the myriad influences that were fed into their machines and regurgitated as a more universal sonic language, liberated from the constraints of national identity. Robots are often depicted as genderless representations of the human form. Similarly, machines have no race or gender. By using them as

---

[24] W Andresen, Computerliebe, *Tip* 22 (1991), p. 202.
[25] Interview with Sylvain Gaire, quoted in Bussy, *Kraftwerk: Man, Machine and Music* (London: SAF, 1993), p. 101.

a channel for their broad spectrum of inspirations, Kraftwerk connected with multiple audiences; black people in Detroit, gay Latinos in New York, people who didn't fit the racially and sexually homogenised mainstream. This was a counter to the dominance of rock music of that era, which embodied a very definite sense of whiteness and masculinity. Not only did Kraftwerk's music transcend race and gender, but it also evoked a very global, transnational appeal, with the band including various languages on tracks such as 'Nummern' or 'Techno Pop'.[26]

'Our music is good if blacks and whites can dance to it at the same time', Hütter once explained.[27] François Kevorkian, who also worked on their *Electric Cafe* LP (1986), observed the universal appeal of Kraftwerk's music first-hand while immersed in New York's vibrant underground club scene in the 1980s: 'What was really remarkable was that their music . . . had that ability to cross over between all the different scenes. Kraftwerk was, like, universal.'[28]

Tim Barr commented on the 'extraordinarily funky bass line' on 'Kristallo' (1973), and that Kraftwerk had 'obviously been paying close attention to the bass parts played by Bootsy Collins on their favourite James Brown records'.[29] Former member Karl Bartos confirms this, explaining that, in the 1970s, 'we were all fans of American music: soul, the whole Tamla/Motown thing, and of course, James Brown'.[30] Atkins commented on his meeting with Schneider at British outdoor rave Tribal Gathering in 1997:

We met up behind the Detroit stage and chatted a bit and I was really surprised to learn that Kraftwerk were hugely influenced by James Brown. Of course, P-Funk was made up of at least half the JB's first line-up, so somehow Detroit techno was a very natural, even 'fated' progression.[31]

Interestingly, Kraftwerk hired a black engineer from Detroit to work on the final master of *Mensch-Maschine* (*Man-Machine*). Leanard Jackson had no idea Kraftwerk were white until he met them in Düsseldorf.[32] Black artists sampling Kraftwerk add up to a considerable list, amongst them as Trouble

---

[26] Compare Toltz, Dragged into the Dance, p. 190.   [27] Bussy, *Kraftwerk*, p. 124.

[28] Quoted in M Rubin, The Heritage of Kraftwerk on Funk & Techno, *New York Times* (4 December 2009).

[29] T Barr, *Kraftwerk: From Düsseldorf to the Future (with Love)* (London: Ebury, 1998), p. 67.

[30] Sicko, *Techno Rebels*, p. 10.

[31] Juan Atkins on Kraftwerk, Electronic Beats (10 November 2012), www.electronicbeats.net /juan-atkins-about-kraftwerk/.

[32] Cf. B Brewster & F Broughton, *Last Night a DJ Saved My Life: The History of the Disc Jockey* (New York: Grove Press, 2000), p. 582.

Funk, Digital Underground, Cookie Crew, Doug Lazy, Kiss AMC, The Fearless Four, Eskimos and Egypt, and Borghesia.[33] The website whosampledwho.com provides more examples, including black music icons like Dr Dre, Timbaland, Sir Mix-a-Lot, Ultramagnetic MC's, Underground Resistance, the late Biz Markie, and others.

The Electrifying Mojo, P-Funk, and the Mothership Connection

The universal appeal of electronic music and its faceless presentation via the radio, meant listeners to influential hosts such as The Electrifying Mojo were often unaware of the racial identity of the musicians he supported. Johnson's reverence and eclectic curation is what Carl Craig describes as the mix of music at the root of techno: 'Techno is that attitude in the music that Mojo was playing that influenced me as a kid. Techno is that cross section – that mix of music that influenced what we know as Detroit techno.'[34] Johnson's ethos was to counter the dominance of commercial organisations.

From my perspective, radio was not going to be an instrument of divisiveness. I would go and bridge the gap that separated old from young, rich from poor, black from white, and informed from uninformed, as opposed to my joining the circle of radio celebs who pretty much dominated the airwaves and psyche of people.[35]

Kraftwerk were among the many avant-garde artists Mojo showcased on his show. Like Frankie Crocker in New York and his peers at WMBX in Chicago, Johnson pioneered a multi-genre approach which tapped into the automated funk that emanated from Kraftwerk's music:

I remember when *Trans-Europe-Express* came out. I played it and they [the station executives] said, 'What the hell is he playing now?' It wasn't a beat that people understood, but I could hear it perfectly. I mean, here's a band who's obviously from the same planet that I'm from, right?[36]

Kraftwerk's music had been relegated to 'production fodder' (i.e. background music) by station management at WGPR but it was salvaged by Johnson and played on his show. A video clip on YouTube demonstrates how well

[33] Bussy, *Kraftwerk*, p. 125.

[34] M Barnes, Label of the Month: Planet E Communications, Beatportal (16 August 2021), www.beatportal.com/features/label-of-the-month-planet-e-communications/.

[35] Sicko, *Techno Rebels*, p. 58.   [36] Ibid., p. 57.

Kraftwerk's music connected with black audiences.[37] Broadcast on local TV station WGPR-TV (the television department of WGPR radio, where Johnson hosted his show) *The New Dance Show* clip features its audience split in two, with audience members parading down the middle – a format copied from the show *Soul Train* – dancing to Kraftwerk's 'Nummern'.

Juan Atkins remembers that the first time he heard Kraftwerk's track 'Die Roboter' ('The Robots') 'I just froze. This sounded like the future, and it was fascinating [. . .] there were other funky electronic bands around – Tangerine Dream and Gary Numan and all that – but none were as funky as Kraftwerk.'[38] Atkins was also influenced by the P-Funk of Parliament Funkadelic, another pivotal group from the seventies whose fantasy-based imagery, and visual presentation (stage and costume design), envisioned black people in space – developing their own brand of psychedelic Afro-Futurism.

Here we can trace the family tree from Motown to James Brown, Kraftwerk, Parliament, and Detroit techno. Members of Parliament (Maceo Parker, Bootsy Collins) were part of James Brown's band The JBs. Parliament frontman George Clinton was a songwriter at Motown, which also influenced Kraftwerk. Mike Banks, of pioneering Detroit techno group Underground Resistance (with Jeff Mills and, later, Robert Hood), was a former studio musician who worked with Parliament. Like Kraftwerk, Underground Resistance adopted a similarly media-averse outlook, and eventually remixed the German group's track 'Expo2000'. Banks refers to Kraftwerk's key track 'Nummern' as 'the secret code of electronic funk': 'That track hit home in Detroit so hard. They had just created the perfect urban music because it was controlled chaos, and that's exactly what we live in.'[39]

Another Detroit outfit that took great inspiration from Kraftwerk is Drexciya. A duo made up of James Stinson and Gerald Donald, who defied music marketing norms to adopt a totally anonymous identity. They never performed live and operated exclusively from Stinson's basement studio, shunning the limelight to focus purely on their music. Stinson and Donald created an entire world and mythology around their Drexciya concept; based around the idea that an underwater colony of aquatic humanoids evolved from the babies of pregnant slave women, thrown overboard

---

[37] Kraftwerk 'Numbers' at The New Dance Show, YouTube video (8 May 2020), www .youtube.com/watch?v=ZOcf9Uq6EjQ

[38] Juan Atkins on Kraftwerk.

[39] Quoted in M Rubin, The Heritage of Kraftwerk on Funk & Techno, *New York Times* (4 December 2009).

during the trek across the Middle Passage (the journey from Europe to the USA).[40]

There are very clear nods to Kraftwerk in some of the track titles and terminology (such as the track title 'Aquabahn' clearly alluding to 'Autobahn') used in their material. Later, under one of the many aliases associated with the Drexciya project, Elekctroids, they paid respects to their German inspirations with a note in their press release from their 1995 LP *Elektroworld*: 'This album, titled elektro world, is a personal, tribute to those well known pioneers of the electro-disco-beat; Kraftwerk.'[41] This homage to the German group not only demonstrates the influence of their robotic funk on black electronic music artists in Detroit but also shows how their conceptual approach had an influence on the generations that followed.

Short Conclusion: Universal Funk and Electronic Spirituality

The transnational flow of musically encoded ideas and concepts between Detroit and Europe hints at a deeper connection. The notion of universal funk pervades throughout Krautrock, the music that influenced it and the music it inspired. Beyond superficial physical identity such as gender, nationality, racial categorisation, and other such limiting signifiers of identity, music is a vehicle for the human experience. As we've seen, machines transcend fixed identity, the listener is presented with sounds that trigger universal responses, memories, thoughts, feelings, and reactions. Accordingly, Ralf Hütter himself hence described the connection between Detroit and Düsseldorf, Germany as 'spiritual':

There's quite a techno connection, Kraftwerk to Detroit. [...] The industrial sound of Motor City and Kraftwerk on the autobahn, there's a spiritual connection. Automatic rhythms, robotic work, robotic music – all kinds of fantasies are going on.[42]

---

[40] Compare H Deisl, Mit dem Zug durch Europa, mit dem Tauchboot durch den Atlantik: Sound-Topografien bei Kraftwerk und Drexciya, in U Schütte (ed.), *Mensch-Maschinen-Musik: Das Gesamtkunstwerk Kraftwerk* (Düsseldorf: Leske, 2018), pp. 275–90.

[41] Elecktroids – Elektroworld, Discogs, www.discogs.com/de/release/1077176-Elecktroids-Elektroworld.

[42] G Dayal, Kraftwerk on Cycling, 3D, 'Spiritual Connection' to Detroit, *Rolling Stone* (26 August 2015), www.rollingstone.com/music/music-news/kraftwerk-on-cycling-3d-spiritual-connection-to-detroit-56548/.

Recommended Reading

S Albiez, Post-soul Futurama: African American Cultural Politics and Early Detroit Techno, *European Journal of American Culture* 24:2 (2005), pp. 131–52.

I Anderson, *This Is Our Music: Free Jazz, the Sixties, and American Culture* Philadelphia: University of Pennsylvania Press, 2016).

D Sicko, *Techno Rebels: The Renegades of Electronic Funk* (Detroit: Wayne State University Press, 2010).

Y Womack, *Afrofuturism: The World of Black Sci-Fi and Fantasy Culture* (Chicago: Chicago Review Press, 2013).

19 | Krautrock Today

ALEX HARDEN

The continued interest in Krautrock several decades after its emergence is testament to its lasting influence and historical importance. Despite a vastly different musical and commercial landscape today, search engine data shows that Krautrock has sustained a wide-reaching interest across English-speaking countries, Europe, Russia, and South America.[1] Yet, most academic work on the topic has largely focused on the canonical artists and albums first associated with the term, with less said about the role of Krautrock in music today. In their respective discussions, Ulrich Adelt, John Littlejohn, and Jan Reetze all provide examples of contemporary Krautrock, but draw primarily from the later work of established bands who were active in Germany during the 1960s and 1970s.[2]

Earlier in this volume, Adelt highlights difficulties with thinking of Krautrock as a single coherent musical practice, yet our engagement, too, with Krautrock today is markedly different from the period in which it was first conceived. This is true both in terms of the contemporary musical landscape and listeners' ways of engaging with music. Historically, Krautrock was encountered by an English-speaking audience primarily in a recorded format and was mediated by publishers and importers who could bring the music to local shores (whereas in Germany it had a greater life in a live performance context).[3]

Today, the availability of streaming services, digital outlets that connect independent bands directly with fans, and various reissues of earlier albums have together afforded renewed accessibility of Krautrock to contemporary audiences. Although incomplete, the works of many well-known Krautrock acts can now be found on digital services, including Amon Düül II, Faust, Neu!, Cluster, and so on. Rarer items are also

---

[1] Google Trends, Krautrock (Musical Genre), https://trends.google.com/trends/explore?date=today%205-y&q=%2Fm%2F01pfpt.

[2] U Adelt, *Krautrock: German Music in the Seventies* (Ann Arbor: University of Michigan Press, 2016); J Littlejohn, Krautrock: The Development of a Movement, in U Schütte (ed.), *German Pop Music: A Companion* (Berlin: De Gruyter, 2017), pp. 63–84; J Reetze, *Times and Sounds: Germany's Journey from Jazz and Pop to Krautrock and Beyond* (Bremen: Halvmall, 2020).

[3] Reetze, *Times and Sounds*; D Stubbs, *Future Days: Krautrock and the Building of Modern Germany* (London: Faber, 2014).

available on streaming services, such as the only release from German Oak, *Down in the Bunker* (1972), which sold few physical copies during the 1970s but became highly sought-after as a collector's item and was previously only available through bootlegs or unofficial releases.

Understanding Krautrock

As a broad anglophone construction, the term 'Krautrock' operates more in common with the commercially motivated umbrella term 'world music' than as a precise musical style category, and the validity of conceptualising Krautrock as a movement has been critiqued elsewhere.[4] Most frequently, Krautrock is understood in relation to a canon consisting of bands who were active during 1968–74 in West Germany and were ascribed the label Krautrock: Faust, Can, Neu!, Harmonia, and so on.[5]

Although musically diverse, for David Buckley, 'Krautrock bands were united by the common *ideology* of wanting to create a uniquely German pop culture after those decades post-World War II when Anglo-American culture was pre-eminent.'[6] This argument for a unifying Krautrock ideology is supported by commonalities in Krautrock bands' approach towards guerrilla gigs, eschewing celebrity, and employing experimental musical vocabulary. Littlejohn also points to some general stylistic norms: extended form, extended instrumental techniques or the use of unconventional sound sources/processing, and (in many cases) instrumental tracks without extended lyrics.[7] Harden also explores how the available music technology informed the 'sound' of *kosmische Musik* (exemplified by Ohr Records' *Kosmische Musik* compilation from 1972) in terms of the creative use of simulated phonographic space (through panning, delay, reverb, and so on), sound-sources that are often either abstracted from acoustical sources or with no acoustical equivalent, and particularities in terms of performance style.[8]

---

[4] Adelt, *Krautrock*; T Boehme, The Echo of the Wall Fades: Reflections on the Berlin School in the Early 1970s, in M Gandy & B Nilsen (eds.), *The Acoustic City* (Berlin: Jovis, 2014), pp. 84–90.

[5] U Adelt, Machines with a Heart: German Identity in the Music of Can and Kraftwerk, *Popular Music and Society* 35:3 (2012), pp. 359–74.

[6] D Buckley, Krautrock, *Grove Music Online* (2001), www.oxfordmusiconline.com/grovemusic/view/10.1093/gmo/9781561592630.001.0001/omo-9781561592630-e-0000049687.

[7] Littlejohn, *Krautrock*.

[8] A Harden, Kosmische Musik and Its Techno-Social Context, *IASPM@Journal* 6:2 (2016), pp. 154–73.

Due to the sweeping changes in music production and reception since the 1970s, this chapter takes a purposefully broad approach, to include: bands who either associate themselves with Krautrock or are ascribed the label in listener discourse; those who share musical similarity with Krautrock's originators; and acts endorsed or supported by acknowledged Krautrock figures.

Krautrock in Contemporary Germany

Following the mid-1970s, many Krautrock acts either disbanded or began to move away from the progressive/psychedelic sounds of their earlier work. Kraftwerk honed their practice with a greater emphasis on popular song structure, while several bands (including Tangerine Dream, Klaus Schulze, and Harmonia) contributed to a growing body of electronic ambient music. Nevertheless, several original bands also reunited in the 1980s and 1990s to release music comparable to their Krautrock origins: the 1980s saw Can reunite to create *Rite Time*, and an offshoot of Amon Düül II form in Britain, led by original guitarist John Weinzierl; in the early 1990s, Frumpy recorded two further studio albums, while Faust also reunited for a series of live performances and studio albums.

Aside from reunions of bands that were already a part of a recognised canon, new generations of musicians emerged who were familiar with their predecessors' musical vocabulary and shared, to varying extents, comparable social complications of post-war Germany. With the ramifications of the Cold War and the legacy of Nazism pervading the public consciousness, several bands emerged from Germany who shared the experimentalism and sonic character of Krautrock. Electric Orange and To Rococo Rot are two such examples, emerging from Aachen in 1992 and Berlin in 1994 respectively. The influence of *kosmische* musicians such as Klaus Schulze and early Tangerine Dream on German prog-rock band Electric Orange can be heard exemplified in 'More End/Cyberdelic' (*Cyberdelic*, 1996). Throughout, the nine-minute track is underpinned by dissonant synthesiser textures, decorative non-diatonic synthesiser effects, and sound effects that resemble reversed tape loops. Although there are two distinct sections in the track, much of the track's textural variation is achieved through gradual fades. In terms of production, several similarities with Krautrock can also be heard, especially in terms of the wide stereo panning and use of effects (in this case, reverb and distortion, which were both common in the 1970s).

Berlin's To Rococo Rot, meanwhile, suggest a greater similarity with Faust, Neu!, and Cluster, quickly becoming known for electronics-led post-punk with accompanying digital media performances. The 1996 release of their eponymous first album led to a career in which the band released eight main albums in total; most recently, *Instrumentals* (2014). As with many canonical Krautrock productions, To Rococo Rot's music is characterised by its instrumental nature, use of electronics alongside bass and guitar, and lengthy repeated grooves. Supporting To Rococo Rot's Krautrock creden-tials, 'Friday' from their 2010 album *Speculation* was conceived with Hans-Joachim Irmler, a founding member of Faust. Throughout, the track avoids clear metre, but does incorporate some repetitive, percussive gestures. A sense of tonal centre is offered by drone textures throughout the track, although there is no melody or repetitive harmonic gestures, in line with various earlier Krautrock tracks.

Also from Berlin, several years later, came Camera, a 'neo-Krautrock' three-piece according to Ben Graham's review of their 2012 debut *Radiate!*.[9] In particular, he argues that Camera 'have more claim than most to be upholders of the kraut tradition, whatever that may be' based on their origin in Berlin, performance in public spaces, joint gigs with Michael Rother (of Neu!) and Dieter Moebius (of Harmonia), and use of improvisation.[10] The band's biography on their record label's website makes a further explicit connection with Krautrock, drawing comparison to Neu!, Can, and La Düsseldorf. It reads:

Julian Cope compared the evolving Krautrock movement of the 1960s and 1970s to Doctor Who's time machine ... In the early 2010s, Camera discovered this very portal which had generally been forgotten by German music history, presumed lost. Without asking for permission, they cleared away the rubble ... and bravely made their way through.[11]

'E-Go', which opens *Radiate!*, offers a helpful example of the band's idiolect: although there is minimal use of synthesisers and little of the sound effect noises used by various Krautrock bands, the track derives its momentum from a repetitive, *motorik*-like beat with occasional embellish-ments, over static harmony, with considerable distortion used on several electric guitar tracks. The track is instrumental and develops a sense of

---

[9] B Graham, Camera – Radiate!, *The Quietus* (5 September 2012), https://thequietus.com/articles/09936-camera-radiate-review.

[10] Ibid.

[11] Bureau B, Camera – *Prosthuman*, Bureau B, www.bureau-b.com/infotexte/BB351_Prosthuman_engl.pdf.

structure primarily using texture rather than tonal ideas. These qualities of texture-driven structure, static harmony, *motorik*-like drum patterns, and noisy texture provide a blueprint for much of the album.

Krautrock Worldwide

When Krautrock was first coined, Germany was not alone in accommodating this sort of musical experimentalism; France, for instance, was home to bands who similarly explored repetition, form, and texture, as heard in bands such as Magma, Besombes-Rizet, and Heldon. Yet, with Germany still occupying the public consciousness, connections remained: Magma derived many lyrics from German phonetics, while Heldon took their name from Norman Spinrad's 1972 novel *The Iron Dream*, which revolves around Adolf Hitler in a fictional alternative history. A similar fascination with German culture is demonstrated by the periods in which Brian Eno, David Bowie, and Iggy Pop spent living in West Germany during the 1970s.

With the availability of music imports, Krautrock helped to shape developing musical scenes elsewhere. In Britain, the burgeoning post-punk scene (including bands such as Cabaret Voltaire, Joy Division, and Simple Minds) drew heavily on the sounds of Krautrock, despite the creative impetus of several Krautrock bands to develop a form of music not associated with anglophone pop or rock. Indeed, throughout the 1980s, prolific Krautrock producer Conny Plank became a key collaborator for new wave acts such as Ultravox and Eurythmics. Accordingly, it is unsurprising that contemporary examples of Krautrock can be found across Continental Europe, Britain, and the United States. Critical discourse has even credited Krautrock as an influence for such high-profile albums as Radiohead's *Kid A* (2000) and Gorillaz' *Plastic Beach* (2010).[12]

Continental Europe

In contemporary France, we can find several examples of bands that draw from Krautrock. In 2010, Biarritz was home to the formation of La Femme, whom *The Quietus* describe as being 'to all intents and purposes

---

[12] K Read, *Kid A* at 20: How the Band's Self-Alienating Album Saved an 'Unhinged' Thom Yorke, *The Independent* (10 March 2020); S Fennessey, Gorillaz: Plastic Beach, *Pitchfork* (10 March 2020), https://pitchfork.com/reviews/albums/14008-plastic-beach/.

a Krautrock band'.[13] In 2013, La Femme released their debut album entitled *Psycho Tropical Berlin*, which was subsequently awarded a Victoires de la Musique award by the French Ministry of Culture. The album consists primarily of roughly four-minute-long tracks combining bass, synthesiser, drums, guitar, and vocals. For the most part, their music consists of a small number of musical ideas that are repeated, often alternating a texted section with instrumental breaks in the same bass and/or harmonic setting (in contrast to the interpolation of a texted chorus). In combination with the use of short, repeated vocal ideas (rather than extended sung phrases), these qualities offer some similarity with the work of Can.

In a comparable manner to Munich-based Popul Vuh, Aluk Todolo formed in Paris in 2004, taking their name from a religious practice indigenous to a mountainous region of Indonesia. In sharp contrast to La Femme, Aluk Todolo's work is characterised by long-form tracks of roughly ten minutes, which incorporate passages of clear metre, and passages in which the band use textural development as the point of focus. Sonically, the use of heavily distorted texture and ambivalence towards musical pitch draw some similarity with aspects of Faust's work or early work by Cluster, while the application of drums (featuring mostly dense, repetitive grooves) reflects a character of the earlier work of Can and Neu! These devices can be heard particularly clearly throughout *Occult Rock* (2012) album.

The Finnish band Circle provide a contrasting combination of Krautrock and heavy metal. Marketing themselves as part of the 'New Wave of Finnish Heavy Metal', the band formed in 1991, described as a combination of 'metal, Krautrock, psychedelia, ambient, jazz, prog, art rock, soft rock, and other assorted fusions'.[14] Yet, despite drawing on a diverse range of musical influences, the band share similarities with Krautrock originators in the form of the sheer range of members' side projects and in their cynical attitude towards the recording industry. Circle's *Incarnation* (2013) album was in fact recorded by different musicians, while the members of Circle recorded *Frontier* (2013) under the name Falcon.

In contrast to Aluk Todolo's use of slowly developing drones, Circle's music incorporates vocals and a clear metric structure. Circle's debut,

---

[13] J Allen, La Femme – *Mystère*, The Quietus (13 September 2016), https://thequietus.com /articles/20925-la-femme-mystre-krautrock-album-review.

[14] J Moores, A Brief Guide to the Weird World of Finland's Circle, Bandcamp (21 June 2017), https://daily.bandcamp.com/lists/finland-circle-guide.

Meronia (1994) includes several clear examples of Krautrock's influence. 'Wherever Particular People Congregate', for example, captures a frenetic quality comparable to Faust's up-tempo works through its use of dissonant textures and manipulation of garbled vocal phrases that take on the character of experimentations with tape manipulation by Neu! Nevertheless, as heard in 'Meronia', the band also apply lengthy repeated segments in which the main musical developments are led by changes in texture, a frequent characteristic of the Krautrock canon.

Unlike several of the bands discussed, the Croatian band Seven That Spells explicitly relate their work with Krautrock via a trilogy of albums released between 2011 and 2018 entitled *The Death and Resurrection of Krautrock* comprising *AUM* (2011), *IO* (2014), and *Omega* (2018). Making such an overt connection between their work and Krautrock is uncommon, although musical similarities can be observed. In each album, the band incorporate instrumentation comparable with a large volume of Krautrock music: drums, bass, guitar, synthesiser, and vocals. Although the band incorporate idiomatic modal elements of metal music not generally heard in Krautrock, the band's use of polymetric rhythms and modal scale patterns do evoke some similarity with Agitation Free and Amon Düül II's early studio releases.

Britain and the Americas

As Alexander Simmeth explores, record imports, radio, and national coverage in music media helped Krautrock to reach significant audiences in both Britain and the United States.[15] Indeed, at the time in which Krautrock emerged, allied troops still maintained a presence within West Germany, contributing to intercultural exchange. As early as the late 1970s, the United States was home to musical scenes that created their own spin on Krautrock. One such example is The Nightcrawlers, who formed in Pennsylvania around 1979 and published many cassette albums, now unavailable, in the style of Klaus Schulze, Tangerine Dream, and the broader Berlin scene earlier in the 1970s. Although mostly unavailable today, there has been some attempt from fans to document and preserve coverage of the band and their contemporaries.[16]

---

[15] A Simmeth, *Krautrock Transnational: Die Neuerfindung der Popmusik in der BRD, 1968–1978* (Bielefeld: Transcript, 2016).

[16] D Campau, The Nightcrawlers 'Crystal Loops', *The Living Archive* (14 July 2015), http://livingarchive.doncampau.com/lost_and_forgotten/the-nightcrawlers-crystal-loops.

The 1990s was a time of particular interest in Krautrock, fuelled by new bands and the publication of Cope's *Krautrocksampler*. In 1990 in London, Stereolab formed from the leader of British indie pop band McCarthy, French vocalist Lætitia Sadier, bassist Martin Kean, and drummer Joe Dilworth. Simon Reynolds' 1994 interview with the band explores a Krautrock influence on Stereolab's music, particularly the work of Neu![17] Such an influence can be heard on tracks such as 'Orgiastic' from the band's first studio album, *Peng!* (1992), conveyed through the use of the *motorik* beat, limited use of lyrics, and prosaic delivery. Sonically, the recording is dominated by low frequencies, giving the track a subdued character (as opposed to the crisper sonic character that comes from a mix balanced with greater strength in higher frequency bands), evoking a 'low-fi' quality compatible with many early Krautrock releases.

Several years later, the duo Immersion formed in 1994, bringing together the lead singer/songwriter of post-punk band Wire and the bassist/vocalist of 1980s Israeli post-punk band Minimal Compact. To accompany the release of their album, *Sleepless* (2018), the pair's website highlights the influence of Tangerine Dream and Popul Vuh.[18] 'Propulsoid' from *Sleepless* perhaps offers the best window into the pair's Krautrock influences, an up-tempo but slowly developing track that is supported throughout by a *motorik* drum beat and a repeated one-bar synth bassline. Instrumentally, the track is comparable to a Krautrock ensemble: the bass synth tone is a simple buzzy timbre with gradual modulation of a low-pass filter throughout, and it is joined later by a simple distorted electric guitar texture and electric organ, which provides the only sense of harmonic movement in the track. Similarly, 'Immersion' from their debut album *Oscillating* (1994) is underpinned by a repeated bassline on a sampled alto saxophone, accompanied later by sustained synth pads, a monophonic lead synthesiser, and sequenced decorative elements. Here, the mobility and ambit of the monophonic lead synth, as well as the modulation of a low-pass filter, reflect common practice for Klaus Schulze.

While Stereolab and Immersion were beginning their careers in Britain, Tortoise were being formed in Chicago. The band incorporated significant Krautrock and dub influences, and soon became an important contributor to the American post-rock movement of the era. 'Djed' from the band's 1996 album *Millions Now Living Will Never Die* provides one such

---

[17] S Reynolds, STEREOLAB Interview, Reynolds Retro (blog) (2 May 2008), http://reynoldsretro .blogspot.com/2008/05/stereolab-interview-melody-maker-july.html.

[18] Immersion, Sleepless: The New Album from Immersion, Immersion, http://immersionhq.uk /index.html.

exposition of their Krautrock-influenced work. The track lasts for more than twenty minutes with several abrupt shifts of musical texture. Here, the opening best illustrates the band's Krautrock influences; a distorted percussive loop provides a polymetric feel against a dissonant modal interplay of electric guitar and bass, accompanied by decorative electronic gestures and a delay sound effect. After two-and-a-half minutes, a motorik drum pattern enters with a slight flange to the high-hat, while the bass and electric guitar grooves change to patterns that repeat for several minutes and together evoke the character of the mid-1970s work of Neu!

Several years later in Orlando, Tonstartssbandht formed and have gone on to release a large number of studio albums, developing a musical style described by Pitchfork Magazine as 'the sound of Guided by Voices swapping out their arena rock fantasies of being in The Who for being a member of Amon Düül's Munich commune instead'.[19] The pair's work incorporates a range of influences to create a psychedelic rock oeuvre that draws in equal measure from Krautrock musical textures and its sense of critiquing or challenging anglophone pop's use of lyrics. 'Midnite Cobras' from Tonstartssbandht's debut album *An When* (2009) demonstrates a more extreme affinity, perhaps, with distorted textures than would be found in Krautrock, but nevertheless shares several telling traits. Thinking of production, the track constructs a large sense of space using panning, delay, and reverb. And, while the track includes extended lyrics, they are delivered with imprecise timing and pitch, evoking the use of unskilled or unpolished textures common in Krautrock.

Towards the end of the 2000s, three further bands of note emerged: Wume (United States), Beak (Britain), and Föllakzoid (Chile). Wume are perhaps the United States's best-known contemporary Krautrock export and even derive their name from the river Wümme in northern Germany (where Faust's commune/studio was located). From a production perspective, the access to, and availability of improved recording technology affords Wume a far cleaner sound than original Krautrock bands. From a musical perspective, however, we can observe several similarities: their music is realised using a combination of drum kit and synthesiser, often incorporating repetitive beats or sequences in complex time signatures or in order to construct polyrhythms.

---

[19] A Beta, Tonstartssbandht – Sorcerer, *Pitchfork* (27 March 2017), https://pitchfork.com/reviews/albums/23026-sorcerer/.

'Control', which opens Wume's *Maintain* (2015) album provides a clear example, lasting approximately four-and-a-half minutes via a gradual development of texture but no repeating sections. It begins with a repeating sequence with gentle delay and the use of a low-pass filter (both common for Krautrock originals). When the drums enter, they too repeat a single idea with minimal variation. Synthesiser textures are also used for bass and harmonic elements, in each case using simple timbres of the sort that were available during the Krautrock era. Two-thirds through the track, a syncopated vocal idea is added, although the lyrics are used primarily as punctuation; the words themselves are unintelligible in the mix.

In the same year as Wume formed, in Bristol, Geoff Barrow (known primarily for his role in Portishead) created Beak. Heather Phares describes Beak's work as 'inspired by dub, Krautrock, and the Beach Boys', going on to describe how the band's debut album was recorded over twelve days without any overdubbing.[20] 'Failand', released in 2014, makes several audible allusions to earlier Krautrock, particularly via a sparse selection of musical ideas across a long form, making use of distortion, reverb, and delay, which were the most widely available (and widely used) effects across the breadth of the Krautrock canon. The track broadly falls into two main sections: from an unintelligible vocal opening, the first section is primarily noise-based with considerable distorted electric guitar; the second, however, makes use of a less distorted, muted guitar-like lead, which repeats a single idea with occasional variations for around four minutes, alongside a *motorik*-like drum beat.

Finally, from Chile hail Föllakzoid, a trio with a large online following who are often connected in critical discourse with Krautrock, although the band themselves instead characterise their music as 'heavily informed by the heritage of the ancient music of the Andes'.[21] Indeed, when interviewed, the band's vocalist appears lukewarm about the association with Krautrock:

After the first record we always got asked about our relationship with Krautrock bands from the Sixties. Bands we love and bands that brought trance into rock. But those guys were aiming at the same ancient music that we are, so we have the same point of inspiration, but it isn't those bands that influence us. It is older music. Ash Ra Temple and Popul Vuh – those guys were aiming at the same ritualistic vibe as we are.[22]

---

[20] H Phares, Beak, AllMusic, www.allmusic.com/artist/beak-mn0001249559/biography.

[21] Sacred Bones Records, Föllakzoid, www.sacredbonesrecords.com/collections/follakzoid.

[22] R McCallum, Collective Trance: An Interview with Föllakzoid, *The Quietus*, https://thequietus.com/articles/17546-follakzoid-interview.

The compatibility that Föllakzoid describe between their music and the 'ritualistic vibe' of canonical Krautrock bands is apparent in a similar use of texture and supported by production aesthetic. Föllakzoid's instrumentation immediately lends a sense of familiarity, combining bass, synthesiser, drums, distorted electric guitars, and sparse vocal phrases. In addition to this textural similarity with Krautrock, the band incorporate extensive improvisation into their work to create free-form musical structures that share similarities with Ash Ra Tempel or, to some extent, Neu!.

Issues in Contemporary Krautrock

Over the past five decades, the intermingling of Krautrock with other styles of music making have diversified an already eclectic body of music, establishing a global community of musicians who illustrate greater diversity in terms of gender, age, and geographical origin. Via this globalisation, the sound of Krautrock continues to be heard in new forms today. And, although this outlasts the association of Krautrock's sound with the development of a distinct German cultural identity (exemplified strongest by Föllakzoid), it reinforces the cultural role that the Krautrock canon has played for modern music. Indeed, the readiness with which critical commentary and bands themselves refer to Krautrock demonstrates the body of work's lasting cultural appeal.

A keyway in which the contemporary bands explored in this chapter diverge from canonical Krautrock musicians lies in the use of the Internet as a tool for distribution and discovery. This democratises Krautrock in the sense that it affords the opportunity for musicians outside of its original context to participate in a shared body of musical practice. However, while the internet also offers ways of reaching fans that were not available in the last century, many of the bands discussed make limited use of social media; few even offer any substantive biographical details about themselves on social media channels or official websites (if applicable). In doing so, they reflect a common approach of earlier Krautrock musicians who similarly avoided celebrity, as David Stubbs describes in his commentary of Can's *Future Days*.[23]

In tandem, Krautrock's cultural place has diversified. For early Krautrockers, their music was intended to run counter to the dominant forms of music making available in Germany and attracted a significant

---

[23] Stubbs, *Future Days*, pp. 143–4.

audience but gained its largest following overseas. Adelt argues that Krautrock's otherness (in terms of both being a foreign import and the unusual sonic palette of Krautrock when compared to Anglo-American music making of the time) helped the music to accrue significant subcultural capital.[24] While this continues in the form of journalistic discourse that reifies Krautrock, we can also observe greater malleability of Krautrock's cultural capital via its role in high-art contexts. To Rococo Rot, for instance, illustrate the successful integration of Krautrock and digital media installations. And, in Britain, exhibitions celebrating the contributions of Tangerine Dream and Kraftwerk both demonstrate a contemporary appreciation of Krautrock within gallery or museum contexts.[25]

The continued practice of Krautrock-influenced music making today provides an opportunity to consider its role in relation to the original Krautrock canon. For both Camera and To Rococo Rot, their interaction with earlier musicians become focal aspects of the bands' narratives. Similarly, both Wume and Seven That Spells acknowledge the genre through their naming choices. In doing so, these later bands contribute to the historicisation of Krautrock, reinforcing a canon of earlier German musicians who – in the main – did not endorse such categorisation. As Föllakzoid illustrate, this can also distract from artistic foci. In their case, they choose to distance themselves from previous Krautrock bands and instead reassert the importance of their work's spiritual origins.

Despite being geographically and historically separate, the bands surveyed in this chapter share in Krautrock's ideological aspects, employ similar creative practices, or hold connections to the genre's surviving originators, allowing them to establish credentials as Krautrockers. For some, the influence of Krautrock is explicit via reference to the style label itself or overt musical similarity. For others, the influence of Krautrock has been less direct, influenced by bands operating in other styles that derived in some part from Krautrock. The long-lasting significance of Krautrock offers several opportunities for further study. One particular opportunity lies in exploring the role of Krautrock as an act of cultural memorialisation; for Andrew Hurley, for instance, the noise and cultural memory of wartime life were key

[24] Adelt, *Krautrock*, p. 172.

[25] B Froese-Acquaye et al., *Tangerine Dream: Zeitraffer* (London: Barbican Library, 2021); J Leloup, *Electronic: From Kraftwerk to The Chemical Brothers* (London: The Design Museum, 2020).

creative impetuses for the 1980s German band Einstürzende Neu-bauten.[26] Such an approach may reward investigation in relation to bands covered above across Europe. On a related note, while Krautrock has received growing recognition from the academic community, similar experimental music scenes, such as in 1970s France, have not yet received comprehensive study.

We have focused on popular music makers in the Western world, primarily as Krautrock itself is a Germanic form of music making by those to whom most available popular music was either German or Anglo-American, however that is not to say that Krautrock has not also inspired music elsewhere. Adelt, for instance, briefly draws a connection between Krautrock and Yellow Magic Orchestra, indicating an opportunity to consider Krautrock's cultural role in Eastern countries.[27] Indeed, bands such as Boredoms, who originated during the mid-1980s in Osaka, Japan have developed an idiolect comparable to Krautrock in terms of texture, repetition, and form.

The musical and geographical breadth of musicians surveyed in this chapter illustrates the diffusion of Krautrock's originators' sonic vocabulary in different musical practices today. In doing so, it opens a plurality of understandings of Krautrock. At its most restrictive, we might conceive of Krautrock as a stylistically diverse range of originators who have since become a part of an acknowledged canon to commenta-tors and fans (those operating in West Germany around 1968–74). At one remove from these canonical acts, we could consider contemporan-eous non-German musicians (including David Bowie or Brian Eno) who created work that drew considerably from their Krautrock contempor-aries. At a further remove, we can consider musical practice that came after the Krautrock era but shared stylistic aspects with Krautrock (including several grunge and new wave artists such as Soundgarden, Joy Division, Orchestral Manoeuvres in the Dark, Love Battery, and Simple Minds). And, finally, in the most inclusive sense, we could view Krautrock as an ongoing, now-global practice, including acts who occupy a vastly different cultural and commercial landscape, but never-theless share some aesthetic commonality with canonical Krautrock musicians.

---

[26] A Hurley, Popular Music, Memory, and Aestheticized Historiography in a Minor Key: Einstürzende Neubauten's Lament for World War I's Dead, *Popular Music and Society* 44:1 (2021), pp. 93–106.

[27] Adelt, *Krautrock*, p. 170.

Essential Listening

Beak, ⋙ (Invada Records, 2018)
Camera, *Radiate!* (Bureau B, 2012)
Föllakzoid, *III* (Sacred Bones, 2015)
To Rococo Rot, *To Rococo Rot* (Kitty-Yo, 1996)
Tonstartssbandht, *An When* (Dœs Are, 2009)

Index

Printed by Printforce, United Kingdom